Kay Francis

KF.6

Kay Francis

A Passionate Life and Career

LYNN KEAR *and* JOHN ROSSMAN

McFarland & Company, Inc., Publishers
Jefferson, North Carolina, and London

Frontispiece: Kay Francis, 1936,
when she was the highest paid actress at Warner Bros.

LIBRARY OF CONGRESS CATALOGUING-IN-PUBLICATION DATA

Kear, Lynn.
Kay Francis : a passionate life and career / Lynn Kear and John Rossman.
p.   cm.
Includes bibliographical references and index.

ISBN 0-7864-2366-8 (softcover : 50# alkaline paper)

1. Francis, Kay, 1905–1968.   2.   Actors— United States— Biography.
I. Rossman, John, 1945–   II. Title.
PN2287.F672K43   2006   791.4302'8092 — dc22   2005035203

British Library cataloguing data are available

Front cover: Kay Francis on the set of *Wonder Bar* (1933);
back cover: in *Mandalay* (1934).

Manufactured in the United States of America

*McFarland & Company, Inc., Publishers
Box 611, Jefferson, North Carolina 28640
www.mcfarlandpub.com*

For James Robert Parish

Acknowledgments

This book would not have been possible without the help of many other people. We're happy to have the opportunity to thank those who were part of the project.

Charles Harthy was invaluable in helping with the section on Homer, Michigan, and the Gibbs family. He is a relentless, first-rate investigator and researcher, and a joy to work with.

Jimmy Bangley was extremely generous with his contacts and quotes. An enthusiastic supporter who became a friend, Jimmy, sadly, passed away in December 2004. He will be missed by everyone who was fortunate enough to know him.

We're especially appreciative of the opportunity to speak to Lesley Lee Francis, Margalo Ashley-Farrand, and Maureen (Fenwick) Quinn. Their candid, frank conversations helped us tremendously in researching some of the important men in Kay's life.

Mindy Hill, a wonderful friend, provided able library assistance. Katrina Callahan helped out with the illustrations, and, along with Mindy, provided friendship and encouragement through the many years it took to finish the book. Jimmy Kirk, another good friend who was always enthusiastic about the project, helped with photocopies and answered obscure library questions.

Writers and researchers who were generous with their time and resources include Amy Schapiro, Clint Jeffries, Eric Gans, Gayle Haffner, Dianna Everett, William J. Mann, John Cocchi, Marc Wanamaker, Christopher Nickens, Margaret Burk, Cari Beauchamp, Allan Ellenberger, Glenn McMahon, and Jeanine Basinger. Jim Parish, as he's done with so many other writers, provided moral support and advice above and beyond the call of duty.

Allen Morrison helped us locate Kay's diaries and the Mielziner Family Papers.

Joseph Yranski, Senior Film Librarian at the Donnell Media Center, provided great insights and information.

Special thanks also go to Larry Johnson at the Oklahoma City Public Library, and Marty Jacobs, Curator, Theatre Collection, Museum of the City of New York.

Since it would have been impossible to write this book without access to Kay's diary and scrapbooks, our special thanks and gratitude go to Leith Johnson and Joan Miller for their professional assistance, encouragement, and unfailing ability to make John's visits such an enjoyable experience. Lea Carlson of Wesleyan University was also gracious and helpful.

Thanks also to Gloria Jean, who was kind enough to reply to an e-mail from a fellow eBayer.

Others who deserve thanks for making this book become a reality include Marsha Hunt, Gloria Stuart, Chuck Tranberg, Joan Seaton, Sidney P. Bloomberg, R.C. Parediz, Susan Caputo, Ray Bean, Valarie Stewart, Ebony Showcase Theatre and Cultural Arts Center, Inc.; Laura Wagner; Jetti Ames; Wade Ballard; Devin Herndon; Bart Francis; Diane

Hirschfield; Dee Camp, Homer, Michigan, Historical Society; Candace Rich; Wanda Gray; Bill Kizer; Dick Moore; Rebecca Peters; and Sybil Jason.

We pestered dozens of libraries and organizations. The following helped fill in some of the gaps: Andrew C. Jelen, librarian, Wichita Falls Public Library, Wichita Falls, Texas; Janis Ashley, William S. Hart Museum; Jane Klain, the Museum of Television & Radio; Alissa Cherry, Yellowstone Research Library; David M. Hardy, Federal Bureau of Investigation; Susan Halpert, Houghton Library, Harvard University, Cambridge, Massachusetts; Roger Stoddard; Erika Ingham, Senior Archive Assistant, Heinz Archive and Library, National Portrait Gallery, London; Patricia H. Svoboda, Research Coordinator, CEROS/CAP, Smithsonian Institution, National Portrait Gallery, Washington, D.C.; Kathy Mortenson, Falmouth Public Library, Falmouth, Massachusetts; Falmouth Historical Society; Ellen Bailey, Pasadena Playhouse; Amarillo Library, Amarillo, Texas; Abbott Public Library, Marblehead, Massachusetts; Allentown Public Library; Atlanta-Fulton Public Library; Berkshire Athenaeum, Pittsfield Public Library; Beverly Hills Public Library; Bermuda National Library; Cedar Rapids Public Library; Central Library of Rochester and Monroe County, New York; Church of the Transfiguration, New York; City of St. Paul Public Library; Cleveland Public Library; Columbus (Ohio) Public Library; Deep River Public Library; Detroit Public Library; Enoch Pratt Free Library; Fitchburg Public Library; Fort Lee Free Public Library; Fort Worth Public Library; Grand Rapids Public Library; Hampton Bays Public Library; Houghton Library, Harvard University; Indianapolis Marion County Public Library; Jacksonville Public Library; Kalamazoo Public Library; Library of Congress, Washington, D.C.; Los Angeles City Historical Society; Louisville Free Public Library; Madison Public Library; Miami-Dade County Library; Museum of the City of New York; New Haven Free Public Library; New York Historical Society Library; New York Public Library; New York Public Library for the Performing Arts; Newport Public Library; Notre Dame Academy; Peoria Public Library; Princeton Public Library; Public Libraries of Saginaw; Public Library of Youngstown and Mahoning County; Reading Public Library; Rockville Center Public Library; St. Mark's School, Southboro, Massachusetts; St. Paul Public Library; Santa Barbara Public Library; Saratoga Room, Saratoga Public Library; South Bend Public Library; Steele Memorial Library, Elmira, New York; Tompkins County Public Library; Wilmington Library, Delaware; Carol Davis, Woodland Public Library, Woodland, California; Worcester Public Library, Massachusetts; Kenneth Cobb, Director, New York City Municipal Archives; Ms. Wiggins, National Archives and Records Administration; Houston Public Library; Rosenberg Library, Galveston, Texas; St. Thomas Church, Fifth Avenue, New York City; Beaumont Public Library; and the Gwinnett County Library.

A special note of gratitude goes to Kaye Kear and Joan Moran for their moral (and other) support.

Alan S. Clarke came along at a great time to provide encouragement and advice. Thanks, too, to Mitch Douglas for reading the manuscript and offering his comments.

Kimber Herndon read draft after draft, watched movies, and listened to Lynn prattle on and on about Kay. Without complaint. For years. She deserves an award, but will settle for this short acknowledgment.

Contents

Preface

I'd heard her name and seen her photo, but her considerable charm, like that of Irene Dunne, Janet Gaynor, and Claudette Colbert, doesn't come through in a photograph — one has to experience Kay Francis to truly appreciate her. I inadvertently found her after taping a Greta Garbo movie on Turner Classic Movies. As I rewound the tape, I discovered I'd also recorded the last part of a different movie. Perhaps it was the husky voice. Or the charming speech impediment. Or maybe that she looked like no one else. But my reaction was, "Oh my *God!* Who is this? And why isn't the world gaga over her?" In any event, that first viewing led to an obsession — and this book.

As for my coauthor John, he first saw Kay Francis on a television broadcast of *Comet Over Broadway* when he was eight years old. The plot was difficult to follow because the movie had been edited to fit an hour time slot. Nevertheless, Kay impressed him. About a year later he saw her photo in a *Cosmopolitan* article on movie stars of the '20s and '30s. He saved the photo and began to carefully scan television listings for her name in the casts of old movies.

The second time he saw Kay she was cavorting with the Marx Brothers in *The Cocoanuts*. He was momentarily confused by her billing as Katherine Francis, but this time her throaty voice impressed him as much as her beauty. After the first viewing of his favorite Kay Francis movie, *Trouble in Paradise,* he became totally entranced. Kay seemed the epitome of what a movie star should be — glamorous, sophisticated, beautifully made-up, gorgeously gowned, and photographed in flattering soft focus— in other words, an Art Deco goddess.

For John, researching Kay's career was a labor of love, and reading her diaries was both exciting and surprising. Co-authoring this biography, then, seemed the inevitable result of his long-time interest in this fascinating star, who occasionally said she wanted to be forgotten, but who deserves to be remembered.

From 1929 to 1946, Kay Francis appeared in more than sixty films, including at least one classic, *Trouble in Paradise.* She acted with the biggest male leads of her day — Cary Grant, Humphrey Bogart, Errol Flynn, William Powell — and earned an astounding $200,000 a year during the Depression.

She also developed a legendary reputation for privacy. If they only knew.... Kay's desire for privacy was essential to her success. Kay lived a rich, uninhibited life that included one-night stands with many of Hollywood's celebrated stars, countless affairs, and carefully hidden abortions. Her diary, uncovered in a university archive, details Kay's life and career in New York, Paris, and Hollywood during Prohibition, the Roaring Twenties, the Depression, and the War Years, including dozens of romantic liaisons.

We were aware that the Wesleyan University archives housed Kay Francis' diaries, but were told they wouldn't be terribly helpful. Of course, curiosity got the better of us, and

John made his first trip to Connecticut only to discover the diaries were not diaries per se. Instead, they were calendar pages upon which two kinds of notes were scribbled, events and appointments (written in longhand), and much more personal, often sexually explicit, comments written in the shorthand Kay had learned in business school.

Kay, the personification of F. Scott Fitzgerald's Flaming Youth, felt compelled to record virtually every romantic encounter. These scraps of paper tell the story of a sexually adventurous woman who lost her virginity in 1922 and consequently took on many lovers— both male and female — over the next decades. For unknown reasons, she stopped recording the entries in 1953.

As great a find as the diaries were, there were several problems with them as a research tool. First, some entries were undecipherable. Kay wrote in pencil, and her handwriting was not always clear. Second, she often used initials, nicknames, first names, or even dashes to identify a person. First names were especially troublesome. For example, at one point in her life she was romantically involved with McKay Morris, whom she referred to as Kay. At the same time, she worked with Kay Johnson and lived with Kay Swan. It certainly didn't help that she herself was named Kay! In some cases, we had to make an informed guess on identity by cross-referencing with other sources. Third, believe it or not, we truly wanted to learn more about her career and her perceptions of people and events in New York, Europe, and Hollywood during this fascinating period of time, but the diary focused on her sex life. Trust us— it became tedious to read through account after account of her sexual escapades.

Despite these obstacles, we're grateful Kay kept a diary. It provides an interesting record of one woman's life, and proved invaluable as we wrote her biography.

However, there remains the mystery of why this publicity-shy woman not only kept these explosive records but *donated* them for future research! Perhaps she'd simply forgotten about them. Or maybe she kept them as notes for a possible book. We'll probably never know, but it struck us as intriguingly out of character for a private woman with a carefully constructed public image to keep highly personal and sometimes unflattering material. Especially a person who famously stated that she wanted to be forgotten. This is the enigma that was Kay Francis.

Through the diary, as well as interviews, historical archives, and recently declassified FBI files, new details have surfaced about Kay Francis. Most of the information in this book is previously unpublished. There are no books devoted to Kay Francis or her career. Written for movie fans as well as researchers, and illustrated largely from the authors' own collection, this is the definitive source on Kay Francis. The biography includes information about Kay's parents, Katherine Clinton and Joseph S. Gibbs, as well as Kay's life from birth to death. We have also included an extensive chronology and filmography.

This undertaking represents our attempt to help others discover "Miss Fwancis"— movie legend, fashion goddess, millionaire investor, and film producer. Although traditionally portrayed as a tragic figure, we see Kay as a multi-dimensional, complicated woman. "I can't wait to be forgotten," she once said; but she also said, "I went into this business because I thought I could make more money in it than any other. I've done everything I set out to do and now I'm going to enjoy myself!"

— Lynn Kear
Fall 2005

CHAPTER 1

The Michigan Playboy and the Actress, 1905–1908

"Being born in Oklahoma City was probably the only un-chic thing Kay ever did."[1]

Oklahoma City was bitter cold. Although mild weather had been forecast, snow began falling late Monday, January 9, 1905. By Tuesday morning, 1½ inches of icy snow covered the streets. On Friday the 13th the temperature dipped to zero, and the high reached only 14. The harsh 10-mile-per-hour wind didn't help matters. The newspaper reported that a young man had frozen to death on Wednesday morning and concluded that Oklahoma City had run into a "ferocious isotherm of zeroality."[2] The cold spell was the worst since 1899. Some, however, delighted in skating parties, and farmers hoped the snow would be good for the wheat crop.

Joseph Gibbs, a 42-year-old steward, was living at the Hotel Threadgill[3] with his 28-year-old wife Katherine when Katharine Edwina Gibbs was born on Friday, January 13, 1905.[4] Oklahoma City, incorporated in April 1889, was then home to 20,000 or so citizens—and an odd birthplace for Kay Francis, one of Hollywood's most glamorous stars. Kay enjoyed telling people she was born there by mistake. "My dad and mother had gone out there on probably the most unusual of business deals," she explained. "Dad, always the master of the magnificent gesture, had heard that he could buy up the Sioux Indian ponies, thousands of them, for polo. He had planned to a nicety just how many ponies he'd keep for his own string, and how many he'd sell and how much money he would make. He got there on his last dollar, and learned that the Government controlled the whole shebang. So while he and mother were wondering what to do in Oklahoma City when you're broke, I was born. In the meantime, he became the manager of a local hotel, so that solved the immediate problem of food and board."[5]

It's a wonderful story, but there were no Sioux in Oklahoma, though the area *was* Indian Territory (Oklahoma wouldn't become the 46th state until 1907), and there *was* a lot of horse trading. Still, like many stories about Joe Gibbs, it *is* telling. In another story, a drunken Joe rode a horse through the hotel's lobby and up the carpeted stairs to his wife's room to greet his newborn. True or not, we get the idea that Joe might have been more entertaining than responsible, more of an amusing character than a good provider.

Kay *should* have been the daughter of a wealthy Michigan landowner and horse breeder. Unfortunately, by the time she arrived, Joe had squandered the family fortune. Joe was much like George Amberson in Booth Tarkington's 1918 Pulitzer Prize–winning novel *The Magnificent Ambersons.*[6] Pampered and selfish, George was an arrogant whippersnapper — and the townspeople fervently hoped he'd get his "comeuppance." George Amberson received his comeuppance when the family fortune was lost — and so did Joe. But before that happened, he had quite a time.

THREADGILL HOTEL, OKLAHOMA CITY, OK
Kay was born in this hotel on January 13, 1905. Opened in April 1904, the building was torn down in 1957, and the site is now the Broadway-Kerr parking garage.

Joe's grandfather, also named Joseph Gibbs, was born January 9, 1789, in Litchfield, Connecticut. A hero of the War of 1812, Gibbs lived in New York, and then moved with wife Polly and children — Mary, Lucy, Marcus, Electa, Philo, Lydia, Volney, and Mason — to Homer, Michigan, in 1836, when the area was "in a state of primitive wilderness and they endured the privations and hardships incidental to pioneer life."[7] Gibbs became a respected Homer citizen, where he farmed more than 800 acres and held elective office. Polly died May 11, 1851, and Joseph[8] on January 12, 1874.

Volney, born in New York on November 11, 1829, married Helen Woolley on March 4, 1861 — making him the only sibling to marry. According to local legend, the siblings drew lots to determine who would marry and inherit the family fortune. Kay's father, Joseph Sprague Gibbs, was born January 16, 1862, in Homer. Helen, born in Madison County, New York, in April 1837, died January 22, 1894. Her obituary in the local newspaper proclaimed Kay's grandmother a living saint. "Since we have known Mrs. Gibbs her life has been an exemplary one. She was a friend to, and was interested in the welfare of all, and those to whom she came in contact were met with regard. Her life was one worthy of emulation, for she reached a degree of perfectness which is not often attained."[9]

Volney farmed, and served as justice of the peace and a city council member. He was also an inventor of some note, credited with patenting a tire-setting machine, a mower apparatus, and the Gibbs Wheelbarrow Seeder. No doubt some of the family fortune came from Volney's successful inventions. He seems a remarkable man, someone who might have been an excellent grandfather to young Kay. Unfortunately, he passed away a little more than five years before her birth. His 1899 obituary began with the headline: "A GOOD MAN GONE. DEATH OF VOLNEY GIBBS — LAST OF A PROMINENT FAMILY." (Since Joe was still around, it seems strange to refer to him as the "last" of the family.) The obituary further described Volney as "inclined to be reticent and unassuming in his demeanor. His mind was judicial in its nature, looking at every side of a question, weighing carefully every consideration that might influence his decision and only making it after he was fully satisfied as to the reason and justice in the case. He delighted in abstruse questions and nothing pleased him more than to reason out some complicated problem that would have puzzled an ordinary intellect. He also possessed a fine mechanical genius. His was a genial, kindly disposition, holding fast the friends he made, though never stepping aside to court a vulgar popularity. He was in every respect a man to tie to, and his loss will be deeply felt by the community."[10]

And then we have Joe. An only child, he was brought up in the huge old farmhouse built by Grandpa Gibbs just outside of Homer. He lived with his parents—*and* Volney's unmarried siblings, most of who remained there until their deaths.[11] As a child, Joe developed a keen interest in horse breeding and racing. After graduating from Homer High School in 1880,[12] he married Harriett (Hattie) Adeline Darrow on September 9, 1884, at Hattie's parents' home. The marriage, described as "the happiest event in the lives of two of Homer's popular young people,"[13] turned out to be something less than that. Despite newspaper reports of sleigh rides, progressive dinner parties, and other social events, the marriage soon ended, and Joe spent the next few years traveling and pursuing a career— as an actor. One report claimed he understudied London theater great Richard Mansfield.[14] He was also said to have helped orchestrate the career of stage legend Maxine Elliott![15]

GIBBS FARMHOUSE, HOMER, MI
Joseph S. Gibbs, Kay's father, was born January 16, 1862, in this farmhouse. Although extensively renovated, the building still stands today (courtesy of Charles Harthy).

"Joseph Gibbs was always attracted to beautiful women, and one of them was Maxine Elliott, whom he introduced to the stage."[16] While this seems to be another myth about the larger-than-life Joe, it's true that Joe liked the ladies—and vice versa.

Joe took another trip down the aisle on August 14, 1891, in New York when he married Mary Connelly.[17] They returned to Homer two years later "with the intention of making it their home for life,"[18] but this marriage, too, ended in divorce. Who was Joseph Sprague Gibbs? Newspaper and historical accounts described him as a well-traveled man who enjoyed the good life. An 1894 county history explained that Joe "has visited many places of interest throughout the United States and foreign countries. We regret that limited space would not allow a detailed account of many of his experiences."[19] So do we, since hard facts about Joe are difficult to come by.

In 1901 the local newspaper provided a brief biography of the man who would sire Kay Francis just four years later: "Mr. Joseph S. Gibbs received his education at the Homer schools from which he is a graduate. Later he learned telegraphy[20] and was in the employ of the Michigan Central Railroad for a period of two years, at which time he made a change in his occupation as he was engaged in the hotel business in New York City. Subsequently, having a natural fondness for theatrical life, he was connected with that profession for four years, seeing life in many of its phases, not only in the United States, but in foreign countries, as he crossed the Atlantic four times. His experiences in his varied life have been many and some of them very interesting, as he is a person of keen perceptions and retentive memory."[21]

When Volney died in 1899, Joe inherited a fortune. According to one estimate, Joe received the 800-plus acre farm, as well as seven smaller properties—and about $100,000 cash. Joe, however, was not the penny pincher his daughter turned out to be. "Joe maintained an estate equal to a country gentleman. The house was rebuilt and patterned and furnished in fashionable manner in the style of an old English country home. When it was completed Mr. and Mrs. Gibbs gave a house warming staged on a most elaborate scale."[22] Newspapers provided frequent reports on Mr. and Mrs. Gibbs, particularly focusing on their travels and parties. One of the most memorable social gatherings was a Tally-Ho party. "A fine two-horse team hitched to a large coach came dashing into town after the guests with a coachman in uniform on the box and Gibbs dressed in keeping with the event on the coach steps. As the homes of the guests were approached, Gibbs signaled with a blast of his tally-ho horn."[23]

Newspapers also reported on Joe's racehorses. "The finest horses bred were to be found in the Gibbs stables, horses for racing, driving or saddle. Many horses were sent from there to racing stables in New York City and Chicago."[24] There was even a mention of Joe as a crack baseball player. "Joe Gibbs makes a good shortstop—in fact, Joe can play anywhere."[25] Truer words were never written.

Most interesting, however, were the accounts suggesting Joe was an amateur actor of some repute. The local newspaper reported in August 1892 that Joe had left for New York City to prepare for an acting role that would eventually put him on a tour winding through the South and up the West Coast. On January 6, 1893, Joe was back in Michigan, playing a role in *The Westerner,* a popular play of the time.[26]

"Many people here [in Homer] were anxious to see a play in which he took part. The trip of eight miles to Albion in those days was quite an undertaking so the Homer people chartered a special train which was made up in Hillsdale and took them to Albion to attend the show."[27] In the following year, the newspaper reported that Joe had returned to New York City for a stage production. Joe also tried his hand at writing, authoring a March 1894 dramatic sketch, "A Mother's Love," which he directed for a local program. Sometimes wife Mary got in on the act, too. In April 1894 they appeared in a comedy sketch written by Joe—"Nellie's Brother." The newspaper critic raved, "The people were more than pleased. The sketch embraces four characters, three of which were taken by Mr. Gibbs, each of which was true to life. Mrs. Gibbs as Nellie was a surprise to all present. The part could not have been better taken. We understand that Mrs. Gibbs has had little, if any, experience as an actress, but the manner in which she carried the part was no evidence of inexperience."[28]

Sometime around 1900 Mary Gibbs became restless. In April of that year, Joe advertised for a housekeeper; and then in May, Mary and Joe adopted a two-year-old girl, Helen Louise, from St. Joseph's Foundling Home.[29] Meanwhile, Joe continued to travel on business and remained active in horseracing circles. In late July 1900, his stallion, Cedric Muscovite, won two races at the Battle Creek Driving Club. Then, during an August business trip, Joe was almost killed when his passenger train collided with a freight engine and caboose near Lafayette, Indiana. Several people were killed, but Joe, though knocked unconscious and bruised, fully recovered. If that was the worst of 1900, the year's highlight came in October when one of his horses won a $5,000 purse at the Minnesota State Fair.

Joe Gibbs was the first Homerite to own an automobile. Like many of Joe's adventures, it made the local paper. "Joseph S. Gibbs is the newest rival of William K. Vanderbilt as an automobilist. While in Chicago last week Mr. Gibbs purchased a locomobile and started home with it Friday afternoon, accompanied by W.L. Hibbard, an expert engineer."[30] All went well until it broke down in Coldwater and had to be towed to Homer for repairs. Joe, quite proud of the car, frequently drove it into town, where he showed it off to locals.

Joe made a strange decision in 1900. He signed over the farm's deed to wife Mary. Perhaps it was an attempt to hide his assets—he was hit hard by the new county inheritance tax law, which required he pay $228.21[31] in February 1901—or maybe Mary demanded it in lieu of a divorce. No one knows, but the decision came back to haunt him a few years later.

Something even more ominous occurred in 1901. Joe was so ill in March that many feared death was imminent. On April 17, the newspaper reported that Joe "lies in a precarious condition at his home south of Homer. He rallied considerably yesterday morning but is very low at this writing and hopes of his recovery have been abandoned."[32] A week later the paper sounded a more optimistic note, and suggested Joe would be out and about in several weeks.

He indeed recovered, and his comings and goings were again dutifully reported, beginning in June. By November, he was spotted in Battle Creek, where a newspaper referred to him as a "well known horseman and sportsman."[33] But his near-death experience triggered wanderlust. Joe took many business and hunting trips, and in January 1902 he and his wife—"the royal host and hostess"—threw an elaborate party celebrating his 40th birthday. "The handsome mansion was a veritable dreamland of beauty and daintiness. Dancing, pedro[34] and music took a prominent part toward the merry making and were augmented by refreshments."[35]

Joe's business continued to thrive. In April 1902, a local newspaper described in detail his state-of-the-art horse breeding facilities. "Mr. Gibbs deals exclusively in high class coach horses and cobs and endeavors to secure only those that will attract the attention of buyers who represent the eastern coach horse trade. He shipped 18 horses to Buffalo yesterday."[36]

Although Joe and Mary continued to make nice in public, the marriage apparently was over. In December 1902, Joe sold off part of his real estate holdings for $8,000[37] and disappeared from Homer. Mary Gibbs filed for divorce on June 23, 1903, citing extreme cruelty and habitual drunkenness, and the divorce was granted on November 19, 1903.[38] Mary received the Gibbs farm—a generous settlement, to say the least, suggesting she'd been abandoned.

"Nothing fazed mother, the darling."[39]

Born in Chicago on May 17, 1874, the daughter of Isabel C. Clinton and Edward Gay Franks, Katherine Clinton Franks Gibbs apparently made up her mind at a young age to become an actress. Little is known of her childhood, except that she lost her mother when she was ten, and her father, a Chicago sugar broker, at the age of twelve. According to a magazine article, Grandpa Franks "wasn't always old, and in his youth the boom-towns of the frontier were his familiar habitat. He married twice, and of the second wedding in his house was born a daughter, Katherine, who became Kay Francis' mother."[40] Katherine attended the Chicago Conservatory,[41] where she likely took classes in theater, speech, and music. She gave an elocution reading in Elgin, Illinois, on April 10, 1898, and was a teacher before beginning her professional acting career, using the stage name Katherine Clinton. In September 1898, she was hired by theater great Augustin Daly.[42] Her first known role was a bit part in *A Runaway Girl*, a musical comedy. In October, Daly assigned her to Ada Rehan's[43] company, where she played Jessica in *The Merchant of Venice* and Bianca in *The Taming of the Shrew*.

Daly died in June 1899, and Charles Frohman took over the company. In 1900, Clinton appeared in *The Great Ruby* and *Marcelle*. A reviewer remarked that she'd "acted very well last season in 'The Great Ruby' and has certainly advanced in her art."[44] A 1901 newspaper clipping suggested she was ambitious and not averse to fame and fortune. "Miss Clinton's dramatic aim is higher than the frivolous class of dramatics. She hopes some day to have her name printed in big type on the programmes."[45]

While with the Daly Company, Clinton toured with Blanche Walsh, traveled to Europe, and performed with Maude Adams in *The Little Minister*. A writer remarked that Katherine had made "remarkable headway in her chosen profession, and it proves Mr. Daly's wonderful insight into the capabilities of the young players in whom he took an interest that he should have seen at once that the girl whom he started in musical comedy would prove a success in the legitimate drama."[46]

Like most young actresses at the time, Katherine sold photographs at shows. Although few remain today, they provide a rare glimpse of Kay Francis' mother. Bearing a slight resemblance to Kay, with dark hair and round brown eyes (Kay's eyes were gray), Katherine Clinton was attractive, but not the beauty her daughter became. Kay once made reference to a Spanish grandmother.[47] It's likely the Spanish grandmother was Katherine's mother, Isabel. Katherine, aware of the possible scandal if Kay was found *too* exotic[48] for American tastes, claimed to have traced her family back to 17th century Massachusetts, adding that Kay was a ninth-generation American.[49]

Katherine Clinton was never a star, though she occasionally received good notices. Still, she made a living in the prestigious Daly troupe—probably the most important American theater company of its time—and had the potential to become a successful actress. Something happened, however, that took her career in a different direction. In June 1902, Katherine left Daly's to join Boston's Castle Square Theatre Stock Company. The Company's star was Lillian Lawrence, a popular stage actor who went on to act in silent films. Clinton, described as "a dark-haired, spirited beauty—with fire and verve,"[50] remained there for a few months, but left for a twelve-week stint in 1903 with a Rochester, New York, stock company. There is no indication why she left the Daly troupe, though it would have been an unwise career move to leave America's top stock company for a less prominent one. In any event, Katherine didn't remain long in Rochester — she ended up marrying Joseph Gibbs before the year ended.

Katherine and Joe, who likely met through the stage, married on December 3, 1903, at the Church of the Transfiguration.[51] Also known as the Little Church Around the Corner, this Episcopal church is located at One East 29th Street (between Fifth and Madison avenues) in New York City. Built in 1849, it became popular with theater actors in 1870 when legendary stage producer Joseph Jefferson, arranging a funeral for fellow actor George Holland, was turned down by local churches. Jefferson, told about a little church around the corner that would accept the funeral, supposedly cried out, "God Bless the Little Church Around the Corner."[52]

KATHERINE CLINTON
Kay's mother in a 1902 publicity photograph for Boston's Castle Square Theatre.

Katherine became pregnant a few months after the wedding. She apparently assumed she'd live the rest of her life in quiet domesticity. Like most plans, life interfered. Very soon after their marriage, Joe and Katherine moved to Oklahoma City. An old-timer still living in Oklahoma City in 1944 gave a different version of how Katherine and Joe ended up there, explaining that Kay's parents were theater performers who'd come to perform at the Delmar Garden, a summer theater. "Perhaps because they were stranded, Kay's father got a job as a clerk or something at the Threadgill Hotel at Second and Broadway, now known as the Bristol.[53] This hotel was just built and was the pride of the city."[54]

Actually, Joe was the manager of the hotel, and he continued to be a socialite — even in Oklahoma City. In June 1904, he entertained a number of friends in the hotel's grand dining room. "The dinner was a princely affair and the viands served in elaborate style, there being three courses of wines. Following the dinner the entire party were the guests of Mr. Haecker at a theater party at Delmar Garden."[55]

It wasn't long before finances became an issue for the newlyweds. In February 1904, Katherine placed an ad in the local newspaper advertising her availability as an elocution and drama teacher. Now using the name Mrs. Joseph S. Gibbs, she indicated her specialty was Shakespeare.[56] Whatever her name, Katherine was apparently expected to contribute to the family finances.

Katherine — or Mrs. Joseph S. Gibbs — made her acting debut in Oklahoma City on October 5, 1904. By this time, of course, she was pregnant with Kay, who would arrive three months later. The show, *Two Hours of Oblivion,* was described as "a dramatic and musical mélange," and was presented by the "Ladies Guild of the Episcopal Church,[57] Arranged and Staged Under the Personal Direction of Mrs. Joseph S. Gibbs."[58] In addition to directing the show, Katherine also performed in "A Happy Pair" with Nels Darling. The local newspaper reported that the show brought out "all society decked out in its very best bib and tucker,"[59] and gave the production a rave review, especially noting Mrs. Gibbs' "airy grace and perfection of acting."[60]

Kay's January birth didn't stop Katherine's dramatic aspirations. In April 1905, C.W. Stater hired Katherine Clinton to be his leading lady at the Delmar Garden theater. On April 14, 1905, Mrs. Gibbs, as she was billed, appeared with Nels Darling in a sketch at the Overholser Opera House. Part of a program titled *Sense & Nonsense,* other participants included "lightning cartoonists,"[61] a magician, monologist, vocalist, "El Reno's Famous Warbler," and other variety show types. This vaudeville-type event was a portent of what lay ahead for Mrs. Gibbs, soon to be Katherine Clinton again.

Stater had ambitious plans for Mrs. Gibbs, scheduling three different plays per week, and giving his leading lady her choice of parts. Mrs. Gibbs indicated she hoped to again play the countess in *The Great Ruby,* a part she'd played with Daly. In May, Katherine appeared in *Woman's Sacrifice,* as Zell, an ex-slave. "Mrs. Gibbs[62] proved herself to be an actress of exceptional ability,"[63] a reviewer wrote. She also appeared in a British farce, *Three of a Kind,* in early May, and, later that month, was in *Union Forever.* The reviewer again applauded her, noting that she "was exceptionally strong in her part and richly deserved the curtain call that she received after the third act."[64] Finally, in late May, Katherine appeared in *Brother John,* again, to good reviews. However, this was the last time she was reviewed in Oklahoma City. Stater denounced a rumor that the theater was on the verge of closing, but it appears the gossip had some truth to it.

A former streetcar conductor claimed to remember Katherine and baby Kay. "Almost daily Kay's mother walked the three blocks to the car line at Seventh and Harrison and boarded my car. There was no paving then, in consequence of which the car steps were so high that a woman with a baby could hardly negotiate them. But I made it my business to hop out and take Kay in my left arm and give Mom a boost with my good right arm."[65]

"I don't believe, even though a baby, Kay will ever forget a rough and muddy journey in our first auto over the then terrible roads to San Francisco."[66]

The Gibbs family — Joe, Katherine, and baby Katharine — remained in Oklahoma City until Kay was nine months old, and then moved to California, no doubt seeking opportunity and sunshine. Perhaps Joe heard of another get-rich-quick scheme, or the harsh winter of 1905 convinced them to move to a warmer climate. It's also possible that Joe, who'd already had at least three different employers in the brief time they lived in Oklahoma City, was encouraged to move.[67]

From Santa Barbara, they moved to Los Angeles. Katherine Clinton granted only one interview about her famous daughter.[68] In it, she briefly spoke of Los Angeles. "We had a horse and buggy in Los Angeles and as soon as Kay was old enough to see and enjoy things out of doors she used to beg for afternoon drives. It was so beautiful here then. There were so many more orange groves and gardens before the city grew large."[69]

Kay rarely spoke of her father, but claimed her first memory was of him. "When I see a red sweater I remember running down a road to a white gate and hanging on the gate waiting for my father on Sunday mornings. We were living at Montecito,[70] in California, and he used to ride to town for the paper and then I would put on my red sweater and run out to meet him. That is the first thing I remember about myself. I wasn't quite four-years-old and we were living on a little ranch and there were a lot of orange trees. I used to sit under the trees and reach up and pick the fruit and sit there eating it. We had a big dog and father had brought a cat for me. The cat and I used to ride all around the yard on the dog's back."[71]

Although no photographs have been found of Joe, it's likely Kay resembled him in a variety of ways. Katherine was a petite woman who attributed Kay's height to her husband. Embarrassed about her height as a child, Kay recalled her mother's reassurance. "Even as a girl I was tall, but mother instilled the sensible attitude. Rather than making me self-conscious, she kept reminding me that my father had been six feet four, that height was admirable."[72]

Katherine saw other qualities in Kay that reminded her of Joe. "Every daughter is one half her father by inheritance. Kay's father had a great personality."[73] Katherine further described him as "a clear thinker who possessed excellent judgment. I attribute the fact that her career has been one of the steadiest and most evenly regulated rises in filmdom to the calm, wise brain she inherited from her father."

The family moved on to Denver and Salt Lake City. There is no record of them in any city directory, suggesting they didn't stay long in any one place, probably moving from one inexpensive rooming house to another. By 1907, Joe was managing the Yellowstone Lake Hotel,[74] though it's not known if Katherine and Kay were living with him at the time.

It was probably in Denver or Salt Lake City that Mrs. Gibbs decided to leave Joe. The frequent moves, financial hardships, alcohol abuse, and regrets about giving up her stage career had taken their toll. Katherine Clinton Gibbs moved back east with her daughter and returned to the stage.

It's impossible to know how much Joe told Katherine about ex-wife Mary and the divorce settlement. The marriage certificate listed Joe as widowed, which may have been the story he told his new wife. Katherine, however, may have discovered more than she wanted to know about Joe's previous life when Mary Gibbs died on September 1, 1907, at the age of 40.[75] Mary died a wealthy woman, thanks to Joe's court-ordered generosity. Before her death, Mary deeded property to Edwin Linton,[76] and then left him her estate. Joe returned to Homer and bitterly complained that he'd been cheated. On April 16, 1908, he filed suit against Linton and H.W. Cavanagh, the will's executor, but the lawsuit was dismissed. This may have been one of his last chances to make things right with Katherine. Mr. Linton,[77] who was in the liquor business before managing Mrs. Gibbs' farm, became a wealthy man. Described as "a well known baseball player,"[78] whose "people were well-to-do," Linton inherited what was left of the Gibbs fortune, which wasn't a small sum.

Joe made further desperate attempts to raise money, selling off real estate until he had nothing more. In 1908, he was living in Milwaukee, Wisconsin, where he was the Republican House's hotel manager.[79] It's likely Katherine — and Kay — had gone east by this time.

There was little contact between Joe and Katherine after they moved. Kay claimed she last saw him in New York when she was three. According to friends, Kay had little regard for her father. However, it does seem that Kay was introduced to Joe's relatives. An intriguing newspaper clipping from one of Kay's 1940s stage tours featured a picture of Kay as a youngster and described how she'd visited Homer when she was young. The clipping quoted a Mrs. Justin T. Cook, who proclaimed herself Kay's aunt. Mrs. Cook was actually married to Joe's first cousin — his mother's sister's son.[80] Although it's unlikely Kay visited the Homer farmhouse, local legend insisted that she not only stayed there, but that a staircase

REPUBLICAN HOUSE, MILWAUKEE, WI
Joseph S. Gibbs managed the Republican House in Milwaukee in 1908. Today the site is a parking lot for the Milwaukee Journal.

was re-routed so the budding diva could make a regal entrance! It's one of those stories that can't be true for any number of reasons, but the story was told and retold; like most legends, it's too perfect. Still, there were Homerites who claimed to remember "the tall slender, dark-haired girl of 11 or 12 years, often seen with Mrs. Cook."[81] For her part, Kay claimed she'd never set foot in Homer.

A Michigan newspaperman reported that Kay last saw her father in 1918. The story is suspect since, upon Kay's death in 1968, her attorney reported that Joe had disappeared and was presumed dead. However, in the reporter's story, Joe returned to Homer in 1916, broke and alone. By 1918, he was near death. "Joe Gibbs is in bad shape and needs surgery," a Homer businessman told an Albion doctor. "If you will perform the operation without charge, I'll pay the hospital bill." A few days after the surgery, Katherine and Kay arrived at the hospital. "Dr. Henderson remembered Kay and that she was called Katherine then, and was a very pretty little girl. He took them to his home for a visit with his wife."[82]

Joe eventually moved to St. Louis, where he found work as a bookkeeper. He made one final effort to regain his fortune. On August 19, 1918, he filed suit against Cavanagh and Linton again, asking that the deed be set aside. Joe died of pneumonia on January 20, 1919,[83] and the suit was dismissed on April 13, 1920. The once wealthy landowner and horse-man, the husband of actress Katherine Clinton, the father of movie star Kay Francis, had nothing when he died. The Homer Masonic Lodge paid for his $15 funeral and burial.[84] At the time of his death, he'd started another family.[85] He was survived by wife Minnie and two daughters, four-year-old Virginia and five-year-old Helen—Kay's half-sisters. Joe's death forced Minnie to apply for relief. It's unlikely Virginia and Helen Gibbs ever learned they were related to Kay Francis.

CHAPTER 2

Kay Comes of Age, 1909–1921

"Don't be frightened! Mother's only acting."[1]

Returning to show business couldn't have been easy for Katherine, especially with a small child in tow. Publicly, Katherine never mentioned leaving or divorcing Joe. In fact, she implied he came with her and Kay to New York. In *her* version of a legendary Kay story, Joe made an appearance. "One evening my husband bought two box seats and brought Kay to a Boston theater where I was playing. Before the drop of the third curtain I died a dramatic death. Just when we had brought the audience to a pitch of tense sobbing, Kay rose in the box and in a shrill baby voice called: 'Don't be frightened! Mother's only acting.' The hysteria of the audience turned into loud laughter and we had to ring down the curtain. After that, when she visited the theater, the baby remained under guard in the wings!"[2]

This story was retold — and embellished — many times, but only in Clinton's version did Joe appear. Kay told several versions, usually with variations in age and city, but all were equally dramatic. "It was in New Haven or New Bedford that I first saw my mother in a play. She made me promise to be a good little girl. 'I'm going to die in the play,' she told me. 'Only I won't really be dead, so don't you worry. You sit there and be good and remember I'm all right.' I was in a box with some other people [notice Kay didn't mention her father], and it was fine watching the stage and seeing my mother and hearing her voice. Then a man came out and shot her and the people all around me seemed to be frightened. I stood up and cried: 'That's all right. That's my mama and she isn't dead. She's just pretending.' I was six-years-old at the time and I don't know what play it was or what part mother had. I remember only standing up in the box and crying out that she was my mama and was pretending. I can't even think what she said to me afterward, but she must have been amused."[3]

In yet another version, Mother was *not* amused. "My childish voice carried everywhere in the theatre," Kay said. "The audience became hysterical with laughter. They had to ring down the curtain. The part I remember best is the spanking I received in the dressing-room. After that episode I saw mother's portrayals from the wings — not from out front."[4]

Katherine Clinton told charming anecdotes about Kay's childhood. While smacking of a publicity writer's hand, they may hold a grain of truth. "When she was four I found her changing from a pair of plain, play panties into party panties trimmed with ribbon and lace. 'I ain't going to wear panties without trimming,' she declared. At six I suggested a black hat with a white plume for Sundays. 'I was planning this winter on a fur hat,' she informed me. So a rabbit muff became an ermine bonnet."[5]

In 1909, when Kay was four, Clinton toured with the Lindsay Morison[6] Stock Company. This was no Augustin Daly repertory company. Little information can be found about the company, suggesting Katherine's brief retirement hampered her professionally and financially. Still, she continued to receive good notices. In a production of *Home Folks*, Katherine Clinton played the role of Sis Durkee. According to a reviewer, "As a creature of the wild, Miss Clinton makes up to look the character, and acts it with skill. Her scene in the third act where she declares her determination to wreak vengeance upon Ruth for stealing the affections and love of the man she loved in her mad, savage way was effective and highly dramatic."[7]

A year later, the Lindsay Morison Company cast Katherine Clinton as Madeline Gray in the *The Bingville Bugle*. Although a critic found her character unpleasant, he added, "Miss Clinton is to be congratulated on the way she acted it. The transition, during the scene in the third act, from the sneering, hardened woman who has tasted the bitterness of life to one softened at the mention of 'Home' and 'Mother' was forced, but that was not the fault of the actress."[8]

By 1914, Clinton was touring with vaudevillian Harry Brooks in the popular show, *The Old Minstrel Man*. A reviewer applauded the group effort: "Mr. Brooks, in the make-up of the 80-year-old veteran of the burnt cork profession, portrayed a delightful blending of comedy and pathos, and the support offered by the two members of Miss Clinton's company was all that could be desired. The playlet carries an atmosphere of the human interest, and is easily one of the best acts of the bill."[9] Another reviewer found it an "excellent study of a quaint type."[10]

In most cases, Clinton and Brooks were the headliners, appearing with various other acts. They sometimes shared a bill with dog acts, comedians, whistlers, jugglers, clog dancers, and the Brightons, artists who "do not paint in oils, water colors, crayons or chalk, but from a heap of miscellaneous rags on black surfaces." A review concluded that the Brightons "manage to put together some very fine pictures."[11] Another critic described the Brightons' act as "a clever way of arranging rags of various colors and shades on a canvas background, forming landscapes and portraits, among the latter being a perfect likeness of Abraham Lincoln."[12]

Another act was the Kurtis Educated Roosters. "These roosters are well trained. They do a lot of interesting things, including wire walking, operating swings and see-saws, crowing at the command of their trainer, and many other things that you'd hardly expect in a bird act."[13] The Clemanzo Brothers were described as having "a queer act. They act alike in size and height, and paint their faces in such a manner as to make it impossible to tell them apart. They do a little acrobatic work, then produce music from their gloves, shirts and clothing. They get some real good music out of their knives, forks, mugs, bologna sausage and roast duck when they sit down to a dinner. They also go through a boxing bout, and the music comes from their boxing gloves."[14]

One is reminded of the old joke: what killed vaudeville *was* vaudeville. Bird and rag acts were a far cry from Augustin Daly's troupe and classic theater, but with a young daughter, Katherine Clinton found work where she could. Kay rarely talked about her mother's career, except to say that she'd toured with "The Old Minstrel Man" for ten years—but had started with Augustin Daly, which, as they say, meant something in those days.

Although Clinton very much desired a stage career, it's unlikely she was able to make a consistent living during those years. Undoubtedly there were times when she was forced to take other employment. George Eells wrote that Kay's childhood revolved around her mother's tours, living in a succession of rooming houses. He further described the two as surviving on popcorn and water. According to a friend, "It was all very third-rate."[15] Kay also intimated in her diary that her mother had secrets, suggesting she occasionally took on unsavory employment. In a March 22, 1927, entry, Kay wrote: "I told them [Kay's friends] about Mother. Damn fool."[16]

When Kay publicly discussed those days, she focused on something more pleasant — her love of movies. Flickers, as they were called then, provided an escape. "Before there was even the possibility of my becoming a screen actress, I adored certain movie stars, with abject worship. I built up all the glamorous illusions for which fans are noted, and the fact that I am now a screen actress myself hasn't changed those illusions one bit."[17] Kay's favorite star? Pola Negri. "She held me enthralled. I thought she must be the most marvelous person in the world. When I met Pola not long ago, I was so awed that I could scarcely speak.[18] Although I tried to reason with myself that she is a person and works very hard, too, I could not overcome my early illusions of her."[19]

"Kay failed in geometry and I was pleased over that. I've always thought it ridiculous for an attractive, glamorous woman to study Latin and Greek."[20]

Frequent moves made it difficult for Kay to attend school. Her mother and family friends provided Kay's early education. Perhaps out of embarrassment and guilt, Katherine Clinton later claimed that Kay was convent-educated. Kay professed an unclear memory of those years. "My childhood was a constantly shifting scene. Mother was on the stage and we were never in one place very long. She sent me to one convent after another and none of them is clear in my mind. Only bits of pictures come back to me now, like the time I had measles in one school and mumps in another and chicken pox in another."[21]

According to Katherine, Kay attended a convent school, Holy Angels in Fort Lee, New Jersey,[22] when she was four, and spent the next two years at Notre Dame Academy in Roxbury, Massachusetts.[23] There is no record of her attendance at either. When Kay was seven, she was sent to live with Katherine's friends in Buffalo, New York, and then supposedly attended Holy Child Jesus School in New York[24] from 1914 to 1916. Again, there is no record of her attendance.

Katherine first envisioned a musical career for Kay. "I wanted Kay to be a pianist. We [this 'we' frequently shows up, though it apparently referred to Kay and herself—*not* Joe Gibbs] began her musical education when she was very young and found her to be a natural musician. I think few of her fans know how very accomplished she is in this other sphere. Kay became very proficient in memorizing and made an unusually fine pianist. In her teens she played exquisitely. I wanted her to study the pipe organ, for picture houses were just installing organs and I felt this would open a new career for musicians."[25]

Yes, it *is* difficult to envision Kay Francis playing the pipe organ at a movie palace. Still, this statement does indicate that Katherine had her daughter's future very much in mind. Katherine, like one of the characters she played, had tasted "the bitterness of life," and it's easy to imagine her warning Kay against making the same mistakes she'd made — mainly, marrying for love. At some point, it must have occurred to Katherine that the key to Kay's future happiness was marriage to a wealthy man. Perhaps the idea came after receiving yet another compliment on Kay's beauty. Or maybe it was after another dinner of salty popcorn and water. There was the sudden click of insight — *yes.* Like many insights, this became an obsession. Once she realized the goal, how to *accomplish* it became the more important question.

Certainly the company Katherine Clinton was keeping would not provide the means for Kay's climb out of poverty. In fact, in Clinton's mind, probably the worst thing would be for Kay to fall for some charming actor. Somehow the funds were found to send Kay to a private school. It's unlikely Joe left any money to Kay after his death. Perhaps his death, however, forced Katherine and Kay to realize they were truly on their own — romantic illusions that he might one day rescue them disappeared with his passing.

According to Kay, she attended the Ossining School from the ages of 10 to 15. It's not possible to verify her attendance for these dates, but it seems an exaggeration. Run by principal Clara C. Fuller, the Ossining School for Girls was a boarding and day school. Sometimes referred to as Miss Fuller's, the school was located thirty miles from New York City in Ossining, New York.[26] Kay described Miss Fuller as "a tiny woman, with white hair and a sweet face who was very kind to me."[27] According to an advertisement, the school provided "special courses in Typewriting, Bookkeeping, Stenography, Secretarial Work, Household Economy, Practical Gardening and Red Cross Work as well as our special courses of Art, Music and Drama."[28]

Photographs show a grand looking mansion on spacious grounds. "Ossining, on the eastern bank of the Hudson River is distinguished for its healthfulness and beautiful scenery. Being within an hour of New York, it combines the advantages of country life with access to city privileges. The school stands in large, well-shaded grounds, commanding a charming view. The building is commodious, carefully planned, heated by steam and indirect radiation, and has a modern and complete system of plumbing."[29]

Kay discussed life in Ossining, usually with the intention of making it sound madcap and carefree. In an incident sounding like a scene from a Mack Sennett Keystone comedy with Mabel Normand, Kay was rescued by the fire department. "It was a cold night and there was ice on the roofs. I had climbed out the window of the dormitory to a porch for

OSSINING SCHOOL FOR GIRLS, OSSINING, NY
Kay attended the Ossining School for Girls for one year, 1919–1920. Ossining, 30 miles from New York, is famous for its prison, Sing Sing.

some reason or other [in another version, it was the result of a dare]. On the way back I slipped and fell and my bloomers caught on a nail. I hung there, howling, and someone turned on the alarm. People came running because they thought the place was on fire and stood in the yard looking up at me, watching the firemen put up ladders and unhook me."[30]

While attending Ossining, Kay apparently made it into New York City on occasion. In an interview, she described attending the September 10, 1919, homecoming parade[31] for World War I hero General John J. Pershing. A policeman hoisted her up on his shoulders so she could see Pershing — she would have been 14 at the time.

Kay also claimed to be quite an athlete, adept at basketball and track. In fact, one popular tale claimed she tied an Olympic record for the 100 yard dash! As late as 1951 Kay was still repeating the story, though it seems a whopper of a fib. "I tied the Olympic record for the hundred yard dash when I was 15. I made it in 12 seconds. Oh it's been done faster since I was 15, but that was the record then. I had beat it in practice. Eleven and a half seconds. But the day of the official competition, I was sick. I didn't let on except to my friends. If the teachers knew I would not have been allowed to run. I took aspirins and all my friends at Miss Fuller's school for girls in Ossining, N.Y., were cheering me on. I remember I was running for them, and for dear old Miss Fuller."[32] There was no official Olympic record for the women's 100 yard dash in 1920. Still, running it in 12 seconds at that time would have been a marvelous, newsworthy feat, especially for an unknown — and *ill*—15-year-old living at a New York boarding school.[33]

With her athletic build, it's easy to believe Kay would have excelled in sports. At Ossining, Kay also claimed to be good at the high jump but not hurdles because of her small feet. Her mother added that Kay "was the crack player on the basket-ball team, for she could easily place the ball in the basket without jumping."[34]

Kay first fell in love while living at Ossining. It was with a boy from the nearby St. John's Military Academy. "He looked wonderful in his uniform and when he kissed me that first time I thought someone had touched a match to my clothing."[35] Nothing more came of it as Kay tagged along with her mother's vaudeville tour when classes ended that summer of 1920. According to a flowery magazine article, "Kay used to view her mother's performances from the wings or 'out front,' alternately picturing herself as a great star and as a rich socialite attending a matinee in quest of a new thrill for jaded nerves. Little did she dream," the article gushed, "that both pictures were to become realities!"[36]

Although no records have been found, she also attended the Cathedral School of St. Mary in Garden City, Long Island. Located nineteen miles from New York City, the Episcopalian school offered similar coursework as Ossining. Kay began attending in the fall of 1920, and left when the school year ended in May 1921. George Eells reported that Kay's grades included a "77 in conduct and 80s in everything else except for a 98 in spelling and a failing mark in geometry."[37] Most importantly, however, Kay made her first attempt at stage acting. *Let's Not and Say We Did*,[38] written by classmate Katherine (Katty) Stewart, featured songs and Katie Gibbs, then a junior, as the male lead. "Katty played the female lead because she was the author, and I played the leading male role because I was the tallest girl in the class."[39] The play was a success, and an encore performance was held for alumni. "Each one of us had the right to bring two guests and I remember that we invited the boys from St. Paul's School and there was a lot of talk about it."[40] Katty, whose literary effort may have been inspired by a crush, remained close to Kay for several years, eventually becoming one of her first female lovers.

Kay won a fashion sketch contest at school and briefly entertained the idea of becoming a fashion designer. She freely admitted she was not a serious student. "I schooled about,

ST. MARY'S SCHOOL   GARDEN CITY, N. Y.

CATHEDRAL SCHOOL OF ST. MARY, GARDEN CITY, LONG ISLAND, NY
Kay attended the Cathedral School of St. Mary in Garden City from September 1920 to May 1921. Located 19 miles from New York, the school has been torn down and the site sold to a real estate developer.

at one institution and another, barely making my grades, indulging in what romances could be carried on despite the usual high walls, and participating in all school dramatics."[41] Katherine Clinton, however, dissuaded her daughter from acting. Instead, she thought Kay should study secretarial science. In a cautionary 1937 magazine article supposedly written by Kay, she explained that "my mother effectively stripped the profession of any false glamour it might have had for me, while I was still in my 'teens, and readily approved of my plan to do secretarial work."[42]

Before starting school, however, Kay fell in love again. "Before I was 16, I met 'Reg' while visiting friends of my mother during a summer vacation on a Jersey Beach. We became engaged, planned to elope, and although I packed my luggage four different times, I could never quite muster courage to write the farewell note and descend the water spout. I've often regretted that I didn't."[43]

Kay's next school was the Katharine Gibbs School of Secretarial Training. The name led some to believe that Kay's mother ran the school. However, the founder was actually Katharine Ryan Gibbs, born in Galena, Illinois, in 1863. Widowed after her husband's boating accident in 1909, she opened her first establishment, a two-room school in Providence, Rhode Island. She began with one student, but quickly expanded to other cities. The New York School opened in 1918 at 101 Park Avenue.[44] Gibbs revolutionized secretarial training, helping to change it from a male-dominated field. Female graduates from her school — considered the elite of secretaries — were required to wear a hat and long white gloves. Gibbs died in 1934, but her school is still around.[45]

According to the Gibbs School advertisement, a student received a "Broad and advanced curriculum covering all phases of business training pertaining to office, literary, social, and home life. All work is individualized so that each student advances as rapidly as she is able." Although no records have been found, Kay claimed she briefly attended the school and then entered the business world.

Kay found work as an assistant to Juliana Cutting, a New York party planner. Mrs. Cutting, who lived on fashionable Park Avenue,[46] hosted parties and social gatherings for the wealthy, especially debutantes. She introduced Kay to the world of the Social Register — exactly the type of men Katherine Clinton wanted her daughter to meet and, hopefully, marry.

As her daughter entered the business world and the land of eligible bachelors, Katherine Clinton's stage career received a boost when she appeared in two short plays at the Garrick Theater in New York. Produced by the prestigious Theatre Guild — definitely a step up from vaudeville — the plays opened on November 28, 1921. Cast as Mademoiselle Lebos in *The Wife with the Smile,* Clinton appeared with Blanche Yurka, Arnold Daly, and Philip Loeb.[47] In the second play, *Bourbouroche,* staged by noted theater and film director Philip Moeller, Clinton played the cashier. Between Katherine's improved roles and Kay's first career steps, life seemed on the upswing for mother and daughter.

CHAPTER 3

Her Most Wonderful Years, 1922–1925

"I love Dwight."[1]

Kay's youthful romances must have been nerve-wracking for Katherine. Torn between maternal protection for her beautiful teenage daughter and a strong — even frantic — desire to see her marry well, Katherine likely experienced Kay's dating with a combination of enthusiasm and apprehension. One imagines Mrs. Gibbs gleefully rubbing her hands together, like ZaSu Pitts in the classic scene from *Greed,* when she discovered her daughter's fiancé came from a wealthy family. Maybe she didn't go this far, but it's safe to say she wasn't disappointed to learn in the fall of 1922 that Kay was engaged to James Dwight Francis.

Kay may have met Dwight Francis through Juliana Cutting. One clue is a small photograph that appeared in a 1961 book, *Berkshire: Two Hundred Years in Pictures.* A pictorial history of the Pittsfield, Massachusetts, area where Dwight grew up, the book featured a turn-of-the-century photo of picnickers, including Juliana Cutting. Twenty or so years after this photo was taken, Mrs. Cutting, who'd moved to New York, likely knew the Francis family. According to Kay's diary, Kay met Dwight on January 3, 1922, shortly before her 17th birthday. They began seeing each other frequently — dining at the Biltmore Hotel, nightclubbing, taking long walks, dancing at the Waldorf Astoria, attending operas, movies, and even hockey matches.

While dating Dwight, Kay found work modeling at Lundihn's clothing store on May 16.[2] The job, however, lasted less than two weeks. Kay reported to work one Monday morning to find that her locker and bag had been searched — three dresses were missing, and an employee was suspected. Insulted at the accusation, Kay promptly quit. Her next employment began on June 5. Employed as a secretary for the McMillan Emerson & Co.[3] investment firm, she earned $30 a week. Later, she worked at the Sinclair Rubber Company.[4]

Kay never regretted her business training or work experience. "The more I think about it the more I am convinced that being a secretary had much to do with my subsequent career. The habit of self-discipline I gained in the business world has been of the utmost use in my acting career."[5] She further credited her strong desire for privacy to these early experiences. "Business training teaches one not to volunteer information. That, I suppose, is the secret of my well-known reticence about my own life. Thanks to my training in the business world I keep a secretary-like silence about most of the matters that concern my employer, who happens to be myself."[6]

Maybe. In fact, Kay needed to keep her private life secret because the truth would have damaged her reputation. 1922 was an important year — she landed her first real jobs, lost her virginity, and began living a life of uninhibited sexuality. While dating Dwight, Kay wrote a vague, cryptic note on April 23: "I am no longer a virgin though I have never slept with a man."[7] This might refer to an experience with a woman or to a sexual act with Dwight that, at least in Kay's mind, was not technically sexual intercourse. If the reference was to a woman, it might have been Katty Stewart, Kay's old school chum, who was now also living in New York. It also might have been new friend Kiki Whitney. Kay later had affairs with both women.

Based on Kay's diary, she and Dwight became physically involved in late April. Kay's June 12 entry simply stated that she thought she might be a mother. The June 27 entry was terse: "My baby died — or rather our baby."[8] Kay and Dwight continued dating. After a few months, Katherine Clinton confronted Kay, perhaps frantic that her worst fears were true. Kay reported a huge blowup with her mother on September 27, but the lecture, if that's what it was, came too late. Kay had her second abortion[9] around October 12, and a third on November 24.

By all appearances, Dwight Francis was a "good catch." On the surface, he seemed near perfect — attractive and wealthy, from a good family, with a

JAMES DWIGHT FRANCIS
Kay married her first husband, James Dwight Francis, on December 4, 1922. They divorced in France in the spring of 1925 (courtesy of Lesley Lee Francis).

bright future. However, traits below the surface — immaturity and a poor work ethic — ultimately doomed the marriage. James Dwight Francis was the son of Agnes Bartlett Francis and Henry Francis, general manager of the Pontoosuc Woolen Company, one of the most profitable Massachusetts mill companies. Eight years older than Kay, Dwight, born January 13, 1897 — the same month and day as Kay — was the grandson of General William Bartlett, a Civil War hero who became a successful businessman.

Privately tutored, Dwight later attended Phillips Academy in Andover, Massachusetts, from 1912 to 1915, but did not graduate. He also attended Harvard University from 1915 to 1917, but was asked to leave because of poor grades. Dwight blamed his lackadaisical study on the distraction of World War I, and indeed joined the military and became a pilot after this first dismissal from college. He was a flight instructor in France when the war ended, and returned to Harvard in 1919, but was again expelled.[10]

The similarities between Dwight Francis and Joe Gibbs are uncanny. Both were only sons of prosperous men — and grandsons of war heroes. And both ended up losing the family fortune and dying in obscurity. Whatever the similarities, it must have been quite a trick for Kay and Katherine to keep the truth about Kay's background from the Francis family.

It's unknown how Dwight explained to his moneyed parents that Katherine Clinton was an unmarried stage actress— and that he wanted to marry the vaudevillian's daughter. Kay and Katherine undoubtedly put together quite a production — one of their finest dual acting performances, one imagines. Whatever story they told, they probably emphasized Joe's sad passing more than his womanizing, divorces, and alcoholism. Mother and daughter plotted, got their scripts straight, and convinced Dwight's family that Kay was worthy of marriage. Dwight and Kay gamely traveled to Pittsfield and met the parents in late October. Although Dwight's parents believed the two were too young to marry, they reluctantly gave their blessing, and the couple announced their engagement on November 2, 1922. Very soon after, Kay was referring to Dwight's father as dad, and even joined him in partridge shooting.

Kay's diary entries for 1922 are heartbreakingly naïve. It's important to keep in mind she was only 17, and saw the world with a teenager's eyes. On September 5 she reported that she'd lost her faith in men, but by September 20 everything was right again as she noted that she and Dwight had been intimate 100 times. On November 17 she received her engagement ring, a Francis family heirloom. Despite her mother's unfortunate marriage, Kay figured *hers* would be different. Perhaps Katherine, too, believed that Kay's marriage promised happiness and longevity. At the very least, her daughter was no longer doomed to poverty. Or so she thought.

Kay and Dwight were married on December 4, 1922 — Kay was 17 and Dwight 25 — at the St. Thomas Episcopal Church.[11] Still located at 5th Avenue and 53rd Street, this was a popular wedding spot for society couples in the twenties. A magnificent stone, cathedral-like church, it was used as a movie set for *Tarnished Lady,* the 1931 Tallulah Bankhead movie. As a youngster, Kay had a premonition she'd marry young. "I had a feeling I'd marry before I was eighteen — and I did. I didn't want a solitaire for an engagement ring and I didn't want to be married in white. That was about the extent of my 'planning.' As it turned out, I had my wishes. Someone had given my husband a diamond set between two sapphires, and that was the ring he had put in a new setting for me. We decided on a small church wedding with only eighty people present. My gown was gray."[12]

Mr. and Mrs. Francis honeymooned in Boston, went duck hunting in Hyannis Port, visited Pittsfield and Kay's in-laws, and then journeyed back on December 17 to their New York home — Dwight's apartment at 21 West 49th Street.[13] While the rest of December was spent getting settled, Kay concluded her 1922 entries with this notation for December 31: "My most wonderful year!"[14]

"People who knew her then, when she was in her teens, say that she was certainly the model wife. Dwight was from one of the Best Families, but there wasn't much money for the young married couple so they lived in a little house in Pittsfield, Massachusetts, and the future Glamour Girl of Warner Brothers cooked three meals a day for her husband. It was all very beautiful and simple."[15]

Actually, the above was a public relations fantasy. Kay and Dwight lived at their New York apartment, though they spent occasional weekends and summers with Dwight's parents— and then their own apartment at Pittsfield's South Street Inn[16] in 1924. One of Massachusetts's largest apartment houses, the six-story building, constructed of steel and brick, featured six-room apartments with French doors leading to private balconies. Oak molding, tiled bathrooms, and parquet floors distinguished these stylish apartments.[17]

Kay's social activities during 1923 included bridge and mahjong parties, tea dances, dinners, luncheons, opera, symphony, skating, swimming, polo, and occasional games of golf and tennis. Diary notations indicated she saw *Tristan and Isolde, Aida* and *Lucia* at the Metropolitan Opera; Katharine Cornell in *The Enchanted Cottage;* W.C. Fields in *Poppy;* and performances by Ruth St. Denis and Arthur Rubinstein. Movies included Harold Lloyd's *Safety Last* and Pola Negri's *Bella Donna.* She also reported a lunch date in April with Katharine Cornell, who was not yet the stage superstar she would soon become.[18] The care-free lifestyle continued throughout the year, and though Kay noted in June that she was searching for employment, there was no evidence she found work — or even looked that hard.

Kay later claimed she took a job — so she could hire a cook. "My husband's parents correctly assuming a newlywed couple should rise on their own merits, I decided I wanted a cook and I went to work as a social secretary[19] to pay her wages. Later, for nine months my husband, who was in the woolen business, was stationed at a factory in Pittsfield, Massachusetts. I lived the simple life there, doing all my own housework, and I was perfectly content."[20]

Kay and Dwight moved from West 49th Street to 61 W. 10th Street in October, and Kay almost immediately entered Roosevelt Hospital on October 5 for a tonsillectomy. After a two-day stay, Kay returned home and jumped back into her social activities. The couple celebrated their first anniversary in New York at a party at the Ritz for Condé Nast's daughter, Natica. By April, Kay and Dwight had moved again, this time to 150 E. 54th Street.

Married for less than two years, it didn't take long before the relationship soured. Unfortunately, Dwight, often described as fun-loving and eccentric, preferred nightclubbing to working. Although some have reported that Dwight had a drinking problem and even physically abused Kay, no evidence has been found to support this. Family members insist Dwight neither drank nor smoked, though they also admit he wasn't career-minded. Kay, still a teenager, discovered she was expected to supplement the family income.

The year got off to a bad start when Kay had a hemorrhoid operation in January 1924. She spent February through April in Pittsfield. While there, she again played bridge — lots of it, mainly with Dwight's relatives — and also skied. Boredom, a problem that plagued her for most of her life, had crept in, and in May a relieved Kay left the small town to return to the big city.

By now, the marriage was hitting rough spots. On May 12, Kay reported that Dwight was unhappy. She blamed herself. The bickering increased, and then, on May 25, Kay did what many women do when they're unhappy — she got a haircut. In Kay's case, since it was the mid–1920s, she had her hair bobbed.

There's no report on Dwight's reaction, but the act portended a change in the marriage — and in Kay. Less than two months later she met Paul Abbott. She may have met him at the West Side Tennis Club, where she spent most of her time in June. They likely flirted until Kay returned to Pittsfield on July 15 and spent the summer and early fall sunbathing, swimming, and playing tennis and bridge — and avoiding Dwight. On July 21, she briefly mentioned Dwight, noting her happiness that he was returning to New York. In fact, after meeting Paul, Kay rarely mentioned Dwight, though her October 12 entry suggested he was unfaithful — "Dwight is such a cad!"[21] There is no doubt that Dwight had an eye for the ladies. In a 1933 interview, Kay made an interesting reference to Pittsfield. When asked about Ronald Colman's adulterous husband in *Cynara,* Kay commented that most women in Pittsfield would be unable to forgive an erring husband. "Women in that town, and it's typical of other towns, would have felt the blow to their pride too severely to make up after a public scandal. I think that's true of so many divorces. It's pride that goads women on to an unforgiving attitude. They simply can't believe it and they can't walk out of the house and know the neighbors are whispering."[22] It seems an odd but telling reference, since Kay lived only a brief time in Pittsfield.

By this time, Kay, too, was unfaithful. She and Dwight separated in October 1924 after she returned to New York City and reunited with Paul. For his part, Paul ended his marriage with Liza in mid–October, and Liza left for Paris the following month for a divorce. For all intents and purposes, Kay's marriage, too, was over. She was not yet 20.

Kay later poignantly looked back on the marriage and made a startling admission about her disillusionment. "When I was first married, at seventeen, to Dwight Francis, I was a much better wife than I am today. I have an idea I was rather more of a person and considerably more of a woman."[23]

Although there were attempts at reconciliation, Kay admitted on October 30 that her marriage was over. She and Paul began a torrid romance that continued into the fall. "What a wonderful night!"[24] she wrote on November 9. "After two years of the other."

Kay claimed to have no regrets about the early marriage to Dwight. "It's a rather wonderful thing to be married very young and know that ecstatic happiness that belongs to the 'teens. I suppose I'd do it all over again."[25] Some believed her failed marriage affected the rest of her life. Producer David Lewis confided to George Eells that Kay never got over her first marriage. That's a sentimental thought, but what might be more accurate is that Dwight's treatment demoralized her. Her lack of self-confidence perhaps propelled her into numerous sexual liaisons. Paul, in other words, was the first of many. The extramarital affair led to a promiscuous lifestyle that included multiple partners, sexual experimentation, and a casual attitude toward abortion. Frankly, there were so many sexual partners that Kay sometimes referred to them by number — and often wrote of them with regret ("My seventh man — God I hate myself!"[26]). One of Kay's last entries for 1924 was this entry: "Bored and scared."[27]

In 1923, an author using the pseudonym Warner Fabian[28] published a novel titled *Flaming Youth*. The book, a fictional account of women in the 1920s, began with Fabian describing a typical young woman of the era: "restless, seductive, greedy, discontented, craving sensation, unrestrained, a little morbid, more than a little selfish, intelligent, uneducated, sybaritic, following blind instincts and perverse fancies, slack of mind as she is trim of body, neurotic and vigorous...."[29] These same adjectives could have described Kay Francis in the 1920s. Fabian further provided insight into American Jazz Age women with this passage: "They're all desperados, these kids, all of them with any life in their veins; the girls as well as the boys; maybe more than the boys."[30]

"Beginning a new year — have a resolution to make — not to be a damn fool!"[31]

Kay's first entry for 1925 was echoed in later years. Seemingly bewildered by her own behavior, Kay found herself involved in many short-lived relationships over the coming years. Shortly after the first of the year, Kay made her first notation about the man who would become her second husband — William Gaston, commenting on his smile on January 2. Bill would have to wait, however; she was still involved with Paul and married to Dwight.

January 13, 1925, was Kay's 20th birthday. Despite her impending divorce from Dwight, she was listed in the 1925 Winter Edition of the *New York Social Register* as Mrs. James

Dwight Francis (Katharine E. Gibbs), 150 East 54th Street.[32] The building, a typical New York brownstone in a chic neighborhood, was on the south side of the street, near the corner of Third Avenue.[33]

Before traveling to France to divorce Dwight, Kay posed for noted British portrait artist Sir Gerald Kelly.[34] He'd arrived with wife Jane in New York in 1924 to take on American commissions, but found New York expensive and disagreeable, and returned to England after only nine months. Before he returned, however, he painted Kay. She posed several times in December 1924, and then again in February 1925. Kelly painted two portraits from these sessions. The first was described as "yellowish velvet."[35] Unfortunately, the whereabouts of this painting are unknown. The second painting's description is "golden charmeuse — sitting on brown velvet cushions against a grey wall — a pale lilac scarf lying on the cushions."[36] This painting was finished in March 1926. Described as "Spanish-looking, with rich browns and yellows,"[37] another critic noted that it was "a portrait of a girl with definite features, in which the deep red of the lips subtly balances the black decision of uncompromisingly straight hair. A strong harmony this."[38] The portrait was also used to illustrate a New York newspaper article celebrating women's new short hairstyles,[39] and was shown at London's Royal Academy in 1926.[40]

Kay, not a woman to forget a kindness, wrote to Kelly in September 1959: "'Shades of 1925'—How kind you were to me when I came to your studio on Central Park S.—but also—you frightened me most to death when you said, 'One day you are pink—One day you are yellow—Why does your skin tone change?' Do you remember?—So many years have passed & now you are Sir Gerald & I am Kay Francis."[41] Indeed, Katharine Francis in 1925 and Kay Francis in 1959 were two very different women, and the contrast must have hit Kay hard when she wrote of the naïve, enthusiastic girl who flounced into Kelly's studio. The last words—"& I am Kay Francis"—were weighted with bittersweet meaning.

FRANKLIN SIMON & CO. ADVERTISEMENT
This ad was published in the February 1925 issue of Harper's Bazaar *when Kay was 20.*

Shortly after Kay wrote this letter, in an impulsive Rosebuddian moment, she purchased the painting from Kelly.[42]

Kay also modeled for the February 1925 issue of *Harper's Bazar*.[43] In an ad for Franklin Simon & Co., the caption read: "Members of New York Society Wearing The Spring Bramleys For Mademoiselles (14 to 20 years)." Three women appeared with Kay in the full-page ad. Kay's spring coat was a $50 topcoat with a velvet collar. It is a wonderful photo of Kay at age 20. One gloved hand is stuffed into her pocket, while the other is draped across her chest, holding what appears to be a glove. To complete the outfit, a cloche hat is pulled low over her eyes.[44]

Kay did turn down one modeling job before she left for Paris. She was approached to appear in M.F. Weaver's "Bathing Beauties of 1925," but apparently thought better of posing in her bathing suit.

"Paris is really a test for an American. Dinners, soirees, poets, erratic millionaires, painters, translations, lobsters, absinthe, music, promenades, oysters, sherry, aspirins, pictures, Sapphic heiresses, editors, books, sailors, and how!"[45]

This was American writer Hart Crane's description of Paris in 1921. It likely was much the same on February 28, 1925, when Kay sailed on the *S.S. Minnetonka* for France. According to friend Beatrice Ames Stewart, Dwight's family blamed him for the marriage's failure. "They loved her so and realized how much in love she was with that poor, dreary, sodden offspring of theirs. So his aunt took her to Paris, and the family paid for the divorce."[46]

Paris divorces were trendy among the wealthy in the 1920s, partly because New York State required proven adultery, and Reno had a six-week residency requirement. Celebrity divorces included luxurious trips on the ocean liners *Leviathan* and *Ile de France,* fittings at the major fashion houses, side trips to resorts, exotic nightlife, even photographs and interviews in the newspapers. A 1923 *Harper's Bazar* article said it all: "The First Divorce Is the Hardest."[47]

It appears that Paul accompanied Kay to Europe, though she rarely mentioned him in her diary, and the affair was over by the time she returned to New York. Kay stayed in France for more than six months[48] and had a wild, raucous time. Ostensibly chaperoned by Aunt Gertrude, who may have been her mother's relative or friend, Kay became very adept at giving her the slip. Her diary recorded much drinking and sex, beginning almost the minute she arrived at the Paris Vendome Hotel on March 8. Word quickly circulated that an American-born exotic beauty had arrived — and invitations started pouring in.

Charles Baskerville[49] and Lois Long[50] agreed that Kay created a sensation in the fashion capital with her dark look and innate sense of style. Baskerville wrote and illustrated articles about Manhattan's nightclub and restaurant scene for *The New Yorker* in his column "When Nights Are Bold." He met Kay in 1922 and became her good friend and occasional lover, sometimes hiring her as a model after their return to New York.[51] According to Baskerville, "She was an extraordinary person. That summer she had no wardrobe but took a paisley — gray, black and white — Persian shawl and had it made into an evening wrap. Whenever we were going to any swell place, she would put the paisley wrap over her gown, and she was a knockout. She carried herself beautifully; her hair was cut as short as mine, and she wore no jewelry, only lipstick. No eyeshadow or anything; she didn't need it. People were stampeded by this creature. They thought she was a maharani on the loose."[52] Lois Long also was astounded by Kay's fashion sense: "Before we left Paris, she managed to get a beige Patou outfit and hat, a black Patou outfit and a hat and a black evening dress[53]—and that's what she wore for two years. And always looked stunning."[54]

Between dinners at Ciro's, Café de Paris, the Ritz and other expensive restaurants, Kay also attended the Follies Bergere, visited the Arche de Triomphe, and even saw future lover Maurice Chevalier at the Palace Theatre. She motored, attended operas, golfed, and traveled to London, Antwerp, and other European cities. In addition, there were several diary notations of illness, implying a hangover.

One intriguing individual who Kay met was Countess Jean de Polignac. Kay ended up having tea and cocktails with the Countess—a noted Parisian fashion leader—one week after she arrived in Paris.

Kay did take time out of her busy social schedule to meet with her attorney on March 16, and then appeared in court on March 26, where she was granted a divorce. Since this was a "civilized" divorce, she met Dwight for tea on April 10.

Then, like Lorelei Lee in Anita Loos' magazine serial *Gentlemen Prefer Blondes,* Kay went on to enjoy the Parisian social whirl and giddy nightlife. She spent April and May as a tourist, attending the opera, taking tea at the Ritz, lunching at the Acacias and Ciro's, dining at Café de la Paix and Jardin de Ma Soeur, and drinking cocktails at Aux Deux Magots and Harry's Bar. On June 10, Kay traveled to London where she toured Warwick Castle, Parliament, 10 Downing Street, and Oxford. She also began a very brief affair with someone named Donald Gillers, which did not get off to a good start when she fell into water and became sick. Ill for days, she finally returned to Paris on June 17, and had a one-night stand with Julien Chaqueneau[55]—her self-described seventh man.

Kay posed for sculptor Roussie in July, shortly after another abortion. Kay admitted in a July 15 entry that she had no idea who the father was. Roussie Sert was the sister of the notorious Mdivani brothers—Alexis and Serge—who, between them, married Pola Negri, Barbara Hutton, Louise Astor Van Alen, and several other vulnerable American heiresses. Married to Spanish artist Jose Maria Sert, Roussie provided a kind of escort service for her brothers, helping them meet wealthy, eligible American women in Paris. In any event, Kay made a notation in August that she'd returned to Roussie's studio to see the completed bust.[56]

While on her European romp, Kay renewed her acquaintance with the infamous Kiki Whitney Preston. Kay had met Kiki, also known as "the girl with the silver syringe,"[57] in April 1922. Born Alice Gwynne, Kiki was a cabaret performer who supposedly was related to the wealthy Whitney family, though no one can quite determine the link. She married Harvard graduate and investment banker Jerome (Gerry) Preston in April 1925, but had many affairs. In 1924, Kay recorded several visits with Kiki, but it wasn't until both were in Europe in July 1925 that their friendship took on a new intensity—dinner dates, drives into the French countryside, and long conversations. In late July, Kay also began an affair with a man named David King, perhaps an artist, which continued off and on, along with a brief dalliance with Charles Baskerville. Most important, Baskerville introduced her to Stuart Walker on August 25, the American stage director with whom she'd eventually work.

By September, Kay was still seeing David and Charles, but also made time for Kiki. Kay noted on September 13 that she'd lunched with Kiki and then spent the night at Kiki's apartment! "Very nice!"[58] They spent the next few days together until, alas, Kay had to leave Paris. Her September 16 notation indicated that she'd dined with Kiki, then left a disappointed and upset Kiki to return to New York. Kay mentioned Kiki a few more times in her diary, seeing her in New York on October 16, 1934, and again socializing with her in Los Angeles in 1937.

Kiki hobnobbed with British royalty and had an affair with the Duke of Kent, somehow managing to get him hooked on cocaine, morphine, and other drugs in the late 1920s. For a time, she and her husband lived in Africa on a ranch they owned at Lake Naivasha. "Kiki's outstanding beauty was much admired. She never rose before dinner, as she loved parties and was up all night, sometimes playing backgammon with her friend Cockie Birkbeck, when Cockie was married to Bror Blixen. Kiki was on the fringe of Lord Errol's so-called Happy Valley set, an infamous group of British settlers living at Wanjohi Valley, on the slopes of the western Aberdares. They were known for wife swapping, drugs, and endless parties."[59] Kiki finally had *too* much fun and committed suicide in New York City in 1946.[60]

Oddly, the European jaunt turned out to be a kind of scouting trip for Kay's future amorous adventures. Although it's unlikely she met him in 1925 — at least no mention was made in her diary — Kay eventually had an affair with French entertainer Maurice Chevalier in the 1930s.

"I found my capital was a certain amount of looks, figure, and youth. Apparently I was most suited for the stage. I would become an actress."[61]

On the return trip to New York, Kay took stock of her assets and decided to concentrate on acting. Her decision to storm Broadway was made shipboard, with the help of friend Margaret Case. Known as "Miss Case of *Vogue*," Margaret devoted her life to the legendary fashion bible. Her favorite dictum — "That is chic as hell!" — certainly applied to Kay in 1925, and for many decades afterwards.[62]

Years later, Kay admitted her divorce and meager finances had much to do with becoming an actress. "Margaret Case and I were returning from Europe on the old *S.S. Lapland*, and the closer we got to the Statue of Liberty, the more certain I became that I needed a job. I had a lot of smart clothes (I bought them at the places in Paris that copied the famous modistes), so Margaret and I figured out that the only place to use clothes and the ability to wear them was the theatre."[63] In another version, Kay added more drama to the story, explaining that the return home was marred by a violent storm that threatened the ship. "She decided that, if she survived, she would be an actress."[64]

Katherine Clinton had an admirable ability to euphemistically describe less-than-glamorous events in her daughter's life. "'One summer,'" she said, referring to Kay's hedonistic divorce trip to Paris, "'on a vacation trip to Europe, my daughter decided she was not happy in secretarial work. She wanted to earn a larger salary in some more interesting vocation.'"[65]

CHAPTER 4

Kay Goes Wild, 1925–1927

"Arriving New York 1:30— met by Bob[1]— flowers from Dwight."[2]

When Kay returned to New York from Europe on September 26, 1925, she mentioned Dwight for one of the last times in her diary—he sent flowers to meet her ship. Dwight remarried in 1928. He'd met Lesley Frost (1899–1983), daughter of poet Robert, at The Open Book, a Pittsfield bookstore. They had two children, Elinor and Lesley Lee,[3] but the marriage was over by the early 1930s. Meanwhile, he lost much of the family fortune in the 1929 Wall Street crash, and suffered a breakdown. At the height of Kay's fame in the 1930s, Dwight was living in Europe, where he studied, taught, and skied. When war approached, he returned to the United States, and married third wife Henrietta Rossiter in 1936. They had three sons—Henry, Robert, and Bartlett.[4] Although he tried to enlist in World War II, he was turned down because of health issues and mistaken suspicions about his pre-war activities in Europe. Dwight moved his family to Santa Barbara, California, where he lived until 1950, when he divorced Henrietta and moved back to New York. In the late 1950s he married Felice Rose, but that marriage also ended. Like Joe Gibbs, Francis faded into obscurity, and died in a Martha's Vineyard rental cottage on January 25, 1988, at the age of 91. According to an obituary, "his principal business activity was as an investment counselor. For much of his life he explored the world with a spirit of adventure, absorbing and enjoying most of the intellectual and artistic disciplines."[5]

"Instead of going west, I took mother's advice and stayed east. I had made various friends in the theatrical profession. I went to see them. They treated my ambition kindly— but weren't impressed. In fact they told me what I have since been trying to tell all girls who write or come to me: that they were powerless to help me get started until I could help myself. If I had sufficient talent and earnestness, they said, the stage would not fail to discover me."[6]

Almost immediately upon returning from Paris, Kay became serious about going on stage. Dwight, who apparently had little or no money of his own, did not — or could not — pay alimony.[7] "I went on the stage for the very simple reason that I was broke and needed money,"[8] Kay later explained. On September 29 — three days after returning to New York — Kay met with producer Edgar Selwyn, and the next day was offered a role in *Hamlet*.

Kay had two liabilities—her height and a speech impediment. Katherine Clinton had warned Kay about the former. "I believed she was too tall for many stage roles. At that time we knew nothing of camera possibilities."[9] Kay's speech impediment caused her to say her 'r's and 'l's as 'w's.[10] She also had a slight stutter. Kay briefly received speech therapy, which improved her speaking — and confidence.

Kay's attempts to get her size 5C foot through the theatrical door were helped by a combination of good timing and sheer luck. There are several versions of how Kay began her stage career. One persistent but inaccurate claim insists she was hired to understudy Katharine Cornell in *The Green Hat*.[11] According to this story, Charles Baskerville introduced her to producers Al Woods and Edgar Selwyn, who hired her because of her ability to look fabulous in a green hat, along with a slight physical resemblance to Broadway star Cornell[12] — sometimes that's all it took.

The real story of what happened with *The Green Hat* was recorded in Kay's diary. On January 14, 1926, she met with producer Arthur Hopkins and saw the play. Five days later she read for Hopkins. On January 20, she got the bad news: "Failed! Damn it!"[13] She didn't indicate which role she was reading for, or whether it was simply to be Cornell's understudy, but she never publicly admitted failing the audition.

Kay claimed that she refused the role because she wanted actual stage experience and received a better offer — the role of Poppy, a degenerate Eurasian drug addict in John Colton's sensational drama *The Shanghai Gesture*. The play's mise-en-scene was a luxurious Chinese brothel run by Mother God Damn, played by Florence Reed. The male lead in the play was McKay Morris, who would later become Kay's lover.

"Al Woods, when we met," Kay explained to Ed Sullivan, "said: 'Sweetheart, you're just the type for Poppy in *Shanghai Gesture*.' I told him, meanwhile, lying furiously, that I had played stock in Kansas City and amateur Shakespearean companies.[14] He asked me to read the part, and I was very bad. 'Sweetheart,' he said, 'You go home and get the wavers out of your voice.' The next day I knew the jig was up, so I demanded that he get Mrs. Leslie Carter,[15] poor dear, to read the part with me. 'I'll call your bluff,' he said, amused at my nerve, and at three o'clock that afternoon, I was in her apartment. 'You're too tall, three inches too tall,' she told me. 'In the last act, when I kill you, it would look ridiculous for little me even to attempt it — a sort of canary-chasing-the-cat idea.' I was so happy that I didn't have to read the part to her and John Colton that I was delighted at the bad news."[16]

Kay's version of how she got the part in *Hamlet*, is, as usual, dramatic and not entirely truthful. "I heard of a manager who was preparing to produce Hamlet in modern dress. It struck me that the whole idea of the play

KATHARINE FRANCIS EARLY IN HER STAGE CAREER.
Kay — a beauty at age 22.

implied taking a chance. Perhaps the manager might be willing to take a chance on a new-comer as well? Fortified by this theory, I went to see him, persuaded him to let me read some lines in a tryout against several other aspirants—and came off with a part."[17] In later years, when asked how she landed her first stage part in such a prestigious production, she laughed and said, with considerable candor, "by lying a lot — to the right people."[18] In fact, when she met with producer Horace Liveright, she claimed to be experienced with Shake-speare. He specifically asked about *Hamlet*. "'I played Ophelia as a child,' she said with dignity. And so she had — at school."[19]

Years later, when asked about regrets, Kay replied that she wished she had the nerve she'd had that day with Al Woods. "If I had that much gall now, Hollywood wouldn't pay any attention to Garbo. I'd make her look like a blushing violet. I'd just sweep through this town, and people would be so overpowered by my sheer assurance that they'd bow and salaam to me in the streets."[20]

"Probably one of the things that made her determined to go on the stage was the fact that no one thought she could act. Her mother, well-known in the theater as Katherine Clinton, tried to discourage her. 'What can you do on the stage?'"[21]

A London production of *Hamlet* had already opened when A.L. Erlinger announced his desire to put together two American companies, one in New York and one to tour. Any United States production, however, had a distinct disadvantage compared with a European one: "We cannot, of course," said Mr. Erlanger, "permit the players to drink wine and whisky on the stage as they say they do in London, but we shall easily find some substitute for that. In fact, if we are going to present an absolutely up-to-date 'Hamlet,' then we must observe all the customs and manners of the day and the Volstead law must be taken into consideration along with everything else."[22]

Hamlet opened on November 9, 1925, and closed after 88 performances. According to theater critic Burns Mantle, "The 'Hamlet in Modern Dress' was by far the most interest-ing of the experimental revivals. For a few weeks the response was hearty and praise extrav-agantly bestowed. Then interest began to lag."[23] Kay remembered the play as a failure. "The revival was not what you might call a success. We moved from theatre to theatre, and the only reason the star [Basil Sydney] tolerated me was because I knew the Condé Nasts and was able to get his picture in *Vanity Fair!*"[24]

It was through *Hamlet* that Kay met stage actress Adrienne Morrison, one of the play's stars. Morrison, mother of Joan, Constance, and Barbara Bennett, took a special interest in the young actor.[25] Years before, in boarding school, stricken with chicken pox, Kay had a favorite teddy bear removed. She feared never seeing it again, but the cleaned toy was finally returned to her, and Kay kept it as a good luck charm. "I had it until I was playing a leading [not *exactly* a *lead*] part in 'Hamlet in Modern Dress,' on the New York stage." Kay further revealed: "The bear slept with me every night and when I lost it I was heart broken."[26] Morrison presented Kay with a little stuffed dog named Huggles. The toy became Kay's constant companion.[27]

Meanwhile, Kay had married again. Her second husband, William Gaston, described by a friend as a "very good-looking bastard,"[28] was one of the first people she saw after her boat docked in September. His grandfather had been a Boston mayor and the first Demo-cratic Massachusetts governor. His father, William Alexander Gaston, graduated from

Harvard and became a successful lawyer and banker. Gaston's parents—his mother was May Davidson Lockwood—married in 1892, and his father later unsuccessfully ran as a Democratic candidate for governor and the U.S. Senate.

Gaston, born in Boston on November 12, 1896, graduated from St. Mark's School in 1914, and enlisted in the Navy in 1917.[29] Tall and handsome, Gaston saw action in England, Belgium, France, and Italy as a pilot, and was awarded a Navy Cross for bravery. Upon his return, he enrolled at Harvard to study law. A member of the football and crew teams, he received his degree in 1923. An attorney, he also enjoyed the arts and was a rare book collector. He reportedly met Kay at a party through her roommate, Virginia Farjeon, a former classmate at the Cathedral School. Upon meeting him, Kay supposedly confided to a friend, "There's a man I would like to marry!"[30]

Kay and Gaston married on November 19, 1925,[31] when Gaston was Assistant District Attorney of Suffolk County in Massachusetts. Gaston's parents envisioned a political career for their son, who was in the midst of a campaign, and expressed reservations about a marriage. Gaston, however, arrived at Kay's apartment one morning with a minister and marriage license. A 1936 magazine article described the wedding: "Because of the exigencies of the campaign and the objections on all sides, Kay and Gaston were secretly married in Kay's apartment in New York one very cold morning with only Gaston's colored chauffeur and a maid as witnesses. And what an amazing marriage it was! There were no ring, no flowers, no wedding breakfast. Immediately after the ceremony it was necessary for the bridegroom to take the train back to Boston, and Kay spent the first four days of her honeymoon alone in New York!"[32] Typical of Kay's puzzlement at her own behavior was this diary entry on November 19: "Married to BG, my God!"[33]

Gaston often stayed in New York, but lived and worked in Boston. This was a modern idea, and one that appealed to sophisticated, unconventional 1920s couples. Another modern idea was a non-monogamous marriage, which Kay and Bill also chose.

A ridiculous 1934 movie magazine article, loaded with inaccuracies and sporting the lurid title, "The Untold Story of Kay's Secret Marriage," turned their little affair into a great romantic adventure. "Upon arriving [in New York after her divorce] Kay went immediately into rehearsals with a new Broadway show. William B. Gaston hurried to his firm in Boston. A pact was made! At a certain hour Kay would send a telegram to Boston and at the same hour William Gaston would send one from Boston to Kay Francis in New York. If Kay regretted her all too brief status as an unmarried lady, or if William Gaston could possibly throw off cupid's hasty love dart, their ceremony of marriage was to be forgotten. Here was romance too great for any film. Here was suspense too trying for any Hollywood producer. [Here was a pack of lies.] But that was the pact they made. And they both seemed sure. They both were sure for within a week Kay Gibbs-Francis secretly married William B. Gaston."[34]

The article explained that the marriage was doomed by Bill's frequent traveling. "All too soon Kay Gibbs-Francis-Gaston learned that her new husband was all and more than she desired. Unknowingly, Boston's busy playboy neglected this tender creature whose artistic soul demanded constant, mellow affection."[35] In truth, the marriage, which was indeed secret, probably resulted from a night of mutual drunkenness. While they stayed friendly, neither was marriage material. Kay reported in her diary that shortly after finding out she'd failed her audition with Arthur Hopkins in January 1926, she had a one-night stand with *Hamlet* actor Basil Sydney,[36] who apparently tolerated her more than she remembered. Once she started working with the Stuart Walker Company, Kay began a series of affairs—it's likely Gaston did the same—and they drifted apart.

"During the entire two-year duration of that secret marriage only the maid, the chauffeur, the minister who performed the ceremony, and the friend with whom Kay shared the apartment, knew of it!"[37] Actually, Kay did admit the marriage to her mother the following day — and told some male friends and a few others, though there was never a public announcement.

Gaston later married beautiful actress Rosamond Pinchot[38] in January 1928.[39] She was the daughter of Paris-born New York lawyer Amos Pinchot,[40] and niece of Pennsylvania governor Gifford Pinchot. Rosamond, discovered by Max Reinhardt, appeared in the 1935 film version of *The Three Musketeers* as Queen Anne, but was better known for her earlier stage appearances in *The Miracle* and *A Midsummer Night's Dream*. Pinchot died at the age of 33 on January 24, 1938, in the family garage in Old Brookville, New York, when she wrapped herself in ermine, stuffed rags in the car windows, and attached a garden hose to the exhaust. The suicide occurred shortly after she received a letter from Gaston asking for a divorce. Her funeral was held on their tenth wedding anniversary. She and Gaston had two children, William and James. In July 1939, Gaston married Harriet Lucille Hutchings — fifteen years younger than he — and they had one child, Thomas.[41] They divorced in 1948, which was also the year Gaston unsuccessfully ran for Congress. Gaston, who worked in newspapers, banking, and law, died August 15, 1970, at his home in Fairfield, Connecticut.[42]

Before the year ended, Kay also appeared, probably as an extra (since her name did not appear in the credits), in a small role on December 6 in a one-night performance of *The School for Scandal*. Produced by Basil Dean, it was held at the Knickerbocker Theatre. The cast also included Kay's friend, Julia Hoyt, and Ian Hunter, who'd eventually play her romantic interest in several films.

"1925 has been a very big year in my life — and on the whole I have behaved like a damn fool! What will 1926 bring forth?"[43]

At the time of Kay's 21st birthday she slept with a stuffed animal and had been married twice. For the first time, she was listed as Mrs. Katharine G. Francis in the 1926 Winter Edition of the *New York Social Register*. Her address was 37 East 60th Street.[44]

On January 15, 1926, Kay received a plum modeling assignment, posing for noted art deco illustrator Porter Woodruff. A few days later, accompanied by friend Virginia, Kay revisited his studio to look at the portrait. It's likely that the unidentified portrait was eventually published in *Vogue* or another Condé Nast publication.

On February 19, 1926, Kay made her first screen test. It was at the Famous Players studio in Astoria. The test was for director D. W. Griffith, and might have been for casting in *The Sorrows of Satan*. Nothing came of it.

Facing an inability to make a living from acting, Kay took the occasional odd job. She briefly went into public relations with Helen Jenkins in March after *Hamlet* closed. Their campaigns included one for Spanish singing sensation Raquel Meller's April 1926 New York debut.[45]

In the meantime, Kay was preparing to tour with the Stuart Walker Company. She'd met Walker in England and reconnected with him in New York. After signing a contract on April 15, 1926, she left to join the troupe in Cincinnati on April 17.

"Sometimes, while I was playing in Cincinnati, I'd get up early to take a train to Dayton, rehearse the next week's bill and get back to Cincinnati

in time to appear that night. My parts were heavies, but I always wanted sentiment. Once, when I was begging for a weepy part, Stuart Walker actually shook me. 'I'll shake some sense into you,' he said. 'If you learn to play heavies well, leads will come easy to you.'"[46]

Walker's Portmanteau Theatre was a popular and well-known dramatic fixture in the Midwest from 1915 to 1930, where many well-known actors, including Beulah Bondi and Will Geer, received valuable training. Kay, a member of Walker's traveling company from April through September 1926, played everything from walk-ons to bits to secondary leads. It's worth noting that there were four different spellings of Kay's name in the playbills — Katharine, Katherine, Kaye and Kay. At this early stage of her career she was already experimenting with shorter versions of her name — years before she permanently changed it after arriving at Paramount.

Kay's friend Ilka Chase also trained with Stuart Walker, and though she respected Walker, she also reported him to be a bit of a bully. "Every summer he would take a few young people for training — they were called disciples. Stuart was a tough taskmaster, using sarcasm like a lash, working himself up into frightful rages, but within his limits he knew what he was about."[47]

Kay acknowledged that the six months she spent touring with Stuart Walker's stock company provided her with her best training.[48] The sheer number of parts and productions expanded her acting range, though the traveling was grueling. "We used to spend most of the time on interurban[49] cars riding among the three cities. We would play one night in Indianapolis, rehearse in Dayton the next day, and go back to Indianapolis for the evening's show. The cars were old and rattled horribly. It was Summer and very hot, and we would sit on the hard seats and study our parts. We had to get up at 5 in the morning to catch the 6 o'clock car, which wasn't so good when we went to bed after midnight."[50]

Kay admitted to envying the Company's stars — Ann Davis, Peggy Wood, Mona Kingsley, and George Gaul. Kay had affairs with several players in the troupe, including George Meeker.[51] Her June 20, 1926, entry again reflected her persistent surprise at finding herself in bed with someone other than her husband — "Slept with George like a damn fool! God, I ought to be shot."[52] The affair with George was unhappy, marred by boredom, drunkenness and arguing.[53]

Kay's next steady affair was with the leading man in Stuart Walker's Company — McKay Morris. Morris, whose stage career began in 1912 and ended in 1946, was born on December 22, 1891, at Fort Sam Houston in San Antonio, where his father, Colonel Louis Thompson Morris, was stationed. Educated at the Germantown Academy in Philadelphia, he studied acting at the American Academy of Dramatic Arts with the legendary David Belasco.

Morris made his stage debut in *The Governor's Lady*. He was Romeo to Ethel Barrymore's Juliet, and a leading man in dozens of plays throughout the '20s and '30s, including *The Laughing Lady, The Shanghai Gesture, The Road to Rome*, and *Death Takes a Holiday*. Newspaper articles noted that Morris was "always in great demand. Every female star likes to have him as a co-star because of his excellent appearance, his height, his voice and his great histrionic ability."[54]

Kay's stay with the Stuart Walker Company was not without controversy. On August 8, 1926, while appearing in Cincinnati, Ohio, Kay attended a party that was raided by Federal prohibition agents. The arrest made headlines — "Actors Held in Liquor Seizure."

Prohibition agents, responding to neighbors' complaints, crashed a party given by McKay Morris and Larry Fletcher. Neighbors were particularly upset about late, loud parties being held in the garden of Morris' rental home at 204 Gerrard Street in Covington, Kentucky.[55] Kay and the others were arrested.

Apparently acting as the group spokesperson, Kay gave an interview, sounding like a not-so-innocent flapper in a Hollywood movie. "'The day's work of any theatrical performer ends very close to midnight, and the early morning hours are his or her early evening hours,' said Miss Katherine Francis, one of the leading women with the Stuart Walker Company. Miss Francis declared that she and other members of the Walker Company live in Covington, near McKay's apartment, and had formed the habit of dropping in on him after the show before going to their respective homes. 'We thought it so funny when the officers came into the garden,' testified Miss Francis. 'We were so certain, you know, that nothing in violation of the law was on the premises. And we certainly were not talking or laughing loudly. Merely sitting there chatting in lowered voices about our work and the general gossip of the profession.'"[56] Upon arraignment, the liquor charges were dropped, and the players fined $15 each for disorderly conduct.

During her tour with Stuart Walker, Kay often wrote about being drunk, and this may have been when the alcoholism she'd fight the rest of her life took hold. On July 31, she wrote that she'd argued with George and had become ill from too much alcohol. She also wrote about her unhappiness, describing how she often cried herself to sleep at night.

Before the season ended, Kay had impressed several reviewers. Some commented on her beauty. "The most stunning actress in the company is Katherine Francis,"[57] one proclaimed. Others focused on her talent, one referring to her performance as "splendid,"[58] and another saw "a flash of genuine ability coupled with a magnetic personality."[59]

On September 14, 1926, Kay left for New York. She then spent the next few weeks drinking at clubs, including Tony's, Club Alabama, and Texas Guinan's, and traveling with friends to Annapolis, Baltimore, and Tuxedo Park. On October 7, Kay had surgery — probably an appendectomy — and remained hospitalized for almost a week. Upon her release, she moved to 381 Park Avenue, where she shared an apartment with Lois Long and Kay (Katherine) Swan.

Like most Kay Francis stories, there were different versions explaining how she broke her collar bone that October. According to one article, it happened the "night of the great Indoor Polo Match of East 51st Street, when a two hundred pound football player, in the excitement of the game, fell on Kay and broke her collarbone."[60] According to Kay, in the Fall of 1926, "I returned to New York broke, went to a party, engaged in a wrestling match[61] and was so badly injured, I was laid up sick and hungry, for nine weeks."[62] Katherine Swan's version was more vivid. "Dances and parties not being exciting enough we invented new amusements. Indoor Polo held our interest until Kay broke her collarbone. One of the rules is that you must play the game on your knees. The night Kay was hurt, there was a four hundred pound, more or less, football star in the game. In the excitement he thought he was playing football and jumped to his feet. Someone yanked at his knees to bring him down — and all of his four hundred pounds fell on Kay."[63] Fortunately for Kay, who was encased in plaster for more than two weeks, her friends, including Lois Long, anonymously sent her a $1,000 cashier's check.[64]

The incident probably happened in mid–October — Kay was x-rayed at the hospital on October 18 — but the injury didn't seem to slow her down. She recorded another big party on October 24, followed by a dinner date with Ann Harding and Harry Bannister on November 24, and then a party at Condé Nast's on December 3.

After her cast came off, an unrepentant Kay was quickly back in circulation. In an evident attempt to prove that Scott and Zelda Fitzgerald were not the only fun couple who could make memorable entrances, Kay and McKay, with Pepe and Wilda Bennett, hopped on the back of a truck in full evening attire one night and hitched a ride to Texas Guinan's. A few weeks later, a fight broke out during a dinner party at Wilda's.[65] Kay was knocked to the floor in the middle of the melee and spent the night recuperating at McKay's. There were no hard feelings, and both couples were soon back together on the cocktail circuit.

Also, on November 1, Kay moved again — this time to the Hotel Marlton at 5 West 8th Street. This move was an effort to live closer to Morris, who also had a room at the Greenwich Village hotel.[66] Their relationship was complicated. According to one friend, "she was madly in love with him. Neither had a job, and she had no money. He was a great actor and very handsome but impotent, which didn't really seem to make a great deal of difference to her."[67] In truth, Morris was gay, and Kay became annoyed upon discovering he was continuing to sleep with men.[68] Still, Kay remained obsessively involved with Morris, and the tortured relationship continued for several years, with Kay making frequent notations in her diary proclaiming her love.

In later years, McKay acted with the Theatre Guild in *Volpone, Marco Millions,* and other plays. He never appeared in a movie, and his last Broadway appearance was as Prince Nisou in *Lute Song* in 1946. He lived at 230 Riverside Drive in Manhattan, where he died in 1955 at the age of 62.

Lois Long, one of Kay's roommates, dated Bill Gaston, and later married and divorced *New Yorker* cartoonist Peter Arno. Long, who wrote for *The New Yorker* under the pseudonym Lipstick, spoke of the Jazz Age with affection. According to her, Kay enjoyed Manhattan's 24-hour party atmosphere. Their set spent virtually every evening in speakeasies, returning home at dawn, usually cockeyed drunk. "We all drank heavily. It was a wild generation. Katherine — or Kay — always had a tumbler of gin for breakfast. We got it for twelve dollars a case from Frankie Costello, who was our bootlegger."[69]

Katherine Swan echoed Lois Long: "We were a bit hay-wire in those days. Life was very hectic but merry. Now and then we cast our thoughts toward the theatrical world where our careers were centered, but as no engagements came forth we filled the interim by stepping high, wide and handsome. Our apartment consisted of two small rooms but such was our popularity that it was necessary for us each to have our individual telephone. It sounded and looked like the stock broker's office in Douglas Fairbank's picture, *Reaching for the Moon.*"[70]

A magazine article described Kay's Manhattan life. "It was in those gay pre-depression days of 1927 to 1930 that our Miss Francis practically became the belle of New York. Charming, chic, poised, and the most smartly dressed woman in any night club, it is no wonder that men went mad over her. At that time she lived with two girls in a small apartment near the corner of 51st and Park and it speaks well for their popularity that although they only had two rooms they had three telephones."[71]

Thanks to the 18th Amendment, or the Volstead Act, which became law on January 16, 1920, New York's nightlife underwent drastic changes. By 1922, Manhattan was home to five thousand speakeasies, with more than a thousand in the midtown area, bounded by 5th and 9th Avenues and 38th to 59th Streets. "Replacing the old corner saloon, they were located in back rooms, 'tea rooms,' cold-water flats, apartments, and 'novelty shops.' All you had to do to win admittance most of the time was to knock twice and murmur, 'Joe sent me.'"[72]

Most establishments provided entertainment for affluent New Yorkers. The biggest clubs offered grand Ziegfeld-type revues. For example, Billy Rose opened the Fifth Avenue Club with *Billy Rose's Sins of 1926*. Some offered dance teams, such as Fred and Adele Astaire, and Clifton Webb and Mary Hay. Broadway stars, including Gertrude Lawrence and Beatrice Lillie, appeared in cabarets after their shows. A few clubs were named after performers—Club (Harry) Richman, Casa (Vincent) Lopez, The House of (Helen) Morgan, and Villa (Rudy) Vallee. Manhattan's most famous nightclub sensation was Texas Guinan, "Queen of the Nightclubs," whose slogan was "Hello, sucker!"

By 1927, there were so many places devoted to drinking, it was "a matter of not *where* to get a drink, but *which* place."[73] Kay spent nights at Club Alabama, Texas Guinan's, Club Richman, the Jungle Club and others, but her favorite was Tony's—sometimes called "The Tony's," to distinguish it from competitors of the same name. Tony's was located at 59 West 52nd Street, home of so many speakeasies the residents living in nearby brownstones hung handmade signs cautioning not to ring—"This is a private residence." Tony's was expensive, and its preferred customers were writers and actors. Libby Holman, Clifton Webb, and members of the Algonquin Round Table were regulars. Legend has it that "April in Paris" was composed by Vernon Duke at Tony's, and Cole Porter occasionally sat at the piano.

Owner Tony Soma "was dark and distinguished looking. His regular patrons often introduced him as Admiral Balbo, the Italian Fascist leader and intrepid aviator. He had an irritating habit of singing Verdi or Puccini arias while standing on his head, a feat he had mastered by studying yoga. And by serving inexpensive Italian food and highly suspicious alcohol, Tony felt he was performing a valuable service for the intelligentsia."[74]

Kay's life in 1920s New York revolved around two things—partying and trying to make a living. Acting jobs weren't easy to find, so she occasionally turned to modeling—and once costumed a play. "The producer probably figured that anyone who could dress herself as exquisitely as Kay does could dress others, too."[75] Actually, the real story is even *more* interesting. The play was *Damn the Tears,* written by soon-to-be ex-husband William Gaston, produced by Alexander McKaig, and staged by Sigourney Thayer. Julia Hoyt[76] and Kay Francis received costuming credit.[77] Opening at the Garrick Theatre on January 21, 1927, it played for 22 performances.[78] Gaston, who claimed the tale was based on a real person, wrote about Buckland Steele, a college baseball player and law student. Steele, unable to cope with modern-day life, loses touch with reality, becomes homeless, and is ultimately arrested for vagrancy at his old ballpark. An unusual multi-media hodgepodge, it featured music, puppets(!), drums, radios, pianos, movies, harps, disembodied voices—and sets by legendary designer Norman Bel Geddes. Audience members were given a 1,500-word essay written by Gaston, hoping to explain the play, along with a 1,000-word statement by McKaig and Thayer. The reviews were scathing. Alexander Woollcott described it as "quite as irresolute, as confused and as pitiable as Buckland Steele."[79] Burton Davis was equally perplexed. Describing it as "the queerest play of the season 1926–27 to date," he further noted that, "After sitting through their creation I know nothing whatever about what they were trying to do on that stage nor why they tried to do it. This is not a smart-aleck statement. It is an admission of honest bewilderment."[80] Davis also noted that the first-night audience significantly dwindled before the play's conclusion. Gaston, who enjoyed dabbling in the arts, also started a short-lived production company in 1927—Jack Productions.[81]

Famed illustrator Neysa McMein received a credit for a portrait used in the play, and it's likely this was how Kay met her—and secured a much-needed modeling job.[82] McMein's studio, on the fifth floor of an old West 57th Street building, was a gathering place for intellectuals, including Dorothy Parker and George Kaufman. Kay's portrait was used for the

May 1927 *McCall's* magazine cover, part of the Heroines of Fiction series. The cover bore only a small likeness to Kay, though the pose was typical of her later movie stills—leaning forward, she had a direct gaze, with one hand touching her chest.

"Lost Huggles out of window! Found him!"[83]

Despite her frenetic nightlife, Kay found time to return to the stage on February 22, appearing in *Crime,* where she wore a scene-stealing gold lame evening gown.[84] Burns Mantle noted that *Crime* was one of only two of the 25 plays produced in February 1927 that interested anybody for long. He described it as "a stage melodrama of gunmen, their 'gats' and their 'gals.'"[85] According to Eells, "The critics ignored Katherine Francis, but audiences were enchanted by the beautiful dark-haired girl in a gold dress, and to the end of Kay's life Sylvia Sidney maintained that Kay had stolen the play from her."[86] Kay "gladly" took the small part "because I needed the money"[87]—a common theme during her New York years. Also in the production was Kay Johnson, who would later appear in *Passion Flower* with Kay.[88] They'd met on the train to Philadelphia and immediately hit it off, becoming fast friends.

Kay's personal life at the time was typically messy. Still obsessed with Morris, she was also seeing Dave Carter, and noted several occasions in March and April where she spent the night with Swanee—roommate Kay Swan, whom she'd befriended when they toured together with the Stuart Walker Company. It's impossible to tell from her diary entries whether the relationship with Swan was platonic or more.[89] In any event, in April 1927, Kay was working on a vaudeville sketch with Swanee, one that they hoped might get them some work on the circuit.

Kay also became briefly involved with Adam Gimbel, a member of the Gimbel's department store family, who came off as a cad extraordinaire. After attending polo matches and visiting the beach, they slept together on May 23. Kay noted that he was her thirteenth man, and he gave her perfume and a dressing gown. However, he left for Europe in July without saying goodbye.

Kay also dated Cornelius Vanderbilt and Kirby Hall. In addition, her social circle included

MCCALL'S COVER MAY 1927
Kay modeled for illustrator Neysa McMein in January 1927.

Broadway legend Jeanne Eagels. Kay noted meeting with Eagels several times in her diary, and reported having dinner with her on May 28, 1927, and stopping by for words of encouragement before a show on June 25. Probably best known for playing Sadie Thompson in *Rain,* Eagels, born Amelia Jean Eagles in Kansas City, Kansas, in 1894, died of a heroin overdose in 1929. Her motto was "Never deny. Never explain. Say nothing and become a legend."

In June 1927, Kay picked up another assignment modeling clothes for a fashion show. She was still appearing in *Crime,* but drinking a great deal, literally making herself sick, sometimes missing performances. Dr. Levy attended to her on July 1 and 2, suggesting she had another abortion.

In the summer of 1927, Kay also had a brief affair with Stuart Walker actor George Somnes[90] On July 14, Kay wrote that she'd kissed him for the first time, and then added a cryptic comment about possibly marrying him. While they vacationed in the Catskills, talk of marriage continued, and Kay concluded she'd be a fool *not* to marry him.

The sophisticated, urbane Somnes, however, was out of the picture in late July when Kay began a heated affair with Allan A. Ryan, Jr. His grandfather, Thomas Fortune Ryan, worth more than $100 million, was an art collector and philanthropist who owned rubber plantations, railroads, trolleys, and diamond mines. Allan's father, Allan A. Ryan, Sr., had owned the Stutz Bearcat automobile company and was involved in early aviation. Allan Jr., born in New York City on July 4, 1903, like many descendants of self-made men, was not so successful, though he remained quite wealthy. On August 1, Kay recorded this entry: "Please let me make him happy! I so wish to—I said I would marry Al and I am so happy!"[91]

On August 11, 1927, Kay received the wonderful news that she'd gotten a part in the stage play *The Command to Love.* However, only a few days later she was replaced,[92] probably because the producers decided she wasn't right for the role. "What a disappointment but I guess they are right—But I am so blue!"[93] It was devastating to Kay, especially when the production became a hit. After opening at the Longacre Theatre on September 20, 1927, it played for 247 performances—and then went on a year-long national tour.

Kay and Bill Gaston divorced on September 1, 1927. Meanwhile, Kay had met Allan's parents, and Allan's father apparently asked the couple to wait, something that Kay felt conflicted about. While wondering if they'd ever marry, she also expressed a lack of contentment. "I kissed him again but now am getting bored with that! What a bitch I am!"[94]

That fall Kay met famed polo player Tommy Hitchcock, who ran in the same circles with Kay, Hitchcock was nicknamed Ten-Goal Tommy because of his polo playing skill. Hitchcock was an amazing American story. Born to wealthy parents in Aiken, South Carolina, in 1900, he enlisted with the French during World War I at the age of 17 when the United States rejected him. Shot down in Germany in 1918, he escaped from a prison camp train, walked more than a week before successfully reaching the Swiss border (a one hundred mile trip), and was awarded the Croix de Guerre. When Kay met him in New York City in the fall of 1927, he was still an active polo player, having won a National Open championship and a silver Olympic medal in 1924. His image was that of a clean-living gentleman who neither smoked nor drank, and he was idolized by many Americans. Some think F. Scott Fitzgerald based the character of Tom Buchanan in *The Great Gatsby* on him. He shared an East 52nd Street[95] brownstone with several others,[96] and Kay probably met him at a party there. The brownstone, legendary for its parties and brothel-like atmosphere, was crudely described by a Hitchcock roommate: "If there is any spot in that house, six by four, upstairs or down, where some girl hasn't been laid, I'll eat it."[97] Kay reported that she visited Tommy at home, kissed him, and ended up in bed with him during the first week of October 1927.[98]

Kay found another acting job and spent October[99] touring in *Amateur Anne,* a vanity production designed to showcase co-author Gertrude Bryan.[100] The husky-voiced Bryan had been successful in the 1911 cross-dressing musical play, *Little Boy Blue,* and was now on the comeback trail. *Amateur Anne* opened in Wilmington on October 5 and then traveled to the Bronx and Connecticut that same month. It finally closed in Hartford after terrible reviews, despite the "8 Snappy Broadway Night Club Girls" in the cast. Kay's character was described as blasé and liking gin.

Kay continued her stormy relationship with Allan through the rest of the year, though she was clearly going through the motions. She also maintained contact with ex-husband Gaston, who rekindled the romance by telling her he'd like to remarry, though he knew it—like the first marriage—would be a mistake.

Before 1927 ended, Kay was cast in another production. This time she played an aviator in *Venus.* It began rehearsals in late November and opened on December 25, 1927. She took advantage of a unique opportunity to research the role with aviation legend Charles Lindbergh. Hounded by crowds and the press after his famous flight to Paris, Lindbergh hid out at the home of friend Bill Maloney, who happened to be one of Kay's pals. Kay met Lindbergh at a party on November 26. "In his Sixty-seventh Street and Madison Avenue penthouse, Maloney, who loved gadgets, had a secret passageway leading to a secluded bedroom on the floor below. He offered it to Lindbergh, who, in gratitude, agreed to meet a group of Maloney's friends. Among them was Kay, who mystified everyone by asking such questions as 'Tell me, were you scared?' or 'What makes a man become an aviator?' or 'Are fliers unique in any way?'"[101] Alas, the research couldn't overcome her lack of experience. According to one reviewer, "Katherine Francis and Edward Crandall could limber up considerably. They are not strong at any time, particularly in the first act."[102] Another review remarked on the resemblance between Kay and actor Edward Crandall, and noted they made a handsome couple. The play, called "unimaginative"[103] by *The New York Times,* had a short run.

"I slept with him. God damn me!"[104]

This was one of Kay's last entries for 1927. She was referring to Adam Gimbel, who had returned from his European trip. The notation immediately followed an entry reporting that *Venus,* her latest play, had opened. It would close on December 31 after only eight performances. While alternating evenings with Allan and Adam, Kay also indulged in a brief flirtation with Alexis Mdivani, whom she'd met in Paris in 1925.[105] Unbeknownst to Allan, Kay also saw producer William A. Brady, Jr., on the sly. Brady had offered her a part in *The Road to Rome* the previous August. When Kay locked herself out of her apartment one night, Brady broke down the door for her. Kay noted in her diary that she would not tell Allan about this episode. On New Years Eve, Kay celebrated the end of 1927 by going to Tony's with Allan and then spending the night with him. Such was the life of Kay Francis in 1927.[106]

CHAPTER 5

The Big Break, 1928–1929

"In bed all day — lazy and grand! Allan up at 6:30."[1]

Thus began Kay's diary entries for 1928. What was Kay Francis really like then? Adela Rogers St. Johns provided a glimpse. With allowances for the author's gift for hyperbole, the description probably rings true:

"The people who knew Kay Francis in New York thought of her as a play-girl. Always ready for anything. A lot of laughs was her main object. The men she went around with were nearly always the ones who could make her laugh hearty. She was the life of the party, could always be counted on for wisecracks, quick answers, amusing ideas. Broadway's playgirl. A straight-shooter. A grand kid. But she never took anything, neither men nor work, seriously. They didn't know that she had once taken a man much too seriously and had been badly hurt. No, Kay Francis had decided, as young folks so often do, that the way to beat life at its own game was never to take anything seriously, never to believe in anything and then you couldn't be disillusioned, never to build up any dreams and then you couldn't be rudely awakened, never to throw your whole soul into the keeping of another human being and then you couldn't be disappointed. Be a play-girl. That was the system."[2]

Kay spent New Years with Allan, but their arguing increased. One sore point was Kay's stage career. Allan may have wanted Kay to retire once they married. For her part, Kay perhaps wondered how far her career might take her. She was an avid moviegoer and attended many stage shows as well, often noting the female performer in her diary. In the first few months of 1928 alone, Kay saw Beatrice Lillie, Marilyn Miller, Gloria Swanson, Ina Claire, Laurette Taylor, Vilma Banky, Mae West, and others.

Kay had another abortion in January 1928. She'd made several earlier diary entries indicating she and Allan knew they were taking chances—"Got the curse! Hail and thank God!"[3] Kay and Allan continued seeing each other in the early months of 1928, including a winter visit to Canada to visit Allan's ill father.

Kay also had a brief spring affair with Edmund Goulding, a British actor-director-writer who had immigrated to the United States after sustaining injuries in World War I. He had already written a well-received novel, *Fury*, co-written the hit play *Dancing Mothers* with producer Edgar Selwyn, and was then working for MGM as a writer-director.[4] The notoriously sexual Goulding was known to have a "casting couch" for young stage performers. As for his sexual tastes, one writer remarked, "if there was anything he hadn't tried, it was because it hadn't occurred to him."[5]

In Kay's cryptic diary entry for April 23, 1928, she indicated that she'd performed some unnamed sexual act for the first time with Eddie Goulding. Kay saw Eddie several more times in April, and they remained friendly for years.

In May, Kay returned to the stage when *Fast Company*—later to be renamed *Elmer the Great*—opened on May 3 in Worcester, Massachusetts. The play was about a baseball pitcher named Elmer Kane, and Kay played a small role as a showgirl. The play's star was Walter Huston. "If you act as well as you look, the role is yours!"[6] he had told her at their first meeting.

The production traveled to Boston, where Kay attended a tea party that also included the infamous Evelyn Nesbit, "the girl in the red velvet swing."[7] Kay also spent much time with Walter and fellow cast member Nan Sunderland, with whom Walter was having an affair. Kay made a quick trip back to New York for another abortion.

A day after the abortion, Kay returned to Boston to continue in the play. Ted Newton[8] was another cast member, and Kay enjoyed flirting with him. She considered Ted a boy, even though he was actually a few months older than her. Kay pursued him, and a few days later wrote that she'd gotten him to kiss her. Not coincidentally, this happened a few days after Kay had had a brief but emotional meeting with ex-husband Bill Gaston, who'd come to see the play.

A few days later, Kay spent the night with Allan, who'd joined Kay in Boston. "Allan stayed with me all night — Sweet thing, but God I have to make myself like him physically again!"[9] Allan also met with Aunt Gertrude, who apparently wanted to meet Allan before the two married.

Meanwhile, *Elmer the Great* traveled to Chicago, where it opened on June 18. Less than two weeks later, Kay began an affair with Harold Healy,[10] who played the part of her boyfriend in the play. At first, she and Healy were simply drinking buddies; but it quickly turned into something sexual. It also became distasteful. On July 13, 1928, she recorded this entry after a gambling loss: "Lost $100! Damn fool. Back to Harry's room, and then I said I would sleep with him to pay the $100, but he tried and couldn't get excited. What irony! Thank God too!"[11]

Allan arrived in Chicago in mid–July, again hoping to convince Kay to marry him. Kay briefly considered quitting the show, but, following a few days of indecision, decided to stay on — and rejected the marriage proposal. Apparently Walter Huston also played a part in chasing off Allan. According to a 1935 interview, Kay credited Huston with saving her career. "I owe my entire career to him. We were cast together in *Elmer the Great*, and he did more for me than any coach ever could have done. While we were playing in Chicago, a man came there who wanted to marry me. Walter wouldn't let me do it. I can see him now, telling the man in that powerful manner Walter has. 'This girl has a career ahead of her. She *mustn't* get married at this time!'"[12] The affair with Allan ended when Kay telephoned him on August 28, telling him it was off for good. As with Gaston, Kay and Allan remained friendly, and even made weak reconciliation attempts.

After Allan left, Kay continued her affair with Harold, but they were incompatible, especially when drinking, and frequently argued. By September, the stormy relationship exploded. "Terrible fight — Harold put out of hotel. Awful and I am finished."[13]

Kay's life was out of control. On September 15, 1928, she wrote, "After show still cock-eyed — all the boys in 1129 fed me straight tumblers of gin — Whoopee! Begged Grant to stay with me, but I had no luck."[14] A few days later, she admitted she was in despair. At a party a friend named Ernie [15] hosted for her, Kay spent much of the time crying.

Kay spent much of her free time trying to find relief from the heat and humidity of an unrelenting Chicago summer. She lazed away most afternoons on the Lake Michigan beaches of Chicago's Gold Coast. After each night's show, she motored with friends to the outdoor restaurants and road houses in the suburbs north of the city, or attended parties at the lakeside estates of millionaires such as Cyrus McCormack. Her Sundays were often spent on yachts, socializing with out-of-town visitors such as Bernard Baruch, and going for airplane rides at the Municipal Airport (Midway Airport).[16]

Kay returned to New York on September 23. *Elmer the Great* opened at New York's Lyceum on September 24. Back on her home turf, she occasionally saw Harold, McKay, and Allan. Gosh, even Dwight Francis stopped by for cocktails on October 23, which resulted in yet another loud scene with a jealous Harold.[17]

The play was not well received by New York critics and finally closed on October 27. Apparently the last performance was not anyone's best effort. "Closing Elmer!!!— drunken show—Gordon Hicks wet his pants!!"[18] Despite her messy personal life, reviewers had noticed the "stunning brunette."[19] Critics pointed out that she did "splendidly,"[20] and that she was "attractive and bright."[21]

As usual, Kay immediately tried to find work. She interviewed twice with Fox about appearing in Movietones, but nothing came of it. She was also considered for a role in *Nigger Rich,* but that, too, fell through.

Kay's romantic life continued to be complicated. She briefly saw Paul Abbott in mid–November, but it was McKay Morris who still held the tightest hold on Kay's heart. Her affection for McKay, however, didn't stop her from having one-night stands with other men, including a brief flirtation with a man she referred to as Otis Taylor. This was probably Otis Chatfield-Taylor,[22] who was one of many men who fell hard for the beautiful 23-year-old. "I guess he really does love me, poor dear,"[23] she wrote about him on December 5, 1928. On December 27, she also recorded spending the night with Bayard Kilgour, a Harvard man who became an acclaimed rare book collector.[24]

"There wasn't a more popular girl on Broadway than the laughter-loving, gay, witty Kay Francis, who loved a good time and knew how to have it."[25]

While Kay's personal life unraveled, her mother made what was probably her final stage performance. Katherine Clinton appeared in *Caravan,* which opened on August 29, 1928, at the Klaw Theatre and ran for 29 performances. Clinton played Madre Bourdet, a gypsy queen. After this production, little is found on Katherine Clinton, except in the context of being identified as Kay Francis' mother. It's quite possible this was her last production, and she retired when Kay's film career began in earnest.

Ironically, when Kay's personal life was at its worst, she was close to a huge professional breakthrough. On November 16, 1928, Paramount released its first all-talking movie, *Interference,* at the Paramount Theatre on Times Square. Designed as a class production, the drawing-room drama received rave reviews from film critics, primarily because of its intelligent dialogue and outstanding sound recording. Producer Jesse Lasky announced the slogan for Paramount talkies—"With Casts That Can Talk." Paramount was betting that Broadway's stars would become future movie stars, and many of the movies later filmed at the Paramount studio were adapted from hit Broadway plays.[26] Kay, in the right place at the right time, was on the verge of shifting her career from the stage to motion pictures— and becoming a star.

"Kay was the thirteenth girl tested for the screen role in 'Gentlemen of the Press' after twelve blondes had been tried out. Add to that the fact that she was born in the thirteenth month of her mother's marriage;

that in her first stage part her name was listed thirteenth in the cast of characters; and that her first Hollywood screen part was played on Stage 13, and you may understand why she doesn't share the opinion of some people that thirteen is an unlucky number!"[27]

Like her stage career, there were several versions of how Kay entered the movies. It's possible Walter Huston, Kay's co-star in *Elmer the Great*, recommended her for the part. He'd just been cast to star in *Gentlemen of the Press*, and Kay admitted in a 1936 interview that, "Frankly, I owe my entire career in pictures to Walter. I didn't want to sign with any studio. I was, believe it or not, afraid of the movies and of Hollywood. But after we finished the run of *Elmer the Great*, Walter went to Paramount's Long Island studio to make *Gentlemen of the Press*. He persuaded them to give me a part, then talked me into playing it! I had $1.75 in the bank and $1.50 in my purse when I received my first movie contract. But broke as I almost was, I would not have signed it if Walter hadn't advised me to. He has been the most remarkable and kindest friend a person could have."[28] Another version of the story suggested that Kay — already friendly with Huston and director Millard Webb — simply asked for the part.[29]

Ward Morehouse, one of the screenwriters for *Gentlemen of the Press*, claimed he and co-author Bartlett Cormack were responsible for her movie career. "With the shooting ready to start it was discovered that there was no actress for the role of Myra, siren of the piece. So we all went immediately to Tony's and there, in the haze of that famous back room, with Forney Wyly, the Atlanta wit, making cracks at everybody in sight, and with celebrities of sorts piling over the bare tables, we found Kay Francis. She was resting comfortably behind a Tom Collins. She was tall, dark and interesting-looking but had made far more appearances in Tony's than she had on the Broadway stage. She looked the part of Myra, all right. But the day of just looking it was gone forever. Could she act and how was her voice? She was hustled over to Astoria. In the first test her voice came through strong and clear and vibrant. Her screen career began that very day."[30]

In yet another version, Kay claimed that John Meehan was the person responsible for getting her a job at Paramount. According to Kay, Meehan "engaged me for a role in 'Nigger Rich,' which turned out to be so hot that it was abandoned before we got well into rehearsals."[31] On December 11, Meehan took Kay to see the stage play *Gentlemen of the Press*. The next day he gave her a tour of Paramount, and her screen test came about two days later.

Kay feared the screen test and made excuses, ranging from a blemish on her nose to her mother's broken ankle. She finally took the test, only to be disappointed with the results. "I had a bad cold and when they told me to come to the studio they said they wouldn't have to test my voice. But when I got there they had decided to test it anyway. Walter told me about it in the commissary. I ran up to the dressing room and gargled for an hour. Then I ate a box of throat lozenges and stepped in front of the camera. It sounded very bad to me, but when the studio people saw it they said it was fine. They hadn't heard a low voice like mine before, they said. I never told them about the cold."[32]

In another version, Kay made the story even more dramatic. "After trying every possible remedy to relax her vocal cords, she was forced to go through her scenes uttering lines in the huskiest whispers. The sound men, alert to newcomers, excitedly announced the discovery of another 'Ethel Barrymore voice,' and the deep Francis contralto immediately became an institution."[33]

Kay had two strikes against her with director Millard Webb. He'd had his heart set on a blonde, *and* he feared Kay's gray eyes wouldn't film well. Still, he, producer Monta Bell, dialogue director[34] John Meehan, and the writers were impressed with her test. Kay, however, wanted to hide after seeing it. "I had never thought about working in pictures. In fact, I wanted to stay on the stage. After Millard Webb saw the test, he said he wanted me to see it, too. I saw it thinking that I would look as I imagine angels look, but I got the shock of my life. My face was shiny and I looked like the devil. I disappeared for ten days. When they finally found me and said they wanted me to sign a contract, I nearly dropped dead."[35] Kay explained that she hid out on Long Island until her mother phoned — Paramount was offering $300 a week with a five-week guarantee. "I rushed back into town —for $1,500 I would have jumped off the Woolworth Building."[36] Kay signed the contract and began rehearsals at the end of December, thus joining the parade of Broadway's great and near-great crossing the East River to appear in the new talkies.

Before 1928 ended, Kay appeared in ski togs in the December issue of *Harper's Bazar*.[37] This was her last New York modeling assignment, though there'd be plenty more in Hollywood, for products ranging from soap to cigarettes to silverware.[38]

"It was while we were making 'Gentlemen of the Press' that I had my first taste of studio jargon. I was wearing a pink silk chiffon dress and thought I looked pretty nice. When I came on the set one of the electricians shouted: 'Take the silk off that broad.' I jumped and looked around to tell the man what I thought of him. 'He's talking about a light,' a prop boy told me."[39]

KAY FRANCIS IN 1929
Katherine Francis in early 1929 when she was working at Paramount's Astoria Studio in New York.

When Kay turned 24 she was busy commuting every day to Paramount's sound stage in Queens. This was the final year she was listed in the *New York Social Register*. Her 137 East 58th Street address was a convenient one — only a block from the entrance ramps to the 59th Street Bridge, and a short taxi or limousine ride to the studio.[40]

During production in January 1929, Kay and Millard Webb became an item. Webb, more than ten years older than Kay, may have said something about marriage because on February 11, Kay indicated in her diary that things seemed to be moving too fast. However, less than two weeks later, she wrote that she feared he'd become bored with her.

During the four-week production of *Gentlemen of the Press* (or shortly thereafter), Kay supposedly married John Meehan. Virtually every published reference on Kay lists him as husband number three. The story goes that he worked closely with the novice film actress, providing her with a crash course on movie acting, which apparently led to romance and more. This marriage, according to the story, was so brief that many of Kay's friends never knew about it. In an interview more than a decade after the marriage, Kay insisted it never happened. On the eve of her ill-fated engagement to Erik Barnekow in 1939, she attempted to set the record straight on her marriages. "Reporters insist I have already been married four times and this will be my fifth. When you've been married that many times, one more or less doesn't matter, but I have actually been married three times and this will be my fourth. I'm not trying to make excuses but two of those marriages and divorces took place before I was 22. The first was to Dwight Francis, the second to William A. Gaston. My supposed third marriage was to John Meehan, a writer. When this news broke he sent me a kidding wire: 'When did all this happen? I must have been asleep or on a trip around the world.' He was dialogue director on my first picture and while we're good friends we were never married.'"[41]

Part of the confusion stemmed from a Walter Winchell column tidbit on April 2, 1928: "Kay Francis, the play actress, got sealed to someone or other last week."[42] At that time, however, Kay was heavily involved with Allan, who definitely did *not* marry Kay — and she had not yet mentioned Meehan in her diary. Still, newspaper articles in the late 1930s listed Meehan as her third husband. Kay's attorneys were also confused about the Meehan marriage because when filing Kay's will with the courts after her death in 1968, they mistakenly identified Meehan as husband number three. However, they also indicated that they could find no record of a marriage or divorce involving Meehan.[43]

Kay didn't even seem to particularly like Meehan, describing him as difficult in a diary entry. Meehan is a somewhat enigmatic figure, though he had a successful career, including two Oscar nominations.[44]

It *is* possible that it was Millard Webb — not John Meehan — who married Kay in 1929, but her diary failed to provide the answer. There were no notations about any marriage in 1928 or 1929,[45] and, again, Kay insisted her third marriage was to Kenneth MacKenna.

"Obviously, Kay Francis can't act. Acting is not what she is doing on-screen. Being there is what she is doing, and at that she is an Olympic champion. She is presence, not talent."[46]

Kay wrote remarkably little about her first film experience in her diary, displaying much more concern about her affair with Millard. Still, she, Betty Lawford, Meehan, and Webb worked long hours. In one instance, Kay reported they were at the studio until 3:15 AM. On January 31, 1929, Kay saw rushes of *Gentlemen of the Press*— and started rehearsing for her second film, *The Cocoanuts*. She also signed a new contract that day and received a raise. She was now making $450 a week.

Kay's acting in *Gentlemen* was theatrical and not terribly natural, and *The New York Times* accused her of overacting. *Photoplay,* however, suggested a star had been discovered, crediting her with "one of the most astonishing first performances in the history of motion pictures."[47] She would certainly acquire greater range and complexity, but this first film, produced during the early years of talkies, showed a heavy reliance on her stage and modeling background. There were several mannerisms that stuck with her throughout her career, including the hand-on-the-hip stance with a slight slouch, and smoothing or patting her hair with her hand. She also was seen with a familiar prop — a cigarette. Her hair, styled in a shingle, was extremely short and mannish. In fact, some complained it was too butch, though it does seem a perfect complement to the art deco fashions and sets. Leatrice Joy, Natalie Moorhead, and Dorothy Mackaill were other actresses who wore the shingle. Kay's hairstyle would remain like this for several films until Warner Brothers gave her a new look.

Kay wasn't the only novice in the early days of talkies. Even experienced filmmakers faced new challenges with sound. One difficulty was the number of cameras. The minimum was two — one for the soundtrack, and the other for visuals. However, "if you wanted to cover the sequence in any kind of decent way, you had to have five cameras going. That, in turn, meant that when you lit the set, you had to light it in some strange way that would be appropriate for five different cameras pointing in five different directions."[48] *Gentlemen of the Press* required seven cameras.

Another difficulty was the soundtrack. "Nobody in the movie business knew much about sound. Nobody in the sound business knew much about movies. Microphones were hidden in vases and corsages. Monk's cloth was hung on the walls as if it were soundproofing. Noisy flies drowned out the dialogue of great actors. Casts and crews of thousands were kept waiting for hours while repairmen fiddled with bad connections."[49]

If working on *Gentlemen of the Press* was unusual, the set of *The Cocoanuts* must have been surreal, especially dealing with the improvisational antics of The Marx Brothers, then appearing in *Animal Crackers*[50] at the 44th Street Theatre. According to Kay, "Chico pulled lingerie out of my hat. Harpo chased me all over the screen. Groucho wrestled with me. When they talk of me as the dignified Kay Francis, I think back to the prat-falls that I took with the Marx Brothers, and have a nice, quiet giggle."[51]

While working on *The Cocoanuts,* Kay was called back for retakes on her first film on February 19. Finally, *Gentlemen of the Press* was completed, and Kay enjoyed its preview in Yonkers on February 22.

After Kay completed her first two movies in New York, Paramount decided to transfer her to Los Angeles to continue her movie career at the Melrose Avenue studio in Hollywood. Kay, at first, refused. "I said I wouldn't go. It was too far away, I told them. But I needed the money, and after two weeks of arguing, I finally gave in."[52] On March 13, after a meeting with a studio representative, Kay wrote in her diary that she'd made up her mind to go to California. Partly, Kay didn't want to leave Millard: "Blue as hell at leaving M. I think he is going to miss me too — damn it!"[53]

After saying goodbye to Millard, her mother, Julia Hoyt, and other friends, Kay left from New York on April 11 via two luxury trains — the 20th Century Limited and the Chief. The Limited, a celebrity favorite, was the New York Central Railroad's famous train from New York to Chicago. The service was inaugurated in 1902 from Grand Central Station, and followed the Hudson River and the shore of Lake Erie along the smooth water route. Arriving the next morning at Chicago's LaSalle Street Station in the Loop, Kay and luggage would have been transferred to the Dearborn Street Station to board the Santa Fe Chief, an all–Pullman sleeping-car train that made the trip from Chicago to Los Angeles in a little under 40 hours.[54]

Kay, however, spent one night in Chicago at the Ambassador Hotel with Katty Stewart, who'd fallen in love with the soon-to-be movie star. "Slept with Katty only because she wanted me to — Damn!"[55] Kay wrote on April 12. Kay continued her trip the next day — with Katty on board — and reached California on April 15.

A studio photographer met her at the railroad station and captured the beauty's arrival from the East. The "best dressed" actresses at the time were Constance Bennett and Lilyan Tashman. Paramount immediately started a publicity campaign, making Kay a competitor for the title. "And so, when Kay got off the Chief in Pasadena she found the station jammed with trunks and luggage not her own and a publicity department frantically snapping her *by* trunks, *on* trunks, *in* trunks."[56] Although Kay despised the title, this was the beginning of her Hollywood clotheshorse fame. According to the publicity blurb accompanying the photograph, "Kay Francis, arrived in Los Angeles yesterday, via the Chief, ready to start work under the terms of her new contract with Paramount. Miss Francis is a well known Broadway star, and her sartorial acumen causes much attention in New York. She has just completed two dialogue productions for Paramount at Long Island, *Gentlemen of the Press* and with The Four Marx Brothers in *The Cocoanuts*. Her striking brunette beauty, her ability to wear clothes as well as her mellow voice won her a contract with a ticket to Hollywood."[57]

Indeed, Kay Francis had arrived in Hollywood—her home for the next two decades. Meanwhile, the next few months were a whirlwind of activity—professionally and personally.

KAY FRANCIS ARRIVES IN HOLLYWOOD
Kay arrived by train in Los Angeles on April 15, 1929.

CHAPTER 6

"Overnight" Success, 1929–1930

"Learning to drive — two accidents — nice man downtown and over stone wall."[1]

Upon her arrival in Hollywood on April 15, 1929, Kay met with producer B.P. Schulberg, toured the studio, and then checked into the Roosevelt Hotel.[2] Almost immediately, she was put to work, though she did take time out to do something almost unheard of in New York — learn to drive an automobile. It wasn't easy, according to her comical entry for April 17.

It also wasn't easy adjusting to film work. "When I came out here, I was scared to death. I had heard about how mean picture people could be to people on the stage. I hadn't much self-confidence anyway. I didn't know what to do about the camera."[3]

Her first Hollywood production was *Dangerous Curves* with Clara Bow, which started shooting on April 18, 1929. According to legend, Clara suggested Kay change her first name from Katharine to Kay for marquee value. This may be true, but playbills from Kay's days with the Stuart Walker Stock Company showed previous experiments with shortening her first name. Perhaps more accurate was that kind-hearted Clara gave Kay tips about moviemaking. "It's wonderful how helpful Hollywood folks are," Kay said. "When I worked with Clara Bow, she was simply too grand. She said to me, 'Now, Kay, I'm the star, so naturally they train the camera on me. But if you'll cheat over just a little, you'll get in it just right, too. You've got to keep that face in the camera you know, darling.'"[4]

Cameras, microphones, lighting — many movie tools were new to Kay, but she proved to be a quick study. Alan Brock,[5] who later became Kay's personal agent, knew her during her early Holly-

KAY FRANCIS DURING THE FLAPPER ERA
Kay in flapper finery as she appeared in her first movies in 1929.

wood days. According to him, she was fascinated by all aspects of moviemaking, and often stood at the edge of the sets, watching scenes being filmed, even when she wasn't in them.

While working on *Dangerous Curves*, Kay was asked whether the microphone frightened her—as it did Clara Bow. "No," she barked, already sounding like a pro. "What is there in a mike to scare you after you are used to 1,500 people? And once you get used to observing the camera lines by instinct, there isn't anything to worry about."[6] This interview also showed that Kay was concerned about her future career. "I've played menaces right along, and I suppose I'll have to, for a while. But I'd like to do sophisticated heroines."[7]

Much of *Dangerous Curves* was filmed at night, and Kay's schedule sometimes required her to work until the early morning hours. Still, she socialized and began making friends. In those first few months she socialized with Hal Skelly, Walter Catlett, Basil and Ouida Rathbone, Richard Arlen, Eddie Sutherland, Ruth Chatterton,[8] Joan and Constance Bennett, Edmund Goulding, Gary Cooper, Nancy Carroll, Ben Lyon, William Paley, Bebe Daniels, George Bancroft, Sue Carol, and others.

Kay also took time to reconnect with old friend Kay Johnson, who had already moved to the West Coast. Although the two apparently were never physically involved, they were intimate and toyed with a sexual relationship. Johnson had married director John Cromwell in 1928 and later became the mother of actor James Cromwell in 1940.[9] On April 21, 1929, Kay wrote in her diary that she'd been to Kay Johnson's alone for a talk, and that Johnson pledged her lifelong love to Kay.

Katty and Kay lived together, probably at the Roosevelt, for a couple months until Katty returned to New York in June. The two went to movies and beaches, and Katty accompanied Kay to premieres, the studio, and parties—including at least one at Clara Bow's. It's little wonder that many in the Hollywood community began to assume Kay Francis was a lesbian.[10] On June 1, Kay wrote, "I really adore her—and I guess she really loves me."[11] The next day, however, Katty left by train, and Kay didn't mention her again until the following year when Katty was living in New Orleans. Kay later explained that she'd brought Katty to Hollywood—as a kind of chaperone! "I was scared stiff of the 'iniquities' of Hollywood as well as being financially low when I came here. My friends had warned me I'd probably be inveigled into taking dope, so I actually brought a girl-friend from New Orleans along to stay with me as protection for awhile! When I got acquainted I found Hollywood wasn't a bit dangerous."[12]

Meanwhile, Kay's affair with Millard had ended. Although they'd kept in contact with telegrams and telephone calls, the distance proved too great for the fragile relationship. Still, it was serious enough that at some point he'd given her a ring. On May 13, 1929, Kay and Webb argued on the telephone. Kay promptly removed Millard's ring and resolved to find a new lover.[13]

In May and June, Kay fought off advances from Walter Huston. She enjoyed his company, but wanted no part of a sexual relationship with him. One night, a drunken Walter spent the night—sleeping between Katty and Kay. A persistent Walter finally succeeded in getting Kay to kiss him, but she felt no sexual attraction for him.

On June 21, Kay saw a preview of *Dangerous Curves*. Her response? "Ouch!"[14] Indeed, it was strictly a Clara Bow vehicle—and not a very good one. Kay also had a small role in *Illusion* with Buddy Rogers and Nancy Carroll. According to Rogers, "Kay Francis was stunning. Tall, dark, lovely, and very bright. She was an utterly charming lady. It's a shame they didn't give her a bigger role in *Illusion*. She was very capable and appealing, even if her part was just a bit. She eventually showed Paramount and Hollywood what she could do—and how!"[15]

Hungarian-born Paul Lukas had a bit part in *Illusion* as well, and made a play for the new Paramount player. She managed to avoid his European charm, though he came on strong, telling her he feared he'd never see her again — and that he'd willingly die for her.[16]

The Marriage Playground was Kay's first picture with Fredric March *and* her first mother role, though she was cast as a glamorous actress with little maternal instinct. The picture received good reviews, and Kay did her best work up to that point, demonstrating her comedic strengths.

Kay also appeared in *Behind the Make-Up* — which wouldn't be released until early 1930. Important primarily because it was her first film with William Powell, she was still cast as the vamp. Reviewers dismissed the film but liked Kay. *Variety* found her "subtly convincing."[17] Fay Wray, when interviewed almost seventy years later, couldn't remember the film, but did remember her co-star. "Don't remember much about *Behind the Make-Up*. Kay was new to pictures. She was smart, sleek, and had a panther-like beauty. She certainly knew how to wear clothes! Of course, she went on to become a big star at Warners."[18]

KAY FRANCIS IN A TRAVIS BANTON GOWN
A 1929 fashion still of Kay from Illusion.

"Kenneth stayed for quite a while — he's getting better and better!"[19]

In July 1929, Kay moved into a rental home at 8401 Fountain Avenue in West Hollywood.[20] She also began writing about her newest romantic partner — Kenneth MacKenna — the man who would become her third husband.[21] Born Leo Mielziner, Jr. in Canterbury, New Hampshire, in 1899, his parents were portrait artist Leo Mielziner and journalist Ella MacKenna Friend Mielziner.[22] His grandfather was Dr. Moses Mielziner, a Jewish scholar who taught and wrote books, including *The Institution of Slavery Among the Ancient Hebrews* and *An Introduction to the Talmud*.

Leo and Ella, both Americans, met in Europe in 1892 and married in Boston in 1896. Kenneth, who was called Junior during childhood, spent his early years in Europe, where his parents moved shortly after his birth.[23] Kenneth, younger brother Joe, and his parents lived for a time in the Montparnasse section of Paris, where Leo worked and trained as an artist, and Ella, using the pseudonym Aube du Siecle, was a fashion and theater critic for *Vogue* magazine.

Kenneth spoke fluent French, but his broken English concerned his parents enough to send him to boarding school in England.[24] In 1909, when Kenneth was almost ten years old, the family moved back to America. The transition wasn't easy for Kenneth or brother

KAY FRANCIS AT HOME
A rare shot of Kay posing at home in 1930. This was probably taken at the 8401 Fountain Avenue residence.

Joe, as their accents and Eton-style clothing made them easy targets in New York City's public schools. Their parents finally enrolled them at the Ethical Culture School, which proved to be a better fit. Kenneth, however, left the school before graduating, and worked in a machine shop while attending New York University.

After briefly serving in the Army during World War I, he worked in investment banking with Kuhn, Loeb until he had the opportunity to become an actor. Actress Grace George saw him in an amateur production and spoke well of him to her husband, and producer William A. Brady,[25] who signed him to a three-year contract. When Mielziner made his Broadway debut in 1919 in *At 9:45*, Brady suggested Mielziner change his name. Using his mother's family name — and adding Kenneth because he thought it sounded alliterative — Leo Mielziner, Jr. became Kenneth MacKenna. Soon after, he was no longer Junior to family and friends, but referred to as Kenneth or Ken. "Between 1919, when he started, and 1923, he had been in seven Broadway shows and had gone on the road with two of them. When his three-year contract with Bill Brady was up in 1922, he moved on to other producers[26] and to the Theatre Guild. Along the way, he became known as a promising leading man, good looking, personable, with the air of a college instructor. He read prodigiously, carefully analyzed the theatrical scene about him and was ready to pull [brother] Joe along on his coattails."[27] Joe, who eventually shortened his name to Jo, became one of the theater's most acclaimed stage designers.

MacKenna became a popular Broadway actor, appearing in numerous productions, including *The Immodest Violet, The Endless Chain,* and *Windows.* He was particularly noteworthy with Helen Hayes[28] in the James M. Barrie play *What Every Woman Knows* in 1926. Occasionally, he supplemented his income with appearances in silent productions filmed at Paramount's Astoria Studio, including *Miss Bluebird, A Kiss in the Dark,* and *The American Venus.* When Fox offered him a lucrative deal to act and direct in 1929, MacKenna agreed, mainly because the $130,000 contract offered "absolutely security for all of us,"[29] meaning his entire family. MacKenna felt a strong responsibility to provide for his parents and brother, who often struggled. However, this meant moving to Hollywood, which MacKenna reluctantly agreed to do in early 1929, though it meant leaving his close-knit family.

By September 1929, Kay was still seeing Kenneth, and becoming quite fond of him, though she again feared he might grow bored with her. Also in September, Kay traveled to Hawaii, where she spent a couple of weeks surfing, sightseeing, dancing, and playing tennis. Ken greeted her upon her return, and they continued their passionate affair into the winter months. Like Kay's other affairs, this one was marked by wild sex and drunkenness: "Over to spend night with Kenneth — terribly drunk — Poor Kenneth, he's a ram!"[30]

"Paramount imported a most delightful fashion plate from Broadway. Kay Francis, tall, slender, raven black hair, straight back from the face, gray green eyes, and such clothes! Yellow checked linen suit, fitted at the waistline, white and yellow shoes, and hat and bag to match. Believe me, everybody on the Paramount lot turned to look at her."[31]

Still largely relegated to vamp-like characters, Kay wasn't yet a star and had barely been mentioned in reviews. However, in just a few years she'd gone from making $30 to $500 a week, and the movie magazines had discovered her. She received a prominent article in *Photoplay*[32] (her first magazine cover wouldn't come until July 1930), and the article proclaimed her "the first great vamp of the talking pictures, and standard bearer of the new come-hither school."[33]

While at Paramount, Kay became friends with still photographer John Engstead. "Almost every day Kay would enter the Paramount executive building, scoop up her mail, come to my office, and plop down in a big red chair that faced my desk. If I had time, we'd talk or otherwise I'd go on with my work. If she was in a hurry, she'd just say, 'Hi,' glance over the mail, and leave. It was a no-nonsense friendship."[34]

As the 1920s ended, it wasn't just the end of a decade, but the end of an epoch for the world *and* Kay. The prosperity of the 1920s and the state of mind that propelled it ended with America's most devastating stock market crash. The world slowly drifted into the Depression. Through it all, the poverty-stricken girl, with two broken marriages and a so-so acting career, was on the path to becoming a millionaire, more financially successful than many in the Social Register she'd left behind. While the fortunes of many dwindled, Kay's income and popularity soared.

Perhaps most important, Kay's background didn't follow her. Few knew about Joe, the unconventional childhood, or her scandal-ridden New York life. Elsie Janis, who worked with Kay on *Paramount on Parade,* pretended to be convinced that Kay came from a fine family: "I asked people about her, who she was, where she came from. No one seemed to be quite sure. I met her, liked her low husky voice, and by her manner of speech was more than ever convinced that Kay had stepped from under what families invariably call 'every advantage a girl could ask for' to become an actress. The expression, 'well bred,' should be handled with rubber gloves, and I wear mittens, but having met girls all over the world whose antecedents and background demanded that label I feel qualified to say that it fits Kay as snugly as one of her own conservatively chic gowns."[35] In truth, Janis, who was a close pal of Eddie Goulding's, likely knew about Kay's past but was among the first of many writers who worked to shield Kay's scandalous life from her fans.

Another magazine article — this one published in 1932 — described Kay as an "aristocrat of the screen." It further depicted her as "an aristocrat of today who goes in for dash and some splash with her haughtiness. But we can see by her life that she lives up to Webster's definition of the word. She has the sympathies, the inclinations, habits and temper of the ruling class."[36] The author asked Kay's friend, Katherine Swan, if she considered Kay an aristocrat. "An aristocrat in her tastes. I have never seen Kay do an ungraceful thing. She has breeding and poise. She is a bit different — doesn't make friends easily. Though I do not mean to give the impression that she is high hat because she is anything but that. She is very genuine."[37]

Kay's mother, Katherine Clinton Gibbs, also eventually moved to Hollywood.[38] Because of Kay's success, she, too— at last — achieved financial security. In a 1939 interview, ten years after arriving in Hollywood, Kay explained that one of her first tasks upon arriving in Hollywood was providing for her mother. "I established a trust fund for her when I first began making important money."[39] Katherine Clinton, for her part, immediately went to work keeping Kay's Hollywood scrapbooks, perhaps a bittersweet exercise for the former actress.

Kay and her mother established ground rules early upon her arrival in Hollywood. "Sometimes for days or even weeks, I do not see my daughter," her mother explained. "Mothers on studio sets are more of a hindrance than a help, I believe. During Kay's entire film career, I have only visited her set once. We do not live together, but each maintains a home of her own. Her friends are of one generation, and mine of another. That is as it should be. We love each other just as much and do not see each other so often as to grow tired or quarrelsome. Our mother-daughter relation is unique in Hollywood. But it is very happy and successful."[40]

Kay eventually bought a house for her mother in 1937. Described as "a charming bungalow behind a velvet lawn dotted by fruit trees," it featured "one of the largest and loveliest pansy beds to be found in Hollywood."[41]

But that was all in the future. In 1929, Kay still questioned whether she'd made the right decision to move to Hollywood. However, by the end of that year, Katherine and Kay were giddy with excitement, certain their fortunes had changed for good.

Kay ended her 1929 diary with a surprisingly positive entry: "Well, 1929 is over. I have a good job, but I must try to save money this year — my love life is very happy — Kenneth is terribly sweet and I should be a very content woman!"[42]

"Working — my test for Raffles at 9 — Mary Astor's husband killed in air crash."[43]

The year 1930 began tragically when film star Mary Astor's husband Kenneth Hawks was killed in one of Hollywood's worst on-set accidents. Hawks, a director like his famous brother Howard, died on January 2 when two planes carrying a film crew collided over the Pacific Ocean.[44] Ten people, including Hawks, were killed. Kay spent the first few days of the New Year comforting her friend.

She also became involved in the John Gilbert and Ina Claire marital saga. Kay termed it a mess, and indeed it was. Gilbert, a great silent film actor, and Claire, a talented stage actor, had married in 1929 shortly after Greta Garbo jilted Gilbert. A notorious drinker and womanizer, Gilbert faced career troubles when talkies replaced silents — and he clashed with MGM head Louis B. Mayer. The marriage didn't get off to a good start, and Kay became a confidante of both.[45]

Although Kay had been in Hollywood for only a short time, she quickly became a popular guest at parties and social events. Her diary recorded events with King Vidor, Fredric March and Florence Eldridge,[46] Samuel Goldwyn, Irving Thalberg, Irving Berlin, Alice and Benjamin Glazer, Eddie Goulding, Louis Bromfield, Humphrey Bogart, Lilyan Tashman, Constance Talmadge, Martin Townsend, Kay Johnson and John Cromwell, and others.

Unfortunately, Kay's drinking was sometimes out of control. She recorded many instances of drunkenness, sometimes to the point of passing out. Usually, Kay was contrite and ashamed after the incidences.

In January 1930, Kay was loaned out to United Artists for *Raffles*. Her role wasn't interesting or large, but it was a popular film because of Ronald Colman, and helped make her more familiar to audiences. Again cast as the sympathetic girlfriend, she seemed somewhat adrift among the British actors. Still, others found Ronald and Kay a good team. "Ronald Colman is ideally cast as Raffles, and handles the serio-comic role with a deft touch that makes it one of his best roles to date. He is given beautiful support by the alluring Kay Francis, whose sophistication and charm make her an ideal team-mate for the star."[47] Rumors suggested that Kay and Colman might marry, though Kay denied it. The two did have a brief flirtation in February 1930, but Kay quickly tired of him. Still, she never forgot his acting advice: "When people ask me to reveal the secret of my subtle screen charm and individual technique, I break down and tell them all. 'When I look to the right,' I say, 'that's surprise. When I look to the left, that's fear. When I look down, that's sorrow. And when I look up, that's love.'"[48]

According to photographer John Engstead, Kay made an unintentional pratfall during production. "Kay was a smart, classy lady. An unusual, arresting beauty, she stood five feet nine inches tall, wore size two shoes [sic], and consequently was very uneasy on her feet. Once while filming *Raffles* with Ronald Colman, Kay made an impressive entrance coming down a marble staircase. When she arrived at the bottom, she tripped and fell flat on her face. 'Damned little feet,' she said."[49]

"*Had to sleep with her because she wanted me.*"[50]

Kay traveled by train to New Orleans in March — to see Katty. She arrived on March 22, and they renewed their intimate friendship, though Kay apparently put up a small protest. She spent a couple weeks sightseeing and drinking, as well as seeing old friend Stuart Walker, before gleefully returning to Kenneth and Los Angeles on April 10. The affair with Katty was over. "Gee, Katty was terribly boring and unhappy,"[51] Kay concluded.

Kay, who had been typecast as a villain in a succession of films, was finally allowed to play a different kind of character in Paramount's *Street of Chance* (1930). This time she was the wife of a gambler — William Powell, again. It was her first role as a sympathetic wife, and her first real lead. Kay credited producer David O. Selznick for believing in her. For *his*

KAY FRANCIS IN *FOR THE DEFENSE* (1930)
Kay's role as the sympathetic girlfriend in For the Defense
(1930) was one of her many film appearances in 1930.

part, Selznick took credit for Kay's success: "every single part of importance that Kay Francis played was due to my forcing her."[52] In this case, Selznick also reportedly fought Cromwell, explaining that Kay was added to the cast after a "bitter struggle against John Cromwell."[53] Reviewers liked the film, and Kay's performance was particularly noteworthy. "No woman on the screen could be more stunning than Kay Francis as 'Natural's' wife. She wears her clothes like a thoroughbred and she adds interest to a story in which men are featured."[54]

Unfortunately, Kay's eyes were permanently damaged during the film's production. Director John Cromwell, new to filmmaking, didn't realize how dangerous the arc light could be. "It took a day and a half for them to set up the equipment, and as the arc light came nearer and nearer for the close up, I didn't want to break up the scene by complaining. It hurt my eyes, but we did the scene. It never had to be reshot. When it was over, tears came streaming down my eyes, and I had to spend

10 days in a dark room."[55] Because of the incident, Kay wore medicated dark glasses the rest of her life.

Paramount on Parade (1930) was a revue-type production designed to highlight the studio's stars. Kay's role was interesting because she played an exaggerated version of herself, letting audiences see a glimpse of the real woman, tantrum and all. It also included a sequence with Kay in Technicolor—for the first and only time.

In *A Notorious Affair* (1930), Kay took on the vamp role with relish, stealing the movie from gorgeous Billie Dove, which wasn't easy to do. Kay, who probably became a star because of this erotic performance, apparently decided that if they wanted her to play a man-eater, she'd play it to the hilt. Reviewers noticed her. "The Russian countess with the emotional habits of Catherine the Great is given a smoking enactment by Kay Francis. She provides Hollywood's most disturbing portrayal since *Hell's Angels.*"[56] According to Dove, "The critics thought *A Notorious Affair* was an awful picture. I hear so many compliments and good things about it now. That happens frequently. The reviewers hate, and the fans love. Kay played the vamp, and played her well. She shaded her role with wickedness and nymphomania. Kay and I were both dressed to the nines in that one."[57]

Kay's next film with William Powell, *For the Defense* (1930), provided her with a more complicated role, a combination vamp/sympathetic girlfriend. Reviews were mixed for Kay and the film, but notice was again made of her ability to wear clothes. "Kay Francis again is asked to fill the role of a smart clothes horse, but she does so with dignity and a certain amount of feeling. Furthermore, she possesses one of the few musical feminine voices heard in pictures."[58]

When *Let's Go Native* (1930) appeared, it was clear Paramount wasn't sure what to do with the brunette beauty. The film, a weird musical comedy, featured the inexplicable pairing of Jack Oakie and Jeanette MacDonald. It was a throwback to vaudeville—*bad* vaudeville—and seemed a poor vehicle for Kay, who was even required to sing! It's not unwatchable however—but for all the wrong reasons. While some reviewers admitted she was miscast, others liked her in the role. "Kay Francis was attractive in becoming costumes and is heard in an alluring song."[59] Paramount, too, was pleased with Kay's progress to this point, and in October 1930 picked up her option, which had to ease her mind.[60]

The Virtuous Sin (1930) was notable for several reasons. First, the

A DIFFERENT LOOK FOR KAY FRANCIS
This portrait emphasized Kay's girlish looks, a departure from her usual glamour shots.

co-director[61] was George Cukor, and even though it's not perfect — and proved a later embarrassment to him — it did have its moments. Second, it's the only film in which Kay appeared opposite Kenneth MacKenna. This picture, like *Let's Go Native*, also offered the rare opportunity to again hear Kay sing in her own voice — and she's not bad. Although she wasn't top billed, this was Kay's film, and she appeared in almost every scene. Reviewers tended to agree with Cukor. The picture *was* weak but offered a good role for Kay. *Variety* suggested the movie "should do much to help Kay Francis on her way."[62]

Passion Flower, released in December 1930, once again cast Kay as a man-trap — in this case she stole her cousin's husband. The cousin was played by Kay Johnson, Kay's friend. A glorified soap opera, it was produced at MGM by Irving Thalberg, no less. Kay wore some wonderful Adrian gowns, but the film was no great shakes at the box office or with critics. Co-star Charles Bickford described it as "a dreadful piece of clap-trap."[63] Still, it was the first time Kay Francis received top billing, and most of her reviews were good. *The New York Times* noted that she did "exceptionally well,"[64] but *Variety* missed the boat on this prediction: "Kay Francis is coming along. However, having several pictures to her credit now, it's doubtful if this brunette will ever achieve stardom but that she's an invaluable featured player is something the Coast has already found out."[65]

"Because her vocal chords are very tender, Kay is unable to scream in any of her pictures. To save her throat, somebody is called upon to scream for her. Although she is hailed as one of the best-dressed women on the screen, she dislikes 'fitting.' She is fond of the water and likes to go sailing. She owns a small schooner and goes sailing every week-end. Next to this sport she likes tennis. She is a good bridge player, and likes backgammon."[66]

If Kay had stopped to think about the remarkable series of events that found her in Hollywood, she might have become paralyzed. After all, *Vanity Fair* reminded readers, she'd been "chiefly famous, in New York, a year or two ago, as the lady who was going about doing a good deal of what is known as 'creating a stir' when she entered crowded restaurants and nightclubs."[67] Kay, who'd attended parties at Condé Nast's duplex penthouse at 1040 Park Avenue in the 1920s, was photographed annually in the early 1930s by Cecil Beaton and Edward Steichen for Nast's publications *Vogue* and *Vanity Fair*. In the August 1933 issue of the latter, Kay was included in a double-page color spread of caricatures of the movie colony by Miguel Covarrubias. The illustration was titled "Hollywood's Malibu Beach," and Kay's caricature was number 13 — a number she always considered lucky. Maurice Chevalier and Leslie Howard appeared on her left and right, and nearby were caricatures of three of her closest friends in Hollywood — Constance Bennett, Miriam Hopkins and Lilyan Tashman.

Although Kay admitted to nervousness, she possessed a steely calm that no doubt helped her keep a level head in her competitive profession. "When I first went on the stage, I didn't know whether it was to be merely a temporary way of earning my living, or whether it was to be something more. I just went at it calmly and to the best of my ability, not with any of the feverish, pushing anxiety of the usual stage-struck girl. Perhaps if I'd been all tied up in knots about it, I'd not have had half as easy a time."[68]

Kay's film career was very different from her time on the stage in one important respect. She worked steadily, with virtually no breaks. In her earliest years, it wasn't unusual to appear in six to eight films a year. The former playgirl now professed to love work. "Work happens right now to be the important thing to me," she said in 1931. "It's filled my life. I'm mad about it. I love it. I love acting. I love to come home at night and work out a part, visualize it, think up business, get inside the character. I love shooting, when we work hours to get results. It has satisfied me completely. And it seems to me something that cannot fail me."[69]

She quickly became famous, and it wasn't unusual for her to appear on — and inside — magazine covers. Literally hundreds of articles were written about Kay in the 1930s. Every tidbit of information about her was duly reported, no matter how inane. "I can't remember why I won't undertake anything important, like starting a picture, on Tuesday. I don't know what I have against Tuesday."[70] She also believed in numerology. Twelve and thirteen were her lucky numbers, and ten and five were not. "Over a period of years, she has discovered that whenever anything unpleasant occurs, these numbers have figured in it someway. She'll never start a picture or a trip, never take a hotel room or a ship's stateroom that carries ten or five. Most of the actors with whom she's played, have twelve or thirteen letters in their names."[71] In fact, Kay was very superstitious and often consulted astrologers and psychics. She also owned a lucky pair of earrings. "It's probably very, very silly and doesn't mean a thing, but why take the chance? I care little for jewelry but during my first two pictures I happened to wear a certain pair of earrings, so, ever since then, I put them on for a scene or two."[72]

Beauty secrets were also revealed: "Kay Francis is another dark-complexioned, sun-loving beauty. So is Adrienne Ames. Both use only plain vinegar, which they apply after each sunning. To keep her color down for the camera, Miss Francis has a facial once a week with skin food and lemon juice. She tans so easily that, so to speak, she no sooner gets it than she has to get rid of it."[73] And, of course, the clotheshorse gave advice on fashion, too: "Be miserly with ornaments and costume jewelry and beware of those 'little touches' with which so many of your sisters defeat their desire to be chic. That goes double for evening clothes. There is a very ancient Indian commandment which I like. 'Do not adorn yourself profusely with over-elaborate things because this is a sign of little sense.'"[74]

Kay once explained that she disliked most jewelry. "My dislike for precious stones, I think, is principally due to the bad usage that is so often made of them, rather than the jewels themselves. Diamonds are cold, hypocritical and egotistical; rubies are garish and pearls, or rather their imitations, have become commonplace. If I have a favorite, it is the emerald, because it is warm, honest and friendly."[75] Generally, Kay wore only a utilitarian wristwatch and no other jewelry.

There was even an article that analyzed Kay's handwriting! "Those letters — vertical — not too angular, with the capitals stripped down to just the lines necessary — all this shows brains and a wonderfully receptive mind. This hand shows love of beauty, too, and a desire to achieve it. Gee, the will-power in those firm, strong 't' bars! And that reassuringly even basic line. Kay directs her emotions — they seldom run away with her. Yet she is generous, really generous, when she knows the circumstances of a need. It is no wonder that Kay succeeded in her work. Sometimes, we prefer to idolize two extremes — the thing most like us and the thing least like us. And Kay's popularity is of the first. She is so like thousands of our brilliant, fundamentally fine young girls of today, who look life straight in the face and make it come through with what they want. Incidentally, if Kay wanted to write a novel or turn her hand to interior decorating she could do both with the same success that makes her a motion picture personage."[76]

Kay Francis received hundreds of letters each week. "My fan mail delights me. It comes from such unexpected places — Tasmania, Delhi, Russia! It thrills me to have people bother to write just to say they enjoyed a picture that I was in."[77]

Writers struggled to describe her unique looks—no one looked like Kay Francis. "Kay is a flat, willowy drawing from '*Vogue*' come to life. Sleek black head, green eyes, and mouth made redder with well-disciplined lipstick that neither love, liquor, nor any other modern pastime can disturb."[78] Another wrote, "Kay Francis is very much the nice girl type. Paradoxically, she is wholesome looking, yet at the same time alluring and exotic."[79] Nobody sounded like her, either. *Vanity Fair* decided her voice was "the most seductive one in the films."[80]

Magazines also reported on her home and interior decoration: "All the furnishings of Kay Francis' boudoir are of the Louis XIV period. Green, cream, orchid and canary yellow are the colors incorporated in the hangings, upholstering and carpeting."[81] Kay's decorative style was influenced by her Eastern upbringing; she avoided the stereotypical—and tacky—Hollywood excesses of gold-plated plumbing, fur-covered toilet seats, and animal skin rugs, and focused instead on the traditional, elegant style she'd seen among New York's wealthy.

Much of the public focus, of course, was on her wardrobe. Countless magazines offered fashion layouts with Kay wearing the latest costumes from current films. When she was at Paramount, the chief designer was Travis Banton, who costumed Marlene Dietrich, Claudette Colbert, Carole Lombard, Pola Negri, and Kay. "The girls battled for Banton's most eye-filling designs, and they were battlers from away back. Each fought in her own way for the finest sables, mink, ermine, brocades, and headgear. Mae West was also in that stable of stars, but her clothes didn't interfere with the others. They were cast over a different mold. Mae had the same anatomical features as the other gals, but there were more of them."[82] According to Banton, "Miss Francis is the epitome of feminine allure, and her dark beauty calls for fashions that are extreme and chicly daring."[83] When Kay arrived at the Paramount studio in 1929, the two biggest stars on the lot—Clara Bow and Nancy Carroll—were short and struggled with their weight. That's why Travis Banton fell in love with Kay—she was tall, slim, and wore his costumes with great flair.

Orry-Kelly, the designer most associated with Kay Francis, was an Australian who'd come to New York seeking work as a portrait painter and muralist. He dabbled in stage costuming and set design, and met Cary Grant—then known as Archie

KAY FRANCIS AT PARAMOUNT
Kay on an art deco Paramount set in 1931.

Leach—who recommended him to Warner Brothers.[84] Orry-Kelly was told he'd be hired if Kay Francis and Ruth Chatterton approved of his designs. "The sketches Kelly submitted to the two stars cleverly incorporated accurate likenesses of their faces (in lieu of the usual blank mannequin look then current in fashion sketches) and this bit of personal flattery, plus good design, got him the approval he sought."[85]

Aside from a few disagreements—usually caused by too much drinking on the part of one, the other, or both—Orry-Kelly enjoyed working with Kay. "In the beginning, she was very reserved but well mannered and knew exactly what she wanted. I designed simple unadorned evening gowns in velvet, chiffon and crepes for *One Way Passage*. And I introduced what was the forerunner of the shirtmaker dress for evening. At first, only those with sensitive taste were impressed. Luckily, Kay was the essence of good taste."[86] Orry-Kelly considered Kay's best features to be her back and shoulders—and he dressed her accordingly.

Unlike with her romantic life, Kay took an intellectual approach to movie work, including costuming. She and Orry-Kelly carefully analyzed costumes for each film.[87] "If I were playing a woman good and true, we used tailored, sophisticated clothes ordinarily reserved for the femme fatale. But when I played the heavy, I had them design my clothes with lots of frills. Very fluffy and feminine and sweet. Very girlish. I think it makes more sense to reverse it. To dress counter to the character."[88]

Costume designer Dorothy Jeakins, whose movie career spanned four decades, echoed many who still remembered Kay long after she'd left Hollywood. "Kay Francis had an innate sense of style. Tall, dark, and willowy, she showcased some of the top designers in movie history. Her association with Orry-Kelly gave Hollywood and the world true glamour. With poise and confidence, she showcased the work of Adrian, Banton, [Edward] Stevenson, and Max Ree."[89]

"Money is handy stuff. I don't think I'm mercenary, but when all those horrid bills start piling up the first of the month it's reassuring to know you can write checks with a free hand."[90]

Kay Francis made more money working in film than she'd ever made in theater, modeling, the business world—or through marriage. While she grew to hate the grueling movie-making schedule and the constant scrutiny of her personal life, she didn't mind the money. In fact, she liked it. A lot. Her goal was to make a fortune—and return to New York. Of course, the question became how much money was enough.

Kay so believed her stay in Hollywood would be brief that it was years before she purchased a house in California. In fact, after signing a huge contract with Warner Brothers, she continued renting until 1937. Her last California rental was the William S. Hart house at 8371 De Longpre in Los Angeles, which she moved into in 1935.[91] Often described as modest, it was probably Kay's favorite Hollywood house. "Perched on a high hill, it is white with green trimmings and is small and unpretentious. It is picturesque, however, for it drops its three stories down a steep incline, with a charming garden opening off the living room on the lower floor."[92]

Although her New York life involved much socializing, Kay Francis claimed she rarely went to Hollywood parties. Partly, she explained, it was due to her hectic shooting schedule. She once confided to an interviewer that, "parties are more fun when you work hard and only go once in a while."[93] Kay also hadn't made many California friends. Some accused her of being anti-social, but she claimed she was "un-social."[94] Still, despite her protests that she was a homebody, scanning her diary entries and the social pages throughout the 1930s reveals that Kay was a frequent guest at many parties, openings, and events.[95]

She played bridge and backgammon with Jessica and Richard Barthelmess,[96] Arthur Hornblow, Dorothy di Frasso, and Beatrice and Donald Ogden Stewart. Bea, along with writer husband Donald, hosted many tennis games and parties, and Kay was often a guest, along with Clark and Rhea Gable, Sam and Frances Goldwyn, the Barthelmesses, Lewis Milestone, Grace Moore, Fred and Phyllis Astaire, David Niven, and Elizabeth Allen.[97] In a 1937 interview, Kay described her ideal evening: "My idea of a pleasant evening is to spend it with six or eight congenial friends, where we can sit in the patio or before a fire, and carry on a really interesting conversation."[98]

The Goldwyns' parties were of a different type. Sam, who fancied himself a proper gentlemen, hosted "formal very British dinners where the service was so grand one forgot Goldwyn's bad grammar."[99] The Jesse Laskys' parties—hosted on the beach—were only slightly less formal. Bessie Mona Lasky, producer Jesse's wife, wrote of magical Sunday nights at their beach house when they were joined by the likes of Joan Crawford, Kay Francis, Mary Pickford, Charlie Chaplin, Marion Davies, William Randolph Hearst, and other notables. Lasky recalled one night in particular when she'd gone to bed, only to be roused by the quiet singing of Kay, Maurice Chevalier, Jeanette MacDonald, Eddie Cantor, and Elsie Janis gathered around her bedpost. When Joseph Mankiewicz first arrived in Hollywood, brother Herman took him to his first industry party—at Lasky's beach house. "It was the first time I ever gave my hat to a butler in my whole life, and it's also, I think, the last time in my life I ever wore a hat. I then wandered around, and the spectacle left me gaping. My God, I could see Kay Francis, Clara Bow, Olga Baclanova, Gary Cooper. It was the most incredible sight to suddenly hit the eyes of a twenty-year-old."[100]

Douglas Fairbanks, Jr., then married to Joan Crawford, recalled his first memories of Kay: "I never had the privilege of working with Miss Francis in a film. I knew Kay and Kenneth socially in the early '30s. Kay was lovely and very popular. She brightened many social occasions with her sparkling charm and wit. I don't think she ever warmed up to Hollywood. I think of her as a true bon vivant."[101]

Although most spoke highly of Kay's parties and graciousness, a sour note was heard from Charles Laughton and Elsa Lanchester. According to them, "she served finer food than the Thalbergs [Irving Thalberg and Norma Shearer], but she was boringly, absurdly hostessy, rapping the table and informing the guests in a haughty voice, 'Please be silent. I'm speaking!' She corrected her guests on every possible issue, queening it over them."[102]

Kay, like most stars, acquired servants—a maid/secretary, cook, and gardener/chauffer. One of Kay's closest friends was Ida Perry, her West Indian maid and secretary. Ida, who'd come with Kay to Hollywood, was "a lady's lady if ever there was one," according to Kay. "It is always 'our career,' and she shares its every phase."[103] Kay first mentioned Ida in 1928 while in Chicago performing in *Elmer the Great*. It wasn't unusual for Kay to attend movies with Ida, and her name was often mentioned in the diary. When Ida became ill in 1934, Kay remained by her side. "These were no mere phone calls to a doctor to look after her. Instead, Kay sat by her side with cold towels. In the ambulance to the hospital, a faithful colored maid lay on a cot of pain, while beside her, soothing and comforting, knelt Kay Francis. And then the operation. Outside the door, waiting, handkerchief torn to shreds, eyes wide with suffering, stood Kay Francis."[104] Kay's further admiration is evident in this anecdote concerning Kay's dressing room circa 1935 at Warner Brothers. The dressing room, composed of a suite of rooms, featured signed photographs of Kay's "most intimate motion picture friends, but in her sitting room, the walls are as bare as a monastery, the only bit of adornment being a photograph of her maid, which is framed and placed well on a table near the door. The effect is somewhat startling, for after you gazed upon the placidity of this faithful person, she suddenly arrives in person to bring you a dish of tea."[105]

"I guess I should be very happy."[106]

One of Kay's final entries for 1930 suggested a creeping doubt. Still, she continued her frantic pace of socializing, making movies, and dating Ken. The next year would be even busier, including a new studio and marriage.

CHAPTER 7

Trouble in Paradise, 1931–1932

"Decided to be married and down to city hall. Big fuss in newspaper."[1]

Kay's personal life in 1930 was largely taken up with Kenneth. Though she also had brief romances with Ronald Colman and writer Arthur Hopkins,[2] Kenneth was her steady bed partner — and most of her 1930 diary entries were raves about their sexcapades: "Ken worked until 6 A.M. and then came and fucked me! God, I really do love him."[3] She also admitted to jealousy, especially toward Constance Bennett, with whom Ken worked in the summer on *Sin Takes a Holiday*.

As 1930 grew to a close, there were rumors that Kay and Ken would marry. Kay claimed to enjoy being single. "I like living alone. I have to be alone at times and the only chance I get is when I'm at home. I don't see how people live who are never alone. I couldn't do it. I make a swell bachelor girl, really. I'm not domestic. I want to live simply, comfortably, with as little annoyance as possible."[4]

Still, Kenneth was eager to marry. A few days after the New Year, Kay met Kenneth's family. Kay, who probably worried about becoming a serial bride — she was barely 26, and this would be her third marriage — hesitated upon receiving MacKenna's proposal. She was recovering from a jaw ailment at Cedars of Lebanon Hospital when he popped the question. "Ken asked me to marry him. God, what shall I do?"[5] Kay reluctantly agreed. MacKenna, afraid she'd change her mind, whisked her out of the hospital.

Kay was now a star, and the press frantically followed the story. "He drove her from the hospital directly to the Los Angeles City Hall, and got a ticket for speeding too, where he bought a license. Then the two of them, all alone, boarded his boat and sailed away for the island of Catalina, where they were married in the little town of Avalon in January 1931."[6] Another report gave a slightly different version: "Mr. MacKenna and Miss Francis rode to the marriage license bureau in an ambulance which the actress explained was taking her to her home."[7] The ceremony, conducted at Avalon by a justice of the peace on January 17, 1931, with two strangers as witnesses,[8] was private, though word quickly leaked to the Hollywood press. A few days after her 26th birthday, Kay wrote, "Married. Oh my God, please let it be very happy, and let me make Ken happy."[9] She might as well have wished for world peace.

Kay's plans for a romantic wedding dinner aboard Kenneth's yacht, the *Pamet Head*, were ruined when Kenneth forgot something important — cooking fuel. He'd stocked the boat with provisions, but "had forgotten to put gasoline in the stove tank and in the midst of Kay's culinary display the darned thing sputtered and went cold. There was no gasoline on the boat. 'There must be gasoline somewhere,' said Kay desperately, following it with one of her most classic remarks: 'Fate wouldn't let this happen to me on my wedding night.'"[10] This story might have been concocted by a publicity agent. According to Kay's diary, they were in her Hollywood home on their wedding night. This would have been the 8401 Fountain Avenue rental house.

Kay and Kenneth returned to work, planning to take a honeymoon when time permitted. Ken, who'd been hired by Fox as a director, was co-directing his first effort, *Always Goodbye,* starring Elissa Landi and Lewis Stone.[11] An oft-told Kay Francis legend described a different version of Kay's wedding night. The Earl of Warwick,[12] looking for Hollywood madam Lee Francis, somehow found himself, instead, on Kay's doorstep. "Ringing Miss Francis' doorbell, announcing his distinguished name to the flustered maid, his lordship was shown into the drawing room. Upstairs, Kay, *en negligee,* was sipping champagne with her new husband. Learning of the presence of her guest below, touched that he would call upon her on such a memorable night, Kay bestowed a kiss on the bridegroom's forehead, promising to hurry back as soon as possible. Downstairs, Kay was graciousness itself. The Earl, always gallant, admired Kay's gown, her paintings on the walls, but soon tired of her overstimulated chatter. 'You're delightful, Madam Francis,' he admitted, 'but would you mind bringing in the girls.'"[13] Great story, but one that can't be true for any number of reasons, including the fact that the Earl wasn't even in Hollywood in 1931. Still, the rumor persists, and other versions have Kay dressed in a kimono![14]

KENNETH MACKENNA

Kay married third husband Kenneth MacKenna in 1931. They separated in 1933 and divorced in 1934.

"Keeping attractive is really such an important part of a wife's job."[15]

Once her work at the studio was finished, Kay spent her early days of marriage seeing movies, socializing, buying new furniture, and decorating — Kay and Kenneth had moved to 8487 Franklin Avenue in February 1931. It was a relaxing time and probably the happiest of their short marriage.

Shortly after Kay's wedding, she signed a contract with Warner Brothers. "The contract with Miss Francis, which has been rumored for a week or more, was signed just before she slipped away on Kenneth MacKenna's yacht. It would seem that Miss Francis has had too much excitement for one week, what with being about to acquire a new husband and getting a new contract."[16] Indeed. Actually, her signing was controversial. Warner Brothers had disrupted the business-as-usual approach in Hollywood by signing — for huge sums — such Hollywood stars as Edward G. Robinson, William Powell, George Bancroft, Ruth Chatterton — and Kay Francis.

Kenneth gave few interviews. In one, he was described as a golf fan and avid book collector whose prize possessions included a first edition Bernard Shaw and a 1904 Dove's

Press Bible, for which he paid $1,000. Although Kenneth tried directing, he was unhappy with the projects he was given. "He felt no matter how well they could be done they would still be just average programmers. And finding that with all this there was added worry and work (which he wouldn't have minded if he could have been more satisfied with the results), he decided to don greasepaint again."[17] His leisure time was spent yachting, playing golf, and reading. He and Kay also enjoyed attending boxing and wrestling matches, and were sometimes seen dancing at the legendary Cocoanut Grove at the Ambassador Hotel.

It couldn't have been easy to be in love with Kay Francis. Kenneth believed — or hoped — that marriage would force her to settle down. Though Kenneth himself had been a bit wild during his New York stage days, he sincerely wanted to spend the rest of his life with Kay. Marriage, however, did nothing to stop Kay's promiscuity. It just made it more difficult — and hurtful. Kenneth had convinced her to marry at a low point, and Kay regretted the decision and resented him.

Still, Kay seemed genuinely in love with husband MacKenna at first, and even legally changed her name to Katharine Gibbs Mielziner. Still, she also hired a lawyer to draw up a contract so a divorce would require she owe nothing to Mr. MacKenna. Before her marriage, she admitted to her husband-to-be that she'd been sexually involved with three different women, but MacKenna didn't seem to mind. "Told Ken about the three women I had slept with — probably was a God damn fool, but it seemed to excite him a little."[18]

The MacKennas spent many weekends sailing on Ken's yacht. A favorite spot was Santa Catalina Island, south of Los Angeles. Kay's diary entries mentioned Cherry Cove, Isthmus Cove, Long Point Light, and Avalon as frequent destinations. For the most part, Kay was uncomfortable discussing her private life. Still, interviewers were able to get some news about the newlyweds, especially when she talked about boating. "When Ken and I go out on our boat, I usually wear a bathing suit or overalls. I do the cooking and he does the skippering. We sometimes spend a week at a time at sea."[19] In fact, the yacht was a relatively inexpensive hobby because they hired no crew. "Kay is cook, maid and stewardess. Kenneth is captain, sailor and deck swabber."[20]

The two professed to prefer reading to clubbing, and seemed a good match. "The MacKennas are really happy, probably because they make it a rule never to talk about pictures or picture people. They don't night-life very often, but prefer going to bed early and reading themselves to sleep."[21]

Kay tersely listed her husband's characteristics in an interview. "I am in love with my husband. He is diplomatic. He never becomes angry. He prefers beer to champagne. His favorite dish is wild duck and oranges. He doesn't snore. He doesn't take himself seriously. Doesn't like to have his home life publicized. He is neither temperamental nor moody. His favorite indoor sport is bridge. His screen favorites are Lionel Barrymore and Greta Garbo. When through with the movies, he, too, expects to return to the stage."[22]

Kay made it clear that she and Kenneth were different from the usual Hollywood crowd — they were Easterners. "Our bodies are in Hollywood, but our roots are in the East. We shall remain in Hollywood just as long as we are wanted, so long as we have jobs. We will not stay one minute after our bell has run. And against that possibility and because it is our dream, we have bought a two-hundred-year-old farmhouse near Cape Cod. Some day, we shall go there to live. Perhaps, too, we'll have a little apartment in Paris and some sort of hide-out for the winter months in New York.[23] But that farmhouse is to be our home. It still has its old-fashioned oil lamps. There are quiet, charming neighbors near at hand, people who have never been to Hollywood and who have heard the echoes of it only faintly."[24] The farmhouse, nicknamed "Little Hollow Downs," had been purchased by Kenneth in

September 1928 as a summer home. Some of the neighbors—despite Kay's attempt to paint them as simple rural folk—included artists and writers, such as Edward Hopper. Still, the Truro, Massachusetts, area *was* rustic, and Kenneth had acquired Spot, a cantankerous horse, and a wobbly cart to get around the property. On one of Kay's rare visits, she was reportedly dumped from the cart.

Although Kay's diary reported attendance at many premieres—her films *and* his—Kay insisted that she and Kenneth rarely saw any of her films, and she stayed out of his work, too."I frequently have no idea what he is directing and have never been on any set he has worked on. We never talk about our work when we are at home together. It's just because, I think, there are so many other things to talk about."[25] Still, Kay admitted that she and Kenneth normally attended three or four movies a week.

As for her favorite movie star, Kay named Greta Garbo. "I am quite sure that if I should meet Greta Garbo I would be speechless with admiration and unable to utter a syllable. I adore her as much as any fan and I don't suppose I shall ever be able to look upon her as just another human being who eats and sleeps and works just as all the stars in pictures do."[26] Kay admitted to crying at movies—including her own. "When I go to a preview of my pictures, if there is a sad scene I can cry over my own plight up there on the screen just as if I were weeping over the sorrows of another person. Yet by some strange paradox, I can at the same time criticize my performance and see where I could have improved my acting so that it would make me cry a little harder."[27]

"I wonder if Ken and I will be together a year from now?"[28]

Kay's diary presented a different marital picture than the movie magazine portrayal. In reality, Kay's inability to remain faithful or sober led to troubles in her marriage and personal life. It's also very telling that after Kay's marriage, diary entries about her sex life ceased—until she started seeing others. Furthermore, Kay's busy schedule made it difficult for the couple to see much of each other. Kay admitted as much in a 1931 letter to mother-in-law Ella Mielziner. "Ken and I never breakfast together in fact [*sic*] we have only dined together twice in the last 12 days! He's been working nights and I days and some nights too. Some day we'll meet again and learn all over about each other!"[29]

In September 1931, Kay lost several pieces of jewelry, including her wedding ring. A dog attacked her own pet, and Kay ran to his aid, dropping her purse. By the time all was calm again, she was missing a jeweled watch, a brooch—and Kenneth's ring. Kenneth promised another, but it was a bad omen.[30]

"I want to graduate, eventually, from these siren things and play sophisticated leads—the Katharine Cornell type of part."[31]

The year 1931 proved to be a busy year for Kay. She not only married, but appeared in seven films, often receiving top billing. On January 23, 1931, it was announced that, "she of the sleek black hair and magnetic deep voice"[3] would co-star in Rouben Mamoulian's first Hollywood picture, *City Streets*. Based on a work by Dashiel Hammett, the cast also included Gary Cooper, Sylvia Sidney, and Paul Lukas. Like many film announcements, this one was recast, and, sadly, Kay was never directed by Mamoulian, though she did have an affair with him in the 1940s. Her role went to Wynne Gibson.

This was also the year that Kay joined Warner Brothers and left Paramount. Shocked at the betrayal, Paramount decided to get even by giving her weak roles. Producer B.P.

Schulberg characterized the rumors as ridiculous. "It would all react on us, and why would we take such a foolish revenge?"[33] Still, Paramount's casting decisions indicated they weren't above exacting vengeance. Savvy Kay fought back. For example, when they tried to place her in a maid's role, she produced a doctor's certificate stating she couldn't work because of medical reasons.

Paramount then decided to work her to death until it was time for her departure. *Scandal Sheet*, the first release of 1931, featured George Bancroft, and offered a meaty role as a wandering wife. Again directed by John Cromwell, Kay's performance received good reviews. "Miss Francis has what can be most nearly described as 'sensible seductiveness' in this part. There is none of the incredible, overheated emoting commonly associated with the word in the days when vamps were just too bad to be true. She has an emphasized femininity that is charmingly human, and as natural and unaffected as the wind."[34]

KAY FRANCIS IN *GIRLS ABOUT TOWN* (1931). *Kay, dressed to thrill in* Girls About Town *(1931), George Cukor's sophisticated comedy about golddiggers.*

Ladies' Man, another William Powell film, followed. Although this one featured Carole Lombard, the melodrama didn't pack much of a punch. Not only was the picture not very good, but Kay also had an unattractive hairstyle: "Kay Francis' chief handicaps are an overly romantic, fireless part and a new coiffeure [*sic*]."[35]

Paramount next used Kay in *The Vice Squad,* along with Paul Lukas. Kay warned her mother-in-law against seeing it. "You were sweet about *Ladies' Man* but please don't see *Vice Squad!* I am awful the picture is awful and the part is dreadful!"[36] Neither the picture nor Kay were awful, but one reporter rightly pointed out that she was "seen much too briefly on the screen."[37]

RKO then borrowed Kay for *Transgression,* another strong part where she played a combination vamp-wife. The film also featured Nance O'Neil, pal of infamous ax murderer Lizzie Borden.[38] The *New York Times* gave it a mixed review but applauded Kay for her "clear portrayal."[39]

MGM next borrowed Kay for *Guilty Hands,* a cleverly directed mystery by Woody Van Dyke. It was another seductress role. "I don't want to be a bad woman in too many pictures in succession," Kay complained. "Too much glamour, too much sin, repeated often, become monotonously dull. I'm speaking now about the screen, of course!"[40] Reviewers enjoyed the film and Kay's performance. "Kay Francis is splendid as the friend of the murdered man. It is not an easy role, but Miss Francis is always believable in the emotional fireworks."[41]

In April 1931, Kay was announced as George Bancroft's co-star in *Rich Man's Folly.* Instead, however, Kay began work on a different film. A 1931 highlight, Paramount's *24 Hours* also starred Clive Brook and Miriam Hopkins. The film was excellent, and Kay's performance as a jaded, cynical society wife was polished and believable. Reviews were mixed, though Kay's notices were generally favorable. "Kay Francis as the society woman is alluring and poised as ever, and brings great sincerity and feeling in her role."[42]

Girls About Town, another Paramount film, again directed by George Cukor, gave Kay the opportunity to work with her good friend, the irrepressible Lilyan Tashman, who'd previously appeared with Kay in *The Marriage Playground.* Kay and Lil got to run around in lingerie and play characters who could only be high-priced call girls. "Kay Francis shows off her figure in undies while explaining she's through with the gold-digger racket and intends going straight because she's found love with a rich rube. The undie pose and that bit about going straight all in one has its own satirical kick."[43] Andy Lawler, who would become one of Kay's best pals, also appeared in the film as Kay's no-good husband.

In October 1931, it was announced that Kay would appear with Fredric March in Paramount's *The Master Key* — later changed to *Strangers in Love.* Director Lothar Mendes was quite happy over the casting, and it was also mentioned that Kay would receive her Warner Brothers salary — $2,000 a week — rather than her Paramount $750 weekly check.

Kay admitted that she was worried about leaving Paramount, mainly because of the unknowns at a new studio. Still, she was happy that there were no hard feelings over her departure — after the initial sparring between studio and star, they called a truce. "I know Paramount and like the entire organization. And I was so pleased and happy when they asked me to make one more picture than my contract called for. And they offered to pay me the salary that I will receive at Warners. It is mighty nice to know that I will leave Paramount with good feeling on both sides and that there will be no resentment over my departure."[44] Her last day at Paramount was January 9 — and Kay threw a party for the studio's publicity department, grateful for the excellent job they'd done.

"Money? Is that all she cares about in Hollywood? It is. Exactly all."[45]

When 1932 rolled around, Kay was a Paramount star, but would join Warner Brothers on January 11. By the end of 1932, Kay had appeared in some of the finest films of her entire career. Ironically, while 1932 was one of the worst box office years for the industry, it was a wonderful career year for Kay Francis — and the year she became a full-fledged star.

She did not, however, get all the parts she wanted. Ruth Chatterton was viewed as *the* top female star at Warner Brothers, and in January 1932 when Darryl Zanuck purchased the rights to Faith Baldwin's *Week-End Marriage,* Ruth Chatterton, Kay, and Barbara Stanwyck all vied for the role. "'Tis said around the studio that if Miss Chatterton likes the yarn and thinks it is suited to her requirements, she will win, being the stellar favorite of the film plant at present."[46] About a week later, Warner Brothers bought *A Dangerous Brunette* for Kay — later to be renamed *Man Wanted* — to appease her.

Her first 1932 film, *The False Madonna,* was an oddly affecting picture. She played a burned-out con woman, and was directed by Stuart Walker, her former stage director and mentor. Reviewers again found her convincing. "Miss Francis, always smartly costumed, and convincing in parts of this type, is up to her standard."[47]

Strangers in Love — with Fredric March — followed, and completed her contractual obligation at Paramount. Reviewers liked the March-Francis matchup and found Kay charming. "Miss Francis gets everything possible out of her sec role. She works with a nice restraint throughout, pacing her part with just the proper shading."[48]

The third film of 1932, *Man Wanted,* was notable because it was her first at Warner Brothers. Co-star David Manners was so beautiful, he almost stole the picture. Still, Warner Brothers showcased Kay to great effect in this film. "Miss Francis photographed well and wearing stunning costume creations, as usual, creates a smooth, svelte delineation as the wife who found happiness in the world of business rather than in the smart set."[49]

The next picture was the uneventful *Street of Women,* which featured Gloria Stuart's first movie role. Stuart remembered Kay as "a popular star and a beautifully dressed woman,"[50] and noted that the studio often had to work around Kay's speech impediment. "I remember an amusing story about Kay Francis on this film. She had a line in the film: 'I have to have my room redecorated.' Well, it came out, 'I have to have my womb wede-cowated.' Needless to say, they rewrote the line. I'm sure it's not in the picture."[51] Reviews were mixed, but many again emphasized her wardrobe. "Miss Francis wears some stunning clothes and has been photographed advantageously. Her performance is warm, sincere, and charming."[52]

Jewel Robbery, also made in 1932, was her best film up to that point. Her first comedy lead, it paired her again with debonair William Powell. A wonderful role, it offered Kay the opportunity to be funny, charming, and sinfully sophisticated. Reviewers found it "a daring but amusing picture,"[53] but some criticized Kay's performance as "self-conscious."[54]

One Way Passage, also released in 1932, is one of the best arguments for Kay being considered one of Hollywood's greats. She and William Powell shared wonderful chemistry in this gem of a picture. Production started in May 1932, with the cast and crew using the *S.S. Calawall* as their set. "Because it is five miles by water taxi to their boat, they are living on the ship, anchored a mile beyond the breakwater at Long Beach. Altogether, there are 100 people living on the boat, including players, technicians and cameramen."[55]

Aline MacMahon described the less-than-ideal working conditions: "Warners engaged a broken-down iron boat for location shooting and sent the cast offshore, allowing us some fantastic sum like thirty seven cents a day for food. It was an uncomfortable assignment, and we were all pretty miserable. It was boiling hot. The food was terrible. The kids got drunk, and Tay Garnett took this occasion to be difficult. So the assistants were doing what work there was done — which wasn't much. Finally, the studio lost patience and brought us back to the lot to finish it. Through it all Miss Francis behaved with great dignity and did her work without complaint."[56] MacMahon also explained her take on Kay's popularity. "Kay Francis was in a special class. She was very elegant, and she had taste and special clothes, and she fulfilled a need audiences felt."[57]

A true Hollywood character, director Tay Garnett, once married to the witty and charming Patsy Ruth Miller, wrote about the picture's evolution in his autobiography. While lunching with Harry Joe Brown one day at the Brown Derby, Tay explained that he wanted to direct a sea story — more *First Cabin* than *Moby Dick.* Brown told him about *Transatlantic,* a tragedy that had undergone numerous script revisions but was still unfilmable. When told of the plot, Garnett suggested making it into a comedy.[58] After telling his idea to agent Myron Selznick,[59] Tay and Patsy Ruth went off on a cruise of their own. Tay worked on the script in the mornings, and had completed a forty-page treatment when Selznick informed him that Daryl F. Zanuck wanted Tay to write and direct the movie. In fact, Zanuck asked for the finished treatment in 10 days. After informing a livid Patsy Ruth that their trip would be cut short, Tay returned to Hollywood — only to realize the treatment was lost. "I scrutinized Patsy Ruth long and accusingly, but she merely smiled an inscrutable smile and said, 'Don't look at me.' I burned rubber out to Burbank to confide in Doc Solomon, Warner Brothers studio manager and a great guy. Explaining that I was committed to having that treatment on Mr. Z's desk the next morning, I asked for two offices and two secretaries. For fourteen hours I dictated to first one secretary, then the other. They were the greatest, so the treatment was completed on schedule."[60]

The final script was written with Wilson Mizner and Joe Jackson. "I got a fast nod to my request for Mizner and Jackson, so I tested my luck a little further. For leads I wanted Bill Powell and Kay Francis.

'You had Powell before you came in,' said Zanuck. 'But what about Kay's speech impediment?'

'I can write around that. All I have to do is duck any word beginning with "r" or "l." (I remembered having heard Kay read the line, "It wouldn't be right, even if we are in love,' as "It wouldn't be wight, even if we ah in wuv.').")[61]

One problem remained: How can you have a light ending to a tragedy? The solution was the Paradise Cocktail, a drink Powell and Francis shared when they met — and apparently enjoyed together in eternity as well. The Paradise Cocktail was one of Tay's many contributions to the script, but he was talked out of a writing credit, much to Kay's disappointment: "After the preview, Kay Francis rushed from the theatre weeping wildly. Throwing her arms around me she sobbed, 'It's heahtbweaking. It's the most moving film I've eveh seen. It's unfohettable. But what about yoah cwedit? You wote such lovely speeches foah me. Why isn't youah name given witing cwedit?'"[62] Because of studio politics, Garnett simply took the direction credit — though he regretted it when writer Robert Lord won the Oscar for Best Original Story Written for the Screen.

Critics raved about the film and the Francis-Powell pairing. "Polished acting by William Powell and Kay Francis in a fascinating melodrama which has a credible plot and a strictly logical ending. Very good entertainment of some distinction. The stars are brilliantly in harmony — smooth and sympathetic in their performance."[63]

One Way Passage was Kay's favorite film, and she often showed it to friends and lovers throughout the years. Kay admitted that the only shot of her that she found particularly beautiful was in *One Way Passage*. "And even that was more a matter of lighting than of my face. It was beautiful because Bob Kurle, the cameraman took so much time and trouble shifting his camera fifty different ways, experimenting with the light and shadow. When I saw that, I felt the one pang of pure pleasure I've ever experienced when I've looked at myself on the screen."[64]

There's a fine line between lacking vanity and self-hate, and Kay was just one of many beautiful women who was insecure about her looks. "Usually I'm afraid to look. When I go to previews of my own pictures I feel like cowering in my own chair like a kid afraid of a bogey-man. I'm afraid that I'll see myself walking with a slouch, or that I'll see a run in my stocking, or my clip won't be on straight, or that I'll be running my hand through my hair, or a dozen and one other things."[65] She also thought she had unattractive legs, and didn't like to show them in movies. In fact, there are very few films where you can see Kay's legs, most notably in *Let's Go Native* and *Girls About Town.*[66]

Kay traveled on vacation to the East Coast in June, taking the opportunity to reconnect with people from her earlier life. She even went to Pittsfield to see Dwight and her former in-laws before returning to New York to spend time at Tony's and see old friends Bill Gaston, Allan Ryan, Lois Long, Clifton Webb, Kay Johnson, Tamara Geva and others. She returned to California on July 9. Befitting her new status, this time she flew instead of taking the train.

"I do Lubitsch picture!"[67]

Having made *Jewel Robbery* and *One Way Passage* in 1932, Kay could have quit and called it a career, but her next picture was even better. After completing *One Way Passage*, Warner Brothers gave Kay a vacation. Kay and Kenneth planned to travel to Europe — and have a real honeymoon. Their departure date was June 22. "Just five hours before their scheduled departure, with trunks all packed and most of their goodbyes said, there came the siren call of a big role in an Ernst Lubitsch picture and — the sum of $26,000."[68] Cynics were quick to assume Kay chose the money over a vacation with her husband, but Kay said she accepted the film because she wanted to work with Lubitsch. "The money didn't matter; the money had absolutely nothing to do with it. I proved that because, shortly before Lubitsch asked for me, I had an offer of another picture on the Paramount lot. The same sum of money was involved. I turned it down. But when it came to working for Lubitsch, when I weighed my honeymoon against the honor this meant, against the things I would learn under his direction — well, Lubitsch won."[69]

Trouble in Paradise, one of the finest films ever made, included one of Kay's greatest performances. Herbert Marshall, Miriam Hopkins, Kay Francis — why in the world didn't anyone think to cast these three together again? Of course, it helped that Ernst Lubitsch directed. Rumors suggested that the married Marshall was having simultaneous affairs with Hopkins and Francis, which apparently didn't hurt — and maybe even helped — the chemistry. However, Kay's diary mentioned no affair with Marshall, though she often socialized with him and wife Edna Best.

Production began the last week of July and was completed by early September. "There were the usual minor complications, courtesy of the frantic Miriam Hopkins. In one scene, Hopkins ruthlessly upstaged Kay Francis by slowly turning the chair in which she was sitting until her profile had magically become her entire face. A furious Francis complained to Lubitsch, who assured her the problem would be solved in the next take. It was, by the simple expedient of nailing Hopkins' chair to the floor."[70]

Some have suggested that *Trouble in Paradise* was just another picture to Kay. But she knew it was something special. In a letter to her mother-in-law, she wrote about the picture and Lubitsch: "I am working very steadily and so excitingly — Lubitsch is simply thrilling — I always knew he was a genius but one can't really understand his particular greatness until under his direction. Plus that — the most charming Herbert Marshall — a divine script — a crew who worship 'The Master'— and one is entranced by the really perfect unit. Much as I still regret our trip — this does compensate for me."[71]

Trouble in Paradise was Kay's 28th film, and the peak of her career. Film writer Curt Siodmak was a fan of Kay and the film. "Tall, lovely, and sexy. I think Lubitsch brought out the best in her in the flick *Trouble in Paradise.* It was and is a great film, and Kay Francis was great in it."[72]

Fred Lawrence Guiles considered the film one of 1932's best. "Ernst Lubitsch, its producer and director, had liberated not only movie dialogue but the sound camera as well, and it roamed freely up and down stairs, in and around buildings and streets (one suspects that the more mobile silent camera was utilized here). This was no Marx Brothers farce that even the kiddies could enjoy. This was adult entertainment with the suavest thieves in Europe triumphant at the fade-out."[73] As for Kay, Guiles described her as "the perfect Lubitsch heroine."[74]

Most critics of the time realized it was a masterpiece. *The New York American* offered a typical review. "The director hasn't overlooked a single detail, and as every part is close to perfection, so is the whole production. Assisting Lubitsch is the imperious, provocative Kay Francis, the sprite-like Miriam Hopkins and that new-come beau ideal of the cinema, Herbert Marshall. No more attractive trio ever graced the screen."[75]

Kay had been in the business for less than four years but had already learned much. No longer the stiff stage actress, Kay Francis gave some of Hollywood's best performances in 1932. Her strongest work was in comedies, but she could be powerfully compelling in dramas like *One Way Passage* as well.

Kay's last film of 1932, *Cynara,* found her again paired with Ronald Colman. Although some love this film, it left Kay with the thankless role of the betrayed wife, and audiences didn't want to see Colman as a philanderer. Reviews were mixed, though Louella Parsons liked the Colman-Francis pairing and enjoyed Kay's performance. "She is particularly charming and effective as the wife. No one on the screen can play the lady with more finesse and more realism than Miss Francis."[76]

KAY FRANCIS IN *TROUBLE IN PARADISE*
1932 was Kay's best career year. Here she's in a costume from Trouble in Paradise. *Travis Banton was the designer.*

"Did something and had good time but can't remember."[77]

Most people lack the insight to know when the good times have arrived. Kay, too, apparently looked on 1932 as grueling and unsatisfying. Even during *Trouble in Paradise,* the choicest role she'd have in her career, she complained about retakes that delayed a vacation — and was upset that Miriam Hopkins' name was above hers in the credits. So while viewers look at 1932 as the pinnacle of Kay's film success, to her it was just another long year.

Kay wasn't the only one who was clueless about her career. Warner Brothers, too, must share some of the blame. Surely it must have occurred to someone at the studio that she was best in light, sophisticated roles. Early in her career, Kay made a decision not to fight the studio. It may have been her temperament, or perhaps she truly believed they knew best. "I don't think a star knows when a story is right for her — or him. We read a script with an eye to our own parts rather than to the story as a whole. The studios have done pretty well for me.

They've made me an important star and they pay me good money. If they put me in poor stories they lessen my box-office value and the returns on their investment won't be so good. Why wouldn't I rely on their judgment?"[78]

In 1932, Kay also saw her marriage facing tough times. It was reported that Kenneth turned down a stage role with Katharine Cornell so he wouldn't have to be away from Kay. "He says he couldn't stand the thought of being separated from his Kay for a whole year. And he adds — even when his best-pal-and-severest-critic is in the other room — that his marriage means more happiness to him than all the contracts in the world. Since a lead with the great Cornell is considered a higher honor than the Congressional Medal, Ken now rates in Hollywood as a museum piece."[79]

Kenneth, described as "a quiet, serene fellow with an equally quiet sense of humor," apparently tried very hard to make the marriage work. He turned down the New York stage work because "it would upset our domestic happiness and all we've worked for. I don't think I've made a mistake. After all it was personal happiness at stake, and that's so valuable. In a few years when Kay is fed up with pictures we can return east to the theater, and possibly do a show together."[80]

Sounds great, but Kay's drinking was damaging the marriage. "Eddie Chodorov came to Hollywood in 1932 when Kay Francis was the reigning queen at Warner Brothers. He was no sooner settled into a cottage at the Garden [of Allah] than he received an invitation to a Hollywood party. He was young and very excited about meeting some of the people he had read about in the scandal sheets of the day. He was overwhelmed by the house, and he thought, My mother would like to know about this. He went upstairs to make a call to New York. Entering a bedroom he stopped short seeing Miss Francis sprawled on the bed hanging on to an empty brandy bottle. He said apologetically, 'I want to telephone my mother.' 'Do it, for crissakes,' she said irritably and very drunkenly. Then, 'Come here, kid,' and she pulled him onto the bed beside her. Later he called his mother and when she asked, 'How do you like Hollywood?' he assured her, 'Very much!'"[81]

Kay's drinking was taking a toll, leading her to do things that could have damaged her reputation. In September 1931, she attended a dinner party at Gloria Swanson's, drank too much, behaved badly, and then had to apologize the next morning. She also wrote about a party at Eddie Goulding's in her January 23, 1932, diary entry: "Swell time but got very drunk. T.B. called me a lesbian. E.H. and I were very next to getting queer! Damn fool!"[83] T.B. was probably Tallulah Bankhead, and E.H. might be Edith Head, who was Travis Banton's assistant at Paramount at the time. Though married to first husband Charles Head, Edith was dating writer Bayard Veiller, who occasionally socialized with Kay and Kenneth.

Kenneth finally lost his patience. In March 1932, Kay returned home one night after 3 A.M., argued with Kenneth, and reported in her diary that he'd hit her. Just days before, Kenneth had been fired by Fox, no doubt adding to his fury.

"Signed Warner's — drunk and bed — no dinner."[83]

In October, Kay went to San Francisco to see husband Kenneth in a stage production of *The Bride the Sun Shines On*. While there, she visited with Irene Purcell and Laura Hope Crews, and then took a train trip — with a stopover in Chicago— to her beloved New York. Again, she reconnected with Julia Hoyt, Dwight Francis, Lois Long, Bill Gaston, Tamara Geva, Kay Johnson, Clifton Webb, and met Judith Anderson. She also attended her in-laws' anniversary dinner on October 20, and took time to see old friends Juliana Cutting and Neysa McMein.

KAY FRANCIS POSTCARDS
A selection of commercial postcards showing Kay's changing looks in 1931–1932.

While vacationing, Kay, who'd now worked at Warner Brothers for almost a year, awaited word concerning her option. Louella O. Parsons opined, "Doesn't seem possible the time goes so quickly. If her option is exercised she remains; if not, the chances are she will free-lance. No one has any more offers than Miss Francis, who is so popular options needn't worry her."[84] The option *was* renewed, but considering her upcoming roles, it would have been better for Kay if it hadn't been. Still, Kay admitted that receiving such news was always a relief. "The closer option time draws near, the more nervous I become, and I've never lost the thrill and relief that comes when the studio sends that little notice which begins: 'You are hereby notified that the party does exercise its options on your services, as provided by the clause of your contract, etc.'"[85]

On November 10, Kay returned to New York, where she and Ken attended several Yale football games and numerous parties. She was back in Hollywood in early December — after first stopping to see friends in Chicago — and started working on a new film with George Brent. December diary entries detail party after party — with little mention of Kenneth. In truth, the two were seeing little of each other.

To put Kay's life into proper perspective, while she was enjoying the delights of Manhattan that winter of 1932–33, the United States was in the most desperate financial and economic period in its history. The gross national product was one-third of its 1929 level, the unemployment rate was approaching 25 percent and bread lines and Hoovervilles were a grim sight in every large city. The stock market had finally reached rock bottom in July 1932, and the nation's banking system would be shut down on March 5, 1933, for a week-long "bank holiday." Newly elected President Franklin Delano Roosevelt inaugurated the New Deal to jump-start what became a long and slow economic recovery that lasted until the end of the decade.

As 1932 ended — the phenomenal year when she'd made *Jewel Robbery, One Way Passage,* and *Trouble in Paradise* — Kay went out of her way to stay busy, entertaining herself near to death. A reporter who'd met her in 1929 noticed a change in her. "Kay Francis, 1932 model. Still lovely, much more sure of herself, still with wide, frank eyes — and with the shining veneer of hardness with which Hollywood coats its hectic, successful children."[86] Sadly, Kay had no way of knowing this was the end of her greatest year in film. The upcoming year would be much more difficult for her marriage *and* career.

CHAPTER 8

Merrily We Roll Along, 1933–1935

"I'm not afraid. Of course, everybody knows that a good many players begin to go downhill in prestige after they have been before the public for five years. That has happened to a number of very good friends of mine, whom I won't mention."[1]

She *should* have been afraid, because as early as 1933, her film roles decreased in quality. Like many actors, Kay was often announced for roles that never came to be. For example, in 1932 Kay was cast in *Forty-Second Street*, but ended up not making the picture. Instead, Bebe Daniels ended up with the part. In addition, although it was announced that she'd appear in *Madame DuBarry* (which was made with Dolores Del Rio), *Empress Josephine* (which apparently was never made), *The Key* (with Edna Best), and *The Firebird* (with Veree Teasdale), she was cast into lesser films. There were also rumors that Kay might be cast in *When Ladies Meet, The Narrow Corner,* and *The Worst Woman in Paris.* These roles also never materialized.

The Keyhole, her first 1933 film, featured her earliest pairing with George Brent. There simply wasn't the magical chemistry between Brent and Francis, as there had been between Powell and Francis—or even Marshall and Francis. Reviewers didn't like the film, but found Kay, once again, delightful. "Light entertainment saved by grace of Kay Francis' charming personality. Miss Francis is gorgeous and makes the film entertaining through sheer personality."[2]

MGM next borrowed Kay for *Storm at Daybreak,* a film with Walter Huston. While it was probably lots of fun to work with her former stage buddy, the historical epic was not very good, and

KAY FRANCIS IN PROFILE
Kay's profile shots were always stunning.

reviewers suggested Kay was miscast. "Although Miss Francis is as attractive as always, she hardly seems suited to the enigmatic and mysterious qualities demanded in the role of the wife."[3]

Back at Warner Brothers, Kay was stuck in *Mary Stevens, M.D.,* which might serve as the symbol of the point at which her career went so wrong. It was the type of role that many identified her with — a turgid melodrama with a suffering Kay playing a professional woman. The movie had its moments, but, again, didn't suit her strengths, though most reviewers agreed she was "excellent."[4]

Around 1933 she developed an acting trick in which she simply stared, expressionless, into the camera — similar to the Garbo mask. It's effective, and she used — and perfected — it into the 1934 films and beyond. She was learning, *thankfully,* that film acting required less rather than more.

Kay was next paired with Edward G. Robinson in *I Loved a Woman,* a mediocre film that made neither star happy. Kay begged Warner Brothers not to use her, but the studio insisted. During production, Robinson developed a reputation for being difficult, especially with writers. Producer Hal Wallis admitted that Kay and Robinson were "oddly matched. Kay was so tall we had to put Eddie on a box in some scenes to bring him level with her and, understandably, he was humiliated. Irritable and self-conscious, he argued with Kay frequently."[5] Still, *Variety* enjoyed her performance. "Kay Francis is a grateful and sympathetic opera singer who holds interest even when she is caught double-crossing her benefactor."[6]

The House on 56th Street was another melodrama that actually turned out quite good. This film offered Kay an opportunity to play a giddy young girl and a cynical, tired middle-aged woman. It also offered up a typical plot in the Kay Francis film canon. In this one, a mother loses custody of her daughter after a tragic set of circumstances. Later in life, she meets up with the daughter, and helps her out of a jam. Of course, the daughter never learns that the woman was her mother. The film required thirty-six costume fittings for Kay. "Horrible, isn't it?" she asked an interviewer. "If that looks like the beginning of a life of ease, let any business girl try it."[7] Film historian Lawrence Quirk considered the film a minor classic, and claimed it "contains Kay Francis's finest performance, in the type of role that made her a household name in the 1930s. *The House on 56th Street* is not only the perfect Kay Francis vehicle — it is in its own right a touching nostalgic romance that haunts the memory. The author saw it when he was ten years old — also in several revivals — yet the impression made by certain scenes is still fresh in mind after forty years. What better test of a film than that."[8] Ruth Chatterton had turned down the film, and, according to one reviewer, this afforded Kay "an opportunity to do some of the best dramatic work of her career."[9]

"A really well dressed woman never made people conscious of what she was wearing."[10]

Kay started the New Year by attending the Pittsburgh–USC football game with Gary Cooper. During that first month of 1933 she also socialized with Colleen Moore, playing tennis at Moore's home and then enjoying cocktails. On January 19, Kay left for New York on the Chief, and, as usual, had lunch with friends Ernie and Kitty in Chicago. She arrived in New York on the 20th Century Limited on January 23, and joined Kenneth. They attended the opening of Noel Coward's *Design for Living,*[11] and Kay shopped for antiques to furnish her home. She also went to Bill Gaston's party and spent several evenings at Tony's.

On February 4, Kay met with *Photoplay* magazine for an interview, after which she and Kenneth argued — she ended up spending the night at Julia Hoyt's. Kay spent the next few days in Lake Placid, and then socialized with Allan Ryan.[12] She also saw Herbert Marshall several times, and if they did have an affair, it was probably during this brief time in New York.

Kay returned to Hollywood on February 28, and Ken was back on March 5. A week later they argued again, and Kay went to a movie by herself. Still, they continued entertaining as a couple, spending time with Miriam Hopkins, John and Virginia Gilbert, Kay Johnson, Carole Lombard and William Powell, Lilyan Tashman, Richard Rodgers, Jessica and Richard Barthelmess, and even Zeppo Marx. They also attended films, including *King Kong* and *Zoo in Budapest,* as well as wrestling matches. Gen-

KAY FRANCIS IN *THE HOUSE ON 56TH STREET*
This is a typical publicity pose for Kay in 1933.

erally, when Kay was working on a picture, she was better behaved, at least in terms of her drinking, which meant fewer arguments with Kenneth.

Kay attended a cast party[13] with Kenneth on May 20. Once again, she drank too much, and Kenneth had to carry her out. Shortly thereafter, Kay began — or continued — a flirtation with Gary Cooper. Cooper, who'd been involved in affairs with Lupe Velez and Anderson Lawler, was now seeing Kay's friend Countess di Frasso.[14] Whether it was because of Kay's friendship with di Frasso or another reason, little came of the romance between Francis and Cooper, though they spent at least one night together.

Career difficulties, in addition to marital problems, loomed over Kay in the summer. On June 15, she saw the preview of *Mary Stevens, M.D.,* and wasn't impressed. She and Kenneth went to the Colony, where a depressed Kay drank too much.[15] That same month, Kay wrote about visiting Nils Asther[16] in his MGM studio dressing room and having a kissing session. On July 13, Kay simply recorded that it was her fourth anniversary with Ken, adding no additional comment. Tellingly, Kay was referring to the first time she slept with Kenneth — not their marriage.

The fall of 1933 was spent in typical fashion, with parties, tennis, lunches, dinners, and drinking. One highlight came on September 2, 1933, when Ken and Kay hosted a barnyard party, complete with straw, costumes, and farm animals. However, on September 30, she wrote about a terrible fight and was convinced they'd divorce. Not surprisingly, her next entry indicated they'd made up. But not for long.

Kay stayed busy at the studio working on *Mandalay,* but, again, ran into trouble when the movie wrapped. At a Ruth Chatterton dinner party, Kay went on a toot, and the next day again expressed shame and disgust at her behavior. She did, however, sufficiently recover to attend *another* party the next night at John and Virginia Gilbert's.

Ken left for New York on November 29, and Kay followed on December 13. The marriage, however, was over.[17] Although friends professed to be shocked, on December 19, 1933, Warner Brothers announced that Kay and Kenneth were separating. "The couple, while remaining the best of friends, have decided that they will be happier living apart."[18] Newspapers reported that the timing was particularly surprising since the two had planned to spend the holidays together in New York. Kay didn't mention the announcement in her diary. She recorded entries for a luncheon with Charles Baskerville, dinner at the Colony, a viewing of *Jezebel,* and then drinks at the 21 Club. She did see Kenneth on December 29, but it was apparently to discuss divorce arrangements. On New Years Eve, Kay had lunch with Bea and their usual gang, played tennis, went to Jo Forrestal's for dinner, and then attended Whitney Aldrich's party.

Some attributed the final breakup to Ken's inability to deal with Kay's success. One writer suggested Ken didn't respect her talent. "Ken MacKenna was, and is, a very splendid actor. He is an excellent technician. And it was whispered that his wife's great popular success, her sensational 'draw' at the box office, began to be a thorn in the side of the husband who believed he knew so much more about acting than his charming wife. But whatever the reason, it was apparent to their friends that Kay was beginning to lose confidence in herself. Finally, when the situation became completely intolerable, she filed a surprise divorce suit against MacKenna in Los Angeles, charging 'incompatibility' and 'nagging.'"[19]

After the New Year started, Kay suffered from a bad cold, but still managed to enjoy her new freedom as a single woman. Her companions included Clifton Webb, Noel Coward, Bill Gaston, Charlie Baskerville, George Kaufman, Allan Ryan, and more. Back in Hollywood in mid–January, Kay had a brief affair with Count Alfredo Carpagna. She'd met him through di Frasso, but quickly tired of him, especially when she met her new lover — Maurice Chevalier.

Kay began the affair with Maurice Chevalier at the end of January 1934. Typically, it started with frequent lovemaking. "Had merciless afternoon with Maurice — four times in 2 hours."[20] However, by May, Kay's old bugaboo had arrived. She wrote in May that they took dope, and then the next day wrote of boredom. On May 19, she told Maurice he was selfish; but, then on May 21, she indicated they'd made up, though she feared the argument had caused lasting damage. By late May, Maurice suggested ways to spice up their lovemaking: "Swell evening — very exciting, discussing about lesbians and a threesome. Not practical, I'm afraid."[21]

Meanwhile, in February, Kay described Kenneth's shortcomings in her divorce proceedings. Kenneth nagged and complained, she said. He wasn't happy with how she dressed, where she placed furniture, or even her acting. "She further charged that he assumed an 'air of superiority' and for seven months frequently had made slighting remarks about her in front of friends and acquaintances."[22] When her lawyer asked for additional examples, Kay fired more salvoes. "I would come home late at night after working twelve to fourteen hours and he would keep me up for hours making sarcastic remarks. That made me nervous."[23] Ida Perry, Kay's loyal maid, also testified on Kay's behalf. Kenneth remained quiet, though apparently he could have complained plenty about Kay's drinking, tantrums, name calling, and adultery. In fact, if aware of her diary, he could have created a scandal far worse than the one faced by Mary Astor and George S. Kaufman in Astor's 1936 divorce proceedings.[24] Kay's uncontested divorce was granted in three minutes on February 21, 1934.

Because of Kay's divorce complaint, reporters went wild trying to figure out the identity of her second husband. It was only then that the public learned that the mystery man was William Gaston, who was then married to actress Rosamond Pinchot. Ironically, upon Kay's divorce from MacKenna, Gaston —and Allan Ryan — propositioned their former lover yet again.

> *"Kay Francis was a mistress of understatement. She could create soap-operatic characterizations with such restraint and apparent sincerity that clichéd drama could become moving drama. Kay Francis is nobility without stuffiness."*[25]

Amidst all the personal intrigue, Kay continued her film career. In early 1934, Kay was still waiting in vain for the go-ahead on *DuBarry,* as well as a possible role as Napoleon's Josephine. She was also slated to appear with William Powell and Colin Clive in a picture titled *The Key,* a movie about the Irish rebellion. Just in time, before the Production Code took effect, Warner Brothers released *Mandalay.* Yes, it's another melodrama, but it gloried in its sordidness and is still great campy fun. Kay played a woman sold into white slavery by her bad-boy boyfriend, and virtually spat her lines—finally given the chance to play Poppy in *Shanghai Gesture,* she unleashed an unforgettable performance as Spot White. It will always remain a popular Kay Francis film. One reviewer realized its appeal when it was released. "Make no mistake, you'll like Kay Francis in her clothes, her rich, exotic lure, her drama, no matter how you quarrel with the over-wrought story. The camera presents some lovely pictures of Miss Francis."[26]

Of course, film censors had a fit. Producer Hal Wallis stayed involved with the production through memos. On October 21, 1933, he wrote to director Michael Curtiz. "Generally your stuff is beautiful and I don't want to start limiting you and restricting you. However, when you show Kay Francis in the bathtub with [Ricardo] Cortez in the shot and a close-up of Kay Francis in the tub and show her stepping out of the tub and going into Cortez's arms, then you get me to the point where I am going to have to tell you to stick to the script and not to do anything else. For god's sake, Mike, you have been making pictures long enough to know that it is impossible to show a man and a woman who are not married in a scene of this kind. The situation is censorable enough with Cortez and Francis living [together.]"[27]

Wallis also wrote screenwriter Robert Presnell on the same day, warning him about a different scene. "Naturally, in the scene in the Orient Café, it should be shot carefully, that is, making it more of a nightclub and gambling house than to indicate that it is a hook shop [brothel.] I don't feel we are sacrificing anything by doing this because people will put their own interpretation on it and know what kind of an establishment it is and what Francis is doing there."[28]

Kay described a typical day while working on *Mandalay.* After rising at 6:30, she bathed, dressed, ate, read over the script, and then drove herself to the studio, arriving at 8:00. After sitting in the makeup chair for an hour, she was on the set from 9:00 to 12:45, interspersed with two costume and makeup changes. Her lunch was spent with magazine interviewers. She returned to the set at 2:30 and worked until 5:30, again breaking for another costume change and photo sittings. Her dinner hour was spent phoning guests, explaining she wouldn't be able to attend a party planned for later that evening. She was back on the set from 7:00 to 10:45, and then spent the next hour removing makeup, dressing, and driving home. She greeted husband Kenneth and guests—she was still married to MacKenna during the film's production—but apologized that she must retire to bed as she had to report early the next morning.

"I love this studio."[29]

Wonder Bar was the first time Kay publicly complained about the studio's treatment of her. Although Kay was promised a large role, Dolores Del Rio's part was expanded at Kay's expense. "Frankly, I did not want to take part in that picture. I made no secret of my dissatisfaction with my role. It was a small, inconsequential part, and I believed (and still believe) that I should not have been forced, by my contract, to play it."[30] Kay, however, who valued professionalism, bristled at charges that she phoned in her role. *Variety* wrote, "Miss Francis plays her faithless wife role with a superciliousness and condescension not in keeping with the assignment."[31] Kay responded, "I didn't scowl my way through the picture because I didn't like the part. I felt the woman would be spoiled, petulant and sullen, and I played her that way. I was trying to characterize. I hope I'm too intelligent to let any dissatisfaction I may feel reflect in my work."[32] Kay also made it clear that despite her occasional disagreements with her studio, she was grateful. "I feel I owe them a great deal. After all, they made a star of me. When I was with Paramount I was only playing featured roles. That feeling of gratitude is one reason I haven't complained more over some of the roles given me."[33]

Her subdued mood was also blamed on domestic difficulties. In March 1934, observers noticed that she seemed in better humor. "Since the announcement of her separation from Kenneth MacKenna, she has been sweet, smiling and gracious, and the studio lads are rooting for her once more."[34] Another writer explained that Kay's moodiness could also be blamed on the role she was playing. "She *always* lives her roles. And so if you ever hear stories about her aloofness on the set,

KAY FRANCIS IN *WONDER BAR* (1934)
Kay detested costume fittings and posing for stills.

don't believe them. It isn't Kay at all, but another girl entirely, brought to life by the sincerity of a grand actress and an even grander person!"[35]

Dr. Monica was another film that did little for Kay's career. Yet another melodrama, it cast Kay as a professional woman who really wanted to be a wife and mother. Although Kay told an interviewer that the part was "the most interesting characterization she has had for a long time,"[36] she reported on-set difficulties with director William Keighley. She later admitted that she was tired of such roles. "I want to get away from the 'new woman'—the *Doctor Monicas*—if I can. I want to do something essentially feminine."[37] Reviewers did not like her in this one. *Variety* was especially harsh. "Even in her best moments Miss Francis in this film is mostly a well-dressed lady who is acting: always acting."[38]

By mid–1934, Kay had become bored with her roles. Asked how she liked her performance in *Dr. Monica*, she replied, "I don't particularly like myself in anything any more. Seems to me I'm always doing the same things with my hands and eyes and face. It makes you wonder just how much there is and is not to this acting business."[39] She'd never forgotten Ronald Colman's acting lesson, but added a new gesture that became associated with her — placing her left hand on her forehead. Kay had grown tired of it, and feared her audiences might, too. "Just think how many times I do that in a picture! But directors like it. They say it's characteristic of me."[40]

Kay took time off from studio work in March and spent much of it with Maurice. She also took a trip to the La Quinta resort with Lydia Macy, and then continued her vacation in Palm Springs.[41] During this time, Kay was also friendly with Contessa Tookie De Zappola.[42] The rest of the spring was spent back at the studio for tests and retakes. April was also when Kay's beloved maid and friend Ida became ill and had to be hospitalized.

While working on *British Agent*, Kay had a one-night stand with co-star Leslie Howard. Like most of Kay's brief romances, she immediately regretted it and considered it foolish. In the fall of 1934, *British Agent* was released. Whoever thought of casting Kay as Lenin's secretary obviously needed to find a different career. Still, reviews of the picture, and of Kay's performance, were good. "Miss Francis' straight, breezy charm is well suited to the role of Elena,"[43] one critic wrote.

During the production, Kay suffered a serious—and somewhat mysterious—injury. According to the *Los Angeles Times*, Kay "was virtually rescued from the jaws of death, and largely due to her own presence of mind." The article went on to state that on May 16 Kay had cut the artery in her right hand after breaking the glass in her door, trying to let herself into her locked home. She hadn't wanted to awaken her sleeping, ill maid. "If it weren't for the fact that Miss Francis quickly instructed the maid, whom she had to awaken, to apply a tourniquet to her arm the bleeding would have been disastrous."[44] Like most Kay Francis stories, this one had another, different version. It wasn't her hand, but her arm, and it was because she'd gone out with her dog. "She took her dog out for an airing and the door slammed shut behind her, locking her out. Kay knocked a hole in the window with a chunk of iron. She cut her arm on the jagged glass when she reached through the hole to unfasten the window. Kay lost two quarts of blood and seven pounds from the experience."[45] The story—in any version—doesn't make sense, and one wonders what the real story was. Some thought it was a suicide attempt. According to Jean Muir, who co-starred with Kay in *Dr. Monica*, "I guess Kay Francis was very unhappy. She came in with her wrists bound up once and the rumor spread that she tried to commit suicide."[46] Oddly, the incident received no mention in Kay's diary.

In June 1934, Maurice returned to Europe, leaving an unhappy Kay behind. Shortly after this, Kay traveled to New York and saw Richard and Jessica, Julia Hoyt, Allan Ryan,

Elsa Maxwell, Charlie Baskerville, and so on. And then on June 23, Kay sailed on the Italian liner *Rex* with the Barthelmesses, planning to visit Naples, Rome, Cannes, Nice, Paris, and London. She arrived in Gibraltar on June 28, and reached Naples on June 30. There she met Elsa again — and Paolo, a married man, who became her next passion. This was probably Paolo Garretto, an illustrator who worked for *Vanity Fair, The New Yorker, Harper's Bazaar,* and other magazines. He was born in Naples, Italy, to an American mother and Italian father, and was working in Europe at the time of Kay's trip.[47]

This European trip was similar to her divorce excursion in 1925 — it turned into a sex romp. Now a full-fledged movie star, she visited with William Randolph Hearst and Marion Davies, and was introduced to royalty, including Prince Christopher of Greece, Prince and Princess Del Drago, the Duke of the Spoleto, the Grand Duchess Marie of Russia, and Prince Phillip of Hess, the King of Italy's son-in-law.

Kay was joined in Naples by Dorothy di Frasso's brother Bert Taylor and his wife Olive, along with Allan Ryan — who apparently regretted not marrying Kay when he had the chance. He presented her with an expensive emerald and attempted to woo her again. Typical of Kay's soap opera life, the day after he gave her the emerald they quarreled. "Allan and I had a large battle over Aileen B — back to house — laughed at him and swam with Paolo and Vasinara — later slept with B — very good."[48]

A sprinkling of Kay's diary entries, beginning July 30, 1934, and concluding September 2, 1934, could provide the seed for a pre–Code motion picture featuring a spoiled American heiress:

"To bed again with B. Better."[49]

"P[50] and I fucked until 5 A.M."[51]

"Promised P to meet him in Milan."[52]

"Slept with HRH."[53]

"Michael came to my room."[54]

"Miserable farewell with P — many tears."[55]

On September 12, Kay was informed by a Paris doctor that she was again pregnant. She assumed the baby was Michael's. Kay met Maurice on the pier, and they rode together to Paris, sparking marriage rumors. Kay, however, had another lover on her mind, and was now bored with the Frenchman. She left Paris and met up with Paolo again.

Kay recorded the serious side effects of yet another abortion in September. Still, Kay continued seeing the man she referred to as "P," and wondered if she was telling him the truth about being in love with him. She also compared him to Maurice, and found Chevalier sorely lacking. Kay continued to see Maurice, but between his sad sack personality and impotence, she was over him — at least for the time being.[56]

"The one thing I have is that I will never have to worry about money as long as I live."[57]

Kay returned to New York in October on the *Rex,* and again told reporters there was no truth to the Chevalier-Francis marriage reports, explaining that, first, she hadn't received her final divorce decree, and, second, she had no plans to marry again — "unless it is when I am old and doddering."[58] In the spring of 1935, she admitted that she thought him a "grand person, but he is my dear friend and nothing more serious."[59] For his part, Maurice proclaimed, "Please make it plain that she is one of my closest friends. But marriage — we're not even thinking of getting married, at least to each other."[60]

Kay's diary suggested that after the initial part of their relationship, she and Maurice became more friends than lovers. Behind the Frenchman's smiling face was a deeply insecure, morose person. In many instances, Kay was more his caretaker than a passionate lover. They clearly depended on each other, but for Kay, once the passion was gone in a relationship, she moved on and found a new lover.

Kay was still infatuated with Paolo, and they took turns frantically telephoning each other. Kay spent most of October in New York, hanging out with her usual friends at her usual spots. She returned to Hollywood on October 19 and was ordered to bed by her personal physician, Bill Branch.[61] She apparently ignored his advice, as she attended a party at the Trocadero, made a phone call to Paolo in Italy, had dinner at Pickfair, and fulfilled other social obligations before she was hospitalized on October 27 for either an abortion or its complications.

On doctor's orders, she didn't report to work on her new George Brent film, *Living on Velvet,* until November 10. A notorious practical joker, Brent made life interesting for the carefully prepared Kay. "Since Kay Francis is considered the best-poised woman before the camera and George Brent the greatest practical joker, there is a complete feud going on in the making of *Living on Velvet* to see 'Gawgie' make Kay go up in her lines. Up to date it has only been accomplished once. The two of them have a 'dunking' scene which took four hours to shoot and which practically 'undunked' them forever."[62] Most reviewers focused on Kay's wardrobe in *Living on Velvet,* as well as her comedic appeal, but dismissed the film. "Miss Francis displays not merely a new collection of gowns (which had the feminine members of the audience cooing) but somewhat surprising talent for comedy in the earlier sequences."[64]

In November, Maurice Chevalier returned to Hollywood — to live. He'd recently purchased a new California home, and he and Kay spent time together when Kay wasn't working on the film. Apparently the affair with Paolo was over — she rarely mentioned him again. Kay consented to an interview in which she named her favorite male per-

KAY FRANCIS IN *LIVING ON VELVET* (1935).
Sometimes Kay's wardrobe startled critics. Still, it proved she truly could wear anything.

formers—Jackie Cooper, John Barrymore, Lionel Barrymore, Richard Barthelmess, James Cagney, Ronald Colman, Gary Cooper, Clark Gable, William Powell, and Maurice. "I like pictures, and I like men with character."[64] She also found time in December to visit Chevalier on the *Folies Bergère* set.

For the first time in years, Kay didn't spend Christmas and New Years in New York. She celebrated Christmas with Jessica and Richard Barthelmess, attended a party at the Samuel Goldwyns, and then she, Jessica, and Ruth Chatterton partied away the early morning hours in the city. She celebrated New Years Eve with Maurice, who was ill with the flu. They toasted the New Year at four o'clock in the afternoon — midnight in Paris— and then went to the Charles Boyers, and, finally, to Tim McCoy's for cocktails.

After Christmas, Kay reportedly suffered from makeup poisoning and then an attack of hemorrhoids. Still, she was able to do a radio broadcast with George Brent, which resulted in another one-night stand with one of her leading men. "He told me afterwards that I had helped him tremendously and that he appreciated that. Big fucking! And he got the jitters."[65] In a later interview, Brent shared his thoughts on Kay. "Kay is one of the few women I know who speaks a man's language. He gets from her the same firm, steady friendship he gets from other men — and yet she's so deeply feminine along with it."[66]

In February 1935, Kay came down with the flu. At least the newspaper reported it as such. In her February 5, 1935, diary entry, Kay wrote that she'd had a miscarriage, and was thankful she didn't have to undergo another abortion. It didn't stop her from attending a lavish party given by Fred Astaire at the Trocadero, and then one hosted by Dorothy Parker —or throwing her own party at the Vendome restaurant, which wowed many. Kay had the entire restaurant made into a ship. "Merrily we roll along — without Kenneth MacKenna," was the sign that greeted guests, including the George S. Kaufmans, James Cagney, the Fredric Marches, June Walker, Joan Bennett, Joan Blondell, Virginia Bruce, Walter Wanger, Joseph Schenck, Samuel Goldwyn — more than 300 guests in all. Kay was celebrating her divorce —and taking a poke at Kenneth, who'd had a major success with the Broadway play, *Merrily We Roll Along.*[67] According to writer George Oppenheimer, "It was one of the best parties I ever attended in Hollywood. She rented a stylish restaurant and converted the entrance into the prow of a ship. You went up the gangplank and slid down into the ballroom. There were big photographic blowups like those in front of theaters."[68] Kay dressed as an admiral —complete with suit, tie, and a cap rakishly tilted over one eye. "Standing at the foot of the slide that brought the guests to the floor where the party was getting in full sway, the hostess greeted each arrival with a typical maritime salute. Nearly every feminine star-guest wore white shorts and blue sweaters, with their male escorts attired in varied sea-going costumes, running largely to natty blue and white officers' uniforms."[69]

A couple of days later, Dr. George Parrish, head of the Los Angeles Health Department, wrote Kay a stern letter accusing her of using "anything but good judgment. Probably you gave the influenza to many of your guests. The city spends the taxpayers' money to educate people to remain at home when they have influenza or any other communicable disease, and the fact that you are a screen star gives you no right to do a thing like that."[70] Kay, who was hospitalized shortly after the party's conclusion, explained that she only had a touch of the flu, that her personal physician was one of the guests, and her hospitalization had less to do with the flu than fatigue from overwork. Kay was even more perturbed that rumors suggested the party was expensive. "If anybody believes that party cost me $10,000, they don't know their Kay Francis."[71]

Meanwhile, ex-husband Bill Gaston was having his own marital troubles. He arrived in Hollywood and propositioned Kay, who declined. The next day, Kay, Gaston, Gilbert

Roland, and Countess di Frasso went to Pasadena to see a movie. Their plans were ruined when Gaston and Roland got into a fight.[72]

While Kay turned down a reconciliation with Gaston, she continued to have an up-and-down relationship with Chevalier, marred by occasional stormy fights. Maurice returned to Europe in March, but Kay quickly found a new lover that same month. A couple of days after Maurice left on the Chief, she met Delmer Daves at a Japanese-themed party at Frank Borzage's.

According to Del, their romance began when he visited her home to discuss the script he'd written for *Stranded*. One of Daves' tasks was rewriting the script to remove words with the dreaded "r." The romance with Daves took off quickly. According to Daves, "I went to her house, introduced myself and the object of my visit and it became one of Cole's 'one of those things,' for we hit it off so well I never left, and we were devoted to each other solely for the next three years, traveled together between films, to New York, Europe."[73] Daves, described as "big, blond, anything but handsome,"[74] was Kay's constant companion, leading many to speculate they'd marry. Typical of Kay's relationships, their early days involved much sexual activity. But Kay also found Del intelligent, funny, and an enjoyable companion.

Meanwhile, Hal Wallis announced that Warner Brothers was trying to find good roles for Kay. "He says they are acquiring plays, one by one, suitable for her, so that they will have a list to choose from. A few days ago *I Found Stella Parish,* the dramatic story of an actress, by John Monk Saunders, was purchased with Kay in mind."[75]

On April 16, 1935, Kay helped open the House of Westmore. Makeup man Perc Westmore — rumored to have been Kay's lover, though there was no evidence of this in the diary — and his brothers opened the elaborate salon with much fanfare. Kay turned the key that opened the establishment, and Joan Blondell, Marlene Dietrich, Carole Lombard, Anita Louise, Clara Bow, Myrna Loy, and Claudette Colbert also participated in the public relations bonanza. Kay helped financially as well. The Westmores had run out of funds before the opening, and Perc told Kay of his misfortunes one day while she was in his makeup chair for *Stranded*. "Right then and there, with one eyelash on and the other still in Perc's hand, Kay reached into her purse, brought out her checkbook, tore out a blank check, signed her name at the bottom of it, and told Perc to fill in whatever amount he needed. He filled in $25,000, rushed to his decorators with the money, and the job was completed on schedule."[76]

In April 1935, Kay was torn between Maurice and Del. At this point, however, the magazine writers hadn't discovered their romance. "Kay isn't saying whether it's Maurice Chevalier or the Italian Count who is the attraction; probably both."[77] The Italian count, Alfredo Carpagna, was, of course, long out of the picture.

On April 15, Del left for Annapolis, and Kay began wondering if she'd fallen in love with him. She wrote several heartfelt April entries about her feelings for Del, and told her best friends about their relationship. She left for New York on April 20, and saw him before she left for Europe, boarding the *S.S. Aquitania* on April 26. Tortured because she missed Del — and knew she had to face Paolo again — Kay couldn't enjoy herself. She finally convinced herself that she loved Del — after having sex one last time with Paolo. She explained the situation to Paolo, who by all accounts was a good sport, and continued to socialize with him on the trip. She also saw Roussie, Elsie Mendl, and fashion designer Elsa Schiaparelli, and visited the Bal Tabarin nightclub.

Anderson Lawler, a sometime movie actor and Kay's frequent friend and escort,[78] accompanied her on the 1935 European trip, and it was on this trip that one of the legendary Kay Francis stories occurred — or didn't. They'd met through George Cukor, and Andy had appeared with her in Cukor's *Girls About Town*.[79] According to the story, which likely originated with Lawler, the studio invited him along to keep her out of trouble. In hindsight it doesn't seem like a great idea, but Andy went along, telling friends he was paid $10,000. One night he was awakened by a drunk, nude Kay pounding on his London hotel room door. "I'm not a star. I'm a *woman,* and I want to get fucked!"[80] Andy claimed he earned his money that night.

The incident probably never happened. Andy had a habit of exaggerating his importance to Kay. He was interviewed once by the local Lynchburg, Virginia, newspaper, who asked him a few months later about his *engagement* to Miss Francis. "For a moment it appeared that Mr. Lawler was blushing. He looked fluttered [*sic*]. 'Winchell started that,' he said, and then shook his head. 'You may say,' he went on, 'That I admire Miss Francis more than any woman I have ever known, but — he smiled sadly, " — the rumor, I'm sorry to say, is not true.'"[81] Andy also intimated to family members that Miss Francis had fallen for him, and eagerly showed off autographed photos she'd given him. On the one he was most proud of, she'd inscribed, "Thank God for Andy Lawler."

Andy was gay — his closest friends were George Cukor, Billy Haines, and Jimmie Shields — and Kay certainly knew this. They socialized together a great deal, and Kay leaned on him for advice, though at one point she wrote that she was beginning to wonder if he was competent. At some point they had a falling out, perhaps because she found out about the stories he was telling. Although both moved to New York in the 1940s, and lived within blocks of each other, they had nothing to do with one another.[82] Andy died in Manhattan in 1959.

In any event, Kay didn't mention the incident in her diary. Ironically, this particular European trip was one of her tamest because she was obsessed with Del, who was still in America.

While in London, Kay had successful surgery on May 24 to remove her salivary gland. The surgery was precipitated by an infected wisdom tooth. Her visitors included Andy, Kitty Miller,[83] Bea Stewart, and producer Dwight Wiman. Kay spent several days in the hospital, and then hit the circuit again. On June 5, she saw Maurice and told him about Del. He, too, was a good sport, and a relieved Kay continued on her whirlwind trip, attending friend Grace Moore's debut at Covent Garden, where Moore played Mimi in *La Boheme*. Kay also met the Prince of Wales before returning to New York — and Del — on June 20.

In New York, Del and Kay made the rounds, seeing Lois Long and Bill Gaston, and having dinner with Ed Sullivan, before deciding to get away. Kay and Del — or Red Gyp, as Kay called him — traveled to the Lake Louise area of Canada.[84] Indeed, this Canadian vacation with Del was like a honeymoon, and Kay's entries expressed much joy, although Del's bad back and other medical problems produced some frustration for her sex life. In July, they traveled to Washington State and then returned home to Hollywood on July 19.

Unfortunately, Kay became pregnant again. A woman named Mrs. Wilson performed the abortion, and complications set in, making Kay miserable for more than a month. On August 22, Kay moved to 8371 DeLongpre Avenue — the William S. Hart house — and the relationship continued into the fall of 1935. The couple particularly enjoyed spending time at Del's rustic Lake Arrowhead cabin near San Bernardino, and this period was definitely one of Kay's happiest. Even after she had an unspecified operation on September 25, she expressed contentment with Del.

She was dismayed, however, to learn in October of terrible gossip. Bill Branch, her personal physician, told her that rumors were swirling that she had syphilis. In truth, it's

WILLIAM S. HART HOUSE, 8341 DELONGPRE AVENUE
Cowboy movie star William S. Hart bought this home in 1920 for $25,000. He began leasing it in 1927, and Kay lived here from 1935 to 1937. The house was donated to the City of Los Angeles in 1944 for use as a public park.

remarkable that Kay Francis enjoyed a fairly scandal-free reputation, considering her lifestyle and frequent abortions. After weathering this particular storm, Kay and Del continued to enjoy many trips to the cabin in November and December.

"Hollywood saps your vitality. It demands your strength in a constant struggle. It is like an octopus, always reaching out, always absorbing. It knows no pity. It takes far more than it gives."[85]

It would have been one thing if Warner Brothers was working her to death in interesting pictures, but Kay was relegated to mediocre properties. A few months after *Living on Velvet* arrived in theaters, *Stranded*—again with Brent—was released. *Time* called it "an eminently unimportant little fabrication,"[86] and *Variety* agreed that Kay was "wasted"[87] in the film.

In September, *The Goose and the Gander* with—you guessed it—George Brent was released. This was the best Kay Francis–George Brent pairing, and Kay was able to utilize her comedic talent. *Newsweek* noticed. "In her new film Warners give Miss Francis a chance to display her talents as a comedienne instead of confining her to the role of manikin."[88] However, reviewers also felt the need to point out Kay's speech impediment. "Its chief impediment to an evening pleasantly unimportant in the cinema comes from its insistence on cramming the dialogue with r's, which has an embarrassing habit of becoming w's when Miss Francis goes to work on them."[89]

Kay reported to the studio on September 1 to work on *I Found Stella Parrish*, which featured her sadly miscast as a classic stage actress with a secret past. Elsie Janis, her friend and fan, wrote, "It seems to me that outside of *One Way Passage* (in which she was grand) Kay has been handed a lot of roles that someone must have refused to play."[90] Critics again suggested that Warners Brothers was misusing Kay. "That ceaseless search of Warner Brothers for a worthy Kay Francis vehicle has not ended. Miss Francis, a handsome woman who has still to prove herself a great actress, deserves a good deal better than this hour and a half of heroics."[91]

Meanwhile, once the gossip columnists realized Kay and Daves were dating, they followed them, reporting on their every move. Upset at the scrutiny, Kay and Del engaged in a cat-and-mouse game with the press. One night in September 1935, they attended the premiere of *Shipmates Forever*. Seeking refuge in the balcony, they remained after the preview crowd left and watched the next film as well. "Then Daves came down first and cautiously surveyed the situation. He finally gave Kay the high sign and the two faded away like the G-men were after them."[92]

While dating Daves, Kay went to court to change her name back to Katharine G. Francis, leading some to believe she'd soon marry Daves. Though she didn't marry him, she tried to build a professional partnership, asking him to write an adaptation of Mildred Cram's *Forever*. Unfortunately, that project didn't reach fruition because Norma Shearer owned the book's rights. According to Daves, "Kay's greatest ambition was to do Tristan and Isolde, but I discouraged this, feeling her métier was modern life."[93] Still, Kay continued to try to convince him it was a worthwhile project, though it often led to arguments.

In November 1935, Warner Brothers gave Kay a new contract — even though hers hadn't yet expired. "Jack Warner told her that she had accepted any story given her without a word and had always been gracious and lacking in unpleasant temperament, that he wanted to show his appreciation by handing her voluntarily a three-year contract."[94] It didn't hurt that *I Found Stella Parish* had done well at its New York opening. This was one of the last goodwill gestures on the part of Warner Brothers. Kay's film career, which had been deteriorating since the end of 1932, was going downhill fast.

During the last month of 1935, Kay consoled her friend Rhea Gable, whose husband Clark had left her. Kay also met with Samuel Goldwyn about appearing in *Dodsworth*. Unfortunately, Warner Brothers vetoed the project. Once again Kay didn't go to New York for Christmas. On Christmas Eve, she had dinner with Del, and visited with Grace Moore and friends until five in the morning — a highlight was Jeanette MacDonald singing carols at dawn. On Christmas, Del fulfilled family obligations, and then met Kay for cocktails at the Brown Derby. They concluded the evening with movies at the Goldwyns. After Kay hosted a cocktail party — for 100 people — in honor of Lady Mendl on the 27th, she and Del left for the cabin the next day. On the last day of 1935, they enjoyed a New Years Eve dinner with Jessica Barthelmess and Ruth Chatterton.

Kay seemed a contented woman on the eve of 1936. One of her last entries was on December 28, describing how she and Del had gone to the cabin, and despite the wet, dreary weather, she was happy. However, the following year would prove challenging. She'd face battles with the studio — and Del.

CHAPTER 9

Disillusionment, 1936–1937

"Beginning the New Year with my lover. May he be in the same bed with me next year this time."[1]

Kay's New Year began with an optimistic wish for herself and Del. However, her second entry was more telling: "Read my new script—dear God!"[2] The unidentified script was probably *The White Angel*.

Kay recorded social events in January 1936 with Cole Porter's wife Linda and Clifton Webb and his mother Maybelle[3]—along with a grand function at Pickfair. Coming the day after Mary Pickford's divorce from Douglas Fairbanks, it was a formal dinner party for Lady Mendl—better known as Elsie De Wolfe—and included a Russian orchestra and motion pictures in the drawing room. Guests included Prince and Princess Vaselli, Frances Marion, Ouida and Basil Rathbone, Countess de Maigret, Edmund Goulding, the John Mack Browns, Michael Bartlett, Mrs. Charlie Farrell, Joan Bennett and Gene Markey, the Jesse Laskys, Frances Dee and Joel McCrea, the Leslie Howards, Adrian, Cesar Romero, Miriam Hopkins, the Lewis Milestones, Grace Moore and Valentin Parera, Clifton Webb and Maybelle, Louella Parsons, the Donald Ogden Stewarts, George Cukor, Constance Collier, the Sam Goldwyns, Phillips Holmes, the David Selznicks, Conrad Nagel, and many others.

Kay also visited with Marion Davies and old friend Dorothy di Frasso. Kay enjoyed a surprise birthday party thrown for her on January 13, and continued celebrating her 31st birthday by leaving for New York the next day, where she revisited her usual friends, accompanied by Del. On January 17, 1936, it was announced that Kay had signed a three-year contract with Warner Brothers. By this time, Kay and Del were living together. In fact, they were so domesticated that Kay made a point of noting on February 4 that it was the first time in a long time she hadn't spent the night with Del.

Back in California, Kay's busy social life continued with Jock Whitney, Dorothy Parker, Alfred Vanderbilt, Cole Porter, Johnny Weissmuller, and Marlene Dietrich, among others. In March, she saw McKay Morris, who was visiting Hollywood. Kay admitted in her diary that she still found him charming.

Life, however, wasn't easy for a star. A strange headline from March 25, 1936, hinted at Hollywood's dark side: "Kay Francis Home Guarded By Police ... Girl hunted whose note warns of death plot."[4] It turned out to be a case of mistaken identity. James Crawford, 23, explained that he'd told a young woman named Carol Lawrence that he "had it in for K. Francis, because she and my wife had been arrested together." He said he meant Kathleen Francis, an extra—not the famous actress. "Kay Francis is my favorite star. I wouldn't make threats against her,"[5] Crawford asserted. Carol Lawrence delivered a letter warning of the threats to Kay's residence.

Most of Kay's diary entries during the spring of 1936 indicate she was working, which left little time for socializing. Kay did find time, however, to release her own best-dressed actress list, which included Constance Bennett, Claudette Colbert, Marlene Dietrich, Carole Lombard, and Myrna Loy. "But please list them alphabetically. I don't want to get in any more jams with my friends."[6]

The White Angel, released in the summer of 1936, found Kay again miscast — this time as Florence Nightingale. "Being Florence Nightingale was not such a great departure for me. I've portrayed women doctors on the screen twice. I'm getting to be an old hand at these medical characterizations."[7] Yes, but *Florence Nightingale?!* Graham Greene described how Kay, "handicapped by her beauty, does her best to sober down this sentimental version of Florence Nightingale's character, but she is defeated by the scenario-writers."[8] Later, Kay acknowledged the film was a mistake. "I shudder when I think of that one,"[9] she admitted in 1938.

A writer, interviewing the star for a beauty article, described Kay's arrival on the *White Angel* set: "At seven-forty into the center of all this stepped that angel of mercy, Florence Nightingale — right out of Kay Francis' big black coupe. And in spite of the unearthly hour of her departure from home and the drabness of her heavy woolen cloak and gray nurse's uniform, glamour stepped before the camera when Kay took over the spot held by her stand-in."[10]

Producer Hal Wallis became disenchanted with director William Dieterle — and Kay — during the production. "I felt that he should have gotten more emotion from Kay Francis.

In scene after scene, reacting to the sight of the injured, or clashing with an official who refused to see things her way, she looked completely blank. We weren't too happy with the picture. *The White Angel* was well directed, but miscast, and Kay Francis had lost the box office she once had. It was one of our box office failures."[11]

During production, Kay became a habitual knitter, a hobby she enjoyed the rest of her life. She knitted a coat for her dachshund, Wilhemina (Weenie), and dog coats for assorted crew members. Asked how to measure a dog for a coat, she answered, "Oh, it's easy. You just take their neck measurement and go ahead and knit."[12]

Warner Brothers allowed Kay a brief vacation before she started work on her next film, the much better *Give Me Your Heart.* Kay used the time to visit Del's cabin — which she now referred to as the "Sanctuary" — and also attended William Randolph Hearst's birthday party, given by mistress Marion Davies, though she complained it was boring.

Give Me Your Heart was a melodrama, for sure — with George Brent

KAY FRANCIS IN *GIVE ME YOUR HEART*
Even Kay was dismayed by this outfit from Give Me Your Heart *(1936).*

again — but done well, and Kay's performance rang true. Though she battled director Archie Mayo, this might have been one of her last good Warner Brothers films. In general, critics praised her performance. "Cosmopolitan Productions have turned out an intensely absorbing drama, well devised for the talents of the handsome Kay Francis, who has in this one her best modern characterization to date. Miss Francis gives an outstanding performance, handling the variety of emotions called for by the script with considerable skill."[13]

In May 1936, Kay talked to an interviewer about her acting style — and ability. For someone who'd worked steadily in motion pictures since 1929, she betrayed a remarkable lack of confidence. "I always see the 'rushes' as I'm making a picture. It's like being given instructions. I watch my habits. I don't want to repeat gestures too often. I have a habit of wrinkling my forehead. I've got to be careful not to do this. And I always look taller to myself than I really am. Anything I've ever liked about myself on the screen is what the cameraman has done with me. It's not what I've done. It's what the cameraman did. And they can do plenty. I give all credit to them."[14] Another article revealed why she liked close-ups. "They're kind to her type of acting, which is done largely with the eyes and by subtle changes of expression rather than wide gestures. Then, too, her looks are close-up proof. They will stand any degree of magnification."[15]

In early June, Kay learned of a scandal involving Billy Haines and Andy Lawler. She received a call from Perc Westmore on June 4, 1936, explaining that Andy, Billy, and Jimmie Shields were attacked in Haines' and Shields' Manhattan Beach neighborhood by a mob who accused Shields of molesting a six-year-old boy.[16] She met first with Billy, and then Andy dropped by, wondering if the scandal might interfere with their upcoming European trip. It didn't.

Kay had her own possible scandal to worry about. On June 12, she had another abortion. "Jesus, it's awful. Why do I always get caught and have so little fun."[17] In addition, tensions were growing with Del, even as they tried to collaborate on a project. "Del and I have battle over Legend — Del packed up and left but telephoned and back he came — what a night! Fuck The Legend."[18] This was probably a reference to a screen adaptation of the Tristan and Isolde medieval legend.

Once again, Kay suffered from medical problems. On June 22, she had teeth extracted, was given codeine for the painful procedure, but received little relief when an infection set in. At the same time, Del had his own health issues. On June 25, he had an abscess lanced. Finally, by the end of the first week of July, Kay felt well enough to socialize. Her companions included Douglas Fairbanks and new wife Sylvia Ashley, Clifton Webb, Tallulah Bankhead, Elizabeth Allen, Merle Oberon, David Niven, and Constance Bennett. However, she had a relapse, and surgery was scheduled for July 13.

It's little wonder that she and Del bickered. They occasionally slept apart, and Kay feared he'd fallen out of love with her, especially when she learned that Del was considering a trip alone for five weeks. They also argued several times about her will, though it wasn't clear what the conflict concerned.

Perhaps most tellingly, Kay had ceased recording sexual entries in her diary, indicating the passion was gone. They'd settled into a mundane if stable existence, and both were busy with their respective careers. Many of Kay's fall 1936 diary entries simply told of mutual fatigue and many dinners in bed on trays. She also suffered what she first called a heart attack on September 11, following a tennis game. The incident was probably a panic attack, and Kay's cardiogram a few days later showed no heart damage.

When Kay began to stray, the relationship suffered a major blow. In October, Del caught Kay kissing another man. "Home and David kisses me on the doorstep! And I kiss him back! And Del puts on the light!"[19] Del left Kay's house in a huff, and Kay immediately regretted her behavior. The man in question was probably actor David Niven, one of Hollywood's great ladies' men, and Kay's neighbor.

"Home from mountains — Cukor's for dinner — Tallulah, Roland, etc. — he sees me as Scarlett O'Hara — good!"[20]

Kay was considered for the role of Scarlett in *Gone with the Wind*. Really. The improbable casting idea got started when Kay met with David Selznick on August 26, 1936. He apparently gave her a copy of the book, and Kay finished reading it on August 29, thoroughly enjoying it. According to Kay's diary entry for August 30, director George Cukor[21] told her he could see her as Scarlett. The matter wasn't mentioned again in the diary. There's no question that dozens of actors were considered for the role, but it's odd that Kay was in the competition, since historical dramas weren't her strength.

In November 1936, Kay again vacationed in Europe — this time with Del. She met him at the Newark Airport, and her antics made the newspaper. "Miss Francis was on hand in a limousine fifteen minutes before the American Airlines plane with Daves aboard arrived from Hollywood. When the ship hove in view, she tossed a baby camel hair blanket into a corner, dashed from the car and did a tap dance while the plane came in to land. Then she bucked the line of spectators for thirty yards to greet Daves with a flying tackle around the midriff. 'Can't you leave us alone?' La Francis snapped to photographers between hugs and kisses."[22] Yet again, rumors were rampant that she'd marry Daves. "It is pointed out that the romance seems to have intensified in recent months. The scenarist not only was Kay's constant companion at Hollywood affairs, but, during the filming of her recent picture, *Another Dawn,* spent considerable time on the set."[23] Kay, however, remained adamant that she had no marriage plans. "I'll never marry him. I'll never marry anybody again."[24]

Kay gave an interview before she left, and went to great pains to paint herself as a boring homebody. "My life has been singularly uneventful. It has drifted quietly from one step to another, avoiding anything unusual or outstanding. There are no thrilling or colorful pages in my record and I imagine that I'm entirely different from what the public believes me to be."[25] To complete the picture, Kay actually knitted during the interview!

She also explained that she dresses casually off the set. "In screen portrayals, I wear gorgeous costumes and I adore them. Yet, after dressing up all day for the cameras the feminine desire for pretty clothes is fully satisfied and I like to slip into slacks and sandals when I leave the studio."[26] Frankly, Kay had tired of talking about fashion. "Clothes! I haven't talked about anything else for eight or nine years. I'm not nearly the clothes person the studio has built me up to be."[27]

Before they left for Europe, Kay briefly stayed in New York and saw Elsa Maxwell, McKay Morris, Bert and Olive Taylor, Julia Hoyt, Bea Stewart, Lois Long — and attended a fun party for Clifton Webb, thrown by Libby Holman. She also saw *Red, Hot, and Blue* and *And Stars Remain*. She boarded the *Normandie* on November 25. By now, the Manhattan Beach scandal had blown over, and Andy accompanied her.

While in Europe, Kay saw Eleanor Boardman and Harry D'Arrast, Edna Best, Bill O'Brien, Kay Hammond, Alexander Korda, the Fairbanks, Raquel Meller, Ivor Novello, Merle Oberon, and others. The abdication crisis in England occurred at the same time. In true Zelig-fashion, Kay found herself on the same train as King Edward, now the exiled Duke of Windsor, as she made her way to St. Moritz!

Although Kay caught a cold, she enjoyed shopping, sleigh rides, and her first luge.

KAY FRANCIS IN *STOLEN HOLIDAY*
Kay Francis, costumed by Orry-Kelly, on the set of Stolen Holiday *(1936).*

The cold developed into a severe headache that lasted more than a week. Kay's Christmas was spent in bed. Although she wasn't in perfect health, she enjoyed a packed, if argumentative, New Years Eve watching the Cresta Run, a skiing competition, dining, drinking — and then fighting with Del, who was in a sour mood. She finally got to bed at 5 A.M. This was the not-so-good ending to a not-so-good year.

"No star is better than her script."[28]

Kay did manage to dodge one bomb in 1936. She refused to work on *The Golden Arrow,* and it was subsequently assigned to Bette Davis. Davis agreed to star in the film with George Brent, but asked for more creative control in her next contract.

The Warner Brothers films of the late 1930s simply were not as good as the ones produced in the early 1930s. An example is Kay's first 1937 feature, *Stolen Holiday,* with Ian Hunter and Claude Rains. Certainly it was an expensive picture, and reviewers pointed to Kay's numerous costume changes, but the fault lay in the script. It wasn't interesting or compelling. It's easy to blame the Production Code — and it's true that film quality did deteriorate when filmmakers could no longer show adult behavior and situations — but there were many fine features *after* the Code. In reality, Warner Brothers was putting out a mediocre product, especially in the slate of films they produced with Kay Francis. Kay's description of Warner Brothers as a "man's studio"[29] wasn't far off. "Our executives and writers understand men thoroughly, but they have no grasp whatever of woman's psychology."[30]

Kay finally acknowledged that the studio had made mistakes with her career. "One of the unpleasant angles is being handed a poor story with the idea that your name and popularity will carry it. That's a very foolish notion. Someone once said that no star could survive three flops. I would like to add that no star can rationalize a badly prepared story. I know; I've tried! The public holds a bad picture against a star longer than a good picture is remembered."[31]

She was right. By the beginning of 1937, there was talk in Hollywood about the damage Warner Brothers had done to Kay's career. Kay finally returned to New York in mid–January, but continued to fight various illnesses. Although she socialized with Dorothy di Frasso, Bert and Olive Taylor, Doug and Sylvia Fairbanks, Andy Lawler, William Powell, and others, she was finally diagnosed with bronchial pneumonia on January 24. Still, somehow she'd managed to see stage productions of *The Women, You Can't Take It with You, On Your Toes,* and *Hamlet—and* visit nightclubs like the Cotton Club and El Morocco. She returned to California on January 31, but still suffered health problems, and was rushed to the hospital on February 6. After being released on February 9, she finally seemed to have turned the corner.

Kay's next film, *Another Dawn,* starred Errol Flynn and was even more ridiculous than her upcoming *Confession* wig. But it did have beautiful production values, and there were some wonderfully lit shots of Kay Francis and Errol Flynn. Sometimes that's enough. However, most critics agreed it was mediocre. "This one rings no changes, follows the old pattern faithfully; generates no suspense and no excitement because it is always and completely predictable."[32]

While Kay no doubt longed for a sophisticated comedy role after numerous melodramas, she instead found herself in a remake of a German film, *Confession.* Perhaps because of its European influence, however, it was her best role of 1937, and one that she could be proud of — even with the ludicrous blond wig she wore through much of the film.

Confession was a difficult set. Kay started rehearsals on February 23, and quickly ran into problems with the director. Joe May had seen the original *Mazurka,* which *Confession* was based upon, and decided his film should be a literal duplicate of the original. He resorted to using a stopwatch to film scenes, which made life difficult for the cast. Kay and the director openly sparred on the set. One argument centered on a line of dialogue. Kay thought the line should be "I won't." May insisted on "I can't." When Kay pleaded with him, explaining that there was little difference between the two lines, May insulted her by telling her it was "the difference between you and a good actress."[33] More than once during the making of *Confession,* Kay stormed off the set.

During production, Kay attended a March 6 party given by Ginger Rogers and boyfriend Alfred Vanderbilt at Culver City's Rollerdome. Inspired by Rogers' roller skating dance in *Shall We Dance,* it was newsworthy enough to get written up in *Life Magazine.* According to Rogers, "The guests included Joan Crawford, Franchot Tone, Sally Eilers, Kay Francis, Frank Morgan, Chester Morris, George Gershwin, Ira Gershwin, Harold Lloyd, George Murphy, Simone Simon, Johnny Mack Brown, Jack Oakie, Humphrey Bogart, Mayo Methot, Cary Grant, Phyllis Fraser, Anne Shirley, Johnny Green, Cesar Romero, Eddie Rubin, Florence Lake, Hermes Pan, and Lela [Ginger's mother], too. Alfred and I hired the best band available for our joint party and served plenty of spaghetti, chili, tamales, Boston baked beans, sliced ham, cheese of every kind, hot dogs, and hamburgers cooked to order. The food table covered practically one-quarter of the circle of the rink. You name it, we had it! There never was a better party. Alfred and I agreed on that. Everyone dressed very casually and had a great time."[34] Kay, however, was unimpressed, complaining that the party was dull.

Tragedy struck the next day when Kay's beloved dachshund Weenie died. "Weenie is dead! I can't believe it! Got her from vet — buried her in silks and satins with red ball — oh dear god — why?"[35] Kay reported for rehearsals the next day, but two days after Weenie's death Kay didn't report to the set. It marked the first time since she'd started her career — nine years before — that she'd called in an absence. Instead, Kay went to see *The Plainsman,* and reluctantly returned to work the next day.

She also busied herself during this time by getting her mother's house ready. Kay relished telling the story of how she'd surprised her mother. "I built a house for her and furnished it without her knowing anything about it. When it was all done I planned to move her into it on her maid's day off. The maid, instead of taking the day off, went over to the new house. I had picked up Mother's dogs the day before and told her I was going to take them to the veterinarian to be washed. Instead, I took them to the new house. Then I took Mother driving and when we passed the house I said, 'That's a cute place. Let's go in and look at it.' Her own maid answered the bell. Her dogs jumped up and down in welcome. I had arranged to have her best friend drop in for tea. Afterward, the friend stayed with her when I left and I went home to telephone her so the call from me was the first one she received in her new place."[36]

Confession wrapped on April 14, and the film's crew presented Kay with a special gift — "a big, square cellophane box full of gardenias in the center of which nestled a rare old Eighteenth Century snuff box. Inside the box was a scroll of parchment inscribed with 40 names and the message: 'A confession of our love and appreciation of Kay Francis.' The difficult Miss Francis, frequently reported terror of the sets, promptly broke down and cried like a baby."[37]

Many Kay Francis fans point to *Confession* as one of their favorite films. According to film historian Allan Ellenberger, it's an excellent reason to re-evaluate Kay's career. "Despite being a major actress of the 1930s, Kay Francis is mostly forgotten today, except by film buffs. This is regrettable, considering the immeasurable talent this striking beauty communicated on the screen. Who could forget Francis as Vera in *Confession,* arguably one of her greatest screen performances, who as a woman of means is seduced and ruined by Basil Rathbone. After losing her husband and daughter, she becomes a fallen woman and is forced to entertain in sleazy cafés to earn a meager living. The poignancy and naturalness of her performance shows the range in emotion that she was capable of, confirming her place in film history with such greats as Stanwyck, Hepburn, and Davis."[38]

This wasn't a happy time for Kay. Not only was she distressed with her career, but she and Del frequently squabbled, and Kay admitted in her diary that she'd grown bored with the relationship. Ironically, at her most miserable, Kay Francis was making $227,500 for forty weeks of work, proving true the old adage that money can't buy happiness.[39] Kay was also rated *Variety's* sixth most popular actress behind Myrna Loy, Loretta Young, Claudette Colbert, Ginger Rogers, and Alice Faye, proving fame wasn't the key to happiness, either.

Despite the frequent arguments with Del, Kay became pregnant again in May. A frustrated and depressed Kay had another abortion on May 31, 1937.

Hollywood mourned on June 7, 1937, when Jean Harlow died at the age of 26, a victim of kidney failure.[40] The funeral was attended by Hollywood's biggest stars. "Outside the Wee Kirk o' the Heather Chapel, at Forest Lawn, William Powell stumbled. His face was milk white. Tears streamed down from beneath his dark glasses. Slowly, he reached for Mrs. Bello's [Jean's mother] arm. Together, they entered the flower-banked chapel. A broad-brimmed black hat and dark glasses cloaked her emotions. The chapel was filled with famous faces—all the greats were there. Gable sat, weeping. The usually unemotional Robert Montgomery wiped tears from his eyes, Spencer Tracy, Ronald Colman, Myrna Loy and Norma Shearer hid emotions behind dark glasses. L. B. Mayer openly wept. Howard Hughes was there, pale and motionless. Everywhere you looked, there were stunned, still disbelieving mourners. Somehow, it was incomprehensible that a twenty-six-year-old woman, in the peak season of her life, was gone. Outside the cemetery gates, thousands of fans stood quietly. Everywhere, there were summer flowers, and sprays, and wreaths and bouquets. Joan Crawford and Carole Lombard walked solemnly out of the chapel together. Kay Francis stood comforting Barbara Brown, Jean's stand-in, so hysterical she'd had to leave in the middle of the services."[41]

On July 1, Kay had her own health scare. She was taken by ambulance to the hospital and had surgery the next day. She didn't identify her malady in the diary, but was hospitalized for more than two weeks.

By late summer, Kay and Del were on the verge of breaking up. Kay was so angry with him in July that she ignored his birthday.[42] She relented the next day and gave him a color camera. In August, he left for a time after yet another argument. Kay professed not to care. In addition to her troubles with Del, Kay also reported that her mother had arrived at her house dead drunk. Kay and housekeeper Sylvia[43] took her back to her own home.

By the time she'd finished filming *Confession,* Kay wanted a different kind of role. "I am so tired of suffering for my art. For picture after picture I've had to shed buckets of tears over my little child or my poor, thwarted lover or something. I'm sick to death of crying. It is going to be grand to have unmixed comedy to do. They've promised me there won't be a mite of weeping or hand wringing in the next one."[44] The next one was *First Lady*—indeed a departure from the angst. *First Lady* was light, frothy, and sophisticated. However, a frustrated Kay later wailed that her fans deserted her on this film because her character was *too* light, *too* frothy. Though Kay wanted a change, she was hurt by her fans' reactions. "The fans expect sincerity from me, a certain warmth and 'sympatica.' And if they don't get it they howl. They didn't like me in *First Lady* worth a cent. They told me so, by the hundreds. They don't want me to be flibberty-gibbetty."[45] On the other hand, while critics offered mixed reviews of the film, most praised Kay. "Her performance is splendid and witty, and her costumes striking."[46]

"Lots of people, I expect, certainly those who know me here in Hollywood, call me temperamental. What of it? Who wants to be a dead stick?"[47]

Kay Francis had a habit that was valued in Hollywood — punctuality. Whereas other stars were notorious for being late — or not showing up at all — Kay was legendary for promptness. She insisted that being late made her physically ill. "But though she is rarely late, neither is she inclined to arrive ahead of time. She appears on the moment, not before, not after."[48]

KAY FRANCIS IN *FIRST LADY*
Kay wore this chic daytime ensemble in a drawing room comedy about politics in Washington, D.C.

Kay was different from many stars in another important way. She wasn't a spendthrift. "I live simply, comfortably but unpretentiously. Outside of an occasional European jaunt, which refreshes me physically and mentally, I made every effort to save my money. Silly extravagance has hastened the downfall of a number of popular stars. They went head over heels in debt buying fine homes, remodeling and decorating them like queens of olden times. They bought millionaire's yachts, kept crews. They had retinues of servants. They entertained lavishly. I do not propose to make those mistakes."[49] According to Kay, she believed in living simply. Although her personal life was often messy, she believed large houses and fancy cars only made life more complicated. "Eliminate. That's my philosophy. Eliminate waste of time, energy, effort. Leave yourself as free as possible."[50]

Her frugality was so unusual by Hollywood standards, it made news. The *Los Angeles Times* ran a brief article in 1934: "About three years ago Kay Francis drove into the Warner Brothers studio for the first time in a coupe of well-known make. Yesterday she still possessed the same car, and it is her one and only. Miss Francis says she is satisfied with a modest little chugger because it serves its purpose — gets her places."[51] Another reporter chimed in. "The Francis weekly stipend from Paramount and Warners has not gone into Beverly Hills estates, Duesenbergs, yachts, race horses, furs and star sapphires. On the contrary, it has gone into annuities, trust funds, bonds and similar little knick-knacks. Yes, for a pretty girl Kay has been very intelligent."[52]

Reporters were obsessed with Kay's Ford — and her reluctance to use a chauffer-driven limousine. "If I were to leave the studio in a chauffeured limousine, I should lean back and continue to worry about my problems of my screen work. But in driving my own car, I become lost in the business of avoiding traffic and all that sort of thing. I've never cared for the limousine attitude toward life, anyway, nor do I think it necessary to success. Especially in Hollywood, where success is such a fickle, ephemeral thing."[53]

Kay's mother also applauded her daughter's ability to manage finances. "I have never been Kay's business manager. I take care of her press books and photos and paste all the items in sequence of events. But Kay handles her own money and investments, so why should I presume to give her advice? Kay, I am convinced, has made a far more remarkable success than if I had tried to manage her life for her."[54]

Kay enjoyed playing cards, especially bridge and poker, and supposedly had no interest in high stakes gambling. According to one story, Elsa Maxwell once tried to bully her into raising the stakes. "I won't play," Kay said. "I work hard for my money and I would hate to lose it just as much as I would hate to take yours."[55] The truth is that Kay *did* hate losing, but was a lucky player who frequently won.[56] Diary entries commonly reported gambling parties, often involving Constance Bennett, and it wasn't unusual for Kay to win — or lose — $1,000 or more a night. Bennett teasingly claimed that Kay used her poker jackpots to pay Katherine Clinton's expenses.

Years later, boyfriend Dennis Allen claimed, "she was very funny about money. She often laughed about Hollywood friends calling her Hetty Green[57] because she was so slow to part with a buck. I don't mean she was stingy. She could be incredibly generous, but she did pinch pennies."[58]

One nice story about Kay's generosity involved Ida Greenfield, a wardrobe worker at Warner Brothers. When Kay heard she'd been saving money to buy a car, she spontaneously gave Ida a new car as a gift. In April 1936, *Modern Screen* reported that Kay, "regarded by many as cold and rather haughty, can be credited with one of the nicest deeds that has come to our attention in some time. It seems that several months ago Ruth Jones, secretary to the head of the publicity department at Kay's studio, was severely injured in an automobile accident. As a result, she spent considerable time in a hospital in San Bernardino, some distance from Hollywood. Without fanfare or publicity (up until now), the lovely Kay has paid a good share of the hospital bills, and she and Delmer Daves have been Miss Jones' most constant visitors."[59]

Kay also showed her generous side when she spent the night in the hospital room next to Donald Ogden Stewart's. On November 13, 1937, she'd heard that Stewart had just had a serious automobile accident, fracturing his skull. She phoned Stewart's wife Bea, who was in New York, and camped out in the hospital in a gesture of friendship.

Kay, like most successful actresses, also developed a reputation for being difficult. Basil and Ouida Rathbone socialized with Kay, but Ouida explained, "In many ways she was a lonely lady. People were afraid to approach her."[60] Genevieve Tobin worked with Kay twice, but didn't like her. "I always felt like she snubbed me, and at first I thought it mean of her. But later I decided that behind those velvety, tragic eyes there must have been some tragic thing that made it so she couldn't really be friends with anyone. I went to a party at her home when she was married to Ken MacKenna — whom we all loved and admired — but even then there was friction in the air. I couldn't understand her."[61]

Co-workers spoke of her moodiness and occasional tantrums — usually followed by a heartfelt apology. Kay admitted that Hollywood had changed her. "This business is getting me down. When I first came out here I had a fairly even disposition. I loved people and when I heard someone put me on the pan I usually tried to find something nice to say about them. Now I don't bother. I just pitch in and dish with the best of them. And I snap and snarl at people in a way I never used to. I'm getting to be a perfect harridan."[62]

Although Elsie Janis claimed, "I've never heard anyone say they did not like her,"[63] she probably didn't listen hard enough. Many colleagues defended Kay when Warner Brothers mistreated her, but there were others who felt she got what she deserved. "There were those who, having known her longer and better, claimed at her height she had been a bad-tempered, money-mad bitch, who was now reaping her just desserts."[64]

To many, Kay was an enigma. "Kay makes no pretense of being a professional recluse. She attends parties, premieres and first nights and she frequently entertains. Still she remains a more authentic 'mystery woman' than either Garbo or Dietrich, who have spent their entire Hollywood lives working at the title."[65]

"I hate hats."[66]

After many movies in succession, Kay started to sound a tad burned out when describing a typical day at the studio. "I get up in the morning at a quarter of six if I'm going to wear an evening dress. That sentence sounds a bit ga-ga, doesn't it? But never mind. An evening dress means body make-up. It takes time. Otherwise, I get fifteen minutes more sleep. By nine I am at the studio,[67] made-up, and on the set for work. We stop usually at six-thirty in the afternoon. Then comes a talk, probably with the director and the leading man, sometimes with others, so that we'll be ready with everything thoroughly understood for the next day. After that, we see the rushes of the day's take. At about eight, it's time to go home. I jump into a bath, and am glad to have dinner on a tray in bed. If I don't get to sleep before eleven, I have only seven hours. Just let anyone try to persuade me to go out any evening except Saturday! It can't be done when I'm working."[68]

Kay also complained that her type of role — the weepy, suffering kind — was particularly taxing. "I have seen switchboard operators plugging long telephone cords in and out in so complicated and rapid a maze that it looked as though they were knitting something, but plugging your own emotions in and out at the same rate all day is infinitely more wearing."[69]

She especially detested fittings. "It's one of the chief tortures of my life, and I am required to fit an average of eighteen to twenty-five for every picture."[70] Later Warner Brothers built a special Dolly-Ann — a type of mannequin used for fittings — to spare Kay the agony.

She also disliked posing for still photos. "Getting her into the studio photographic gallery for a fashion sitting is just about equal to accomplishing the impossible. The still camera lens, for some reason or other, brings out the worst in Kay and she can usually be counted upon to go into a temperamental rage and tell off everybody in sight."[71] Kay wasn't a huge fan of being made up, either. "She loathes the powder brush part of her make-up. [Perc] Westmore always begins some little interesting anecdote or story just before he begins to brush off the excess powder. He saves the punch of the story for the brush to keep her mind off it."[72]

"Stardom looks alluring when you haven't achieved it."[73]

On September 4, 1937, Kay filed suit against Warner Brothers. The last straw came when Warner Brothers gave Claudette Colbert the lead in *Tovarich*. Kay had been promised the

KAY FRANCIS HAIRSTYLES
A selection of commercial postcards showing Kay's changing hairstyles from 1934 to 1937.

role, along with others, in August 1935 when her option clause was due to expire.[74] Also, according to Kay's suit, the studio had put her in roles "of inferior quality and had posted her name in a special interstudio register which kept other studios from bidding for her services."[75] Kay's lawyers requested that the contract be cancelled, and an injunction issued to prevent the studio from exclusively claiming her services. Warner Brothers responded by assigning her to *Return from Limbo*. After much discussion in the press—and frenzied meetings between lawyers—the two parties announced a settlement in December. The agreement stipulated that Kay's contract would end in September 1938, but that she'd appear in the dreadful *Return from Limbo*—which was renamed *Women Are Like That*. Whatever its name, it was one of Kay's worst films. *Variety* called it "another disappointment for Kay Francis,"[76] and *Film Daily* called it a "dull routine piece" and observed that Kay "walks through scenes rather indifferently."[77]

Warner Brothers retaliated against Kay, and the rest of her career at the studio was sheer misery. While Kay fought the studio, she and Del were nearing the end of their relationship. "I am sick of his superiority,"[78] she wrote on September 20. Although Kay continued to see Del for a time, a new man entered her life in the fall of 1937. In fact, Erik Barnekow swept her off her feet so thoroughly, she reconsidered her decision to never remarry.

CHAPTER 10

The Actress and the Spy, 1937–1940

"The thing I envy most about Kay Francis is not her appearance, nor her ability, nor her position. It is her laugh. I've never heard anyone laugh so wholeheartedly or who seemed to enjoy laughing as much as she."[1]

According to Delmer Daves, he and Kay had agreed to never marry. Kay "designated herself lousy-wife — happy-lover. Thus, our happy pact and our rather enchanted life for three years. We broke off in much the same manner — because my career had flourished. So we had to face this change — and to do it without gossip columns; so I went to Europe alone — and suggested she find a new love while I was gone."[2] In truth, Del and Kay broke up for good when Kay became interested in Erik Barnekow. Del indeed traveled to Europe, but it was after Kay and Erik began seeing each other.

Baron Raven Erik Barnekow was probably one of Kay's most improbable romances. She'd met him October 24, 1937, at one of Countess di Frasso's Beverly Hills parties. "When these two looked at each other over formal words of introduction," a movie magazine later gushed, "a vague and inexplicable something passed between them. It must have been a harbinger of love, because love came so quickly and overwhelming soon after that."[3] The romance was private and quiet for some time, as Kay was still seeing Del. Once Del left for Europe, however, Kay introduced Erik to her friends — and became sexually involved with him.

According to Kay's diary, she and Erik first became intimate in late November, around the time she moved into her residence at 9033 Briar Crest Lane. She spent Christmas with him in the new house. "We baptized the library floor. Good fucking."[4]

Kay's home in Coldwater Canyon was in an area called Gopher's Gulch.[5] Kay proudly used this quaint term on her stationery. The house's construction was complicated by the fact that the area was fairly remote. In fact, new roads were being built along with the house, and one day, while Kay was checking out the home's progress, she found herself stuck at the site the entire day.

Kay made sure the house wasn't extravagant. "It's what you might call 'a big little house' or 'a little big house.' It's all paid for and I have managed to save enough money that I can always keep it up on my income. It isn't an expensive place to run and the investment isn't so large I can't afford to close it up when I want to go away — although I'm thrifty enough to sublet it, probably."[6] It was, however, large enough to include a theater/projection room.

Normally private, Kay was so proud of her new home she hired a producer to film — in color — the home's construction. Narrator Pete Smith provided commentary, and the film was shown at Kay's housewarming party. She also allowed a photo crew in for a piece in *House and Garden*. The magazine explained the house was in the Santa Monica foothills near Beverly Hills. "It is a low, rambling house, of white brick, gray roofed, commanding from its mountain-top site an incredible spread of surrounding hills and sea."[7] The architects were Levine & Frederick, and the interior designer was former actor turned decorator Tom Douglas.[8] "Inside the house, one color — gray — is used throughout, creating a brilliantly sophisticated scheme highly complementary to Miss Francis's own distinguished tastes. This soft shade carries through every room — even on the terrace, where the chairs wear gray outdoor linen. In the living room the basic tone is enlivened by rose, mauve and emerald green; in the dining room it is accented with pink and in Miss Francis's bedroom with yellow."[9] The home, decorated with antiques, was more elegant than flashy, more upstate New York than Hollywood. Leonora Hornblow, wife of producer Arthur, commented on Kay's home. "I remember going to her house for dinner, and her dining room was the most elegant thing I'd ever seen in Hollywood. The walls were antique gunmetal-gray mirrors with ivy designs painted on them. The ceiling was covered in a gray linen-fringed canopy, and the chairs were covered in pink and gray."[10]

Although Kay and Erik were very different, Kay initially chose to focus only on their similarities. "We enjoy the same things, you see," she told an interviewer, explaining that they enjoyed watching boxing and playing tennis. "And we equally dislike night club life."[11] One of the things they did *not* agree on was Kay's use of makeup — the Baron wanted her to stop using it, considering it cheap.

Of German and Scottish decent, Erik was variously described as a nobleman, aviator, inventor, stock broker and businessman. His maternal grandfather was Count Sholto Douglas, and, like the Douglas family, the Barnekows traced their lineage back to medieval days. Similarities abound between Erik and William Gaston, Kay's second husband. Not only did the two have impressive family trees, but both were World War I heroes — though on opposite sides.

Born on March 10, 1897, he first served with the 2nd Guards Uhlan Regiment and then the 4th Guards Foot Regiment. In February 1917, he joined the Luftstreitkrafte, flying an FEA 5. Transferred to Jasta 4 in September, he served under the command of Kurt-Bertram von Doring, and flew with ace legend Ernst Udet. In March 1918, he transferred to Jasta 20, and on May 12 shot down and killed Royal Air Force pilot Henry Dolan. He added three more victories before being wounded on August 23. After returning to action in September, he was eventually reassigned to Jasta 1. When the hostilities ended, he had 11 victories. Although Germany wasn't allowed to have an air force after the war, it entered into a secret agreement with Russia to have airplanes built, and in 1924 Barnekow was one of the pilots sent to Lipezk, Russia, to train with the Red Army.

He later came to the United States, where he worked for a time in the New York offices of General Motors. He was also reported to be a Diesel airplane engine manufacturer. He met Kay in Los Angeles while in business talks with Trans World Airlines. Heir to a mining fortune, Barnekow had little money of his own and often depended on friends, including Udet, to find employment. He'd also struck out at least once matrimonially, marrying New York socialite Ingeborg Sielken in 1924. They had one son, but divorced in 1929.

"I'm ready for any story they name. And they won't find me too far from the studio."[12]

In early 1938, Kay was falling in love with Erik, but increasingly bitter and depressed about her career. Although she'd been announced as the star of *The Sisters*, Bette Davis ended up with the part. Kay asked to be considered for the lead in *Carlotta*,[13] but Warner Brothers turned her down, hoping she'd ask to be released. For her part, a determined Kay continued to collect her paycheck while waiting out her contract's end. "There'll be no contract breaching on my part. I'm going to be a good girl and do everything I'm told — waiting all the time for the dawn of that great day, September 12."[14]

Warner Brothers entered into negotiations to acquire *Dark Victory* in January 1938. A studio memo written to Hal Wallis on January 14, 1938, suggested Kay would be a good choice. "I think you would have a good Kay Francis picture in a reasonably short time," an executive wrote, "and one that would not cost a fortune to make. Moreover, Kay herself, is, I understand, very much in favor of it."[15] The property was acquired by Warner Brothers in May 1938, but Kay didn't get the part. It's been suggested that Kay changed her mind because she didn't want to play a dying woman. However, Kay had already played such a role in *One Way Passage.* In truth, the studio reassigned the picture, first to Merle Oberon, and then, finally, to Bette Davis, who received an Academy Award nomination.[16]

"Dinner with Andy, Erik, Hedy Lamarr, Reginald Gardiner — so bored."[17]

Kay's $209,100 salary made her Warner Brothers' top-paid actor.[18] Still, one imagines her solemnly crossing out each day of the calendar, looking forward to the end of her association with the studio. Warner Brothers continued to put Kay in terrible films. The first, *Women Are Like That,* was awful — but not as bad as the next, *My Bill.* Anita Louise played Kay's daughter. Kay, only ten years older than Anita, couldn't have been happy, especially when her part was that of a 46-year-old mother! According to *The New York Times* film review, "It is all too pat, too incredible, too unimportant."[19]

Producer Bryan Foy replaced the original writer with Vincent Sherman. According to Sherman, "He [Foy] had assigned another writer to work on the script but asked me to take over, and he informed me that the film had to start the next week. Thus, he needed a script by Monday morning. It was now Thursday afternoon. (Brynie [Foy] thought it should take no longer to write than to type.) After working until midnight Thursday and all day Friday, Saturday, and Sunday with my secretary, Helen Fahringer, who was one of the fastest typists on the lot, I turned over on Monday morning the script of *My Bill.*"[20] This was typical of the lack of care taken with Kay Francis pictures during this period.

Secrets of an Actress was so weak, one reviewer suggested an evil plot on the part of Kay's studio. "There is absolutely no excuse for releasing such a picture as this one proved to be. If Vitagraph wants to kill off Kay Francis, they are doing a swell job of it."[21]

Comet Over Broadway, which followed, was another poor film. Co-star Sybil Jason, born in Cape Town, South Africa, was Warner's answer to Fox's Shirley Temple. Although there were reports that Kay was difficult on the set, Sybil Jason claimed that Kay not only presented no problems, but was the "most caring, compassionate and professional actress and woman I have ever had the pleasure to meet and work with. And she was like that towards fellow stars as well as the extras on the set. She did not differentiate!" Miss Jason added that she particularly enjoyed working with Kay because the actress was "the spitting image of my own mother."[22]

Director Busby Berkeley had been warned about Kay's behavior. "Kay had a reputation for being a bit difficult. I had been told by other directors that she had sometimes been tactless with co-workers and studio executives, but I saw no evidence of it on this picture. I do know she was unwilling to participate in the publicity game. That didn't interest her at all. And it seemed to me she lacked that driving ambition an actress needs in order to get the best parts in the best films. I found her to be cooperative and humorous, perhaps because she knew this was one of her last films for Warner's. She had been under contract since 1932 at the rate of four pictures a year, and I think she was rather glad the grind was coming to an end."[23] Kay's diary entries suggested that she and Berkeley did occasionally spar, though they made up after the film wrapped. The film opened to negative reviews, and one critic stated that Kay's career had reached "a sorry state of affairs."[24]

"I'm going to be Paul Muni in skirts."[25]

Warner Brothers used its B-movie unit for three purposes. First, it was an apprenticeship program for new cast and crew. Second, it was a moneymaker because its low costs resulted in sure-fire profits. Finally, the unit was used to punish ungrateful, uppity actors. This was how Kay Francis and Humphrey Bogart ended up in *King of the Underworld.*[26] The production suffered numerous delays, and when it was finally re-edited and released, it was a Humphrey Bogart film, with Kay relegated to the sidelines. Vincent Sherman explained why Kay was cast in this picture: "He [Jack Warner] thought: I'll give her to Bryan Foy. She won't want to make a picture with Foy, so she'll walk out on her contract. But Kay said, 'As long as they pay me my salary, I'll sweep the stages if they give me a broom.' So Foy called me one day and said, 'I'm going to do a picture with Francis. We're gonna remake *Doctor Socrates,*' which had been made originally with Paul Muni. I said, 'Well, which part is Francis gonna play?' He said, 'She's gonna play the Paul Muni part' and she did. We made the picture. Nothing I'm proud of, but we made it in sixteen, seventeen, eighteen days—something like that."[27] Sherman added that he admired Kay for taking a stand against Warner.

Kay worked on the picture in the summer of 1938, and it was released in early 1939. The movie was so bad it caused a *New York Times* critic to gallantly come to her aid. "We simply want to go on record against what seems to us an act of corporate impoliteness." The writer pointed out that the movie appeared to be "deliberately bad. The script writers, knowing as they perfectly well do that Miss Francis always has 'r' trouble, have unkindly written in the word 'moronic.' Indeed, considering the plot and everything, it is our settled conviction that meaner advantage was never taken of a lady."[28] Another critic stated that Kay "deserves better."[29]

Sounding like a woman who'd had a particularly bad day, Kay went on a rant about stardom in a movie magazine. "'I hate all the attention a star is supposed to give her precious self. I do nothing in particular to keep physically 'fit.' I do not diet. I have no beauty secrets. I wash my face with soap and water when it needs washing, and I let it go at that. I don't know yet what is meant by 'glamour.' I'll be glad when September comes, and I won't have to worry about what others think I should or should not do about myself. I want to get fat. I want to do *nothing*. I want to sit on my back porch, in a rocker, and not even think. I can't imagine anything more divine than stepping off a gangplank one of these days, and looking down into a sea of faces to find them all staring blankly away from me, disinterested.'"[30]

During this time, she sometimes sounded clinically depressed. "I not only do not enjoy seeing myself on the screen, but I don't even see myself any more when I look in the mirror at home. Even the pleasures of a woman's vanity, the fun of 'prinking' are mine no longer. It has all become mechanical, impersonal, and boring. I look in the mirror, and I know there's a face there. And it's probably mine. I know that I must go through the motions of pulling it together, and I do, but I have no personal pleasure or interest in the process."[31]

Warner Brothers went out of their way to make Kay's life difficult. One former employee described it as "one of the more sordid chapters in our history."[32] When Kay rejected their settlement offers, they devised a plan. "Since there was too much money at stake for us to allow her to graciously decline our final offer of a 50 percent settlement, the only other means at our disposal was to force her to quit. So began a campaign of harassment and humiliation."[33] The studio assigned Kay to help with screen tests. "It was unthinkable to use high-salaried actors, let alone stars, for the embarrassing task of playing second fiddle to raw newcomers, but again, contractually her refusal would have resulted in an immediate suspension. Swallowing her pride and pocketing her paycheck, for the next six days she reported to the test stage. Although her call was for nine A.M., she was seldom used before mid-afternoon, at which point she would be called upon to mainly feed lines to the youngsters while the camera focused on them, shooting over her shoulder. Uncomplainingly, she spent her days sitting on the sidelines, knitting and drinking gin from a silver flask."[34]

One of Warner Brothers' worst offenses occurred when the studio denied her lunch pass request for two guests at the studio commissary. When told the news, Kay stoically commented: "'I understand. Thank you anyway.' She joined her friends for lunch off the lot, reporting back within the allotted hour."[35]

Still, Kay refused to break her contract. She did, however, start a particularly juicy rumor — one that had to make some more than a little nervous. Kay told friends she was writing a book — "and what a book, say her intimates!"[36]

Warner Brothers received criticism for their treatment of Kay. In fact, Bette Davis and James Cagney demanded an audience with Harry Warner to discuss the situation, but Harry claimed the decision was Jack's. According to Stuart Jerome, "it was Harry who instigated the campaign. Much as J.L. might have approved, he was carrying out his brother's orders."[37] When the press began portraying Kay as an innocent victim of big, bad Warner Brothers, the studio decided to simply throw her into mediocre pictures until her contract ended.

In the fall of 1938, it was reported that Bette Davis would star in *The Lady with Red Hair,* a biopic about Kay's old audition buddy Mrs. Leslie Carter — a picture that had been earmarked for Kay.[38] Furthermore, Davis had just signed a new contract that paid her substantially more salary —*and* gave her greater say in her roles. Everyone, including Kay, knew Davis was being groomed to replace her as the Queen of Warner Brothers.

"I abhor having to show off. I detest sycophants. I avoid gossips as I would the plague. And this business is ridden with all three pestilences."[39]

In the spring of 1938, Kay was 33 years old. Perhaps because of her career frustration, she turned to Erik Barnekow for comfort. Convinced she was in love with Erik, she wanted to settle down. Still, she worried about their future. An odd entry on March 1 suggested she even considered having a child with him. On that same day, Kay announced to Louella Parsons that she'd retire from films and marry Barnekow.

Kay may have done stupid things, but she wasn't a stupid woman, and doubts increased about her lover. She loaned Erik money, purportedly for a business venture in aviation. "Gave Erik another $1,000. That makes $1,300 all together. I wonder if I will ever get it back?"[40] Kay also wondered if they were truly compatible. "Worried stiff about money, about Erik being a bum, about his never wanting to go out!"[41] By July, she was frantic. "Oh my God, what am I getting into, I have no idea! Pray that it will come out all right, that's all!"[42]

Nothing seemed to be going right. In August, while working on *Comet Over Broadway,* Kay's face broke out in pustules. The studio was worried enough to call in their own doctor. Antibiotics were prescribed, but her condition worsened. Weeks passed before her face improved. Kay also faced weight problems. In the past, she'd proudly told interviewers that she never needed to diet. However, now in her 30s, she was alarmed at her weight gain and tried a variety of fad diets, including a grapefruit diet.[43]

Meanwhile, Kay and Erik agonized over their romance. On September 9, 1938, Kay's wedding dress was fitted, but she doubted that the marriage would ever take place. She also fretted over the inability to rent her house.

Still, Kay continued to insist she'd retire from films when her contract ended. "Barring an Act of God, my retirement will be permanent. I'm through. I'm getting *out.* It's *over.* And I can hardly *wait* for September!"[44] A reflective Kay admitted that part of her career problems stemmed from her reticence to criticize the studio. "Perhaps I'd have been better off if I had fought for better stories, but the end didn't justify the means. I'd have been suspended and the time I was under suspension would have been added to the end of my contract. So, instead of being free now, I would probably have had another year to go. And, even then, I'd have no guarantee the stories I picked would have been any better. Even if they had been, the only difference would have been that I would be retiring in a blaze of glory instead of more or less inconspicuously — and this is the way I want it. I'll be forgotten quicker this way."[45]

During the shooting of *Women in the Wind,* Kay gave an interview to *Photoplay* that turned out to be one of her most quoted interviews. The title and the first line read, "I can't wait to be forgotten." According to the reporter, Kay had repeated this line to him many times. When pressed, she clarified, "I don't say I'll never make another picture because if I should happen to be in Hollywood and some producer offered me a good part I'd jump at it. But as far as another contract or making a career of pictures any more is concerned, I'm through!"[46]

Asked by a reporter when she'd marry, she refused to answer, but did say, "When I am married it will be as a private citizen of no consequence. I won't be in the limelight any more and there is no reason my wedding should be given more than passing comment." Kay explained to another interviewer that she planned to renovate the new house for Erik, and that because of his business ties, it was necessary for him to spend six months in the United States and six in Europe. "We'll take side trips during the time we're abroad and of the six months we're in this country some of the time will be spent in New York (which I adore) and some of the time here in Hollywood."[47]

The last film on Kay's contract, *Women in the Wind,* was mediocre and a sad finale to her days at Warner Brothers. One critic got it right when he described it as "the sort of picture that is so simple and is made so fast that everyone exudes a feeling of let's-get-it-over-with."[48] She gave up her personal dressing room the last week of the shoot and used the main dressing room.[49] While Kay didn't mind saying goodbye to Warner Brothers, it was more difficult leaving her co-workers. "This is the first picture I've finished out here that I haven't had a party for the cast and crew afterward. But this time is different. I knew I'd start crying and so would some of the others. I didn't want to say good-bye that way. I want to remember all these people as friends with whom I used to kid — with whom I had swell times. I don't want to remember them — or have them remember me — with long faces and red eyes. I want to saunter off the lot and out of their lives as casually as though the picture weren't finished and we'd be meeting again in the morning."[50] In a final tribute, "the cop at the Auto Gate performed an unheard-of-gesture to an actor: He saluted Kay Francis."[51]

At 5:30 P.M. on September 28, 1938, Kay ended her employment with the studio and became a free woman. She'd been making movies for a little less than ten years, though it likely seemed an eternity to her.

"The parade is passing me by — and I don't care."[52]

On October 13, Louella Parsons reported that Kay was leaving for a cruise with secretary Dorothy Wagner.[53] Kay, who'd finally leased her house, wanted to go to Europe, but settled on a Caribbean vacation because of the war threat. Barnekow, too, was leaving for a two-month business trip. "He returns here in December," Parsons reported, "and the marriage is now definitely set for the first of January."[54]

Before Kay left on her trip,[55] Erik told her about additional debts he owed, totaling almost $2,000. On October 12, Kay finished packing and wrote checks, convinced she'd be broke by the time she returned. Before she and Erik parted, they exchanged gifts. He gave her a soap box, and Kay gave him a belt, studs, and scarf. Erik also gave her a letter to read on the train, and enclosed a four-leaf clover his mother had given him years before. It was particularly meaningful because Erik's mother had died in Germany in the spring of 1938.

On Oct. 27, the *New York Times* reported that Kay was in San Juan, Puerto Rico, and that a large crowd had filled the Plaza Colon when word spread that Kay was having her hair done at a local beauty salon. On December 1, Parsons reported that Kay had been sending postcards to friends. "Personally," Parsons wrote, "I will be surprised if that marriage ever takes place, for it does not seem to this writer that she would be content to remain away all these months if she intended to marry. Talk is that Kay may sign with RKO when she returns. There are several movie jobs in the fire for her and I look to see her back, hard at work before many months, with her romance with the Baron a closed chapter in her life."[56]

Louella, apparently obsessed with the Kay-Eric romance, reported on December 8 that Kay had returned and the marriage was on. "The good looking baron met her at the plane and, from the welcome he gave her, it was easy to see that he was glad to have her back."[57] Indeed, Kay hurried back to Erik and met him on December 7 in a joyful reunion.

Barnekow, however, had cold feet about the wedding. "Baron Barnekow can't make up his mind about fiancée Kay Francis. One day he tells friends they'll be married soon and next day he's doubtful."[58] Still, they continued to see each other, and Kay prepared for Christmas. She socialized with Laurence Olivier, Vivien Leigh, and Isabel Jeans, and attended Jessica and Richard Barthelmess' Christmas Eve party. Unfortunately, the party was ruined when Kay drank too much and then argued with Jessica over a perceived slight concerning Erik. Jessica visited Kay on December 29, and they attempted to repair their friendship. The estrangement with Jessica, however, continued for some time. In addition, Kay Francis was now essentially unemployed. With no studio contract, she needed to look for work.

"Had my ears pierced — started 4-day diet — 142 lbs.!"[59]

Kay's career, which had started so promising ten years before, seemed a burden by 1939. Still, she'd made more than 50 films — a few of which were brilliant — and had become a millionaire. "I've done everything I set out to do and now I'm going to enjoy myself. I've given ten years of my life to accumulating enough money to do the things I want to do. Ten years of never being able to travel when I wanted to, never being able to entertain when I wanted to, or go out when I wanted to — because picture schedules always had to be consulted before I could make plans. Now, I'm free!"[60]

When Kay left Warner Brothers, she did something out of character — she got her ears pierced. She later told a reporter, "I had my ears pierced right after I was thrown out of Warners. You know, they threw me out lock, something and barrel."[61] Although she made light of it, there was no doubt that she was hurt. Still, after ten years in Hollywood, Kay felt free, hopeful that she could now have the kind of career she wanted — without a long-term contract to tie her down.

"Got job at RKO for Lombard picture — that helps!"[62]

RKO signed Kay for *In Name Only*[63] on February 22, 1939, at the urging of Kay's friend, Carole Lombard. Kay, who'd gained at least twenty pounds amidst her Warner headaches and romantic troubles, was so disturbed by her appearance during wardrobe and makeup tests that she promptly lost the weight. While the film was only fair, Kay showed she could act, playing a vindictive, bitter wife. Her role, more complicated than the two leads, was the highlight of the film. Critics gave her some of her best reviews. "What impressed preview critics most forcibly about *In Name Only* was the performance of Kay Francis, who has been delivering good performances for years, but hardly anyone was aware of it because her abilities were stifled in inferior picture products and her frantic efforts to assert herself were without avail. In this case, she is the root of much evil, and by this role wherein she inflicts the position of a hateful woman on her luckless victims, she will call attention to herself again as an actress of first rank."[64]

The role was unlike any she had been given when she was a star, and Kay considered it an opportunity to show her range. "When I played the heavy in 'In Name Only,' my friends told me I was crazy. I said I *had* to be seen in some other type of part than the mush I had been playing."[65]

A hired hand for this production, Kay delighted in it. "I believe that as a free-lance I can learn more about acting than if under studio contract. I'm happier at it, for life takes on new interest. And the more we players free-lance, the better served will the public be."[66] Kay, always money-conscious, also pointed out that free-lancing was more lucrative. "Due to the intricacies of the income tax, I can actually work less yet have more to show for it at the end of the year."[67]

Kay could now choose her own roles. At first, this arrangement seemed ideal. "I can do better for myself. An arrived player, under contract to a studio, becomes pretty much typed. The studio finds a type of role which proves profitable at the box-office, and keeps the player doing it over and over in picture after picture. That is considered good business. Well, it may be for the studio, but it isn't for the player. It offers the latter greater job security, certainly. But that isn't everything in life."[68]

In March, Kay made her first appearance on *Lux Radio Theatre* in an adaptation of *One Way Passage* with William Powell. Kay, who wasn't scheduled, took over when friend Norma Shearer became ill. The program was terrifying for most actors. "It was always an elaborate production. Actors did not merely show up and read scripts; there was a full week's rehearsal beforehand with a director. A live studio audience at show time. Top stars received several thousand dollars for appearing on the program, a respectable stipend for a week's work."[69] That same month, Kay also appeared in a *Gulf Screen Guild Show,* "Never in This World," with Leslie Howard and Virginia Weidler. For someone who no longer received a regular paycheck, these income opportunities were very welcome.

It was also in March that tension grew between Kay and Erik. "Erik dislikes the publicity attached to my work as much as I do, understands it even less than I do, never having experienced anything of the sort."[70] As it turned out, Erik had a very good reason for not wanting the press snooping into his business. Kay told friends he'd disappear for days without telling her where he'd gone or on what business. Kay's friends suspected the worst — Erik was playing Kay for a fool or was a German spy. Kay's friends had never warmed to Barnekow, and strained friendships resulted when Kay defended him.

Inexplicably, in late March 1939, Erik claimed Dorothy di Frasso accused him of being a Nazi spy and announced he'd file a slander suit. Erik, apparently forgetting his distaste for publicity, took his case to the newspapers. "I am an American citizen, and I am a manufacturer of motors, and such false remarks as this may damage my business."[71] Kay, who abhorred publicity, especially this kind, was dumbfounded. Dorothy di Frasso was equally puzzled. "Someone must be mad. I never said anything of the sort. I haven't seen the Baron Barnekow in weeks. I didn't know the baron in Europe or Germany. I do not know what his politics are, and I must say, I couldn't care less."[72]

Barnekow probably *was* a German spy, but likely a reluctant one. He did meet with Ernst Udet in New York in 1933 and discussed joining the Nazi party, but neither man was enthusiastic about Nazis or Hitler. Meanwhile, the FBI became interested in Barnekow when they were tipped that he had a supposed interest in poisonous gases.[73]

Perhaps Barnekow's bigger problem, however, was that he presented himself as something he wasn't to Kay and her friends. He simply was *not* the wealthy industrialist war hero. To Germans who knew Udet and Barnekow, the latter was a sort of alcoholic loser who depended on Udet to find him jobs, give him money, and bail him out of difficulties. Barnekow considered himself a failure, once drunkenly railing at Udet, "You've got everything — a villa at the expense of the state, a general's uniform, but I've remained a small man. I can hear what they say behind my back. He owes everything to the general who protects him."[74] And this was *after* his affair with Kay Francis! Erik may have left the United States for several reasons, including loyalty to his country. But he also realized his tissue of lies with Kay was unraveling.

"England at war 2:15 A.M. our time, 11:15 A.M. England time — Oh dear god — Goodbye to my Erik."[75]

In May, Erik was living and working in San Francisco. He frequently threatened to return to Germany, which made Kay frantic. Kay traveled that summer to Chicago and then to Ohio, where she stayed with writer Louis Bromfield on his farm. She also took a trip to Reno, Nevada, accompanying Miriam Hopkins and son Michael so Miriam could divorce director Anatole Litvak.

Meanwhile, Erik returned to Europe — without Kay — and made his way to Germany on an American cargo ship. On September 3, 1939, England declared war on Germany. Kay managed several phone calls to him, but he was aloof and distant. A severely stressed Kay became ill with stomach problems and a cough. She spoke to Erik on September 14, and managed several other phone calls, including one on September 21, when he continued to profess his love for her. Meanwhile, Kay battled depression and occupied her time by taking Red Cross courses, including first aid, administering a hypodermic needle, and sewing. She also visited with old friend Bea Stewart, now married to Ilya Tolstoy, but her mind remained on Erik.

In November, Kay tested for a role in *My Son, My Son,* but didn't get it.[76] She also socialized with Hedy Lamarr, Doug and Sylvia Fairbanks, Andy Lawler, Billy Haines, Basil and Ouida Rathbone, Fanny Brice, and others. Kay ate Thanksgiving dinner at the Lubitsch's with Miriam Hopkins, but continued to reflect back on Erik, noting in her diary the anniversary of the first time they'd been intimate.

More bad news came on December 12 when friend Douglas Fairbanks died. Much of the month was spent with Sylvia — Kay even interviewed maids for her recently widowed friend. Kay did find time in December, though, to successfully test for a role in a Deanna Durbin movie, *It's a Date.*

Kay also attended Ouida Rathbone's Christmas party, "A Night at St. Moritz," a benefit for the Hollywood Guild, which was held at the Beverly Hills Hotel. An article gave a preview. "Workmen are already setting up the elaborate wind and snow machinery which will create a real snowstorm for this wintery wonderland of snow and ice. An ice ballet has been engaged to top the ice rink program."[77] Guests included Bette Davis, Gary Cooper, Benita Hume and Ronald Colman, Herbert Marshall, Freddie Bartholomew, Jessica and Richard Barthelmess, Louis Bromfield, and Irene Dunne. Kay pronounced the party a dud, complaining that rain ruined it.

Kay's Christmas was no better. She continued to battle depression, and often found herself crying, even while decorating the tree, dining with her mother, and drinking cocktails with Miriam Hopkins. She declined an invitation to Jessica's, simply too sad to enjoy an evening out. Before the year ended, she attended the preview of *Gone with the Wind,* but her New Year's Eve was marred by illness.

Kay did have an enjoyable birthday, dining with writer Dorothy Parker and Alan Campbell. Kay was a longtime friend of Parker's, and may have known her in New York in the 1920s or met her in the early 1930s in Hollywood. Parker, born in New Jersey in 1893, was one of the wits who held court at New York's Algonquin Hotel. She married Alan Campbell in 1933, and they went to Hollywood where they wrote screenplays, including *A Star Is Born* (1937).

In January 1940, Kay worked with Deanna Durbin and Walter Pidgeon on *It's a Date,* playing Durbin's mother. Deanna, of course, was the main attraction, but Kay didn't embarrass herself in the role of an aging star who's forced to compete with her daughter for roles. Critics were kind to Kay and the movie. "Kay Francis, who still avoids an 'r' as if it were a social error, never looked better — or younger — in her entire career."[78]

Kay finished *It's a Date* on February 28, and started dating again, but found the results less than satisfying. She had brief affairs with her personal physician, Bill Branch, and old friend producer Arthur Hornblow — married to Myrna Loy at the time.[79] She

KAY FRANCIS MODELING TURBAN
Kay modeling one of the new turbans popular in 1940, and also revealing more décolletage than usual.

complained about the lovemaking abilities of both men. Apparently neither man could equal Barnekow's charm.

In March, Kay also performed on two radio shows, appearing on *The Silver Theatre,* hosted by Conrad Nagel, and then later that month on a live radio adaptation of *When the Rains Came.* The movie version of *Rains,* which starred Myrna Loy, had been one that Kay campaigned for—to no avail.

Meanwhile, Barnekow was back in Germany, once again asking Udet for a job. Udet made him his aide, referred to him as "my breakfast director,"[80] and assigned him to read international newspapers for military news.

"It may sound like sour grapes, but I wouldn't be a star again for anything."[81]

Kay signed with Universal for *When the Daltons Rode,* an unremarkable western. However, she enjoyed working with co-stars Brian Donlevy, Broderick Crawford, and Randolph Scott, and often had drinks with them. Between social occasions with Andy Lawler, the Humphrey Bogarts, and the Louis Bromfields, Kay received unhappy letters from Erik. San Francisco columnist Herb Caen reported that Barnekow was in Germany—recovering from a heart attack. "The Hollywood chatterers might want to know that during his illness, she [Kay] phoned him nightly from Hollywood (until a censorship on personal phone calls was clamped on three weeks ago.)"[82]

Between Red Cross classes and social engagements, Kay next had an affair with director Rouben Mamoulian.[83] A relieved Kay commented favorably on Mamoulian's lovemaking skills. In that same month, she began a short-lived affair with Eddie Mayer, but this relationship was doomed because she simply didn't find him appealing, though she did feel sorry for him. Edwin Justus Mayer worked on screenplays for *Desire* (1936), *Gone with the Wind* (1939), *To Be or Not to Be* (1942), and others. Born in New York in 1896, Mayer lived at the legendary Garden of Allah and was a longtime friend of F. Scott Fitzgerald's. According to Fitzgerald's girlfriend, Sheilah Graham, Eddie was brilliant but homely. "Eddie was always hoping that lovely women would fall in love with him. But he was rather fat and his blind eye bulged and didn't help with the girls he coveted."[84]

Kay still pined for Erik, whom she hadn't heard from in weeks, often reading and rereading his letters. On May 1, she hosted a party for producer Charles K. Feldman. After drinks at Ciro's, they went back to her house. "Slept with him and he may be the best of them all! Christ, I am a slut."[85] Feldman, born in New York in 1904, was a former talent agent who became a producer in the 1940s, eventually receiving an Oscar nomination for *Streetcar Named Desire* (1952). He married actress Jean Howard in 1934, despite the efforts of MGM studio head Louis B. Mayer, who'd fallen in love with Jean.[86] Kay occasionally socialized with the Feldmans, but it's unclear whether Jean ever learned of the affair.[87]

Throughout May, Kay continued to juggle Charles, Rouben, Eddie, and even Harry Crocker. Crocker, born in San Francisco in 1893, was a silent film actor who frequently worked with Charles Chaplin, and later was an assistant to William Randolph Hearst.[88]

On June 7, while working on *When the Daltons Rode,* Kay received the startling news that Erik had been seriously wounded. It upset her terribly, but the incident may have only been a rumor. In fact, there were many unfounded rumors about Barnekow. For example, there was a February 1942 report that he'd flown a mission over England and was imprisoned there. It was also rumored that his name was on a German casualty list—shot down flying for the Nazis. The truth was even more tragic. Barnekow, loyal to his fellow World

KAY FRANCIS AT A PREMIERE
Kay attending the 1940 premiere of Buck Benny Rides Again, *accompanied by agent Cornwell (Corny) Jackson.*

War I pilots and country, reluctantly rejoined the German military. Although he served on General von Doring's staff again, his heart wasn't in it. On November 17, 1941, Ernst Udet, who'd feuded with former friend and colleague Hermann Goering, committed suicide after being blamed for the Luftwaffe's military failures. Though the German government publicly claimed Udet[89] was accidentally killed while testing a new weapon, Barnekow knew the truth, and, shortly after Udet's death, Erik resigned his position, refusing to work for Udet's replacement, Erhard Milch. Poor Barnekow, perhaps planning to reunite with Kay after the war, gave up hope when America entered the war on December 8, 1941. A few days later, he explained he was going hunting and shot himself on property his family owned in Alt-Marin, Pomerania. Barnekow's suicide was kept quiet, and it's unlikely Kay ever found out what happened to her former lover. She continued to mark their anniversary dates in her diary.

As a free-lancer, Kay's workload was considerably less, but the parts weren't much better than what Warner had offered her. Her last film in 1940, *Little Men,* was an RKO picture that never rose to the level of any version of *Little Women.* To make matters worse, Kay was asked to meet one of the stars at the Los Angeles train station. Elsie the Cow's owners, in fact, requested the presence of Kay Francis, a parade, *and* a brass band in return for the free use of the bovine! The *New York Times* found the picture "maudlin and smarty-smart, too obviously rigged for tears and laughs," and criticized Kay's performance as "just too sweet and good."[90]

In July 1940, Kay began a romance with director Fritz Lang.[91] Like most of Kay's sexual affairs, this one was intense and brief. The two had socialized many times, but became sexually involved on July 13. By the end of July, they were inseparable, attending premieres, horse races, parties, romantic dinners, and dances. By September, gossip columnists suggested a wedding might be in the future. However, by late fall, the affair was, for the most part, over, though they continued to be friendly. Lang friend, writer-producer Gottfried Reinhardt,[92] suggested Kay belonged to a certain type of female star who was easy to seduce. "To have an affair with one or two of these actresses was ... well, how could you avoid it? I slept with one or two of them myself. They were all no-conquests."[93] Kay found Lang to be intelligent, charming, and complex. It's a shame the two never worked on a film together.

Kay's next serious lover was Australian Ivan Goff.[94] The handsome Goff, whose parents were classical musicians, started as a newspaperman in his home country, and moved to America in the early 1930s. By 1936, he was working as the Hollywood correspondent for *The London Daily Mirror.* Kay met him in July when Mamoulian escorted her to a party at producer Henry Blanke's. The romance with Ivan became serious in September, though Kay sailed to Honolulu with Rouben in November, where they stayed at the Royal Hawaiian Hotel. She felt close enough to Ivan to feel guilty when she slept with Rouben on the trip. In fact, after her return, Ivan became her steady companion through the remainder of 1940, though she did make a diary entry on November 23, again noting that she and Erik had first made love three years before.

Typically, Kay suffered health problems near the end of the year. She and Ivan enjoyed dinners at Chasen's and Ciro's in early December, and she then appeared on *The Silver Theatre* radio show on December 15. However, Kay endured yet another hemorrhoid operation at Hollywood Hospital on December 20. She wasn't released until Christmas Eve, and then spent Christmas Day with her mother, the Rathbones, Ivan, and Jessica. For New Year's Eve, she attended a party at Dorothy Parker's, and then had dinner with Ivan. Her diary entries for 1940 ended on an ominous note: "I'm in an ornery mood."[95]

CHAPTER 11

Four Jills in a Jeep, 1941–1943

"The public is not entitled to the details of my private life. I have as much right to keep my home and social life private as I had in the days before the name Kay Francis meant anything to anyone outside of my own particular circle of friends."[1]

Writers have variously described Kay as heterosexual, homosexual, and bisexual. According to George Eells, one friend insisted Kay was interested only in men, but finally admitted that Kay may have ended up in bed with a woman or two after drinking too much.

Diana McLellan wrote that Marlene Dietrich had an affair with Kay Francis, though no evidence of such a tryst has surfaced. The rumor may have stemmed from Dietrich's lengthy FBI file,[2] which included two mentions of Kay. "During her [Dietrich's] Paramount days, she verged from the norm for an affair with Kay Francis (known Lesbian)."[3] In another, an informant noted that Dietrich "had affairs with well-known women in Hollywood, one of these being Kay Francis."[4] Other women rumored to have been romantically involved with Kay include Lilyan Tashman, Tallulah Bankhead, and Mary Martin, though, again, no mention of affairs with any of these women was made in Kay's diary. Still, it's almost inconceivable that the bold and irrepressible Lilyan wouldn't have made a pass at Kay. Lil considered Kay one of Hollywood's most beautiful women, and pointed out that Kay was not catty — a rare quality among Hollywood actresses. There is the possibility that Kay — a very sexual woman — was reticent when writing about her lesbian activities in her diary. It wouldn't be surprising to find that Kay occasionally edited certain activities from the written record.

Kay's lesbian activities were also rumored to have caused her dismissal from Warner Brothers. Bette Davis detailed one of the more lurid Kay Francis rumors. The story goes that William Powell "went around telling anyone who would listen that she *must* be a good actress, because she played convincing love scenes with men.[5] What I heard, elsewhere, was that Miss Francis had girlfriends, but only in between husbands."[6] According to Davis, Kay left Warner Brothers after she was discovered in a compromising situation with a woman.

There *was* a lesbian scandal at Warner Brothers involving actresses, but it's unlikely Kay was implicated. Supposedly, Josephine Hutchinson and Margaret Lindsay were photographed at a lesbian orgy, and Warner Brothers was blackmailed.[7] In Kay's case, it seems Warner's disagreement with her was strictly financial.

Kay's lesbian rumors also might have arisen from guilt by association. Kay's friends included many lesbians, including designer Elsie de Wolfe,[8] Elsie Janis,[9] Tashman, Linda Porter, and Elsa Maxwell.[10] She was comfortable around homosexual men, and spent considerable time in the company of Cole Porter, Andy Lawler, Billy Haines, Jimmie Shields, Clifton Webb, and Tom Douglas.

According to her diary entries, Kay was bisexual, with a definite preference for male lovers. She once told an interviewer, "*Everything I have been or hope to be I owe to men* [emphasis in original]. They have helped me in my life far more than women have. But most of all I have been fortunate in the men I have known."[11]

Perhaps the most scandalous aspect of Kay's life was her frequent abortions. While married to Kenneth MacKenna in 1932, she provided some clue as to her mindset about children. "We'd like to have a baby. Because I feel that it would be a pleasant thing to have — not at all because I feel that I *must* [her emphasis] have the experience in order to have 'lived,' as so many women do. I'm not a bit sentimental about it. But, in the first place, I do not believe that a baby would enjoy *being had*— right now. What have we to give a child as we live to-day? When I come home from the studio at night, I am full of it. I am dead tired. I can think of nothing but getting into a tub and removing my make-up. I know that I could not, at the same time, be full of the nursery and imbued with a desire to get the *baby* into the tub. And then, on the other side of the scales, I think 'Supposing I should *never* have a child? Well ... I have had so much that other women never know that perhaps it would all balance quite perfectly.'"[12]

Surprisingly, Kay believed most women shouldn't have careers. "For the glorification of Self that we get, for the fun and the fever of fame, for the money we make and the abnormal independence we know, there is so much that we lose. In the first place we are, necessarily, masculinized."[13] For her, however, Kay admitted there was no choice. "I weigh both sides and I find, whatever kind of a person this makes me, that the joy I get from working outweighs the things I lose. But I do know that I lose them."[14] When Kay toured with Jetti Preminger[15] in the stage play *Windy Hill* in the 1940s, she gave the young actress interesting advice, suggesting that for the newly married Preminger, children were the right decision for her — and advised Jetti to take time off to raise her family.

"The thing about it was that she had this exotic exterior, and people who were attracted to that were always disappointed because she was a regular guy."[16]

Some went out of the way to let the public know that Kay wasn't glamorous in real life. "The last time I saw Kay Francis," one reporter wrote, "she was at the smart cocktail party which Merle Oberon gave before leaving for England. Kay wore a rather dowdy sports coat and no hat. Hardly the Best Dressed Woman."[17] Another described her disappointment in meeting her. "I found Kay Francis unsmart that day. The gardenia of the Hollywood hothouses looked more like a faded sweet-pea. Where was the glamour, the whiteness, the still lovely quality like water-lilies in moonlight that had always, for me, distinguished her from all other stars of the screen?"[18] No wonder Kay wanted out of Hollywood.

Good friend Elsa Maxwell explained the difference between the on-screen Kay and the private Kay: "You who watch her on the screen playing those dangerous sirens and fatal women may not realize that there is nothing sirenish or dangerous about this delightful woman. Well-groomed, beautifully but discreetly dressed, she does not look like an actress, least of all like a Hollywood star, when she walks into a restaurant in New York or sits on the beach in Venice. You would easily take her for a young society matron when encountering her in a shop or at a concert. She does not raise her voice or wear a whole collection of bracelets. She does not go for crazy hats or exotic coiffures. She does not hire a liveried chauffeur. She does not attach three hundred dollars worth of white orchids to her shoulder.

She does not travel in a private car or especially chartered plane. In short — she does none of the things which a 'Great Star' is supposed to do."[19]

At the beginning of 1941, audiences saw Kay in RKO's *Play Girl*. *Variety* correctly pointed out that Kay remained beautiful and skilled. "Miss Francis is still the glamour girl who displays an eye-arresting figure in either negligee or smart fashions. She's still plenty poised and attractive regardless of story requirements. Miss Francis capably handles the role of the fading glamour girl."[20]

Kay next appeared in Universal's *The Man Who Lost Himself*. Again, Kay was undoubtedly compensated well, but the picture was only slightly entertaining.

In yet another comedy, Kay appeared with Jack Benny in Twentieth Century–Fox's *Charley's Aunt*. A bigger hit with audiences than critics, reviewers noticed that Kay seemed ageless. "The wealthy Donna Lucia is portrayed by Miss Kay Francis, upon whom the years seem to be sitting lightly."[21]

KAY FRANCIS IN 1941
This glamour shot from 1941 shows that Kay was still beautiful well into her fourth decade.

Kay's next film was MGM's *The Feminine Touch* with Rosalind Russell and Don Ameche. Once again, the movie looked good, but the script was mediocre. One critic saw it as a setback for Kay. "Rosalind Russell, Don Ameche, Kay Francis and Van Heflin are the unfortunate notables taking part in 'The Feminine Touch.' Maybe the whole thing wouldn't have been so hard to bear with if lesser lights had been doing and saying the utterly silly things that such charming players are forced to do in this film. It's too bad that Ameche, away from stereotyped roles at 20th Century–Fox, wasn't given something to do that would increase his popularity. The same goes for Miss Francis, who, up to this one, was making a fine comeback."[22]

Stylist Sydney Guilaroff, who worked with Kay on *The Feminine Touch*, was a fan. "I loved Kay Francis. One of the great movie-going pleasures in the 1930s was Kay. She was exotic, poised, dark, and lovely. I did her hairstyle in a film with my good friend Roz Russell ... Kay was a joy to work with. She possessed incredible eyes that were very expressive. She wore hats and turbans with such style and grace. She was very elegant on and off the screen."[23]

"Took long walk in hills alone — Fritz here at 5:30 for cocktails — dinner with Ivan."[24]

Kay's unaccompanied walk was a rare thing. Years earlier, on the eve of her marriage to Kenneth MacKenna, she'd praised the pleasures of being alone. However, by this time in her life, she didn't like it, and became panicky and depressed if she wasn't immersed in a frantic social world, complete with a melodramatic romantic life.

As 1941 began, Kay continued seeing Ivan Goff, though the romance was hitting rough spots. Again, alcohol was causing problems as they both behaved poorly when drinking. She also spent much time with Fritz Lang, but it appears their romance was now a friendship, one that would last for years. Kay also had time for a quickie with Reginald Gardiner, who would remain her friend for years.

Kay's reduced work schedule meant she could frequently socialize and relax — and she did. In fact, she often invited friends over to her house for music; and on at least one occasion, neighbors called the police when the music was still going strong at 3 A.M. Her diary entries for this period recorded social events with Ann Sothern and husband Roger Pryor, Jessica Barthelmess, Miriam Hopkins, Rouben Mamoulian, Basil and Ouida Rathbone — even a Lady Mendl dinner party for Alfred Lunt and Lynn Fontanne. In addition, Kay performed in a radio adaptation of *My Bill* with Warren William. Still, Kay felt overwhelmed by it all. On March 8, she wrote, "I must get off merry-go-round."[25] Two days later, she made a notation about Erik Barnekow's birthday, and also recorded a typically hectic day, including a publicity photo shoot for the war charity Bundles for Bluejackets, shopping at Saks, tea with Kendall Milestone,[26] dinner with Hugh Fenwick at Chasens, and then drinks at the Mocambo. It should be noted, too, that Kay was a habitual moviegoer. In the first few months of 1941, alone, she saw *Burning Secret*, *Fantasia*, *Meet John Doe*, and *Citizen Kane*.

KAY FRANCIS IN *FEMININE TOUCH* (1941)
Throughout her career, Kay was known for her movie wardrobe.

It was around this time — March 1941 — that Kay met her newest romantic partner, Hugh Fenwick, though she'd keep Ivan in the picture for some months to come. Hugh remained in Kay's life off and on for years, seeing her in New York and Los Angeles or whenever the opportunity presented itself. A throwback to Kay's previous lovers, Hugh was an aviator from a wealthy family who turned ne'er-do-well. In fact, there were numerous similarities, especially, to Dwight Francis and Bill Gaston. Born February 17, 1905, Hugh grew up in California, the son of Frederick McLeod Fenwick, heir to a lumber business. Mostly raised away from his parents on a timber ranch, he attended public and private schools in Eureka, California; New York City; and Germantown, Pennsylvania. Though Hugh was never a good student, his father somehow convinced Harvard, his alma mater, to accept his son. Hugh joined the polo and football teams, but was asked to leave after a year or so because of failing grades. Hugh, who'd trained as a pilot at the U.S. Naval Air

Station in Florida, then joined the New Jersey National Guard, where he became a lieutenant. This, too, ended when his recklessness resulted in tragedy. "His career came to an abrupt end when he flew dangerously low over a Bernardsville [New Jersey] apple orchard. Hugh, leading two planes, disappeared into a low patch of clouds. Before he knew it, the planes were much closer to the ground than he had expected. He pulled up, but the two planes behind him didn't have time to compensate for their low altitude and plunged to the earth below. Two men died."[27] Undaunted, Hugh continued to fly privately, often using his piloting skills to impress dates. By the time he met Kay, he'd already been married twice. His first wife was Dorothy Ledyard, daughter of the President of the New Stock Exchange. His second was Millicent Hammond Fenwick, who later became a Congresswoman. Still married to Millicent at the time he was seeing Kay,[28] he was also the father of two children. Hugh, who'd deserted Millicent in 1938 when he went to Europe to sell airplanes, was asked to leave England when he had a dalliance with Lady Maureen Stanley, wife of Oliver Stanley, England's Secretary of State for War.

Apparently Hugh, despite his womanizing, lying, and coarseness, could be quite charming. "He has a lot of charm, ghastly as he is," one woman said about him. Oh, he's full of charm. He can charm the birds off the trees."[29] Hugh, who also dated Kay's friend Rosalind Russell, was witty and fun — and capable of tenderness and patience. Perhaps that's why Kay fell for him. The relationship with Hugh, however, didn't start well. Kay reported that though they slept together in the spring of 1941, she found him boring.

In April, Kay, accompanied by Louella Parsons, Frank Capra, and Sylvia Ashley, traveled to Mexico City for the Motion Picture Producers Goodwill Fiesta, which was sponsored by an organization headed by Kay's friend Jock Whitney. The occasion was the premiere of *Pot o' Gold*. When Kay returned, her life was taken up with a tennis party at the Goldwyn's; dinner with Judith Anderson, Rosalind Russell, and Cole Porter; a party at Jack Benny's; dinners at Romanoff's; cocktails at Mocambo; and so on. Her companions included Barbara Hutton and Cary Grant, David and Irene Selznick, and Connie Bennett and Gilbert Roland.

In June and July of 1941, Kay was busy with the Motion Picture Production Defense Committee, helping entertain troops stationed in California. Other performers included Lucille Ball, Desi Arnaz, Pat O'Brien, Ann Miller, Kay Kyser, and Judy Canova. The group appeared at various camps, including Ford Ord, Camp McQuade, Hamilton Field, Camp Hunter Liggett, Camp Callan, Camp Haan, and Moffett Field.

On June 19, 1941, Kay sold her house and began looking for another property. It was an unhappy time. She and Ivan frequently argued as the relationship was nearing its end. During the summer months of 1941, Kay juggled Ivan and Hugh — and frequently saw both of them on the same day. She was also briefly hospitalized, probably for a kidney ailment. Fortunately, it didn't prevent her from playing tennis with Charlie Chaplin on at least two occasions that summer. Kay also visited Louis Bromfield at his Ohio farm in August. From there, she traveled to New York and saw her usual friends— Lois Long, Elsa Maxwell, Bill Gaston, McKay Morris, Stevie Wiman, Bea Stewart, Rouben Mamoulian, socialite Dolly O'Brien,[30] Grace Moore, and others. She recorded visits to the 21 Club, the Monte Carlo, Stork Club, El Morocco, the Colony, and the Ritz Tower. When Hugh arrived in New York, she began referring to him as "Hughsie-Woosie."

In October, Kay appeared on the NBC radio program *Cavalcade of America* in an adaptation of "Waters of the Wilderness." The cast included Gale Gordon, Agnes Moorehead, and Bea Benaderet. In that same month, Kay moved into a new house at 1735 Angelo Drive in Beverly Hills. On November 8, Kay showed off her new residence at an elaborate dinner party for Grace Moore. Grace wrote about the party in her autobiography. "When I visited Hollywood late in 1941, Kay gave me what I think was the last big glamour party before Pearl Harbor. According to a story in Louella Parsons' column, Kay had announced this as a small sit-down dinner of my twelve most intimate friends. I arrived to find a houseful of Hollywood's elite crowded into Kay's little place and a profusion of tables decorated with orchids, gardenias, and *leis* from Hawaii."[31]

Kay was still dating Hugh and Ivan, but spending more time with Hugh. In fact, Hugh and Kay spent Thanksgiving with Cary Grant and wife Barbara Hutton. Shortly after Thanksgiving, she traveled to New York for the holidays, seeing her usual crowd. However, Bill Gaston once again proved he was no gentleman. He showed up at her hotel room, dead drunk, and Kay made him leave. Kay also argued with Hugh, who'd joined her on the East Coast.

During this New York visit, Japan attacked Pearl Harbor. Kay described her surreal trip back to Hollywood. "Stopped at every port! Frightening trip!"[32] It was around this time that Kay's former lover, Erik Barnekow, committed suicide in Germany.

KAY FRANCIS MAKING A WORLD WAR II PERSONAL APPEARANCE
Kay making one of her many personal appearances, with unidentified officers at a Navy hospital during World War II.

Kay spent the rest of the year working with the Red Cross and Bluejackets. She had dinner on Christmas Eve with Ivan, and spent Christmas Day with her mother and two soldiers she'd invited to stay in her home. By the 26th, Hugh was back in town. She spent Near Year's Eve dining at the Arthur Hornblows, followed by drinks at Romanoff's. Her companions included Hugh, David Selznick, and Johnny McMullen.[33]

"Crying all night — hell of a New Year — no plans — I guess I am a pretty stupid unattractive person. Wonder if I will live the year out? Hope not!!"[34]

Thus began Kay's entries for 1942. Kay's depression no doubt stemmed from boredom as well as fears about the war. She worked infrequently — and too much free time was *not* a good thing for Kay Francis. She made only two pictures in 1942. The first was *Always in My Heart* with Walter Huston. The Warner Brothers movie was a futile attempt to make a star out of a young woman named Gloria Warren. However, Kay must have gotten some satisfaction from the fact that Warner Brothers hired her back at her asking price. It also must have been bittersweet to work again with old pal Walter Huston. More than a decade had passed since they were novice stage actors, and both could no doubt tell — and retell — war stories about their disillusioning Hollywood days.

Later that fall, Kay appeared in Universal's *Between Us Girls,* a vehicle for Diana Barrymore, which was also disappointing. A Universal press release tried to put a happy face on Kay's demotion to character roles. "While she enjoyed doing her romantic leading roles in former seasons, Miss Francis gets even more pleasure from her present assignments. She finds these roles represent film acting in its most agreeable phase. All she has to do now is concentrate on acting. Gone are the interminable fashion and coiffure fittings and sittings, the hundreds of portrait 'still' photograph poses, which are part of every leading lady's work. Now she has leisure to study her lines and work out the character she is to play, in minute detail. Thus, Miss Francis' current work in pictures contains many of the best features of her former acting assignments, with most of the drudgery eliminated."[35] Critics considered the film lightweight slapstick, but continued to marvel at Kay's beauty. "Better looking than so many younger actresses, she is still good to look at."[36]

This particular set was the scene of an ill-conceived practical joke. Charles Laughton, hoping to surprise his friend Henry Koster, instead sent Kay to her dressing room in tears. While Koster was directing Kay, the lights suddenly went out and shots were heard. "Kay, who hated guns, was horrified, screamed, and grabbed Koster's arms saying, 'Somebody's shooting.' Then the lights went up and Charles came down the stairs in a long nightgown and nightcap he had worn in *It Started with Eve,* singing 'Happy birthday, dear Henry!' accompanied by the entire cast and crew."[37]

A common sight around the Universal lot was Kay knitting while waiting to be called to movie sets. According to Gloria Jean, then a child actress at the studio, "I used to visit Kay Francis on the set when we were both under contract at Universal Studios. She was always so nice to me and took the time to try to teach me how to knit between shooting scenes. She was a beautiful knitter and it was fascinating to watch her knit so fast. I never did master the art and knew I would never be able to knit as well as she did or as fast. However, she tried!" Gloria Jean found Kay to be pleasant company. "There are only very nice things I can say about her. She was just as lovely to be with as she was to look at."[38]

At this point in her career, Kay decided to concentrate on what she could do to aid the war effort. World War II was uppermost in people's minds, and Kay volunteered — for her country *and* herself. It was partly due to the loss of Carole Lombard. The tragic death of her friend on January 16, 1942,[39] in an airplane crash was devastating to Kay, and all of Hollywood. But Kay also wanted to busy herself since her film career was slowing. Like most things, she went into it with gusto, eventually being named head of the Hospital Unit of the Naval Aid Auxiliary.

Meanwhile, Kay continued to see Ivan, Hugh, and occasionally Fritz. The relationship with Hugh was winding down, though Kay would occasionally see him once or twice a year for the next few years. By 1942, Hugh was vice-president of Vultee Aircraft and would become known, at least briefly, as a visionary because of a speech he gave on "The Challenge of Air to American Business Men."[40] During this time, Kay also suffered from a myriad of health problems, ranging from frequent colds to chronic pain.

During the winter of 1942, Kay worked with Myrna Loy at the Long Beach Naval Auxiliary Canteen, handing out refreshments and clothing. Kay described her work as providing good cheer and maintaining high morale for the sailors in the naval hospitals at Corona and Long Beach. Once a week, joined by actresses such as Joan Bennett, Lynn Bari, and Carole Landis, Kay distributed cigarettes, games, books and magazines to the boys, and

KAY FRANCIS, MYRNA LOY, AND VIRGINIA ZANUCK
Left to right: Virginia Zanuck, Myrna Loy, and Kay Francis on duty for Bundles for Bluejackets at the San Pedro Harbor.

spent the afternoons chatting and posing with them for snapshots. A typical day's schedule involved leaving Beverly Hills at 10 A.M., arriving at the hospital at noon, leaving at 5:00 P.M., and arriving home about 7:00. In 1943, Kay noted in a report that the visits were becoming problematic because of restrictions on gasoline and cigarettes.

According to Myrna Loy, Kay "was a little ahead of her time, using four-letter words that shocked me terribly; but I liked her. We shared a reality beyond titles and organizations at Long Beach, handing out coffee and doughnuts and whatever reassurance we could to draftees bound for Hawaii. We saw untrained kids inducted, all so young and bewildered, an endless stream totally unprepared for war. It broke our hearts."[41] Shortly after midnight, during the predawn hours of February 25, 1942, they were told the area was on a yellow alert and ordered to quickly leave. "Kay and I, bordering on hysteria, were trying to drive home when we passed what is now Los Angeles International Airport. Then it served as a private landing field for Howard Hughes and other fliers. This night — I will never forget it — there were dozens of planes lined up ominously in the dark with their propellers just turning, waiting for something to happen. I barely reached home before all hell broke loose. It sounded like the end of the world. When I peeked from the tightly drawn curtains, the boys from Brooklyn were firing. Artillery fire, flares, and spotlights crossed the sky. Arthur [husband Hornblow], who'd been asleep, came running downstairs in a panic. When I got through to my family, Mother was in hysterics. 'Take it easy,' I said. 'We're all right.' Which turned out to be true. We had experienced the famous false air raid of 1942 that no one has ever really explained."[42] Explanations ranged from war jitters to weather balloons to UFOs.

There was more excitement in April 1942. Kay and Constance Bennett, co-hosts of the Bluejackets Ball in Culver City, agreed to mingle with servicemen. Constance offered to dance with all, and the ensuing hysteria resulted in a fistfight between Hyman Curson and Ralph Abbott. Ralph got the worst of it, and was taken to the hospital, accompanied by Kay and Constance. Kay not only phoned Abbott's mother from the hospital with an update on his condition, but also brought him home. "Imagine my surprise when a lady called me from the hospital and said she was Kay Francis. Then later, about 8 o'clock, who drives up in a limousine with a chauffeur, bringing Ralph home, but Miss Francis and Constance Bennett?"[43] Connie and Kay finally got to bed around 9 A.M. the following morning.

"God, I am lonely!"[44]

Kay's social events in April included meeting Greta Garbo at a dinner party at Basil and Ouida Rathbone's. Almost a week later, Kay had dinner with her *Between Us Girls* co-star Diana Barrymore. In the late spring and early summer, she was also preparing to move into her last California home. Located at 1010 Benedict Canyon Drive in Beverly Hills, Kay moved into the house on June 20, 1942. A busy day, she also had dinner with Cole and Linda Porter, went to a party for Elsie Mendl, and then joined Rosalind Russell for drinks at Romanoff's.

Kay's new house came with a pool, and she often hosted pool parties. In fact, she and producer Larry Fox enjoyed an intimate evening in July: "Naval Hospital with Joan Bennett and Lynn Bari — Larry Fox. Then spent night — swimming pool — never done that before!"[45] The affair with Fox never developed into a full-blown romance, but Kay's juggling of Ivan and Hugh eventually led to trouble when Hugh found Ivan's car in Kay's driveway early one morning.

In September, Kay met director Otto Preminger, who'd shown up at one of her pool parties.[46] Her first sexual experience with Preminger was not enjoyable, but Otto apparently improved because Kay began writing raves about his lovemaking less than two weeks later. However, the next few weeks left little time for Otto as Kay prepared for her first major USO[47] trip. She received a set of typhoid shots, said goodbye to friends and mother, got her passport in order, and spent her remaining time in New York, seeing Grace Moore, Dorothy Parker, Lillian Hellman, and Stevie Wiman.[48]

On October 30, 1942, Kay, Martha Raye, Mitzi Mayfair, and Carole Landis took off for Bermuda. Kay and her troupe stayed for eight days and then left for England on November 9.

Raye, Mayfair, and Landis were intimidated by Kay. She was, after all, a major Hollywood star and still a great beauty. In fact, Kay had been one of Carole's favorite stars while growing up.[49] However, "as soon as the younger girls discovered that Kay Francis did not have any stuffy ideas about protocol, the tension disappeared. They began bantering and joking as the plane hop-skipped its way through the darkness across the Atlantic, stopping at various military bases."[50]

In mid–November, the troupe arrived in war-torn London, staying at the Savoy Hotel. Like other buildings, the hotel was darkened at night to avoid being a target. However, during the day, the four Americans saw the damage. According to Martha Raye's biographer, "The wounded city lay exposed, piles of rubble marking the most recent sites where Nazi bombs had exploded."[51]

The first English performance was held in a high school auditorium, now converted into a barracks and mess hall. "This was the first in a six-week series of shows, six days each week, during which the four entertainers adapted their acts to a variety of stages ranging from 12' × 24' platforms in tin-roofed Nissen huts to velvet-draped huts."[52] Sunday was a day off, which the women used for laundry, fixing their hair, and resting.

Kay often began the show by telling the soldiers, "I'd rather be here than any place in the world," and then adding, "There's no place we could be the only women among several thousand men."[53] She also served as emcee, read a motivational 'letter' from 'back home,' and participated in sing-alongs to "America" and "God Save the King." The grueling schedule—"Each night the entertainers were slowly driven some fifty miles or more along darkened country roads by a U.S. Army Special Forces officer who maneuvered his vehicle, headlights hooded, through the blackness to the next military camp"[54]—finally got to Kay and Mitzi. Kay was hospitalized in London with laryngitis. Mitzi soon joined her in the hospital after straining her back and shoulder. "The two 'casualties' have been placed in a special room of the nurses' barracks of the army hospital in the Midlands. The day before they were hospitalized all four actresses were entertained by Major Gen. John Lee of the Services of Supply at an army camp. After dinner they put on their show and then the two went to the hospital."[55]

Only one show was canceled. Arriving at one camp, the women learned that the squadron had lost several fliers that day. "In a somber mood, the surviving pilots and bombardiers and the American women ate their evening meal by candlelight in a tavern with a wood-beamed ceiling. The survivors offered toasts in memory of their friends, then took candles and burned into the ceiling the names of those who had not returned from the mission."[56]

The tour was an extensive one. They traveled 37,500 miles and gave 125 performances and 150 personal appearances. Venues included England, Algiers, and other locations in North Africa. They performed in theaters, hospitals, on improvised stages, and even in a boxing ring. Kay, who brought along only seven dresses and a black dinner gown, insisted there was no glamour, adding that they were lucky to get one bath a week. "Throughout the trip the actresses washed their own laundry and often traveled about without changing clothes for as long as six days at a time. In England, through the offices of a soldier, they were equipped with G.I. winter woolens, decidedly oversized. In Africa, they were provided with regulation khaki shorts."[57] Kay, however, noted that their audiences were easy to please. "They would have been perfectly happy if all you said was boo to them."[58]

The tour was dangerous, and Kay described being bombed every night in Algiers. "We stood in the general's house and watched several Jerries come down in flames."[59] Kay also explained that she *slept* through one attack over the Bay of Biscay when she and her companions were on a B-17 bomber, headed for North Africa. Although the tail gunner was killed during the encounter with two German fighter planes, Kay's friends agreed to let her sleep. Meanwhile, Mitzi, Martha, and Carole were in fetal positions, praying during the battle.

The highlight for the entertainers was the December 4, 1942, command performance for the Royal Family. Although King George was not in attendance, Princesses Elizabeth and Margaret, Queen Elizabeth, and Queen Mary saw the Windsor Castle show. In fact, Princess Margaret learned to jitterbug from Mitzi!

The trip's highlight for the press was Carole Landis' London marriage on January 5, 1943, to Captain Thomas Wallace. "You can't be sure. You haven't known him long enough,"[60] Kay cautioned. Landis adored Kay, but ignored the advice. The elaborate Catholic wedding featured Mitzi Mayfair as maid of honor. By October 1944, Wallace and Landis had separated, and Landis divorced him in Reno in the summer of 1945.

In early January 1943, the troupe left Europe for North Africa. In fact, Kay arrived in North Africa on her 38th birthday. Among those in Algiers at the time were Bea Lillie, also performing for the troops, and photographer Margaret Bourke-White, who was there on assignment. The troupe was a big hit, and one soldier was particularly impressed by Miss Francis: "The real surprise to me was Kay Francis. As the M.C. and leader she had great charm and some very good material."[61]

"Mitzi and I start home — Algiers to Oran — filthy — unable to sleep in sheets — meet pilots for next day — Sileer — shot at and I slept!"[62]

Finally, after enduring a bout with influenza and then a torn leg ligament, Kay returned home in late January 1943. On January 29, Kay arrived in Alma, Georgia, surviving a forced landing. Still, she was grateful to be back on American soil and promptly enjoyed a chocolate ice cream soda. She flew first to Washington, D.C., where she filed an official report with the War Department, and then to New York. According to Grace Moore, the trip deeply affected Kay. "When she returned, she was so shaken by her experiences she found it unbearable to sit through a little dinner party I had arranged for her first night home. Our Land of Plenty was more than she could take after what she had been through."[63]

Kay returned to Hollywood on February 20, where she was met by Frances Goldwyn and Bart Marshall and wife Lee.[64] She quickly reconnected with her mother and old friends, including Cole Porter, Lady Mendl, Irene and David Selznick, Harry Crocker, Rosalind Russell and husband Frederick Brisson, and Ina Claire. She also attended yet another formal dinner at Pickfair.

It took Kay a long time to fully recover from the tour, though she was seen frequently at Ciro's with date Lieutenant (and eventual film producer) Bert Friedlob.[65] As often was the case with Kay, her first dates with Bert did not go well, and she complained about his sexual performance. While seeing Friedlob, Kay also dated Otto and Hugh, though she and Otto argued when he accused her of being too busy for him. Kay *was* busy during this time, working on the film version of *Four Jills in a Jeep*, along with several radio broadcasts, including *Cavalcade of America*, *The Silver Theatre*, and another appearance on the *Lux Radio Show*. She also continued her USO work. A typical entry described sleeping on cots in tents and arriving back home in the early morning hours.

Born in Vienna, Austria, in 1906, actor/producer/director Preminger was yet another talented European working in Hollywood who had an intense affair with Kay. Kay's attraction to European men may have been a combination of personal taste as well as their more relaxed attitudes toward sexuality. Kay had few sexual hang-ups and was comfortable with the idea of sex for sex's sake — it didn't have to be a prelude to marriage.

Preminger had worked with German stage director Max Reinhardt before coming to the United States to direct plays. He directed some minor films at Fox, but became best known for playing Nazis — ironically, he was Jewish — in such films as *The Pied Piper* and *Margin for Error* in the early 1940s. His big break came when he directed the brilliant film noir *Laura* in 1944. Although he'd married Hungarian actress Marion Mill in Vienna in 1932, Preminger was known as a ladies' man. "His reputation for sexual appetite and prowess which had followed him from Vienna was enhanced when he was seen with some of Hollywood's prettiest faces and best figures. To escape the pressures and frustrations, he slipped away for long weekends in the company of some very slim, very tall, very long-legged and very willing partner[s] — they all had to be slim, tall, long-legged and willing.... When his companion for the night or the weekend was herself well known, as happened not infrequently, Otto was scrupulously discreet. There were rumors galore linking his name with Hollywood headliners but by the time the whisper got around, the affair was usually long over."[66]

"Dinner with Bert — then Mocambo — I hate that damn place!"[67]

Kay's social companions in 1943 were a diverse lot, including William Paley, Bill Thornton, Jean Feldman, Ann Warner, Elsa Maxwell, Fritz Lang, Cole Porter, Dorothy di Frasso, Jane Wyatt, Howard Cushing — even Jane Wyman and Ronald Reagan! Many nights were spent at dinner parties, Romanoff's, and — despite Kay's professed hatred — the Mocambo nightclub.

She continued to help out several nights a week at the Hollywood Canteen.[68] It was here that film actor Roddy McDowall met Kay. "I adored Kay Francis. I got to know her at the Hollywood Canteen when I was just a starstruck lad. She was a real trouper. Warm and energetic. There was a regal quality to Kay Francis. She was one of the true movie stars of the 1930s."[69] In addition to her charity work, Kay worked in radio, appearing on July 4, 1943, on *The Silver Theatre* in an episode titled "Murder Unlimited."

In July 1943, Kay was approached by Corporal Ambrose DuBek, a costumer and set designer, to see if she'd allow servicemen to use her swimming pool once a week. This was one request that Kay refused. In a polite and gracious letter, she enumerated her reasons, including the small size of her pool, the fact that her household staff now numbered only one, her busy schedule, and so on. She also wrote about her desire for privacy. "I do a great deal of defense work and honestly feel that the little privacy I have should at least be within the four walls of my own home, and to have strange boys running in and out is impossible, though I am sure they are charming and I well appreciate their need for recreation. I also must consider my own need for relaxation with a few of my friends once in a while.

Practically every weekend (besides my hospital work Tuesdays and Thursdays) I am busy entertaining for USO-Camp Shows, Government broadcasts, etc. and naturally I cannot leave my house open for soldiers to come in at will during my absence."[70]

"Pickfair at 4 — tea for 200 soldiers — Otto here at 7:30 — script reading for Four Jills in a Jeep — *Nervous!"*[71]

Four Jills in a Jeep was based —*very* loosely — on the tour and resulting book, supposedly written by Carole Landis. The movie added a fictional Kay Francis romance and specialty numbers by the studio's biggest musical stars and popular big bands. The movie was not without controversy, not only because it glamorized a decidedly unglamorous tour, but also because some Hollywood entertainers thought the four received too much attention — others, some claimed, did far more for the war effort.

According to writer Snag Werris, Kay was a delight: "This was a true fun assignment. They were swell gals. Kay was a real pro and a joy to work with. Her troubles with 'r's were well known. So for a gag I was asked to bring in a new page of script. I don't recall the lines, but one was something like 'I ran into Ralph in Roanoke and rapidly wrung his neck.' When Kay got to it, she read through it and yelled, 'Where is that son of a bitch Snag? I'll kill him!' but none of the four took herself too seriously. They got along well — although the assistant director had orders to make sure the A.M. calls for all the girls were at the same time."[72]

Phil Silvers explained that it was difficult coming up with a viable script: "Each [actress] had her own version of what actually happened, and wanted the script changed to fit her 'truth.' Director William Seiter had to explain over and over that this was entertainment. Who cared about reality?"[73] Indeed, the film took liberties with the truth. Although the actresses rarely wore makeup and often dressed in bulky clothing while touring, the movie showed them coiffed and in beautiful gowns. Oddly, the command performance at Windsor Castle was left out. The film even replaced the airplane's aluminum bucket seats with lush upholstery. The film would have been much more entertaining if a documentary approach had been followed. Critics applauded the patriotic gesture of the four women but lambasted the film. "The claptrap saga is just a raw piece of capitalization upon a widely publicized affair. It gives the painful impression of having been tossed together in a couple of hours."[74]

While working on *Four Jills in a Jeep,* Kay may have had an affair with fellow USO trouper and actress Carole Landis. Although Kay was definitely seeing a lot of Otto during this time, she made a notation on October 19, 1943, that Carole Landis had dinner at her house and spent the night. A couple of months later, Kay attended a party thrown by director William Seiter. Kay wrote, "Girls here 6:30 —fight Carole but good!"[75] Phil Silvers, who also appeared in the film, intimated that Kay had been after several female cast members. In his autobiography, he wrote, "Kay Francis was shown falling in love with an officer [in the film]. This was a tribute to her acting skill, because she had very little interest in men."[76]

Ironically, Kay and Otto's relationship was becoming more intense at this time. On October 25, a diary entry applauded Otto's kind treatment of her, while her more realistic side wondered what kind of future they might have. Meanwhile, Otto was house hunting near Kay's neighborhood, and the two enjoyed dinner together almost every night.

Kay was hospitalized again on November 8, 1943 — this time for kidney problems. Otto visited often, and accompanied her home when she was released on November 11. Before the year ended, Kay appeared in a couple more radio programs, including an NBC

Thanksgiving radio show with Bob Hope, Jack Benny, Frances Langford, Carole Landis, Mitzi Mayfair, Pat O'Brien, and Merle Oberon. (Although Kay didn't act in any movies in 1943, she did appear in a newsreel filmed at one of the Lockheed plants in Los Angeles, and newsreels of her USO work were included in *The March of Time*.)

At the end of 1943, Kay met her newest boyfriend. Tim Howard worked for the government, and Kay met him on December 5 — which was Otto's birthday. She spent the rest of the year dating Otto and Tim. Her last entry for 1943 indicated that Tim was, at least for the moment, her favorite. That night they dined at the Savoy and then attended a party at the Goldwyn's — and had a wonderful time.

The next year would be one of great change for Otto and Kay. Otto would become a father and an acclaimed director, and Kay was on her way to becoming a film producer. She would also dump Tim and find a new boyfriend — yet another pilot —*and* make a triumphant return to the stage.

CHAPTER 12

Goodbye Hollywood, Hello Broadway, 1944–1946

"Tim by at 3 — over to Marshall's at 5 — saw Song of Bernadette — *And Otto stayed the night here. Hope next year will be as nice."*[1]

Kay saw both Otto and Tim the first couple of weeks of January 1944, but Otto soon caught her in a fib. He'd unsuccessfully tried to phone Kay, but she explained she'd been at the Mocambo. In truth, she was entertaining Tim. Otto attempted to verify her story. "Otto called at 12 —furious— having checked Mocambo! Well, that's that! The end of a beautiful friendship?"[2] It wasn't — at least for a time. Meanwhile, Tim was ordered back to Washington, D.C. on business on January 11, and Otto helped Kay celebrate her 39th birthday.

The first month of 1944 was spent on USO work and socializing. Kay attended Cary Grant's birthday party on January 18, and also enjoyed dinner and cocktails with such friends as Ann Warner, Fritz Lang, Rosalind Russell and Freddie Brisson, Moss Hart, the Mendls, and Lawrence Rockefeller. Kay also took a brief vacation with Charles Feldman's wife Jean to the Arrowhead Springs resort.

On February 18, Kay left for Canada and Alaska on a USO trip with dancer Patty Thomas, actress/singer Marsha Hunt, singer Teddi Sherman,[3] actor — and old friend — Reginald Gardiner, and musical accompanist Nancy Barnes. They traveled on a C-47 and performed in front of U.S. and Canadian Air Forces— and even some German POWs. Their pilot was Don King, who would become Kay's next lover. "Our pilot, Don King, was chosen to ferry us all over western, central and northern Canada and Alaska because he was considered the very best bush pilot in the Arctic," fellow traveler Marsha Hunt wrote. "Certainly, he was, as far as we were concerned, and whatever the changes and threats of weather and flying visibility, we trusted Don to deliver us safely, and so he did, despite a few rather dicey occasions. He also was handsome and a fine companion."[4] The affair with Don was probably only a flirtation at this point, but would become a full-fledged romance after Kay returned to the States.

Kay, by now an old pro on these USO tours, was endearingly referred to as "Sarge, our fearless leader"[5] by her fellow travelers. Although Kay dressed practically for this tour, she was still Kay Francis. Marsha Hunt, who admired Kay, found her unconsciously glamorous— as had Kay's 1920s Parisian friends. "With her distinctive raven hair and classic beauty, Kay was known for her fashion chic both on and off screen. She had worn so many gorgeous evening creations in films, no doubt her GI audiences expected more of the same. Instead, she usually went on stage in a simple dirndl skirt and blouse, but she couldn't resist trailing a long chiffon hankie. I suspect it answered the gnawing query: 'But what shall I do with my hands?' just as pockets answered that question for men. The peasant-look helped her and the boys out front feel informal and anyhow, nothing could rob Kay of her own innate glamour."[6] According to Miss Hunt, Kay packed only two silk gabardine pants suits and several blouses and sweaters. Kay's biggest problem was staying on her feet. "We were kept busy pulling her upright after frequent slips and spills on the ice. Miraculously, these falls left her unhurt and cheerfully resigned to them."[7]

The tour went remarkably well, and the troupe got along famously. "By great good luck, we proved a uniformly game group, cheery, compatible and even relishing the trying conditions of extreme cold, the bare bones dressing and sleeping quarters, long hours, fatigue, delays and boredom, making chitchat with constantly changing hordes of eager strangers, forever packing and unpacking, and living for six weeks in a cargo plane, lacking even passenger seats and consistent heating. It was our home away from home, where we repaired after each stop, to whisk us to our next one, and where we swapped stories, napped, read, set our hair, polished our nails, mended our costumes and worked up the freshness needed for the next port of call performance. I truly can't recall a single sour note among us in all that time."[8]

After the tour ended in March, Kay and Reggie traveled to New York, where Kay met up again with Tim. She also saw Betsy Whitney, Jessica Barthelmess, Elsa Maxwell, Ivan Goff, and Joan Payson; attended Annabella's[9] Broadway performance in *Jacobowsky and the Colonel; and* shopped at Saks, Cartier, and Bergdorf's.

While in New York, Kay fretted about not hearing from Otto or new flame Don. Unbeknownst to her, Otto was busy with beautiful stripper Gypsy Rose Lee — nine months later, Erik Preminger would be born in New York.[10] Don, however, soon began phoning, and the romance was on. As for Tim, Kay pronounced herself finished with him. "Dinner with Tim — arrived 8:30 — long repeat discussion! Finally went to bed with him and Christ, that is the end! The worst ever! Goodbye!"[11]

On her return trip to California, Kay, as per usual, stopped in Chicago, where she enjoyed a romantic rendezvous with Don. "Such a sad but wonderful night! Hell, why do I fall in love with the wrong guy?"[12] Unfortunately, Don was married to Ann, whom Kay had met in Edmonton in March while on her USO trip.

On March 31, Kay left Chicago and returned home to attend Mitzi Mayfair's April 7 wedding to *Four Jills in a Jeep* musical director Charlie Henderson. But Kay's mind was on Don, eagerly awaiting his phone calls. Meanwhile, she and Otto ostensibly broke up (again) on April 12. But they weren't really through. They saw each other several more times until Kay left for Canada on April 21 for speeches, radio broadcasts, and luncheons to aid the war effort.

Kay was interviewed about her USO work, and the articles were printed in Canadian newspapers in both English and French. A highlight of the trip was Kay's appearance on *The Victory Star Show,* which was broadcast from Montreal on April 26, 1944. The next day full page ads stating "Kay Francis Canada Thanks You" appeared in the newspapers.

When Kay returned to the States, she and Don reunited. Their romance, however, was complicated by Don's marriage. When Kay returned home on May 6, Don stayed behind in Canada.

Otto was briefly back in the picture. However, he became upset with Kay, accusing her of not being supportive of his career troubles, especially in light of problems on the set of *Laura.* Preminger, hired by Daryl Zanuck to produce *Laura,* had difficulty finding a director willing to take on the project. Lewis Milestone, Walter Lang, and others turned it down. Finally, Rouben Mamoulian — Kay's former lover — accepted the job, but he and Preminger rarely saw eye to eye. One problem was casting. Mamoulian wanted to hire Laird

Cregar to play Waldo Lydecker, while Preminger insisted on stage actor (and Kay's friend) Clifton Webb. Mamoulian started filming, but an unhappy Zanuck finally asked Preminger to fire Mamoulian and direct the film himself. Preminger eventually received an Oscar nomination for *Laura.*

Kay's hectic wartime schedule continued, despite romantic and health troubles. In June, she made a trip for the War Department to her birthplace, Oklahoma City, where she visited hospitals during the day and performed at army shows at night. It was, she reported, the first time she'd been back to Oklahoma City since she'd left with her parents at the age of nine months. When asked if she'd make any more movies, Kay insisted the war came first.

In a letter dated July 25, 1944, Kay described a typical tour: "The Victory Committee very thoughtfully sent with me one of their very best men but I knocked him off the first day with heat prostration and Ptomaine poisoning, so I had to struggle on alone until I picked up a flyer, Bob Butler, who toted me around under his wing and then literally had to fly me in his C-45 through some of the lousiest weather I've had the pleasure to be up in (and that's saying something, Brother!) so as to catch a connection in Dallas. One of these days, I'll probably end up sitting on top of a nice white cloud playing a harp to entertain the dear Lord and his angels. Oh well, I'm tired but certainly shouldn't kick at the jobs I have to do."[13]

Next on her agenda? "Believe it or not, here I go again! This time they are sending me out alone to cover all of the largest Navy and Army hospitals on the west coast in San Francisco, Palo Alto, Seattle, Spokane, Walla Walla, Pendleton and Portland. It's one hell of a schedule and I travel during the nights in everything from jeeps to trains to planes and then am expected to be gay and bright from morning to eve going through the wards. I only hope they don't kill me off here in America before I have a chance to make the South Pacific."[14]

Hollywood was understandably subdued during the third year of the war, but Errol Flynn did his best to brighten the mood when he hosted a July 1944 pool party at his San Fernando Valley digs for serviceman Bruce Cabot. Back from Africa, Cabot was joined by Kay, Mary Pickford and Buddy Rogers, the Paul Lukases, Paulette Goddard and Burgess Meredith, David Selznick, the Reginald Gardiners, the Jack Warners, the Darryl Zanucks, Elsa Maxwell, Sir Charles and Lady Mendl, and Errol's date, Nora Eddington. "Tables were set up around Flynn's pool, and the tented terrace made the dinner picturesque as well as delicious. There was outdoor dancing, plus a floorshow put on by swimming and diving stars, who performed somewhere between the suckling pig and the ice cream."[15]

"I've decided to produce pictures."[16]

In a July 25, 1944, letter, Kay described her next project — she'd accepted an offer to produce and star in movies at Monogram Pictures. "My first one (co-producer, Jeffrey Bernerd) starts about the 20th of September and the tentative title is *Divorce.* The writers are now working on a story treatment and will begin the script while I am 'spreading cheer' up north."[17]

Despite her obsession with Don during this time, Kay truly was a trouper. On July 26, while on a hospital tour in San Francisco, it was discovered that she had a fractured rib. Medical personnel ordered her home, but she refused and continued on to Seattle. It was here that she and Don again had the opportunity to see each other. They saw *A Guy Named Joe,* and enjoyed several days together until Don returned home.

In the fall, while worrying about what would become of her relationship with Don, Kay socialized with Otto, Michael Arlen, and Harry Crocker. She also went to another dinner at the Goldwyn's—this time the guests included Oona and Charlie Chaplin.

Kay began attending meetings at Monogram in October, preparing for her first production. In November, she traveled to Seattle to see Don. The meeting was tense, but they continued to keep in touch by telephone. In mid–December, Kay traveled to Chicago for the N.A. War Fund, and then continued on to New York to see her usual friends. She also attended friend Grace Moore's performance in *La Boheme* and visited with George and Valentina Schlee.[18] Kay spent Christmas outside New York City with this group of friends, and then returned to New York City where her New Year's Eve was one of the most uneventful in years. She ended up in bed — alone — well before midnight.

During the Christmas season of 1944, Kay again toured army hospitals. Gossip columnist Hedda Hopper saluted Kay: "It's unbelievable how much Kay does in her quiet way."[19] Considering Kay's grueling schedule, it's strange to think this was the same woman who claimed to be lazy. "I should have been born in a harem, with slaves to wait on me, even to feed me. Never to raise my little finger again is my idea of heaven."[20] Kay's war efforts may have tested her physical stamina, but a grateful U.S. military awarded her with citations and letters of commendation after the war ended. Jimmy Bangley interviewed Bob Hope in 1997, and Hope still spoke highly of Kay: "What a looker! A great star! A great dame! They called her 'ravishing Kay Francis.' Nowadays, people forget what a trouper Kay was. She did a lot for the USO and gave her time to many patriotic causes. She was a real class act."[21]

In January 1945, Kay celebrated her 40th birthday with a party at El Morocco. Don gave her forty red roses—and one white one. The relationship, however, was difficult and unsatisfying, as Don was often unavailable to her. By March, Kay had had it. After not hearing from him for days, she wired his office. He finally telephoned, but Kay was livid, and told him the relationship was over. Kay continued to keep in touch with him, but their communication and visits became less frequent.

By now, Kay was busying herself at Monogram trying to jumpstart her film career.[22] Monogram Pictures was one of Hollywood's second-class studios. Some called it a poverty-row studio—the home of burned out has-beens. Other stars who ended up here included Bela Lugosi and Harry Langdon.

Writers have claimed for years that these films were the worst of Kay's career. They weren't. One benefit of working at a small B-movie studio was that there was little scrutiny by censors, resulting in films with a cutting edge. "The sight-unseen dismissal of *Allotment Wives* made sense in theory. Critics and audiences hardly noticed it in 1945. It was made by Monogram Studios, which cranked out a lot of awful B movies. And Francis, a lifelong heavy drinker, already looked puffy, swollen and over the hill by 1940. Who could have expected that five years later she'd emerge as a sleek, sexy and stylish 42-year-old [she was actually closer to 40]—or that the film would have the expensive, glossy look of an MGM feature?"[23]

In truth, none of the Monogram films were as bad as her later Warner Brothers films, especially *My Bill* and *Always in My Heart*[24]—and Kay was ahead of her time in terms of producing her own films. It was a smart choice for her because it not only allowed her to call many of the shots, it was also lucrative. She was a persuasive producer — very aware of budgetary constraints—who charmingly convinced established actors such as Otto Kruger and Paul Kelly to work for less. In addition, Kay often had a hand in rewriting screenplays. Many diary entries included notes about working long hours on the scripts.

Kay worked on *Divorce* and *Allotment Wives* in early 1945. Though *Divorce* was weak and resulted in poor reviews, *Allotment Wives* was a film noir classic, one that hinted at the roles Kay might have played if she hadn't left Hollywood to return to the stage. The final film of the trilogy, *Wife Wanted,* was produced in the summer of 1946 and released in November. Unfortunately, it was the worst of the three — and Kay Francis' last film. Critics were correct in pointing out that it was "somewhat vague and confusing."[25]

Between filming *Divorce* and *Allotment Wives,* Kay went on yet another USO tour — this time to South America. The trip started in April, and Kay returned in early May. She first traveled to Puerto Rico, and then to bases in Trinidad, British Guiana, and Brazil. Kay spent most of this tour flying in C-45s up and down the coast of Brazil, including a two-day side trip to Ascension Island, a strategic refueling stop near the equator in the middle of the South Atlantic Ocean. On a typical day she would be up at 6:30. During breakfast, she'd discuss the day's plans with the officer assigned to accompany her, and then tour the base and ships, lunch in the mess hall, visit hospitals in the afternoon, enjoy cocktails and dinner at the officers' club, and perhaps attend a dance or movie. Finally, she often shared a nightcap with the commanding officer(s), and then climbed into bed, exhausted. Some of the pressure was off during her three days in Rio — she stayed in Copacabana, visited the offices of *Vogue* and *Renault,* made a trip up Sugar Loaf for a panoramic view of the city and bay, and took a ride in a blimp. On her May 4 return flight back home, Kay received the wonderful news that peace had been declared.[26]

The exhausting trip kept Kay sidelined for at least a month before she turned her attention to the second Monogram picture, *Allotment Wives.* Production started on June 19, and Kay finished the picture on July 12. A week later she took a gambling vacation to Las Vegas with frequent companion "Miss P," who Kay never fully identified.[27] In typical Kay Francis fashion, she approached the trip with gusto, describing how she and Miss P arrived at the El Rancho Vegas Hotel at 11 P.M., dressed, and gambled until 4 A.M. Hotel guests were treated to the sight of the glamorously gowned and jeweled Miss Francis traipsing through the hotel dining room one night with a brown paper bag; she'd befriended a stray dog and provided gourmet treats to the lucky mongrel during her stay. After a few days, Kay had lost $3,000 and was ready to return home — to work on a new stage show.

"In the theater you can go on acting with a double chin or lines about the eyes. Those things don't matter, but with the camera, well, you know what I mean!"[28]

In 1945, Kay took a break from Monogram and returned to the stage for the first time since 1928. During her Hollywood years, Kay had wanted to work on the stage, but the studio refused permission. In 1934, she told an interviewer, "I do want to return to Broadway. To begin with, I feel the need of *audience contact* [her emphasis]. There is something electric and inspiring about stage work. The *feel* of an audience lifts one. That inspirational touch is lacking in motion pictures, where acting is a cold, cut-and-dried proposition."[29]

For her return to the stage, Kay chose a vehicle written by silent-screen actress Patsy Ruth Miller, and directed by stage and screen legend Ruth Chatterton. Like Kay, Ruth had defected from Paramount to Warner Brothers in early 1932, the result of a highly publicized talent raid. The lure of higher salaries and promises of class productions had proved illusory, and both actresses likely regretted switching studios. Ruth and Kay had spent much time together in Hollywood in their early days, and the friendship played a major role in Kay's casting.

Ruth first approached Kay about the part on May 30 when Kay and Miss P were working on the script for *Allotment Wives*. According to Patsy, she and Ruth thought of no one else but Kay for the lead role. "Who looked the part—could play it—and would fit in with our feminine, but not exclusively feminine group: With one accord we said it together ... Kay Francis! Kay had been interested from the beginning, just because two gals she knew were trying to do something together. She had stopped over to New York several times on her way to entertain the troops in Europe, India and China [*sic*], and had sort of sat on the side lines, cheering. Kay had been planning on going to the Pacific—but the idea of making a third appealed to her. (As a matter of fact, I think she had been told to take an extended rest before going on another tour, as she had knocked herself out in China. [Patsy must have confused Africa with China!]) A rest indeed! Little did she know!"[30]

Kay traveled to New York—frantically studying the script—and began helping with casting in early August. The play's cast included Kay, Roger Pryor, and—very briefly—the then relatively unknown Judy Holliday, who, according to reviewers, stole the show.[31] According to Patsy, "I couldn't have asked for better actors, and Ruth turned out to be a damn good director."[32] Patsy's description of *Windy Hill* in her autobiography makes the production sound like an ice cream social. In truth, the tour, like most stage shows, was anything but. "From now on hell—only play, fights, trouble and nerves,"[33] Kay wrote on August 4.

1940S PROGRAM COVER
Kay often used this photograph to promote her stage tours in the late 1940s.

On August 13, 1945, the tour of *Windy Hill* began with a tryout in Montclair, New Jersey. The result did not bode well for the show's future. The performances were uneven, and script changes distressed Patsy so much she left Montclair. A few days later, Kay described Ruth as being "on warpath!"[34] Somehow, though, the production started coming together. Despite noting Kay's hoarse voice, *Variety* found her "very smart and attractive."[35]

Before the play opened in New Haven, Kay took time to relax with friend Grace Moore at her Connecticut home. She also went into New York and socialized with Millicent Hearst, Dolly O'Brien, Richard and Jessica Barthelmess, fashion designer Sophie Gimbel, and others. Kay also enjoyed a brief meeting with Don, and then went back into rehearsals with Ruth Chatterton and the *Windy Hill* cast.

The play opened at the Shubert Theatre in New Haven, Connecticut, on September 20, 1945. Grace Moore and husband Val attended one of the first shows—as did Bill Gaston. *Windy*

Hill closed at the Harris Theatre in Chicago on May 25, 1946. In between, the production moved up and down the East Coast and throughout the Midwest. In spite of tepid reviews, the tour was successful enough for the company to return to three cities—St. Louis, Washington, and Toronto—and enjoy a lengthy run in Chicago. *Theatre World 1945* gave Kay the credit. "Managed to stay 12 weeks at the Harris on the strength of the movie magic in Kay Francis' name."[36] Age-obsessed Hollywood studios might not have been interested in Kay anymore, but the tour proved she was still a potent box-office draw on the road. She was also a hit with most reviewers. "It really was a pleasure to see Kay Francis in person. Kay Francis's presence adds a great deal to the play. Miss Francis, moreover, is one of our most pleasing theatrical personalities."[37]

In her memoirs, Patsy Ruth Miller acknowledged Kay was a smart businesswoman—Kay's contract allowed for a salary *and* a percentage of the box-office. Miller also wrote that "Kay

1940s PORTRAIT
Kay in a typical 1940s hairstyle and with ever-present cigarette in hand.

preferred the sure thing of the road to the uncertainty of a New York opening. We finally had to close due to Kay's contract with Monogram Studios, who had a picture ready for her, and threatened a breach of contract suit if she didn't return. That effectively closed our show, as the producer wouldn't hear of putting anyone else in Kay's part. To my regret, *Windy Hill* never did get to New York. By the time Kay was again free the producer had died, his estate was involved in a legal battle, and I got tired of the whole thing and went back to California, which was probably stupid of me. But it had been a great experience, and I had come to love Kay."[38]

Not everyone recalled the play with such fondness. The Pittsburgh show ended in disaster. "Leading man Roger Pryor found the door jammed, and no amount of tugging would loosen it. With the substantial-looking walls seemingly hit by a second San Francisco quake, Pryor finally entered through a door that had been firmly established as leading to a clothes closet. The audience yelped with delight. The cast broke up, and the curtain fell on pandemonium. A moment later it inexplicably rose to reveal the elegant Kay, arms akimbo, stamping her tiny foot and screaming, 'Shit on this production!'"[39]

For a time, Patsy Ruth Miller lived with Ruth Chatterton during rehearsals. "I nearly lost my mind. Ruth was a brilliant actress, and it turned out, a good director, but she was one of those people who knew everything, and would brook no contradiction. It was during the War, hotels were so crowded I couldn't get a reservation for love or bribery, so I stayed with Ruth and went slowly mad. To give you an example, she made a pronouncement about our 94 senators being hopelessly archaic. At that time, before Alaska and Hawaii joined us, there were 48 states, therefore 96 senators. When I pointed this out to her, she replied firmly, No, dear, there are 94 senators. I happen to know."[40] Finally, friend Gloria Swanson took pity on Patsy and invited her to live with her until the play opened.

Patsy wrote with great fondness about Kay. "One of the endearing things about Kay — although she didn't think so — was her difficulty with the letter 'R.' One evening, as we were sitting chatting after a long rehearsal she said plaintively, 'Why did you have to pick that poem ...'"Bweathless we flung us on a windy hill, laughed in the sun and kissed the lovely gwass" — by Wupert Bwooke. Why couldn't you have chosen "Now I lay me down to sleep" by anonymous?'"[41]

Kay and Roger Pryor had a brief affair during the production. Pryor, who Kay had met in 1936 when he was dating actress Ann Sothern, was the son of orchestra leader Arthur Pryor. Born in 1901, Roger went on stage at the age of 18 and became a successful Broadway performer. Lured to Hollywood, he became known as "the poor man's Clark Gable." He appeared in several films but never became a star. Pryor, like his father, hit the road with his own orchestra — sometimes featuring singing by Ann, whom he'd married in 1936.[42] Pryor returned to Hollywood in 1940 to work on radio shows. During World War II, he was an Air Force flight instructor for more than two years. Divorced from Ann in 1943, his affair with Kay appeared to be a matter of convenience and companionship.

Kay's diary entries for the tour detail a relentless trip that had them packing and traveling day after day. It's no wonder there were occasional tantrums. In one outburst, Kay described breaking four liquor bottles. She spent Thanksgiving with Roger Pryor and a new actress who'd been added to the cast, Jetti Preminger.[43] Kay quickly became quite fond of Jetti and often wrote of their activities.

In addition to cast changes, the script was still being fine-tuned, much to Kay's distress. "Toledo — discussion on new version and how to put it in — rehearsal — will cut my own throat!"[44] Kay, needing a break, took her New York City vacation in mid–December, but was back on stage for a Buffalo, New York, Christmas show. She spent Christmas Eve with Jetti and Don King, while Christmas Day was spent at a crew party at the Hotel Statler.

Kay began 1946 with a New Year's Day show at the Royal Alexandra Theatre in Toronto. The coming weeks were a grueling combination of shows, traveling, rehearsals — and more of the same. By now, Kay and Jetti were steady companions. Jetti, who'd joined the show in November 1945, replacing Eileen Heckart, was not only a friend

"WINDY HILL" PUBLICITY PHOTOGRAPH
Kay returned to the stage in 1945 and toured for eight months in a romantic comedy written by Patsy Ruth Miller and directed by Ruth Chatterton.

who occasionally spent the night, but also an able assistant who helped Kay rehearse, assisted her with hair and nails, and even shopped for her. On January 3, Kay wrote how Jetti had finally found some boots for her. Alas, two days later, Kay reported that the boots had been stolen.

For those who have never taken a show on the road, it's hard to imagine just how tedious and tiring such an endeavor can be. It's also difficult to understand why Kay, certainly a millionaire at this point in her life, would choose such a life. Her diary entries chronicle the uncomfortable train trips, frequent illnesses, fatigue, revisions, and arguments. By February 13, Kay wrote that the cast had grown bored with the play.

In March, Kay was in Chicago, and it wasn't unusual for her to write about alcohol abuse at this point: "Matinee — pills, liquor and sleep!"[45] During this time, she was occasionally in contact with Don, but like most of her romances in their second year, it was no longer passionate. Perhaps remembering her former wild days in Chicago in the 1920s, Kay had several brief affairs with businessmen Carrington Clark, Ed Davis, and Bill Kroger. She also saw old friend Teddy Newton. Indeed, it must have been surreal for Kay to talk to Ted, the actor she'd once shared kisses with in 1928. It had been eighteen years since they'd appeared together in *Elmer the Great*. He'd known Kay Francis before she *was* Kay Francis.

"The tissues of our bodies are altered every seven years. Our eyes change every four years. That is an acknowledged physiological fact. I am convinced the same is true of our personalities. Because of this, I now feel capable of acting roles which would have been difficult for me a few years ago. I suspect that as time goes on, my changing personality will enable me to portray roles greatly different from anything I have done so far."[46]

While in Chicago in May, Kay met with director Phil Karlson about her next Monogram picture, *Wife Wanted*. Kay didn't like the first script, and she and Karlson immediately went to work on a new one. Meanwhile, *Windy Hill* closed on May 25, and Kay returned home two days later. She immediately went to work at the studio, trying to hammer out the script. Back in her own home after months on the road, Kay socialized with Hugh Fenwick, Otto Preminger, Jessica Barthelmess, Elsa Maxwell, Jean Feldman, and others. Filming started on *Wife Wanted* on June 19, and Kay immersed herself in the work. She was so busy, in fact, that she turned down an invitation to Constance Bennett's wedding.[47]

"Worked till 5:30 — saw Hayward to talk re State of the Union *— so excited!"[48]*

While Kay completed *Wife Wanted*, stage producer Leland Hayward contacted her — he needed a replacement for a pregnant Ruth Hussey in *State of the Union*. Kay was first contacted in August 1945 about appearing in the play, but decided the role wasn't right for her. After apparently regaining her confidence, she readily agreed when Hayward asked again in June 1946. She finished *Wife Wanted* on July 3, 1946, and simply wrote, "Finished *Wife Wanted* — dead."[49] She had no way of knowing this was her final film appearance.

The next day — Independence Day — she started packing and arrived in New York on July 7. After brief stays at the Hotel Gotham and Hotel Drake, Kay moved into the Hotel

New Weston at 34 East 50th Street. This would be her New York residence from 1946 to 1948 until she moved into an apartment on Madison Avenue and 61st Street. Rehearsals started a few days later, giving her little time to socialize with Grace Moore, Ivan Goff, and other friends. The first weeks of rehearsal didn't go well, and Kay insisted Jetti come to New York to help prepare for the production.

By mid–August, Kay began mentioning the man who would become her next lover, stage manager Happy Graham. He'd graduated from Kansas State Teachers College in 1934, and then subsequently received his masters in 1938 from Northwestern University. After graduation, he taught at the City College of Chicago and then became head of the speech department at Amarillo College in 1940 and 1941. From there, Howard 'Happy' Graham worked at the famed Pasadena Playhouse[50] in the mid–1940s, where he was an actor, stage manager, and director for two years. Happy, who was several years younger than Kay, ingratiated himself with the star by joining her for drinks and listening to baseball games on her radio. Happy also apparently shared Kay's love of drink.

HOTEL NEW WESTON

HOTEL NEW WESTON, NEW YORK, N.Y.
Kay moved to the Hotel New Weston in August 1946 when she returned to New York City to appear in State of the Union. *In May 1948, she moved out and bought an apartment at 61st Street and Madison Avenue.*

Kay made her first appearance in *State of the Union* on September 2, 1946, at New York's Hudson Theatre. Her guests that first month included Greta Garbo paramour Mercedes D'Acosta and old flame Bayard Kilgour — this time he came with his wife, though Kay later met him alone in her hotel on several occasions during the run of the play.[51] Friends who attended the show and visited Kay backstage included Ronald Colman and wife Benita Hume, Elsie and Charles Mendl, Jane Wyatt, Kendall Milestone, Joan Payson, Margaret Case, and others. The reviews were generally favorable, though most focused on her wardrobe. "Kay Francis can still wear clothes. She's handsome in her first act gray suit, lovely in a canary yellow crepe robe and night dress, striking in her second act green traveling suit, sensational in her black dinner dress, and a DRU-EAM in her third act white crepe with sequins evening dress."[52]

Unfortunately, Kay became ill in November, suffering from abdominal pain. Cancer was feared. She continued in the production for several more weeks, but finally left the show on November 30 and returned home, where she underwent successful surgery on December 3.[53] The operation was probably a hysterectomy. It was two weeks before Kay saw visitors, and then there was a steady procession, including Otto Preminger, Van Johnson, Walter Van Peet, Maybelle Webb, and so on.

Kay celebrated Christmas Eve at Kendall Milestone's party, but was ill on Christmas Day. She briefly visited with her mother, and then quickly returned to bed. It was a slow recovery for Kay. She listened to the Rose Bowl on the radio on New Years Day — after turning down an invitation to celebrate at Douglas Fairbanks, Jr.'s. Indeed, Kay took it easy the first few days of 1947, hoping to conserve her energy so she could return to New York and *State of the Union.*

The following years—1947 and 1948 — would be some of Kay's most difficult. Although she continued to be successful on stage, she lost one of her true good friends in a tragic accident — and almost died herself.

CHAPTER 13

Disaster, 1947–1949

"Grace Moore killed — Copenhagen air crash! God!— cooked dinner for Happy."[1]

After saying goodbye to her mother and friends, Kay left for New York on January 4, 1947, where she was greeted by Jetti and husband Louis Ames at Penn Station. On January 20, 1947, Kay returned to the cast of *State of the Union* and restarted her affair with Happy. Although one of their favorite activities was making fried chicken in her suite, they were now arguing frequently. It's interesting to note that Kay's diary entries now rarely included critiques of her sexual activities, a change that seemed to have coincided with Hap. While Kay was probably just as sexually active as before, she was now in her 40s and no longer wrote about her experiences with a schoolgirl's enthusiasm.

Kay was eager to work again, but wasn't feeling physically well, and may have returned to the stage before she was ready. On January 26, 1947, during the Broadway run of *State of the Union*, Kay's good friend Grace Moore was killed in a plane crash. Moore, who'd known Kay since Grace's first stint in Hollywood in 1930, was one of Kay's most intimate friends. Grace wrote about Kay in her 1944 autobiography. "One of our [she and husband Val] boon cronies was— and still is— Kay Francis, who, if anything, has grown more beautiful through the years. When Kay and I get together, it means late nights of fun and gossip or a houseful of mutual friends, for Kay's hospitality is famous. She's shrewd, she's wise, she's completely adult, completely lovable. She doesn't sing, she doesn't dance, she hasn't the experience and training that the legitimate stage might have given her, and she has always frankly said that Hollywood was her road to financial security. Yet with it all she's intensely sincere. She's done the best she can with her screen work, and by it has won a great following as well as the financial security. Never one for swank, she has put her money into safe investments, has foregone fancy real-estate plunges and the usual Hollywood splendor, and has lived with all the simplicity and grace that is the hallmark of her charm."[2]

Born Mary Willie Grace Moore in Slabtown, Tennessee, in 1898, Grace was raised in nearby Jellico. Her successful singing career led to an invitation to Hollywood in the late 1920s. However, Irving Thalberg refused to renew her contract after two pictures—*A Lady's Morals* and New *Moon*.[3] Grace's struggles with her weight and the fact that her films had done poorly—combined with what was perceived as temperamental behavior—sealed her fate. A few years later, Moore, however, triumphantly returned to Hollywood to appear in 1934's *One Night of Love*—and received an Oscar nomination. Through it all, Kay remained a loyal friend. Like Kay, Grace was known for her beautiful gowns. Named by Flo Ziegfeld as one of the world's ten most beautiful women, the "Tennessee Nightingale" was still hugely popular when her plane crashed in Copenhagen, Denmark, on January 26, 1947. She had just played to a sold-out audience and was on her way to Stockholm, Sweden. Also on the plane that tragic day were Sweden's Prince Gustav Adolph, Danish actress and singer Gerda Neumann, film producer Jens Dennow, and eighteen others. The crash was blamed on pilot error — the pilot failed to disengage the elevator-lock. Kathryn Grayson later played Grace Moore in the 1953 movie *So This Is Love*.[4]

Kay was unable to attend Grace's memorial service because of rehearsals for *State of the Union*. She did, however, go to the 21 Club on the night of the memorial to reminisce with Grace's close friends Louis Bromfield and Clifton Webb.

During the first part of 1947, Kay and Hap argued so often it's difficult to understand why she — or Hap, for that matter — put up with it. Still, Kay did manage to see plays and movies and visit old friends. For example, on February 6 she saw Ina Claire in *The Fatal Weakness*— and noted that Noel Coward and Neysa McMein sat behind her. She also attended a party for Noel hosted by Margaret Case. On March 22, Kay received an award at the Waldorf-Astoria Hotel from the Fashion Academy, naming her the best dressed woman on stage.[5] A day later, accompanied by Hap, she attended a Maurice Chevalier one-man show at the Henry Miller Theatre on March 23, 1947.[6] Kay and Hap also saw *Finian's Rainbow*[7] on April 13, which, for some reason, precipitated yet another fight: "Home and real knock-out fight! Whew!"[8]

Kay and the *State of the Union* cast vacationed from May 18 to June 15. Kay visited Grace Moore's widower Val, and also socialized with Margaret Case, Jessica, Elsa Maxwell, Millicent Hearst, and other friends. Additional activities included working crossword puzzles, listening to ballgames— she'd become a Brooklyn Dodgers fan — and even a couple of appointments at Elizabeth Arden's salon. Kay also noted attending *Brigadoon*, but didn't enjoy it.

During the summer, Kay struggled with health problems, sometimes missing performances because she'd lost her voice. *State of the Union* closed on Broadway on September 13, 1947, and five days later she took the show on the road. Kay's company was basically a "bus-and-truck company" tour, albeit by train. The first ten weeks of the tour involved 60 play dates, 48 of which were one-night stands. By the time the tour began, Kay's relationship with Hap was on-again, off-again, marked by frequent fighting, often precipitated by drinking. None of this bode well for the future.

Kay and company arrived in Wilmington, Delaware, on September 18, and then moved north through Pennsylvania. Here, Kay gave a brief interview, explaining how thrilled she was with the play. "It is a magnificent role in a magnificent play, and any actor would want to do much more than his best when provided with such excellent material. I have never worked so hard, but I don't remember when I have had as much fun and pleasure — and work — appearing in any play or picture."[9] The tour continued into New Jersey and western New York State, with major bookings in Schenectady, Syracuse, and Rochester. It was in the latter city where things first turned ugly.

On October 12, 1947, the local newspaper reported that Kay paid legal fees so her escort could be released from jail. The escort was Howard Graham, and he was charged with assault for hitting Rudolph Duro, a 22-year-old fan who had shown up at the Hotel Seneca lobby one Saturday morning. Apparently Duro brought photos of Kay's African USO tour and wanted to share them with the star. Somehow this led to an argument and the arrest, though Duro later agreed to drop the charges.

"I never wanted to be a star. I have loathed being a star. There's too much heartbreak to it. There's too much strain, too much publicity, which means too little privacy, too much of everything I detest, and far too little of everything I value. There is too much responsibility attached to being a star. Non-stars have a much better time of it. I loathe the business of stardom. I hate planned interviews. I hate being 'snapped' when I'm walking down the street. I hate being stared at when I go out to lunch with my friends. I hate taking stills. I hate being mobbed when I go to have my hair done."[10]

Playbills for the tour, one of which featured a striking photo of Kay in a basic black dress and pearls, capitalized on Kay's connection to fashion. A two-page spread, captioned "Let's Go Shopping with Kay," included piquant instructions for women in the audience. "A firm foundation is definitely essential! Looking for date bait? Then hie yourself down to the French Shop and see their dreamy collection of Jonathan Logan styles. Your perfumes and cosmetics should match the sophistication of autumn's mood. The wind-blown look is definitely out for fall. Bandbox grooming is an essential part of the new 'elegant' fashions."[11]

The tour—an interminable grind of one-night stands and numbing overnight rides on crowded "milk trains"—made Kay cranky. Her diary entry for October 25 provided a clue as to her state of mind: "Did we go by bus or train?"[12] Upon arriving in one city, she surrendered to her longstanding, innate dislike of reporters and interviews. "Miss Francis stepped off the Lehigh Valley train from Ithaca and granted a one word interview at the station. The word was 'No.'"[13]

Residents of Homer remember her as Katherine Gibbs, but to the theater-going public she is known as Kay Francis. Miss Francis is Homer's one connection with the movie world. She is the granddaughter of one of this community's foremost pioneer families, and her father was the late Joseph Gibbs, a well-known actor of three decades ago and a nationally known horse fancier. For a number of years and up until she was 12 or 13 years old, Miss Francis (then known as Katherine Gibbs) used to spend her summers here with her father's cousin, Mrs. Justin T. Cook. Older residents remember her as a slender, dark-haired girl."[14]

The tour continued through Ohio and reached southern Michigan by the end of October. Local newspapers in Ann Arbor, Lansing, and Kalamazoo reported on her hometown connection—apparently to Kay's consternation and irritation. One article included a photo of Kay at age eight, supplied by an "aunt," a Mrs. Justin T. Cook of Albion, Michigan, with a caption noting that Kay had spent her childhood summers on the Gibbs farm in nearby Homer. A second article, "Homer Claims Kay Francis," provided a brief but flattering biography of Kay's father, Joseph Gibbs. Another article, published on October 29, 1947, reported that Kay gave a four-minute telephone interview (she also gave a different reporter a *two-*minute interview!) in which she was "charming, but business-like."[15] Kay explained that she had no desire to visit her father's grave. "I've never seen him since I was three years old. That was in New York."[16] Someone had the poor taste to ask if Kay — or her mother — would be interested in old correspondence from Katherine to Joe. The letters had been kept by a local attorney, who was looking forward to cleaning out his files. "Miss Francis said she was certain her mother wouldn't care to have any of her old letters to Joe Gibbs."[17]

Kay had no interest in Gibbs genealogy, and also claimed she'd never set foot in Homer. Still, she told the reporter she'd be visiting "with two of her mother's aunts,"[18] one of whom was Mrs. Justin T. Cook, who most definitely was her *father's* relative —*not* her mother's. Kay also thought it important to point out that she was a Democrat — not a Republican — as had been printed in the latest edition of *Who's Who*. She wisely refused to comment on the House Un-American Activities hearings — no doubt wanting to avoid being called to testify. "I have nothing to say. Don't get me into that. I refuse to be quoted."[19] Kay concluded the interview with a snappish response to a society editor's question about how she'd learned to make a bed so quickly, part of a key scene in *State of the Union*. No doubt with an eye roll, Kay replied, "An actress has to know how to act. After all, I've been doing this part for almost two years."[20]

Kay's visit to Michigan created much excitement. One can imagine she was quite unhappy when one article pointed to a parallel between her career and her father's. "Many Homer people will journey to Jackson Oct. 27 to see Miss Francis in her stage appearance at the Michigan Theater just as others did three generations ago who chartered a special train to go to Albion to see her father, Joseph Gibbs, in 'The Westerner.'"[21]

Kay, as usual, had health problems on this tour, including sore throats and head colds. Several articles pointed out that Miss Francis was suffering from "a bad cold and a coarse voice."[22] In November, the company moved into the Midwest with one-night stands in Kansas City, Topeka, Wichita, and Kay's birthplace, Oklahoma City.[23] Texas followed, and then New Orleans and Atlanta. Relieved to be away from Homer and the relentless questions, Kay had no inkling the New Year would bring worse luck.

"I was interviewed hundreds of times. Do you like rice pudding, Miss Francis? Do you advocate spinach for children? Do you believe in roller skates? You get so you stop knowing the difference between roller skates and rice pudding."[24]

January 1948 brought more one-night stands and a seemingly endless succession of small cities in Illinois and Indiana, followed by a week in Detroit at the Shubert Theatre. The frustrations and strain in her personal relationship with Graham, combined with the stress of the tour and inability to shake her respiratory illness, eventually proved too much. The explosion occurred in Columbus, Ohio, almost two weeks after her forty-third birthday — and only a few days from the first anniversary of Grace Moore's death. Kay's diary entry described what happened on January 22: "Shopping — early dinner — after show all hell broke loose and me too many pills."[25] Her entry for January 23 was equally dramatic: "Out and almost out for good! White Cross Hospital at 7 am — ambulance — Dr. Rusoff— Hap in jail 5 hours — murder charge!!"[26]

Newspapers around the country reported that Kay had been rushed to White Cross Hospital in critical condition, and Howard Graham was in police custody for investigation of attempted murder. Mr. Graham had called the police to Kay's hotel room. Found in a semi-conscious state, with suspicious bruises and second-degree burns, she was rushed to the hospital. Journalists were quick to report that two partly-consumed bottles of Scotch whiskey were found in the room, suggesting a "wild party."[27] Articles also ungallantly noted that Graham was 37 and Kay 43.

The story Graham told police — and Kay later corroborated — makes little sense until one realizes alcohol was involved. And then it makes wincing sense. Kay, still suffering from the cold that had been hanging on for weeks, opened *State of the Union* on January 18 at Columbus' Hartman Theater. She left her hotel with wet hair — covered with a turban — for a radio interview, and the cold worsened. Audience members who saw her performance on January 22 told reporters that it was obvious she had a bad cold, but added that, "Miss Francis gave a magnificent performance."[28] Graham told police he'd left Kay's room at the Deshler-Wallick Hotel about 2:30 A.M. on the morning of January 23, but she phoned him around 6:30 A.M., complaining of illness and telling him she'd overdosed on sleeping pills. When he returned to her room, he called Dr. Maurice Rusoff, whose advice was to give Kay fresh air. Graham opened a window and propped Kay up, putting her head out the window into the cold air. Kay, semi-comatose, leaned against the hot air register under the window and severely burned her legs. Graham compounded things by accidentally pouring hot coffee on her neck. When Kay fainted, he called a doctor. Police took Graham into custody at the hospital, and detained him for five hours.

Hap made no friends at the police station. Officer Clifton asked Graham to submit to a urinalysis. Graham refused and then engaged in a snippy exchange:

"I'm not doing anything," Graham said.

"You're not on the stage now,"[29] Clifton told Graham. "You're in jail."

Graham reportedly had the last word: "You can conduct your own investigation."[30]

When Kay regained consciousness, she confirmed Graham's story and explained that she'd been ill for two weeks. She added that it'd been a tough tour, and admitted mistakenly taking too many sleeping pills. Assistant Chief of Detectives Jay Steele released Graham and announced the case was closed. William Blair, the company's manager, described Graham's arrest as "a ridiculous mistake."[31]

During her hospitalization, Kay's stomach was pumped, and she was placed in an oxygen tent. Her legs were burned from her knees to her hips. Embarrassed, Kay insisted on leaving the hospital. She especially wanted to escape from the press, who were all over the scandalous story. Well-meaning friends, including Miss P and Kay's maid Eunice Hawley, first took Kay to Louis Bromfield's Malabar Farm in Perrysville, Ohio,[32] on February 4. However, the delay complicated her recovery. A few days later, with the help of Jetti and Louis Ames, Kay was moved to New York and seen by Dr. Russell Cecil, who ordered her admitted to the New York Hospital burn unit. She registered under the name of Mrs. Francis Thompson and underwent her first surgery on February 7. In the next month, she had at least six more operations. The pain was tremendous. On February 24, she wrote, "Some kind of day — [Dr.] Conway and [Dr.] Stark here at 6:30 — turned me over and I cussed like hell while redressed."[33] Kay would continue to endure tedious and painful therapy, and eventually had to wear special support garments to strengthen her muscles during a lengthy recovery.

"Feeling lousy — legs bad, etc. — Adnia here for lunch — Hap at 6:30 and our usual battle — guess that's the real me."[34]

Visitors streamed in, including Bill Gaston,[35] Adnia Rice, Jetti and Lou Ames, Jessica Barthelmess, and even Hap — who, believe it or not, continued to be in Kay's life. Adnia was a new friend, but one who became an intimate one for the next several years. Rice had graduated with a master's degree from the Pasadena Playhouse in 1947, and then made her stage debut in Los Angeles that same year in *State of the Union*. She likely knew Happy Graham and got to know Kay when she toured with her in *State of the Union*.[36]

By March, Kay was improving but suffering from depression and crying jags. By the middle of that month, she finally was able to walk, though stiffly. She left the hospital on March 21 and checked into the New Weston Hotel. Almost immediately, she began talking to agent Alan Brock about possible new shows.

Although Hap continued to be in her life, his role lessened after she interviewed actor Joel Ashley on April 14 for a role in *The Last of Mrs. Cheyney*. Meanwhile, Kay, who'd been looking at New York apartments for months, finally decided to leave Hollywood for good. She sold her Beverly Hills home to Solly Gluck for $100,000, thus severing all connection with Hollywood, and moved into an apartment building at 31 West 61st St., on the corner of Madison Avenue.[37]

In truth, Kay never liked Hollywood. As early as 1934, she'd told an interviewer she was biding her time. "Oh, I hope when my time comes and I'm through, I'll have vision enough and sense enough to clear out."[38] She also had little respect for Hollywood's product. "With the finest talent in the world right here in our midst, nothing great ever goes out of Hollywood."[39] She lived for her trips to Europe and New York. "I can't understand people complaining when they have to go on a location trip. They should give thanks for the opportunity to go away from here for a while, whether it's only for a day or a week."[40]

"We never stand still in this life. We either go forward or we go backward. That seems to be an eternal law of nature and I'm going forward!"[41]

In order to salvage her career — and life — Kay made a decision that determined the course of events for the next seven years. She decided to concentrate on Atlantic Coast summer theater.

Dramatic changes in East Coast summer theater began in 1946 when gasoline restrictions were lifted and automobile production resumed in Detroit. "The warm weather months of 1946 saw remarkable activity and revived interest in the 'straw hat' theatre. When we consider that in both the previous summers there had been less than 30 theatres in operation, and that during the current season there were more than 100, we get a good idea of the increase in business. It was, in fact, one of the most successful seasons in summer theatre history. It was the small eastern 'barn theatres' that were the heart of the movement. Many of them were poorly equipped as to stage facilities, and had small seating capacities, but vacationists and natives alike eagerly turned out to see the shows. Some of the companies used the resident stock system. More popular, however, was the visiting star system, and many well-known names from the legitimate stage as well as from Hollywood helped keep business teeming."[42]

The timing could not have been more perfect for Kay. She recovered well enough from her injury to begin working again in the summer of 1948. Kay selected Frederick Lonsdale's 1925 hit, *The Last of Mrs. Cheyney*, which had been a huge success for Ina Claire, Broadway's premiere drawing-room comedienne. The play had been filmed twice — first as an early talkie with Norma Shearer in 1929, and then as a vehicle for Joan Crawford in 1937.[43]

Kay played Fay Cheyney, a jewel thief posing as a society woman. She steals from her rich acquaintances until she is caught. However, the guests, fearful that she'll reveal their secrets, offer to pay her off. Instead, the gracious Mrs. Cheyney confesses and gets a marriage proposal from a stylish Lord who loves her.

"Opening Princeton — rehearsing all day — shambles of a show — so what?"[44]

Kay began her first season of summer stock the week of June 7 at the McCarter Theatre in Princeton, New Jersey, and concluded it the week of September 20 at the Montclair Theatre in New Jersey.[45] The critics were unimpressed with the play, describing it as dated, not terribly amusing, and ersatz Oscar Wilde — but were charmed by Kay, and, of course, noted her fashion flair.

Kay discussed her summer stock experience with a reporter. "It really is a grind," Miss Francis said. "Each week I'm in a different place and playing with new actors and actresses. Then there are rehearsals, broadcasts and many other appointments before moving on to the next engagement. I opened the summer season June 7, and before it ends, I will have toured eight theatres on the straw hat circuit and four on the subway circuit around New York. I arrived at Whalom at 4 o'clock Sunday morning from Gloucester with a very bad cold. Next week I'll be in Marblehead and then Saratoga, New York."[46]

She had her reasons, however, for continuing to tour. According to agent Alan Brock, Kay went back on the stage after her Hollywood career ended because she felt she owed the public for her career. Perhaps equally important, she wanted to show everyone she could still make a dazzling appearance on the stage and carry a star vehicle. It also was lucrative, and Kay wasn't ready to retire — especially now that she had a handsome new leading man.

By fall, romance was in full bloom between Kay and Joel Ashley, her co-star in *The Last of Mrs. Cheyney*. Ashley's closest brush with fame came in 1944 when he appeared on Broadway with Mae West in *Catherine Was Great*. The rest of his career was the classic story of the attractive actor who never quite made it to leading man status. Ashley was born on April 7, 1919, in Atlanta, Georgia. He never knew his father, and spent much of his early youth living with his grandparents in Macon, Georgia. He attended military schools, including the Georgia Military Academy and Peekskill, before he and his mother moved to California after his aunt, Barbara Rodgers,[47] married an MGM studio executive. Mother Beulah worked as a script girl at the studio, and Joel attended the Black Foxe military school.[48]

By his late teens, Joel was hanging out on studio lots, and entered show business as a double for Errol Flynn in *Captain Blood* (1935). After attending the American Academy of Dramatic Arts, he worked on various radio soap operas and on stage. His theatrical career was interrupted by a stint in the Marines from 1940 to 1941, from which he was honorably discharged because of a bad knee. Ashley next appeared on Broadway in *The Sun Field, Another Love Story, War President* (as Abraham Lincoln), and *The American Way*. On August 2, 1944, he appeared on Broadway as Prince Potemkin in *Catherine Was Great* with Mae West, who had personally chosen him for the part. Just before meeting Kay, he'd toured with Elizabeth Bergner in *The Two Mrs. Carrolls*.[49]

Joel, fourteen years younger than Kay, proved to be a less-than-ideal boyfriend. He had a worse drinking problem than Hap, and was married and a father of two daughters. He'd married Margalo Francis Wilson[50] on June 6, 1942. Their daughter, Margalo Francis, was born July 26, 1944, and a second child, Laurel, was born July 11, 1947.

His first child, now known as Margalo Ashley-Farrand, recalled meeting Miss Francis when she was about four at the Ashleys' 24 Gramercy Park apartment. "Mom was not too pleased, because Kay was too interested in Dad." Kay, however, came bearing a gift for Joel's oldest daughter. "She gave me a blue sweater that I wore till I was eight, and wore it out. My mother was not happy with that. I knew she wasn't happy I was wearing that sweater." Kay left a huge impression on the four-year-old. "I mean, she had all this charisma.

I definitely remember her. I'll bet everybody liked her. She had a huge amount of charisma. You have no idea. She walked into that room and you could feel her energy. You could just feel it. It was kind of overwhelming."[51]

By November, Mrs. Ashley, who was not as charmed, had had enough — she ordered Joel to leave. For the next few years, Joel would go back and forth between Kay and Margalo. He'd also battle his heavy drinking, periodically going on and off the wagon.

Favorite Stranger, a comedy by novice playwright Eleanore Sellars, had a plot that sounded like one of Kay's scripts from her Warner Brothers days. A handbill, with a glamorous portrait of Kay as Chalice Chadwick on one side, described the play as "a gay comedy which handles the modern problem of love affairs and divorce with consummate tact and humor. Chalice Chadwick (Kay Francis) is the long neglected wife of a man who has forgotten to return from Paris at the war's end. A handsome bachelor moves in next door and, being a doctor, prescribes a more interesting social life. But a naval commander moves faster than the doctor and Chalice finds herself in the enjoyable position of breakfasting with two charming men every Sunday morning. When her husband returns unexpectedly, ready to resume his marriage but with one eye cast wistfully toward the delights of love in Paris, Chalice is truly in a dilemma."

Kay hoped the show might eventually make its way to Broadway. The tour began on December 25, 1948, in Elmira, New York. Kay thought the production was uneven, but, fortunately, the reviews were flattering. Indeed, a reviewer called it "a splendid Christmas gift."[52] The production continued through the winter of 1949, closing on April 2, 1949, at the Nixon Theatre in Pittsburgh, Pennsylvania. The reviews were tepid, but enthusiastic about Kay's performance. "Miss Francis tries very hard to make her end of things go. She gives her character a lot of charm and vivacity."[53] Some reviewers were even more excited about her wardrobe, reporting its cost and describing individual costumes in detail. "Women in the audience were anxious, and well pleased, to see Miss Francis $3,500 wardrobe, cut out to make the most of her reputation as one of the theatre's best-dressed. She appeared in an especially fetching black dinner dress of taffeta with a perky bustle of shocking pink roses."[54]

"Finally got a doctor for Joel — a mess! — 2 shows — closed "Favorite Stranger"— left for New York on 12:42 A.M. train."[55]

In many respects, Kay's choice of Joel matched previous choices such as Harold Healy and Hap Graham. He was a drinking companion who also proved a willing lover. Like Hap, he was a younger man who may have eased some of Kay's fears of aging. However, Joel was an alcoholic binger with a violent streak. On April 1, 1949, Kay and Joel were in Pittsburgh appearing in *Favorite Stranger.* After the performance, they went to the Dixon Café. According to Kay, they unwisely "picked up 3 guys and back to my room — Joel beaten up!"[56] Kay and Joel returned to New York — after canceling two shows scheduled in Wheeling, West Virginia — where they continued to drink and argue.

Meanwhile, Kay considered other shows, including *Portrait in Black,* written by former boyfriend Ivan Goff, which she eventually turned down.[57] For his part, Joel continued to act out, sometimes showing up drunk, and other times disappearing, forcing Kay to hunt for him.

After *Favorite Stranger,* Kay prepared another package deal for the summer of 1949. She chose Rachel Crother's 1929 hit play *Let Us Be Gay* — again selecting Joel as her leading man. MGM's first lady, Norma Shearer, appeared in the 1930 film version, playing Kitty

Brown, a role created on the stage by Francine Larrimore. *Let Us Be Gay* is a typical 1920s drawing-room play about weekend guests at a Long Island estate and their romantic problems. The hostess has invited a sophisticated lady of affairs to seduce an older man with whom her granddaughter is infatuated, hoping to prevent them from having an affair before the young girl's impending wedding. It turns out that the gentleman in question was formerly married to the lady, who successfully entraps him again.

Kay's season began the week of June 3, 1949, at the Bucks County Playhouse, and her appearance garnered favorable reviews. This time the local critics commented more on the play and Kay's performance, and less on her wardrobe. "'Let Us Be Gay' is the type of vehicle in which Miss Francis is at her best. It shows her vivacious character, the clever manner in which she can read lines with that peculiar but effective voice which endeared her to millions, and her ability to be dramatic without resorting to heroics. This sterling actress has lost none of her charm, nor poise, nor those fetching mannerisms made so telling in screen close-ups. Take for instance the little trick of wrinkling her nose as a flashing smile lights her features."[58]

In addition to her stage performances, Kay continued to participate in local radio broadcasts to promote her tour. For example, the week of June 21, residents of Worcester, Massachusetts, tuned in to hear Kay Francis talk about grooming on WTAG's *Curtain Call* with "Julie 'n' Johnny."

Radio, stage, and film — Kay had successfully conquered all in her career. Television, however, would prove more vexing. She had a push-pull relationship with this medium. On the one hand, it was lucrative, and the offers, especially for experienced actors, were plentiful. However, it terrified her. As the 1950s approached, Kay had the opportunity to forge a career in television. However, her phobia ultimately led, instead, to sporadic television appearances, followed by more stage work and then, finally, retirement.

CHAPTER 14

The Comeback, 1949–1955

"To tell you the truth, I'm afraid of television."[1]

Kay's first attempt to overcome her television phobia came in the fall of 1949. Her debut was scheduled for September 19 on the *Chevrolet Tele-Theatre* in the teleplay "Leo and Sagittarius," written by Jack Bentkover. Although Kay was a Capricorn, the plot sounded tailor-made — she'd play a fashion designer who falls in love, though a horoscope complicates matters. The cast included Joel Ashley, Marjorie Gateson, Enid Markey, and Adnia Rice. It was wise to include the moral support of Joel, Adnia, and Marjorie, who'd appeared with Kay in *False Madonna* back in 1932.[2] At the last minute, however, Kay withdrew "on orders of her physician,"[3] and Vicki Cummings replaced her — too late to change *TV Guide* listings, which has resulted in some confusion as to whether Kay actually appeared on the show.

Kay wasn't shy about stating her main reason for avoiding television. "Women look too darn old on it." Obviously a keen observer, Kay added, "I have the utmost admiration for it, but from the standpoint of an actress, it's bad. For a singer or dancer it doesn't hold the same problems. You see, the image is so small that all expression is lost on the video screen. Of course television still has a long way to go. Right now, it compares with the flicker days in the motion picture industry. There are a lot of things that have to be ironed out. Television doesn't permit much mobility as far as a legitimate show is concerned. And the lights, and the cost, and — oh, any number of things."[4]

Kay felt much more comfortable appearing on stage. Encouraged by the success of *Let Us Be Gay* on the summer circuit, she briefly toured with the play in October and November 1949. Then, in January 1950, Kay revived *The Last of Mrs. Cheyney* for an Atlanta engagement. While Kay and her wardrobe were praised as usual, the critics couldn't understand why she bothered.

Kay, accompanied by Joel and Eunice, returned to New York after the Atlanta shows and began preparations for a more ambitious project — *The Web and the Rock*. Kay was delighted by the project and looked forward to the challenging piece. Her most constant friends during this time were Joel, Adnia, and actor Jerry Shaw. By now, she'd comfortably settled into her life as a New Yorker. She also, like many other well-to-do Americans, had bought a TV set and become a regular watcher. In Kay's spare time, she also occasionally played canasta and saw movies, including *Samson and Delilah* and *The Third Man*. On February 1, 1950, she celebrated old friend William Powell's sixty-first birthday at the 21 Club.

In March, Kay appeared in *Let Us Be Gay* in Phoenix, and then later that month traveled to Jacksonville, Florida, for the same production. She next appeared in *Goodbye, My Fancy* on May 23, 1950, at the Flatbush Theatre in Brooklyn, and then made the rounds again on the subway circuit in the Bronx, Coney Island, Passaic, New Jersey and Rockville Centre, Long Island. The subway circuit of theaters was operated by producer George Brandt, who provided five weeks of "legit" theater in the greater New York City area.

Goodbye, My Fancy had been a Broadway hit in 1948, first with Madeleine Carroll and then Ann Harding, and was popular in summer stock with Sylvia Sidney. A film version with Joan Crawford was released in 1951. The setting for Fay Kanin's romantic comedy is the Good Hope College for Women. Congresswoman Agatha Reed returns to the campus to receive an honorary degree from the college that expelled her 20 years before. She discovers that the man she loves, her former history professor and now college president, may no longer share her ideals. Her visit forces her to choose between two suitors, and prompts the college community to reexamine its values. The tour closed the week of July 10, after two additional play dates at summer theaters in Norwich, Connecticut, and Somerset, Massachusetts. A typical review spoke of Kay's talent and charm. "The star's genuine acting, coupled with the attractiveness of her unique voice, provided that polish in a production which seldom will find its equal. Miss Francis will not be forgotten by local theatre-goers."[5]

Kay finally made her television debut on July 15, 1950, on the CBS television show *This Is Show Business*. Kay, Herb Shriner, and Patrice Munsel were guests on the program's first anniversary broadcast. The variety show's odd premise was this—guests dropped by with a problem, and panelists, including Abe Burrows and George S. Kaufman, endeavored to solve it.[6] Sadly, there appear to be no copies extant today as this would have been America's first glimpse of Kay on the small screen. People who knew her often commented on her warmth, charm, and energy—no doubt these were the qualities that audience members saw that night. Although her vivacious, gracious personality was different from her film siren image, Kay likely would have been welcomed into American homes—if she'd only had the confidence to choose the new medium for her future career.

Kay chose instead to return to the stage. Her next project was Lester Cohen's dramatization of Thomas Wolfe's novel *The Web and the Rock*. The John Huntington production, which opened on August 14 in Saratoga Springs, was advertised as a pre–Broadway tryout, and hopes were high that Kay would return to New York in a hit. Unfortunately, while the reviews were favorable to Kay and Joel, the production itself generated no great excitement, probably due to the difficulty of converting a 700-page novel into a three-act play. The second—and final—play date for *The Web and the Rock* was in Marblehead, Massachusetts, the week of August 21. Critics and audiences agreed it was a nice try, but after two rather low-key receptions, all involved agreed not to bring the play to Broadway.

Summer stock was a long way from Hollywood, and probably more reminiscent of Kay's days with Stuart Walker's company. A Marblehead resident recalled the conditions. "In Marblehead there was no air conditioning, just the open windows with curtains drawn at matinees to keep out the hot sun. The audience and the actors suffered the heat together. During evening performances the train whistles at the crossings could be heard in the theatre and often came at just the wrong moment in a serious play." Despite this, the writer added, "Miss Francis was always a delight to see."[7]

On November 7, 1950, Kay made her second television appearance, this time on a live broadcast of CBS' *Prudential Family Playhouse*. The teleplay, "Call It a Day," was based on a movie released by Warner Brothers in 1937, and concerned the romantic effects of spring's first day. Kay's co-stars included Peggy Ann Garner and John Loder. The *Playhouse*, an hour-long drama, was one of television's most prestigious early shows, known for hiring Hollywood and stage stars, such as Helen Hayes, Ruth Gordon, Bert Lahr, and even a young Grace Kelly.

The year 1951 began with Kay's January 8 appearance in "The Long Way Round," a skit on ABC's *Hollywood Screen Test*. The program, which first aired in 1948, provided an opportunity for would-be stars to appear in a scene with an established actor.

Kay turned 46 a few days later and spent the early months of 1951 looking for a new apartment — always an angst-ridden occasion for Kay. She also attended the opera and saw friends such as Jetti and Lou, Jessica, producer Richard Barr,[8] Adnia, and Joel. In addition, she discussed with Patsy Ruth Miller the possibility of reviving *Windy Hill*— with Joel as her co-star.[9]

Later that spring, gossip columnists dropped hints that Kay and Joel Ashley had married. "Members of the Sardi set are spreading a rumor that Kay Francis is a secret bride," the *Boston Globe* reported. "How about it Kay?"[10] Kay and Joel denied any marriage had — or would — take place. They were right. In fact, Joel was still married to Margalo— and continued to show up late for appointments and drink too much. The relationship with Joel was so stormy that Kay made a special note when things were going well.

Perhaps out of desperation, Kay had a brief March affair with composer Deems Taylor, who was twenty years older. Born Joseph Deems Taylor in New York in 1885, Taylor attended New York University and was a respected opera composer, music critic, and radio personality. Probably best known today for his narration in Disney's *Fantasia* (1940), Taylor was a ladies' man whose lovers included Dorothy Parker, Mary Astor, and Ginger Rogers. Taylor divided his time between California and New York, and probably knew Kay from her movie acting years. In 1945, Taylor married for a third time — this time to twenty-year-old costume designer and painter Lucille Watson-Little. They were still married at the time of his affair with Kay.[11]

Meanwhile, Kay, eager to line up additional jobs, met with George Oppenheimer to discuss his play *Mirror, Mirror,* and was hopeful about being cast in a *Somerset Maugham TV Theatre* adaptation of "Rain," which apparently was never made. At first glance, it doesn't seem ideal casting. In truth, Kay was probably too old to play prostitute Sadie, but it *is* intriguing to consider what she might have done with such a juicy part. Kay was disappointed to learn she lost the role. "Nothing happened and lost Somerset Maugham show — damn!"[12]

More positive news, however, came with the announcement a few days later that she'd been voted the "Most Co-operative Star" in summer theater.[13] Not content to rest on her laurels, Kay continued to make many phone calls during the spring of 1951, trying to find another play.

Unfortunately, Kay suffered another setback when she broke two toes on April 24. She didn't describe how the accident occurred, but was in bed and out of commission for a time. After the recuperation, she made a May appearance on another TV show, the *Betty Crocker Show*. Hosted by Adelaide Hawley, this afternoon program offered recipes and household tips.

Kay next appeared on the *Lux Video Theatre* on June 4, 1951, in "Consider the Lilies." Much like the *Lux Radio Theatre*, this television anthology series featured stars such as Peter Lorre, Edward G. Robinson, and Grace Kelly. In Kay's episode, the plot concerned an author caught between her moral beliefs and her publisher's efforts to spice up her manuscript. Her co-stars were Jerome Cowan, with whom she'd acted in *Divorce* (1946), and Joel Ashley.

Now a veteran of several live television broadcasts, Kay still had reservations about the medium. "Television is the most frightening form of the theatre. It's worse than the first night in the theatre. You do it once, and that's it. Thousands of people can watch every boner!"[14]

"You have to compromise with life. I found that out. You have to get the best out of what you're given — and that 'best' doesn't mean anything pretentious. It doesn't matter what you do, really — if you put your heart into it. Live for the day."[15]

After trying an experimental work that failed the previous summer, Kay returned to more familiar if less adventurous fare for her summer appearances in 1951. She first revived *Let Us Be Gay*, appearing in Pittsburgh the week of June ninth. Performing in an arena-style theater was a new experience for Kay — not one she supported whole-heartedly. "The medium is fun. But entirely new. I'm a bit old-fashioned because I like the footlights in front of me and the audience behind them."[16]

Kay once more chose a new play for a pre–Broadway tryout. This time, however, it was a comedy by George Oppenheimer, *Mirror, Mirror*, based on G.B. Stern's novel *The Back Seat*. The tour included nine dates, beginning in Westhampton, Long Island, the week of July 9, 1951. According to Oppenheimer, "Before rehearsals began, we rented a house in Westhampton with the idea of whipping the script into shape. Kay was great fun. Charming. I was very fond of her. She was a good scout — a good scout and a bad actress. The play wasn't a very good play, and the result was chaos. She wasn't the greatest person to work with because she couldn't remember lines easily. She was drinking in those days, too. She always claimed that she never drank when she worked, but she'd quit at eight and start again at eleven."[17]

In a lengthy Rhode Island interview, Kay and Joel Ashley discussed life on the straw hat stage circuit. Kay began by noting that her mother was still keeping scrapbooks detailing her career. "This scrapbook has been my mother's hobby ever since my career began, which is a long, long time ago. I send her some clippings, but she gets them all anyway from a clipping service. Once I built her a special room for the scrapbooks. The room turned out a lot smaller than it looked in the plans."[18]

In response to the usual comments about her well-known ability to wear clothes, Kay provided a reality check. "We travel with so much luggage that is just clothes for the stage, that we can't take a great deal of personal wardrobe along." When she began the road trip, she traveled with two trunks of her own, and one each for her maid and Mr. Ashley. "We learned," the tall actor commented.[19]

Kay had a lighthearted attitude about touring. "These days the Kay Francis theatrical package travels reasonably light, with Annabella the Third, Mike, Amos and Andy, Arrabella the Second, and Melissa. We give everything a name. It makes traveling more interesting. You know, we do a show for a week somewhere, and then leave Saturday night for the next theatre, arriving Sunday for rehearsal. So, I'm the delicatessen. I'm responsible for the coffee and the sandwiches, and the cigarettes and that sort of thing for the trip. I light cigarettes and I play the radio. I have to keep Joel awake. He drives. Then in the back seat, my maid and Jeanie Flanigan who plays my daughter in the play, have to keep me awake. So we give everything a name. The coffee jug is Mike, and the car is Arrabella the II, and Annabella III is the ice bucket, our third one, and Amos and Andy are cups and saucers, and Melissa is the theatrical trunk."[20]

Kay also discussed her unusual co-star — a feline. "The kitten in my show is a Rhode Island cat belonging to Mrs. Emma Lynch of Matunick. The cat is stage struck and a very competent actor. I've had all kinds. Every theater gives us a different cat. Some cats love the part in the play, are wonderful at rehearsals, good at the opening night, and then after that, they lose interest and go to sleep on my neck on the stage. It's discouraging."[21]

Once again, Kay's affinity for fashion came up. The reporter noted that Kay wore "an oyster gray linen dress especially designed for her by Bernard Newman of Bergdorf-Goodman. Open necked, with buttons to the waist, the garment had wide bands of Irish lace on the skirt. Her linen shoes matched the dress, and she carried an enormous natural colored Madagascar straw bag."[22]

George Oppenheimer later explained that, "Kay was more or less the manager. After the thing opened she wanted to go on with it. But there was very little money, and she wanted me to continue touring and rewriting without expense money."[23] He refused, and the play closed the week of September 3, 1951, in New Hope, Pennsylvania. Kay's reviews were mixed. While one wrote that, "the beauteous Miss Francis accomplishes a fine job,"[24] another complained that, "The role does not, unfortunately, suit Miss Francis very well. She acts it fussily without much show of the heartbreak underneath."[25] On September 8, Kay wrote, "End to horror season!"[26]

"Would you be a little careful when you write this story. My mother keeps a scrapbook."[27]

Before returning to Manhattan in the fall, Joel was in an automobile accident. Kay found him a doctor who tended to his injuries and then drove him back to New York. Kay was increasingly irritated with Joel — and frustrated with the search for the perfect apartment. On September 13, at the end of her rope, she wrote, "Damn everyone but me!"[28]

Gossip columnists were no longer reporting that Kay and Joel would marry. Instead, they mentioned frequent public squabbling. Joel became a less frequent companion, as Kay had found a new drinking partner. "Kay Francis is giving her parties at One Fifth Avenue these evenings. Her comedienne protégée, Adnia Rice, is laughing things up there."[29] One Fifth Avenue, a well-known building in the Village, housed a nightclub on the ground floor where Adnia performed.

Remarkably, Joel and Margalo remained married during his affair with Kay. In fact, they were still married, though in the process of divorcing, in September 1960, when Margalo died. After the affair, Joel liked to tell people that Kay had offered Margalo a significant sum of money to divorce him. According to daughter Margalo, "My father used to say that Kay offered my mother $100,000 to divorce him. But I think that was probably just my father pumping himself." While there's no doubt Kay found Joel desirable, it is highly unlikely, considering her distaste for spending a buck, that she would have made the offer. Margalo also believed that her father was likely using Kay. "I'm sure that my father had a thing going with her, and I'm also sure my father was smart enough to keep on her good side and let her think whatever she wanted to think so he kept working. Do I think he was ever in love with her? No. I don't think so. He never said so, and he would have."[30]

Joel finally took his last drink on December 12, 1962. He had married again, in February 1961, to Erna Maria Rade, and she helped him get off the bottle. Erna Maria died in 1984, and Joel soon found a companion in Connie Egan. Daughter Laurel passed away in 1997, and when Connie died in June 1998, Joel lost his will to live. He finally died on April 7, 2000 — his birthday. Margalo Ashley-Farrand explained that Joel expressed regrets while on his death bed. "When he was lying there in bed, starving himself to death, he was saying how much he was sorry — the thing he kept talking about is how sorry he was ... what he had done to my mother. That was the thing that he really felt bad about. He didn't talk about anything else. He wished he hadn't done that. He would talk at some length about how much he loved my mother, and she was the one."[31]

In the fall, Kay had another unidentified surgery on October 3, 1951. A little more than a week later, she again appeared on television. This time it was a panel game show—*Beat the Clock*. Hosted by Bud Collyer, the show also featured Ilka Chase, Peter Donald, and John Murray. Also in October, Kay considered the script for a television adaptation of "Bleak House," which apparently was never made, and then appeared on *The Frances Langford–Don Ameche TV Show*, a daily variety show.

"Saw new apartment 32 East 64th St.— to buy— can only hope!"[32]

Kay finally found her "perfect" apartment in November 1951. The co-op, on the corner of Madison Avenue at 32 East 64th Street, was previously owned by Mrs. Jack Donahue, the widow of the Broadway dancer. The building is still there today, and Kay resided in this chic East Side neighborhood, a block from 5th Avenue and Central Park, the rest of her life. The locale must have brought back memories of the early days of her career, since the apartment building was only a few blocks from some of her addresses in the late 1920s.[33]

The apartment was, of course, exquisitely furnished. While touring in *Theatre* the following year, Kay visited the Ferris Galleries in Winter Park, Florida, to view their porcelain collection. Her photo appeared in a gallery ad. "Miss Kay Francis is no novice to fine antiques in furniture. She leans toward period French which has been carefully selected over a number of years and adds to the décor of her New York home. She collects 18th century Meissen porcelains and has admired the museum quality collection of our galleries in Winter Park."[34] Kay's taste remained traditional, influenced by her East Coast Social Register background.

On November 6, 1951, Kay saw protégée Adnia Rice in a nightclub opening and very much enjoyed her show. She also appeared on ABC's prime-time quiz/talk show *Celebrity Time* with Red Smith. In November, she discussed plans—which, like many of her television proposals, never came to fruition—to star in a television adaptation of "The Web and the Rock."

On December 2, Kay was scheduled for an appearance on Ed Sullivan's *Toast of the Town*, but cancelled. She was in the midst of ending her relationship with Joel, as well as putting the finishing touches on her apartment. The electricity was rewired in the apartment so Kay could have an exciting new invention installed—air conditioning. Typically, the year ended dramatically. Kay had bought a dog earlier that month, but for some reason the dog didn't work out, and the SPCA picked him up. Sadly, Kay had already become attached to Baden, and her Christmas dinner was marred because of his absence.

Before the year ended, Kay attended Katharine Cornell's performance in a revival of Somerset Maugham's *The Constant Wife*. Finally, on New Year's Eve, Kay was invited to lunch by Margalo. It's not known if the lunch ever came off, but the drama was apparently resolved because Kay reported a quiet New Years Day alone.

"I have a sort of motto which expresses my philosophy— if you can forget yesterday and live only in today, tomorrow can't be too bad."[35]

Kay's apartment was finally ready, and the first part of 1952 saw Kay celebrating her 47th birthday amidst her move to 32 E. 64th Street. A tribute to Kay—billed as "Kay Francis in photo highlight"[36]—was scheduled on Ed Sullivan's variety show *Toast of the Town* on January 20, 1952. However, Kay's salute was cancelled. Again, it was probably because she was too nervous to appear. It's likely word was spreading through the television industry that she had a propensity to cancel live events—and that was not favorably viewed.

Kay again chose to return to the stage. Her next project was also her most successful — it kept her on the road for almost two years, and earned her some of her best reviews. The role, an aging actress, might have hit close to home. The plot dealt with the actress' attempts to prove herself sexually attractive to her husband. Somerset Maugham's play *Theatre* had received a mild reception on Broadway in 1941, with Cornelia Otis Skinner in the lead role of Julia Lambert. Kay made her debut in the play at the Central Florida Drama Festival in Winter Park, Florida, the week of March 5, 1952.

Two names listed in the playbill were interesting for different reasons. The role of Kay's teenage son was played by Anthony Perkins,[37] then an inexperienced young actor. Author Jess Gregg, who reviewed the opening, noticed that in the last act, Kay suddenly went off script. "She was a very funny, savvy woman, and she was being marvelous. But it was obviously improvisation, and I realized she was covering for someone."[38] That someone was Tony Perkins, who, thinking his role completed for the evening, had taken off his makeup. He was shoved back onstage at the last minute, finishing the final scene. "Kay Francis later told Gregg it had been the worst five minutes of her life. And she kidded Tony about it mercilessly, but kindly, from then on. She had to be kind in the face of talent. 'He's very raw in many ways,' she confided to Gregg, 'but you watch him. He's going to be big.'"[39]

The playbill also included the name of Miss Francis' new leading man — on and off stage, whom she'd met on January 18, 1952. Dennis Allen, born in Wichita Falls, Texas, began his acting career as an apprentice at Charles Coburn's Mohawk Drama Festival. He later toured with Flora Robson in *Suspect,* and appeared on Broadway in *The Moon Vine.* Allen was drafted and served in India, where he worked with Melvyn Douglas' Special Service Company. After returning to the United States, he toured with the Diana Barrymore Company in *Joan of Lorraine.* He also performed in stock throughout the United States, including Atlanta, New Orleans, and Miami. Allen, perhaps feeling his strengths lay off-stage, became interested in directing. His first attempt was *Candlelight,* which starred Jean Parker. He also produced *Rain,* starring Lawrence Tibbett.

Dennis was Kay's last romance. He also stayed with her longer than any other lover. By all accounts he adored her, found her lisp charming, and considered her the last of a line of elegant drawing room actresses like Ina Claire, Jane Cowl, Hope Williams, and Katharine Cornell. He failed to persuade her to expand her repertoire with plays by Shaw, Wilde, and Coward. Unfortunately, Kay no longer wanted the challenge of demanding new roles. It was easier to stick with the familiar, if less interesting.

Still, Kay was a sensation in *Theatre,* earning rave reviews. "Very much at home in highly dramatic roles, Miss Francis also proves herself adept as a comedienne in several scenes. Among the more serious moments of the play, the scene between Miss Francis, as Julia Lambert, and her son, Roger Gosselyn, played by Anthony Perkins, is outstanding. Miss Francis with her world crumbling around her, plays a heartbroken woman with commendable reserve, and Mr. Perkins, a drama major at Rollings College, is excellent as the son, who finds his actress mother unreal."[40]

Stage manager Jerry O'Brien described her effect on audiences. "She entered an empty stage lighted with that brown jell she liked so much. She was wearing this black dornfelt cape with a little ermine collar. She moved as if she were bone-weary and sank onto a chair. Suddenly, she threw off the cape, which was lined with ermine. She was in black chiffon and her diamond necklace, bracelet and earrings. And it was pow! Like every light in the world had suddenly been turned on."[41]

Off-stage, however, Kay preferred to dress more casually. According to Dennis, "I guess everyone who'd seen her movies expected her to be chic in private life. You'd go into a stock theater, and the kids were appalled at the way she dressed. She always wore the same thing — a denim wrap-around skirt, a blouse and little wedgies. Of course, we're taking about the private Kay — not when she was on display. She had fantastic taste when she chose to use it."[42]

"Dennis and I to see 'Don Juan in Hell'— Sardi's for one drink and then to Bon Soir — fun evening."[43]

Kay continued to make public appearances, including serving as presenter for the Stock Managers Association awards at the Hotel Astor in April 1952. Along with Basil Rathbone, Kay presented plaques to Edward Everett Horton and Lillian Gish[44] for their support of stock theater. In March and April, Kay was a special guest at fashion shows in Winter Park, Florida, and Albany, New York, where she discussed the new spring styles and her personal fashion credo. Also in April, Kay made an appearance on the television show *The Stork Club.* Hosted by Sherman Billingsley, this live program offered performances and interviews in the New York nightclub, which Kay had been frequenting since the early 1940s.

Kay and Dennis often attended movies, plays, and the opera. For example, she and Dennis saw *Don Juan in Hell,* and also saw *I Am a Camera* and Otto Preminger's *The Moon Is Blue.* They also frequented local bars, especially Chablis, which is where she first met Wayne Sanders, who, with his partner Goldie Hawkins, became a close friend.

"I didn't give a shit. I wanted the money."[45]

Kay was still ambivalent about television, commenting again on how unflattering it was to women. "All actors seem to loathe doing a live TV show. We women look pretty goshawful, you know. It's fine when we make films for television because the lights are right and if you fluff a line, you can do a retake. But on a live show there's always that awful feeling that 10,000,000 people are staring at you just waiting for you to do something wrong. So you do! You can't really act — you just show off. Television films, of course, are something again. I think we're all going to like that sort of medium."[46]

Shortly after airing her thoughts, Kay appeared on *The Ken Murray Show* on May 17, 1952, in a skit with Lola Albright. Two days later, she was in Bermuda, where she appeared in *Theatre* at the Bermudiana Theatre in Hamilton. The audiences in Bermuda enjoyed seeing Kay in person, and so did the critics — her reviews were excellent. The return flight to New York was as dramatic as anything that happened on stage. Kay posed for publicity photos for the airline, arriving at the airport two hours ahead of time. Her maid Eunice was supposed to watch the luggage, but instead drank herself into a stupor in the airport lounge. By boarding time, Eunice was unable to mount the plane's stairs, and the pilot bounced her from the flight. When Kay and Dennis arrived at New York's Idlewild airport, they discovered that the declaration slips needed at customs had been left behind with Eunice in Bermuda. Kay, a drama queen on and off stage, was told she had to pay duties on a case of liquor. After reluctantly paying, she opened the carton and passed out all of the bottles to other passengers at the terminal. She then made a dramatic exit, "clutching her handbag containing her rubies, diamonds and emeralds — which they hadn't even bothered to look at."[47]

The postwar boom in summer theater had begun to sag, partly because of television and air conditioning. Between 1946 and 1951, the number of television sets in U.S. homes increased from 10,000 to 12 million, and in the summer of 1951 the first home window air-conditioning units appeared on the market. The new innovations meant more people were staying home — not attending stage shows.

Fortunately, Kay's 1952 appearances in *Theatre* were the exception to the rule — they were popularly attended and earned great reviews. She started the season at the Pocono Playhouse the week of June 23 and closed the season the week of September 8 with the Kenley Players. When Kay appeared at the Ogonquit Playhouse the week of August 18, 1952, Bette Davis called on her backstage, and after the evening performance, the two former Warner Brothers stars retreated to a bar and commiserated about life and the Brothers Warner. Legend has it that Bette declared she hadn't cared about the money, only the roles — while Kay harrumphed that she'd only cared about the money.

After Kay and Dennis returned to New York, Kay was scheduled to appear in a television broadcast of "Theatre" on *Broadway Television Theatre*. Despite her affinity for the role and previous television appearances, Kay cancelled. Sylvia Sidney instead played Julia Lambert on September 24, 1952, though Kay's name appeared in the *TV Guide*.

Since audience reaction to Kay's appearances in *Theatre* was still enthusiastic, she continued her marathon tour, beginning with a January 6, 1953, performance in St. Louis. From there, Kay and Dennis went on to Wichita Falls to visit Dennis' family. They also traveled to New Orleans, where Kay socialized with friends Clay Shaw and Eva Gabor, who was touring in *Strike a Match*.

In February, Kay and Dennis were in St. Petersburg, Florida and Memphis, Tennessee, for additional performances of *Theatre*. Kay continued to charm audiences as Julia Lambert, and when she appeared at the Sombrero Playhouse in Phoenix, Arizona, the week of March 2, 1953, a local newspaper reported that Katherine Clinton Gibbs attended one of the performances. "What does an actress consider the best seat in the house? Kay Francis picked sixth row center for her mama for last night's show at the Sombrero. 'Twas the first time her mother (yep, Kay calls her 'mama') had been within flying distance of her stage engagements."[48]

By summer, there were already problems between Kay and Dennis. They still saw the occasional movie and play, such as *The 5,000 Fingers of Dr. T* and *The Seven Year Itch,* but most of the evenings were spent at home in front of the television. Kay was bored. On July 19, she wrote, "Dull day & dull stupid people."[49] She also referred to non-speaking days and frequent arguments. Kay sometimes blamed herself: "Very quiet — non-speaking day!— so sick and I am an ass!"[50]

Kay's tour closed the week of August 4, 1953, at the Lakewood Playhouse in Skowhegan, Maine, almost exactly a year after she'd appeared there in 1952. Kay returned to her Manhattan apartment, and she and Dennis attended a showing of *Trouble in Paradise* at the Museum of Modern Art on August 26. Kay termed it a "great evening."[51]

Not long after, she made another television appearance — this time, believe it or not, as the mystery guest on *Anyone Can Win*. Similar in premise to *I've Got a Secret* and *What's My Line?,* the show was hosted by cartoonist Al Capp. Ilka Chase, Jimmy Dykes, and Patsy Kelly tried to guess Kay's identity — while she was disguised in Hairless Joe's mask!

Kay had more health troubles in the fall, which limited her socializing. She did manage to attend the opening of *An Evening with Ethel Waters,* and become immersed in the Brooklyn Dodgers' fortunes.

Interesting rumors also began to circulate that Kay would return to Broadway — in a musical. "The Broadway success of Roz Russell and Bette Davis has onetime movie star Kay Francis in a mood to be in a main stem show this fall. She is wanted for 'Las Vegas'—

a musical! Sam Coslow did the tunes—and with her velvety voice Kay should do okay."[52] This improbable rumor remained just that. Kay and Dennis took a six month break and didn't return to the stage until the spring of 1954.

Meanwhile, Kay and Dennis spent Thanksgiving in Bucks County. In December, Kay socialized with writer Terence Rattigan, and she and Dennis saw *The Robe* and *Tea and Sympathy*. Kay had a rough Christmas again as she suffered from what was probably the stomach flu—and then Dennis came down with a head cold. Still, on Christmas Day, Kay and Dennis managed to see *The Solid Gold Cadillac*.

Meanwhile, after 32 years, Kay finally ceased keeping a diary. Her last three entries detailed Dennis' illness, the viewing of *Teahouse of the August Moon,* and a cocktail party at Johnny Bartles.' Her entry for December 31, 1953, was the last: "Dinner at home here Dennis—quiet evening TV."[53]

Truthfully, most of the entries from the late 1940s on were sparse and often included only play dates and cities. Still, the diary was something she'd been keeping since 1922— and ending it in 1954 perhaps signified an end of sorts, though she'd continue to live for more than a decade. Interestingly, Katherine Clinton continued to keep Kay's scrapbooks, though there were fewer clippings to paste onto pages.

In 1954, Kay appeared on the summer theater circuit for the last time. At this point in her career, Kay agreed to make appearances—but on her terms. According to Alan Brock, when she wanted to do a play, she'd appear at his office with three suitcases full of costumes and jewelry, which she'd spread out all over the office with the help of his receptionist, Hazel Dawn, a musical comedy star in the 1910s and 1920s. Kay would then ask, "What plays go with these clothes?" They'd proceed from there. She didn't care whether the play was a drama or comedy, and had no aspirations to expand her repertoire.

She appeared in *Theatre* at the Biltmore Playhouse in Miami, Florida, the week of May 25, 1954. A month later, she returned in her last new role, that of Alicia Christie in *Black Chiffon*. Flora Robson originally starred in the Broadway play in 1950. The production, directed by Dennis Allen, played the week of June 22.

This role was out of character for Kay. On the eve of her son's marriage, Alicia Christie steals a black chiffon negligee from a store and is arrested. A psychiatrist called in by the defense discovers that Mrs. Christie has an unconscious, unnatural attachment to her son, and committed the theft in order to prevent his marriage. Rather than have this presented in court, Alicia pleads guilty and is sentenced to three months in prison. A critic described her performance as "almost flawless," and added that, "The rest of the cast suffers some-what in comparison to her smoothly professional job."[54]

Kay then returned to her old standby, *Theatre,* appearing in Birmingham, Alabama; Indianapolis, Indiana; and Lake Nuangola, Pennsylvania. In an interview in the *Indianapolis Star,* Kay was surprisingly enthusiastic about life on the road. "A new audience every night. It's wonderful. There is nothing like the stage. I'll never—well, perhaps I shouldn't say never—but doubt seriously if I'll ever go back to Hollywood."[55] Kay said she was "casting about for a Broadway show." Two, she claimed, were being considered, but nothing was settled.

This, one of Kay's last interviews, had her reminiscing. She happily recalled her early stage experiences, refused to name her favorite leading man, and then read a lengthy letter from her mother. "From Mama," she smiled, "in California. Eighty years old and still going strong." Kay again noted that her mother has "kept scrapbooks for me all my life. And she's filled 51 of them. Can you imagine?" She gave a hint of her complicated relationship with her mother, when she added, frowning, "And she's my severest critic, too."[56]

"I'm not an actress. I'm a personality."[57]

No one, including Kay, realized that her final glamorous exit through the audience[58] at the Grove Theatre the week of August 9, 1954, would be the last of her acting career. Kay was scheduled to reopen the Niagara Falls Theatre on January 24, 1955, in *Travelers Joy,* a comedy by Arthur Macrae. It wasn't to be. She fell, fracturing her shoulder in December, and newspapers reported that she was recovering and hadn't made any plans for the summer.

CHAPTER 15

I Used to Be Kay Francis, 1955–1968

"Seeing one's name in lights is a thrill, and don't let anyone tell you it isn't. I've yet to glimpse Kay Francis on a marquee without glowing a little inside. Call it vanity, call it pride. Whatever you want to name it, there's a tremendous ego satisfaction in being a star on the lot, instead of one of hundreds of more or less nameless stock players."[1]

When Kay turned 50 on January 13, 1955, she'd been acting for nearly 30 years in every medium — stage, film, radio and television. A local newspaper noted that she was staying at the Boxwood Club on the Cape, but wasn't discussing plans for the coming season, still recuperating from her fractured shoulder.[2]

In the next years, Kay divided her time between her apartment on 64th Street in Manhattan and summer rentals on Cape Cod. Dennis Allen gave up his stage career. He occasionally worked in non-theatrical jobs, such as selling ties at Bronzini's, a luxury men's apparel store. His primary job, however, was companion to Kay.

Kay's maid, Eunice Hawley, often traveled with Kay and was a member of the household. Reportedly half Indian and half African-American, Eunice was a handful. The connection between actresses and their maids was amusingly illustrated by Bette Davis and Thelma Ritter in *All About Eve*. While Kay and Eunice shared affection, they also shared a weakness for liquor. Not coincidentally, their relationship was contentious and sometimes violent. Once, when Eunice drunkenly attacked an equally inebriated Kay for using a racial epithet, the result was a brief hospitalization for Kay.

Kay and Dennis frequented Goldie's, a cozy East Side nightclub located at 232 E. 53rd Street. Owner Goldie Hawkins was a popular pianist who'd appeared on Broadway with Uta Hagen in *In Any Language*.[3] Goldie and partner Wayne Sanders provided a hangout for celebrities, and achieved enough of a following that an LP, *An Evening at Goldie's New York,* was released in the 1950s. The album's liner notes described the club's atmosphere: "He [Goldie] is occasionally surrounded by the people who help make New York the crossroads of the world — Faye Emerson, Julia Meade, Rosalind Russell, some Hungarians named Gabor, Gene Kelly, Sydney Chaplin, Fred Astaire, who are apt to use Goldie's combined bar, grill, and music room as clubhouse and rehearsal hall.... Because people who sit up as late at night as Goldie's companions don't feel comfortable at conversation unless at least one piano is going in the background, Goldie's has two all evening — the proprietor's and Wayne Sanders. Sanders is a Juilliard pianist who went night club instead of classic, and aside from seeing every play and movie in town, coaching half the city's young girl singers, and working all night at Goldie's, he leads a life on [*sic*] complete idleness."[4]

Kay and Dennis were among those who enjoyed the club's atmosphere. Occasional items about Kay and Dennis appeared in the gossip columns, including one that the couple was seen holding hands at Goldie's. Another commented on Kay's jewelry. "Goldie Hawkins nearly gave Kay Francis a fast case of apoplexy the other night when she dined at his New York bistro. Kay was wearing a huge bib necklace with a five-inch bracelet to match. And Goldie complimented her with a Suth'n accented 'Mah, what pretty beads!' The 'beads' were genuine rubies and topazes — over 50 of each in the necklace alone — and, worth a maharanee's ransom."[5] Although they later had a falling out — Kay accused Goldie and Wayne of using her for publicity — Kay remembered Sanders in her will.

Unofficially retired, Kay and Dennis studied scripts and contemplated Kay's return to Broadway. Some of the plays they considered included *Brock Hollow, But Quite Unbowed, Obelists at Sea, Larger Than Life,* and *The Human Voice.* In 1957, one proposal, *Celia,* a murder mystery written by George Batson, nearly became a reality. Jessie Royce Landis had hoped to take *Celia* to Broadway in 1953, but this dream ended when her Bucks County Playhouse tryout received lukewarm reviews. Four years later, Kay briefly considered the juicy role of Alexandra, a former torch singer turned recluse. Kay and Dennis contacted several producers, came up with a budget of $43,000, and commissioned costume sketches. Kay's attorney recommended that she and Dennis try it out in summer stock with a first-rate cast, but advised against a proposed one-week engagement in Spring Lake, New Jersey, for $1,000. Kay's project never reached fruition, though Tallulah Bankhead toured with it in the summer of 1958 under a new title — *House on the Rocks.*

In the meantime, Kay threw a party in her apartment for a Texas investor. Although the entrepreneur decided not to invest in *Celia,* he wrote Dennis about the "delightful time we had at the cocktail party at Auntie Kay's. I think she is a wonderful person and most entertaining, much more than any show we saw, and we enjoyed every minute of our visit."[6]

Unfortunately, tastes had changed, and old-fashioned star vehicles no longer seemed sure-fire money-makers to the new breed of Broadway producers. Despite her professed lack of interest in returning to movies and Hollywood, Kay contacted Jack Warner about playing Helen Morgan's mother in the Warner Brothers biography of the legendary torch-singer. Warner coldly told her the studio had never considered her for the role. When the movie was released in 1957 as *The Helen Morgan Story,* Ann Blyth starred as Helen (with vocals dubbed by Gogi Grant), and the mother character was evidently eliminated from the final screenplay.

Katherine Clinton, Kay's mother, died on January 29, 1957, at the age of 82. Before her death, she wrote a touching letter of gratitude to Kay, mentioning her own meager finances and estate. "My Precious Babe, I want you to know what a wonderful daughter you have been but really darling I never thought I'd live on so long to be a burden to a very smiling child. I have loved you always more than anyone in this world — but you know that. I wish I could have left more as you have given so much but a very great many things have unexpectedly had to be done and I have tried to keep the place in good condition for you to dispose of as you see fit. I have no debts and the only bills will be the monthly ones. I wish I could have been of more help to my one ewe lamb but just remember me a loving and devoted Mother."[7]

After Katharine Clinton's death, Anna Weissberger, mother of Kay's attorney and friend, L. Arnold Weissberger,[8] became Kay's surrogate mother. Anna physically resembled Katherine Clinton, and Kay enjoyed her company. Kay even requested that Anna be made executor of her estate, but Arnold suggested it wasn't a good idea, considering his mother's age. Arnold and his partner, theater agent Milton Goldman, were known as "one of Manhattan's foremost homosexual power couples."[9]

Kay and Dennis were still mentioned in the gossip columns. "Former movie star Kay

Francis whose most faithful escort is Dennis Allen — they were at Goldie's the other night — insist it's no romance and denies the printed report that a marriage was nearing."[10] Unfortunately, as in her other intimate relationships, this one, too, unraveled amid bouts of drinking and bickering. Finally, during the summer of 1961, Kay broke off her relationship with Dennis. The situation had become unpleasant, and they'd spent the summer apart. When Dennis returned from Fire Island — Kay had gotten wind that he'd met someone — he found his bags packed. He neither saw nor heard from Kay again.[11]

"A woman can feel old, very old — very desolate — very neglected, very unwanted, even at twenty, if she has no one to love her."[12]

Kay became reclusive during the last seven years of her life, though she kept in contact with a few old friends, and maintained a limited social life, similar to another famous Manhattan recluse, Greta Garbo. While most of Kay's friends from the theater and Hollywood had drifted out of her life, she remained in contact with Stevie Wiman — ex-wife of producer Dwight Deere Wiman[13] — and Beatrice Stewart, who'd known Kay since the early 1920s. Kay also made new friends who came and went in her life — Alan and Priscilla Brandt, owners of an East Side art gallery; stage producer Richard Barr; hospital administrator Eva Paton; New Orleans businessman Clay Shaw, who gained notoriety during the John F. Kennedy assassination investigation;[14] Cape Cod innkeeper Hilda Coppage; and stage actor Paul Lipson.[15]

Another friend was Billy Matthews,[16] stage manager for Maurice Evans' theater company. Matthews, who also had been stage manager for *Bells Are Ringing, Dial "M" for Murder,* and other Broadway plays, lived in a penthouse apartment on 82nd St., just off Fifth Avenue. His favorite Kay story concerned the time he escorted her to a Broadway opening in her limousine, complete with a full bar in the back. During the conversation, he asked Kay if it'd been difficult to sell her home in California, move back to New York, and end up in a co-op. She responded by asking if he'd like to see her Bel Air home, and, when he said yes, she directed the chauffeur to drive them down 9th Avenue to a warehouse on the lower West Side. Kay took Billy to the third floor, opened the door with a key from her purse, turned on the lights, and showed him three rooms of furniture arranged exactly as they had been in her California home. Everything was immaculate, so it was obvious someone came in periodically and cleaned. Kay went through this routine several times with different friends, and Billy accompanied her a number of times, always waiting to see the reactions of Kay's guests.

Kay frequently dined at Manhattan's chic East Side restaurants. Several times a month, she and Dennis ate at Fedora's in Greenwich Village, which featured openly gay waiters, infamous for their uninhibited manner with customers. In a 2004 interview, co-owner Fedora Dorato recalled that Kay was tall and made quite an impression. She further noted that many patrons recognized Kay from her Hollywood days. Henry, Fedora's husband and Dennis' friend, always asked "Anyone for Dennis?" and seated the couple at a specific table — the second table from the door, facing the bar. This was a prominent spot that allowed anyone coming inside to see them.[17] Kay's favorite dish was spaghetti with oil and garlic.

In 1963, movie historian and author Jim Parish was a prop master at the Cape Playhouse in Dennis, Massachusetts. Since Jim was a longtime fan of Kay's, colleague Gene Ringgold informed him that Kay was spending the summer a few miles away in Falmouth.[18] Jim sent Kay a note, and she unexpectedly called during the middle of a dress rehearsal at the

Playhouse. "She talked about 20 minutes, mostly saying I was too young to know about her career and how badly Hollywood had treated her. She didn't want me to visit, but one off day I stopped by the resort. I asked at the desk for her. She was summoned and came out and said hello. Outside of salt/pepper hair, she looked much the same."[19]

Parish later wrote about other impressions of Kay. "When we met briefly, she looked remarkably fit in her white tennis outfit, tall and regal. She was the same vibrant if brusque personality as before." Jim continued to send her notes at her New York City apartment, including a copy of an article he'd written about her for *Films in Review*. She sent him a telegram. "She said there were lots of mistakes, but didn't offer any facts. Later, when I learned she had cancer, I sent her a montage of Kay Francis memorabilia."[20]

Eventually, Kay's drinking destroyed many of her relationships. After she got drunk at an East Side restaurant, and then fell flat when trying to leave, Charles Baskerville and other dinner guests declined further invitations. Beatrice Stewart sadly related that she once discovered Kay in her cups and out of sorts in Bergdorf's fur department one summer day. With Bernie Newman's help, Bea whisked Kay into a dressing room. When finally calmed, Kay purchased a mink stole and returned home.

Actor-director Harold J. Kennedy explained Kay's drinking. "Kay was not a big drinker and she certainly was not an unpleasant drinker. She simply couldn't drink very well and the liquor invariably went to her legs. She could be sitting with you in a restaurant carrying on a perfectly sensible conversation and get up to go to the ladies' room and fall full on her face." He described how Kay kept her sense of humor during one incident, even in an undignified situation. "I remember taking her one night to a little restaurant upstairs in the East Fifties when she fell down and it took three of us, the head waiter, the owner, and myself, to carry her down the stairs and out into the street. The owner and the maitre d' were holding Kay slumped between them while I was trying to hail a cab when a young sailor went by and stared at her.

'Is that Kay Francis?' he said.

Kay half-opened her eyes and smiled that million-dollar smile. 'It used to be,' she said."[21]

"Kay Francis was a beauty on the screen and off. She was a warm, lovely, gracious, and generous woman and at the end she was one of the loneliest women in the world."[22]

In 1966, Ross Hunter offered Kay her last movie role, the part of Estelle Anderson, Lana Turner's villainous mother-in-law, in *Madame X*. Kay turned down the role, which was also rejected by Myrna Loy, before Constance Bennett finally accepted.

Declining health became a problem for Kay, the result of years of tobacco and alcohol abuse. A kidney and lung were removed. She had to wear a back brace, and broke an ankle. Finally, she was diagnosed with cancer, underwent a mastectomy, and permanently retreated to her apartment. Stevie Wiman said Kay spent her last days in bed, reading, watching television, drinking, and taking medication. Wiman visited every day and talked to Kay late at night when Kay, frightened and lonely, would often phone. By this time, Kay had a hospital type of bed set up in her apartment, and employed a uniformed housekeeper-nurse.

The final year of Kay's life must have been frightening. Not only was she terminally ill with the cancer that would ultimately kill her, but the world seemed to have come undone.

Civil rights abuses, war protests, assassinations—it was certainly a different era than her childhood, the years she spent in Hollywood, and even the relative quiet she'd spent in New York in the 1950s.

It's sad to think of Kay Francis in the psychedelic era of 1968. Outside her windows came the sounds of the Young Rascals' "Groovin'" and the Doors' "Light My Fire." Popular movies included *Bonnie and Clyde*, *Guess Who's Coming to Dinner*, and *2001: A Space Odyssey*. Now bed-ridden and an avid TV watcher, she may have tuned into *Gomer Pyle, U.S.M.C.* or *Family Affair*. Perhaps she watched some of her past colleagues making surreal appearances on her most feared medium. Ann Sothern had become the voice of an automobile on *My Mother the Car*. Joan Bennett confronted vampires on *Dark Shadows*. Joan Crawford and Bette Davis opted for work in low-budget horror films.

This was no longer the world of Kay Francis. Sadly, she'd outlived her own elegant era. Many of us prefer, instead, to think of her on an Ernst Lubitsch art deco set with Cole Porter's music playing in the background. It's a black-and-white picture, and she's lying on an impossibly long chaise lounge, gowned in Orry-Kelly, drinking a Paradise Cocktail, smiling her dazzling, hopeful smile.

"A star is marked as long as she is a star. Of course they let you alone when you're through."[23]

Years before, Kay had discussed her philosophy of life. "When I say my only ambition is for a life worth living, I mean by that a life in which I'll make the most of myself and a life which will be of some service to others. I live, essentially, for *today*. Never have I planned ahead. I try to live, daily, in the fullest sense and I have implicit confidence in things being smooth in the long run. They have always worked out satisfactorily. Happiness, I figured when very young, is a daily condition of one's own creation. It is not to be anticipated,"[24] she concluded.

On the weekend of April 26, 1968, a small New York film club held a Kay Francis "film festival." *The Vice Squad* and *The Man Who Lost Himself* were shown to the devoted members. If Kay had been aware of the tribute, it's likely she would have been bemused, wondering why in the world anyone would be interested in such relics.

Kay Francis, who once told an interviewer, "you've no idea what a sense of freedom being nobody brings with it,"[25] died in her apartment on August 26, 1968, two days after being discharged from New York Hospital. Her remains were cremated. She told Arnold Weissberger that, "she wanted no funeral, no memorial service, no tombstone, no mark that she'd ever lived."[26] When Jim Parish learned of her death, he called the law firm and asked if anyone knew where her ashes were scattered. He heard one secretary yell to another — "*Hey*, do you know where they threw Kay Francis's ashes!" They didn't.

Kay's fifth will was drawn on March 13, 1967. Filed for Probate in Manhattan Surrogate Court on December 16, 1968, she left an estate of almost $2 million, most of it going to Seeing Eye, Inc., a Morristown, New Jersey, organization that trains dogs to guide the blind. Other bequests included $2,000 and a small gold box to Helen Cornwell; $1,000 to former business manager Milton Cashy; $1,000 and a silver box set to Eva Paton; $1,000 and a photograph of Kay to Wayne Sanders; $5,000 to Jetti Preminger; $2,000 and a silver boat to Fern Cobbs; $350 to Christopher Kemp; a Picasso sketch called "Guitar Player" to Mrs. Priscilla Brandt; jewelry to Hilda Coppage and Mrs. Stephens Wiman[27]; $2,000, two 11th century "piss boy" sculptures, and her dog Chig to Helen Morgan; a crystal set to Anna

Weissberger (who *did* outlive her); and a drawing of Kay by Leo Mielziner, Sr., and two drawings by Jo Mielziner, to lawyer Arnold Weissberger. She also left bequests to doctors who'd cared for her mother and herself.[28]

The bequest to Seeing Eye was a surprise to the organization. According to executive vice president George Werntz, "I never met Miss Francis. I can't say how she became interested in our organization, but I am greatly surprised and gratified."[29] The organization, still in existence today, used the funds for research. The bequest shouldn't have been a great surprise to Kay's friends because she'd been a dog lover all of her life.[30]

Fortunately for the authors and future researchers, Kay left memorabilia to two institutions. Four scrapbooks for the years 1925–1929 and 1947–1954, and four boxes of clippings, letters, and photographs are stored at the Theatre Collection of the Museum of the City of New York. A diary covering the years 1922–1953, along with scrapbooks from her Hollywood career, are kept at the Wesleyan Cinema Archives at Wesleyan University in Middletown, Connecticut.

Thus, the woman who wanted no record of her existence preserved made darn sure there was indeed a record. Partly, it might have been that she couldn't stand to discard her mother's hobby—decades of tedious work, recording every minute detail of Kay Francis' career. Still, that doesn't explain why Kay kept the diary. Perhaps it had simply been forgotten, stored away long ago and then simply gathered up with her scrapbooks. However, we prefer to think that she kept it near, perhaps even occasionally glancing at some of the entries, a written record of her oh-so-pash life. What a record—and what a life!

Thank you, Katherine Clinton. And *thank you,* Kay Francis.

In recent years, Kay Francis' fame has returned. She has a star on the Hollywood Walk of Fame,[31] and collectors have gone wild over her memorabilia, purchasing movie stills and posters, lobby cards, and magazine covers. There is also renewed interest in her career and life, and, most particularly, in her film performances, which often appear on Turner Classic Movies (TCM). In 2004 TCM scheduled a movie marathon on her birthday in what, hopefully, will become an annual event.

Film historian Cari Beauchamp described Kay's influence: "She elevates every film she's in. Incredibly comfortable within her own skin, her smile radiates her confidence in both her sexuality and her ability to take on all comers. Almost all of her characters pushed the envelope for women. She was very warm and intelligent on the screen."[32]

According to writer Margaret Burk, Kay had a tremendous influence on her era. "What moviegoers remember most about Kay Francis is her exquisite form and sophisticated grooming. She was a first style setter for American women.... And her fans would sit through two or three films in admiration of her acting, more particularly her wardrobe.... She left a valuable message of style and fashion. Aprons and house dresses disappeared, and Kay Francis' elegance came in."[33]

Writer Christopher Nickens believes that many of her films are still interesting today. "In an era that produced the most fabulous female stars in Hollywood's history, Kay Francis carved a unique niche for herself. Her dark, good looks, trend setting styles, and ability to play a wide range of roles made her an enduring audience favorite in dozens of films, many of which are enjoyable today as they were decades ago."[34]

By no means perfect or saintly—or a pretender to these qualities—Kay was a real woman who left behind a body of work that still seduces and entertains. Complicated, enigmatic, and contradictory, Kay Francis lived a discreetly scandalous life, richer than any Hollywood movie or stage production—and one that deserved to be told. We suspect she's secretly happy.

Chronology

January 16, 1862	Joseph S. Gibbs born in Homer, MI.
May 17, 1874	Katherine Clinton Franks Gibbs born in Chicago, IL.
December 3, 1903	Joseph Gibbs and Katherine Franks marry.
January 13, 1905	Katharine Gibbs born in Oklahoma City, OK.
January 20, 1919	Joseph S. Gibbs dies in St. Louis, MO.
December 4, 1922	Katharine Gibbs marries James Dwight Francis.
March 26, 1925	Kay and Dwight Francis divorce.
October 19, 1925	Kay Francis and William Gaston marry.
November 9, 1925	*Shakespeare's Hamlet in Modern Dress* opens.
December 2, 1925	*The School for Scandal* opens.
April–September, 1926	Kay Francis tours with the Stuart Walker Company.
January 21, 1927	*Damn the Tears* opens.
February 22, 1927	*Crime* opens.
September 1, 1927	Kay Francis and William Gaston divorce.
October 1927	Kay tours in *Amateur Anne*.
December 26, 1927	*Venus* opens.
May 3, 1928	*Fast Company* [*Elmer the Great*] opens in Worcester, MA.
May 7 1928	*Fast Company* [*Elmer the Great*] opens in Boston, MA.
June 18, 1928	*Elmer the Great* opens in Chicago.
Sept. 24, 1928	*Elmer the Great* opens in New York City.
May 11, 1929	*Gentlemen of the Press* released.
May 24, 1929	*The Cocoanuts* released.
July 13, 1929	*Dangerous Curves* released.
September 27, 1929	*Illusion* released.
December 13, 1929	*The Marriage Playground* released.
January 6, 1930	*Behind the Make-Up* released.
January 31, 1930	*Street of Chance* released.
April 19, 1930	*Paramount on Parade* released.
April 25, 1930	*A Notorious Affair* released.
July 18, 1930	*For the Defense* released.
July 24, 1930	*Raffles* released.
August 20, 1930	*Let's Go Native* released.
October 24, 1930	*The Virtuous Sin* released.
December 19, 1930	*Passion Flower* released.
January 17, 1931	Kay Francis and Kenneth MacKenna marry.
February 6, 1931	*Scandal Sheet* released.
April 30, 1931	*Ladies' Man* released.
June 5, 1931	*The Vice Squad* released.
June 12, 1931	*Transgression* released.
August 28, 1931	*Guilty Hands* released.
October 2, 1931	*24 Hours* released.
October 30, 1931	*Girls About Town* released.
January 10, 1932	*The False Madonna* released

March 5, 1932	*Strangers in Love* released.
April 15, 1932	*Man Wanted* released.
May 26, 1932	*Street of Women* released.
July 21, 1932	*Jewel Robbery* released.
October 13, 1932	*One Way Passage* released.
November 8, 1932	*Trouble in Paradise* released.
December 24, 1932	*Cynara* released.
March 30, 1933	*The Keyhole* released.
July 21, 1933	*Storm at Daybreak* released.
August 3,1933	*Mary Stevens, M.D.* released.
September 21, 1933	*I Loved a Woman* released.
December 1, 1933	*The House on 56th Street* released.
February 15, 1934	*Mandalay* released.
February 21, 1934	Kay Francis and Kenneth MacKenna divorce.
February 28, 1934	*Wonder Bar* released.
June 20, 1934	*Dr. Monica* released.
September 20, 1934	*British Agent* released.
January 4, 1935	Kay appears on *Hollywood Hotel*.
March 7, 1935	*Living on Velvet* released.
June 20, 1935	*Stranded* released.
September 12, 1935	*The Goose and the Gander* released.
November 1, 1935	Kay appears on *Hollywood Hotel*.
November 4, 1935	*I Found Stella Parish* released.
May 29, 1936	Kay appears on *Hollywood Hotel*.
June 25, 1936	*The White Angel* released.
September 25, 1936	Kay appears on *Hollywood Hotel*.
September 17, 1936	*Give Me Your Heart* released.
November 1936	Fashion Academy names Kay "Best Dressed Woman in America."
February 1, 1937	*Stolen Holiday* released.
June 18, 1937	*Another Dawn* released.
August 19, 1937	*Confession* released.
November 26, 1937	Kay appears on *Hollywood Hotel*.
December 23, 1937	*First Lady* released.
April 11, 1938	*Women Are Like That* released.
May 13, 1938	Kay appears on *Hollywood Hotel*.
July 9, 1938	*My Bill* released.
October 8, 1938	*Secrets of an Actress* released.
December 16, 1938	*Comet Over Broadway* released.
January 14, 1939	*King of the Underworld* released.
March 6, 1939	Kay appears on *Lux Radio Theatre*.
March 26, 1939	Kay appears on *Gulf Screen Guild Show*.
April 13, 1939	*Women in the Wind* released.
July 30, 1939	Kay appears on *The Chase and Sanborn Hour*.
August 4, 1939	*In Name Only* released.
December 11, 1939	Kay appears on *Lux Radio Theatre*.
December 17, 1939	Kay appears on *The Silver Theatre*.
March 3, 1940	Kay appears on *The Silver Theatre*.
March 18, 1940	Kay appears on *Lux Radio Theatre*.
March 22, 1940	*It's a Date* released.
August 23, 1940	*When the Daltons Rode* released.
December 7, 1940	*Little Men* released.
December 15, 1940	Kay appears on *The Silver Theatre*.
January 29, 1941	*Play Girl* released.
March 3, 1941	Kay appears on *Lux Radio Theatre*.
March 21, 1941	*The Man Who Lost Himself* released.
May 18, 1941	Kay appears on *The Jack Benny Program*.

August 1, 1941	*Charley's Aunt* released.
October 13, 1941	Kay appears on *The Cavalcade of America.*
December 12, 1941	*The Feminine Touch* released.
March 13, 1942	*Always in My Heart* released.
September 4, 1942	*Between Us Girls* released.
October 1942–January 1943	Kay travels to Europe and North Africa on USO tour.
February 11, 1943	Kay appears on *Stage Door Canteen.*
March 1, 1943	Kay appears on *Lux Radio Theatre.*
March 24, 1943	Kay appears on *Stage Door Canteen.*
November 25, 1943	Kay appears on *Soldiers in Grease Paint.*
November 28, 1943	Kay appears on *The Silver Theatre.*
December 11, 1943	Kay appears on *Command Performance.*
May 3, 1943	Kay appears on *Cavalcade of America.*
July 4, 1943	Kay appears on *The Silver Theatre.*
February–March 1944	Kay travels to Canada and Alaska for USO tour.
April 6, 1944	*Four Jills in a Jeep* released.
April–May 1945	Kay travels to the Caribbean and South America for USO tour.
August 18, 1945	*Divorce* released.
September 1945–May 1946	Kay tours in *Windy Hill.*
December 29, 1945	*Allotment Wives* released.
September 2, 1946	Kay opens in *State of the Union.*
November 2, 1946	*Wife Wanted* released.
March 27, 1947	Fashion Academy names Kay "Best Dressed Woman on Stage."
September 1947–January 1948	Kay tours in *State of the Union.*
January 23, 1948	Kay is hospitalized in Columbus, Ohio.
June–Sepember 1948	Kay tours in *The Last of Mrs. Cheyney.*
December 1948–April 1949	Kay tours in *Favorite Stranger.*
January 9, 1949	Kay tours in *The Last of Mrs. Cheyney.*
June 3–November 1949	Kay tours in *Let Us Be Gay.*
March 1950	Kay tours in *Let Us Be Gay.*
May 14, 1950	Kay appears on *This Is Show Business.*
May 23, 1950–July 1950	Kay tours in *Goodbye, My Fancy.*
August 1950	Kay tours in *The Web and the Rock.*
November 7, 1950	Kay appears on *Prudential Family Playhouse.*
January 8, 1951	Kay appears on *Hollywood Screen Test.*
May 24, 1951	Kay appears on *The Betty Crocker Show.*
June 1951	Kay tours in *Let Us Be Gay.*
June 4, 1951	Kay appears on *Lux Video Theatre.*
July–September 1951	Kay tours in *Mirror, Mirror.*
October 20, 1951	Kay appears on *Beat the Clock.*
October 31, 1951	Kay appears on *The Frances Langford–Don Ameche Show.*
November 11, 1951	Kay appears on *Celebrity Time.*
March 1952	Kay tours in *Theatre.*
April 22, 1952	Kay appears on *The Stork Club.*
May 10, 1952	Kay appears on *The Ken Murray Show.*
May–September 1952	Kay tours in *Theatre.*
September 1, 1952	Kay appears on *Anyone Can Win.*
January–March 1953	Kay tours in *Theatre.*
August 1953	Kay tours in *Theatre.*
May 1954	Kay tours in *Theatre.*
July–August 1954	Kay tours in *Theatre.*
June 22, 1954	*Black Chiffon* opens.
August 9, 1954	Kay appears in *Theatre*—her last stage appearance.
January 29, 1957	Katherine Clinton Gibbs dies.
August 26, 1968	Kay Francis dies.

Filmography

Gentlemen of the Press (Paramount, 1929) 75 min. Released in New York on May 11, 1929, Paramount Theater.

Credits: Producer, Monta Bell; director, Millard Webb; based on the play by Ward Morehouse; screenplay, Bartlett Cormack; dialogue director, John Meehan; camera, George J. Folsey; editor, Morton Blumenstock.

Cast: Walter Huston (Wickland Snell); Katherine Francis (Myra May); Charles Ruggles (Charlie Haven); Betty Lawford (Dorothy Snell); Norman Foster (Ted Hanley); Duncan Penwarden (Mr. Higgenbottom); Lawrence Leslie (Red); Harry Lee (Copy Desk Editor); Brian Donlevy (Bit Part); Victor Kilian (Bit Part).

The Cocoanuts (Paramount, 1929) 90 min. Released in New York on May 24, 1929, Rialto Theater. U.S. release date: August 3, 1929.

Credits: Producers, Monta Bell, Walter Wanger; associate producer, James R. Cowan; director, Monta Bell; musical numbers directed by Joseph Santley and Robert Florey; based on the play by George S. Kaufman and Irving Berlin; adaptor, Morrie Ryskind; original music and lyrics, Irving Berlin; camera, George Folsey; editor, Barney Rogan; choreographer, Erna Kay; musical director, Frank Tours; art director, William Saulter. Songs: "Florida by the Sea," written by Irving Berlin, sung by chorus, danced by Gamby-Hale Girls and Allan K. Foster Girls; "When My Dreams Come True," written by Irving Berlin, sung by Oscar Shaw and Mary Eaton; "The Bell Hops," written by Irving Berlin, danced by Gamby-Hale Girls; "Monkey-Doodle-Do," written by Irving Berlin, sung by Mary Eaton, danced by Gamby-Hale Girls and Allan K. Foster Girls; "Ballet Music," written by Frank Tours, danced by Gamby-Hale Girls; "Tale of the Shirt," Music from Bizet's Carmen, lyrics by Irving Berlin, sung by Basil Ruysdael and chorus; "Gypsy Love Song," written by Victor Herbert, performed by Chico Marx.

Cast: Groucho Marx (Hammer); Harpo Marx (Harpo); Chico Marx (Chico); Zeppo Marx (Jamison); Mary Eaton (Polly); Oscar Shaw (Bob); Katherine Francis (Penelope); Margaret Dumont (Mrs. Potter); Cyril Ring (Yates); Basil Ruysdael (Hennessey); Sylvan Lee (Bell Captain); Allan K. Foster Girls, Gamby-Hale Girls (Dancing Bellhops); Barton MacLane (Bather).

Dangerous Curves (Paramount, 1929) 73 min. Released in New York on July 13, 1929, Paramount Theater.

Credits: Supervisor, B.F. Zeidman; production supervisor, Ernst Lubitsch; director, Lothar Mendes; story, Lester Cohen; screenplay, Donald Davis, Florence Ryerson; dialogue, Viola Brothers Shore; titles, George Marion, Jr.; camera, Harry Fischbeck; editor, Eda Warren; original music, W. Franke Harling.

Cast: Clara Bow (Pat Delaney); Richard Arlen (Larry Lee); Kay Francis (Zara Flynn); David Newell (Tony Barretti); Anders Randolf (Colonel P.P. Brock); May Boley (Ma Spinelli); T. Roy Barnes (Pa Spinelli); Joyce Compton (Jennie Silver); Charles D. Brown (Spider); Stuart Erwin, Jack Luden (Rotarians); Oscar Smith (Porter); Ethan Laidlaw (Roustabout); Russ Powell (Counterman).

Illusion (Paramount, 1929) 80 min. Released in New York on September 27, 1929, Paramount Theater.

Credits: Producer, B.P. Schulberg; director, Lothar Mendes; based on the play by Arthur Cheney Train; adaptor/dialogue, E. Lloyd Sheldon; titles, Richard H. Digges, Jr.; sound, Harry M. Lindgren; camera, Harry Fischbeck; editor, George Nichols, Jr. Song, "When the Real Thing Comes Your Way," written by Larry Spier; musicians, Abe Lyman and his "Californians" in "Believe It or Not."

173

Cast: Charles "Buddy" Rogers (Carlee Thorpe); Nancy Carroll (Claire Jernigan); June Collyer (Hilda Schmittlap); Regis Toomey (Eric Schmittlap); Knute Erickson (Mr. Jacob Schmittlap); Kay Francis (Zelda Paxton); Eugenie Besserer (Mrs. Jacob Schmittlap); Maude Turner Gordon (Queen of Dalmatia); William Austin (Mr. Z); Emilie Melville (Mother Fay); Frances Raymond (Mrs. Y.); Catherine Wallace (Mrs. Z); J.E. Nash (Mr. X); William McLaughlin (Mr. Y); Eddie Kane (Gus Bloomberg); Michael Visaroff (Equerry); Paul Lukas (Count Fortuny); Richard Cramer (Magus); Bessie Lyle (Consuelo); Colonel G.L. McDonell (Jarman, the Butler); Lillian Roth (A Singer); Harriet Spiker (Midget); Anna Magruder (Fat Lady); Albert Wolffe (Giant); Virginia Bruce (bit); Phillips Holmes (bit).

The Marriage Playground (Paramount, 1929) 70 min. Released in New York on December 13, 1929, Paramount Theater.

Credits: Director, Lothar Mendes; based on the novel *The Children* by Edith Wharton; screenplay, J. Walter Ruben; adapter/dialogue, Doris Anderson; sound, M.M. Paggi; camera, Victor Milner.

Cast: Mary Brian (Judith Wheater); Fredric March (Martin Boyne); Lilyan Tashman (Joyce Wheater); Huntley Gordon (Cliff Wheater); Kay Francis (Zinnia La Crosse); William Austin (Lord Wrench); Seena Owen (Rose Sellars); Philippe De Lacy (Terry Wheater); Anita Louise (Blanca Wheater); Little Mitzi Green (Zinnie); Billie Seay (Astorre Wheater); Ruby Parsley (Beatrice [Beechy] Wheater); Donald Smith (Chipstone [Chip] Wheater); Jocelyn Lee (Sybil Lullmer); Maude Turner Gordon (Aunt Julia Langley); David Newell (Gerald Omerod); Armand Kaliz (Prince Matriano); Joan Standing (Scopy); Gordon De Main (Mr. Delafield).

Behind the Make-Up (Paramount, 1930) 65 min. Released on January 6, 1930, State, Norfolk, Virginia.

Credits: Directors, Robert Milton, Dorothy Arzner; based on the story "The Feeder" by Mildred Cram; adaptors/dialogue, George Manker Watters, Howard Estabrook; songs, Leo Robin, Sam Coslow; original music, W. Franke Harling, John Leipold; sound, Harry D. Mills; camera, Charles Lang; editor, Doris Drought.

Cast: Hal Skelly (Hap Brown); William Powell (Gardoni); Fay Wray (Marie Gardoni); Kay Francis (Kitty Parker); E.H. Calvert (Dawson); Paul Lukas (Boris); Agostino Borgato

(Chef); Jacques Vanaire (Valet); Jean De Briac (Sculptor); Torben Meyer (Waiter); Bob Perry (Bartender).

Street of Chance (Paramount, 1930) 76 min. Released in New York on January 31, 1930, Rialto Theater. Released in United States, February 8, 1930.

Credits: Director, John Cromwell; producer, David O. Selznick; story, Oliver H.P. Garrett; dialogue, Lenore J. Coffee; adapters, Howard Estabrook, Ben Hecht, Charles MacArthur; titles, Gerald Geraghty; sound, Harry D. Mills; camera, Charles Lang; editor, Otto Levering; original music, John Leipold; costume design, Travis Banton.

Cast: William Powell (John B. Marsden [Natural Davis]); Jean Arthur (Judith Marsden); Kay Francis (Alma Marsden); Regis Toomey ("Babe" Marsden); Stanley Fields (Dorgan); Brooks Benedict (Al Mastick); Betty Francisco (Mrs. Mastic); John Risso (Tony); Joan Standing (Miss Abrams); Maurice Black (Nick); Irving Bacon (Harry); John Cromwell (Imbrie).

Paramount on Parade (Paramount, 1930) 101 min. Released in New York on April 19, 1930, Rialto Theater.

Credits: Supervisor, Elsie Janis; producers, Albert S. Kaufman, Jesse L. Lasky, Adolph Zukor; directors, Dorothy Arzner, Otto Brower, Edmund Goulding, Victor Heerman, Edwin H. Knopf, Rowland V. Lee, Ernst Lubitsch, Lothar Mendes, Victor Schertzinger, A. Edward Sutherland, Frank Tuttle; writer, Joseph L. Mankiewicz; songs, Elsie Janis and Jack King; Ballard MacDonald and Dave Dreyer; Leo Robin and Ernesto De Curtis; L. Wolfe Gilbert and Abel Baer; Richard A. Whiting and Raymond B. Eagan; Whiting and Robin; David Franklin; Sam Coslow; Samuel Pokrass; incidental music, Howard Jackson; dance/ensemble director, David Bennett; set designer, John Wenger; camera, Harry Fischbeck and Victor Milner; editor, Merrill G. White.

Cast: Iris Adrian, Richard Arlen, Jean Arthur, Mischa Auer, William Austin, George Bancroft, Clara Bow, Evelyn Brent, Mary Brian, Clive Brook, Virginia Bruce, Nancy Carroll, Ruth Chatterton, Maurice Chevalier, Gary Cooper, Cecil Cunningham, Leon Errol, Stuart Erwin, Henry Fink, Kay Francis, Richard "Skeets" Gallagher, Edmund Goulding, Harry Green, Mitzi Green, Robert Greig, James Hall, Phillips Holmes, Helen Kane, Dennis King, Jack Luden, Abe Lyman & His Band, Fredric March,

Nino Martini, Mitzi Mayfair, Marion Morgan Dancers, David Newell, Jack Oakie, Warner Oland, Zelma O'Neal, Eugene Pallette, Joan Peers, Jack Pennick, Russ Powell, William Powell, Charles "Buddy" Rogers, Lillian Roth, Rolfe Sedan, Stanley Smith, Fay Wray, Jane Keithley, Rosina Lawrence, Jeanette MacDonald, Al Norman, Ernst Rolf, Jackie Searl.

A Notorious Affair (First National Pictures, 1930) 70 min. Released in New York on April 25, 1930, Strand Theater.

Credits: Producer, Robert North; director, Lloyd Bacon; based on the play *Fame* by Audrey Carter and Waverly Carter; adaptor/dialogue, J. Grubb Alexander; set designer, Anton Grot; assistant directors, John Daumery, Irving Asher; costumes, Edward Stevenson; original music, Cecil Copping; conductor, Leo S. Forbstein; sound, Oliver S. Garretson; camera, Ernest Haller; editor, Frank Ware.

Cast: Billie Dove (Patricia Hanley Gherardi); Basil Rathbone (Paul Gherardi); Kay Francis (Countess Olga Balakireff); Montagu Love (Sir Thomas Hanley); Kenneth Thomson (Dr. Allen Pomroy); Philip Strange (Lord Percival Northmore); Malcolm Waite (Higgins, the Butler); Gino Corrado (Extra); Ellinor Vanderveer (Society Lady); Blanche Frederici (Lady Keon); Wilson Benge (Briggs, Sir Hanley's Butler).

For the Defense (Paramount, 1930) 62 min. Released in New York on July 18, 1930, Paramount Theater.

Credits: Director, John Cromwell; story, Julius Furthman; screenplay/dialogue, Oliver H.P. Garrett; sound, Harold M. McNiff; camera, Charles Lang; editor, George Nichols, Jr.

Cast: William Powell (William Foster); Kay Francis (Irene Manners); Scott Kolk (Jack De Foe); William B. Davidson (District Attorney Stone); John Elliott (McGann); Thomas E. Jackson (Daly); Harry Walker (Miller); James Finlayson (Parrott); Charles West (Joe); Charles Sullivan (Charlie); Ernest Adams (Eddie Withers); Bertram Marburgh (Judge Evans); Edward Le Saint (Judge); George "Gabby" Hayes (Ben, the Waiter); Billy Bevan (Drunk); Robert Homans (Lineup Lieutenant); Kane Richmond (Young Man at Speakeasy); Syd Saylor (Evening Sun Reporter).

Raffles (United Artists, 1930) 70 min. Released in New York on July 24, 1930, Rialto Theater.

Credits: Producer, Samuel Goldwyn; directors, Harry D'Arrast, George Fitzmaurice; based on the novel *The Amateur Cracksman* by Ernest William Hornung, and the play *Raffles, the Amateur Cracksman* by Hornung and Eugene Wiley Presbrey; screenplay, Sidney Howard; assistant director, H. Bruce Humberstone; technical directors, Gerald Grove, John Howell; art directors, Park French, Wm. Cameron Menzies; sound, Oscar Lagerstrom; camera, George S. Barnes, Gregg Toland; editor, Stuart Heisler.

Cast: Ronald Colman (A.J. Raffles); Kay Francis (Lady Gwen); David Torrence (Inspector MacKenzie); Frederic Kerr (Lord Harry Melrose); Alison Skipworth (Lady Kitty Melrose); Bramwell Fletcher (Bunny Manders); John Rogers (Crawshaw); Wilson Benge (Barraclough); Frances Dade (Ethel Crowley); Virginia Bruce (Debutante).

Let's Go Native (Paramount, 1930) 75 min. Released in New York on August 20, 1930, Paramount Theater.

Credits: Executive producer, Adolph Zukor; producer and director, Leo McCarey; screenplay/dialogue, George Marion, Jr., Percy Heath; songs, Richard A. Whiting, George F. Marion; dances/ensembles director, David Bennett; sound, Harry D. Mills; camera, Victor Milner.

Cast: Jack Oakie (Voltaire McGinnis); Jeanette MacDonald (Joan Wood); Skeets Gallagher (Jerry); James Hall (Wally Wendell); William Austin (Basil Pistol); Kay Francis (Constance Cooke); David Newell (Chief Officer Williams); Charles Sellon (Wallace Wendell, Sr.); Eugene Pallette (Deputy Sheriff Careful Cuthbert); Iris Adrian (uncredited); Earl Askam (Mover); Harry Bernard (Mover); Virginia Bruce (Secretary); E.H. Calvert (Diner); John Elliott (Captain); Charlie Hall (Mover); Pat Harmon (Policeman); Oscar Smith (Cook); Rafael Storm (Argentine Producers' Representative); Grady Sutton (Diner).

The Virtuous Sin (Paramount, 1930) 80 min. Released in New York on October 24, 1930, Paramount Theater.

Credits: Directors, George Cukor, Louis Gasnier; based on the play *A Tabornok (the General)* by Lajos Zilahy; screenplay, Martin Brown; scenery, Louise Long; original music, Sam Coslow, Karl Hajos, Howard Jackson, Ralph Rainger, Leo Robin, Max Terr, Richard A. Whiting; sound, Harold M. McNiff; camera, David Abel; editor, Otto Levering/Otto Lovering.

Cast: Walter Huston (General Gregori Platoff); Kay Francis (Marya Ivanova); Kenneth

MacKenna (Lieutenant Victor Sablin); Jobyna Howland (Alexandra Stroganov); Paul Cavanagh (Captain Orloff); Eric Kalkhurst (Lieutenant Glinka); Oscar Apfel (Major Ivanoff); Gordon McLeod (Colonel Nikitin); Youcca Troubetzkov (Captain Sobakin); Victor Potel (Sentry).

Passion Flower (MGM, 1930) 78 min. Released in New York on December 19, 1930, Capitol Theater.

Credits: Director, William C. de Mille; based on the novel by Kathleen Norris; adaptor/dialogue Martin Flavin; additional dialogue, Laurence E. Johnson, Edith Fitzgerald; art director, Cedric Gibbons; gowns, Adrian; sound, J.K. Brock, Douglas Shearer; camera, Hal Rosson; editor, Conrad A. Nervig.

Cast: Kay Francis (Dulce Morado); Kay Johnson (Cassy Pringle Wallace); Charles Bickford (Dan Wallace); Winter Hall (Leroy Pringle); Lewis Stone (Antonio Morado); ZaSu Pitts (Mrs. Harney); Dickie Moore (Tommy Wallace); Ray Milland (party guest); Ellinor Vanderveer (party guest).

Scandal Sheet (Paramount, 1931) 75 min. Released in New York on February 6, 1931, Paramount Theater.

Credits: Director, John Cromwell; story, Oliver H.P. Garrett; screenplay, Vincent Lawrence, Max Marcin; sound, J.A. Goodrich; original music, Karl Hajos, W. Frank Harling; camera, David Abel; editor, George Nichols, Jr.

Cast: George Bancroft (Mark Flint, the Editor); Clive Brook (Noel Adams, the Banker); Kay Francis (Mrs. Flint); Gilbert Emery (Franklin, the Publisher); Lucien Littlefield (McCloskey, the City Editor); Regis Toomey (Regan, the Reporter); Mary Foy (Mrs. Wilson); Harry Beresford (Arnold); Jackie Searl (Little Boy); James Kelsey (Malloy); Irving Bacon; William Arnold; Vince Barnett; Davison Clark; Monte Collins; Adrienne D'Ambricourt; Robert Dudley; Perry Ivins; Broderick O'Farrell; Leslie Palmer; Robert Parrish; Victor Potel; Jack Richardson; Syd Saylor; Nick Stuart; Frederick Sullivan.

Ladies' Man (Paramount, 1931) 76 min. Released in New York on April 30, 1931, Paramount Theater.

Credits: Director, Lothar Mendes; story, Rupert Hughes; screenplay, Herman J. Mankiewicz; sound, Harry Lindgren; camera, Victor Milner.

Cast: William Powell (James Darricott);

Kay Francis (Norma Page); Carole Lombard (Rachel Fendley); Gilbert Emery (Horace Fendley); Olive Tell (Mrs. Fendley); Martin Burton (Anthony Fendley); John Holland (Peyton Weldon); Frank Atkinson (Valet); Maude Turner Gordon (Therese Blanton); Hooper Atchley (Headwaiter); Richard Cramer (Private Detective); Edward Hearn (Maitre D'); Lothar Mendes (Lobby Extra); Bill O'Brien (Elevator Starter); Frank O'Connor (News Clerk); Lee Phelps (Desk Clerk); Clarence Wilson (Jeweler); Wilbur Mack; Bess Flowers.

The Vice Squad (Paramount, 1931), 78 min. Released in New York on June 5, 1931, Paramount Theater.

Credits: Director, John Cromwell; story, Oliver H.P. Garrett; original music, Rudolph G. Kopp, Ralph Rainger; sound, E.C. Sullivan; camera, Charles Lang.

Cast: Paul Lukas (Stephen Lucarno/Tony); Kay Francis (Alice Morrison); Judith Wood / Helen Johnson (Madeleine Hunt); William B. Davidson (Magistrate Tom Morrison); Rockliffe Fellowes (Detective Sergeant Mather); Esther Howard (Josie); Monte Carter (Max Miller); G. Pat Collins (Pete); Phil Tead (Tony); Davison Clark (Doctor); Tom Wilson (Court Attendant); James Durkin (Second Magistrate); William Arnold (Prosecutor); Lynton Brent (Court Clerk); Irving Bacon (uncredited); Juliette Compton (Ambassador's wife).

Transgression (RKO, 1931) 72 min. Released in New York on June 12, 1931, Mayfair Theater.

Credits: Producer, William LeBaron; director, Herbert Brenon; based on the play *The Next Corner* by Kate Jordan; adaptation, Elizabeth Meehan; dialogue, Benn Levy; original music, Max Steiner; sound, John E. Tribby; camera, Leo Tover; assistant director, Ray Lissnerr; assistant to asst. director, Sammy Fuller; costumes and set design, Max Ree; editor, Arthur Roberts.

Cast: Kay Francis (Elsie Maury); Paul Cavanagh (Robert Maury); Ricardo Cortez (Don Arturo); Nance O'Neil (Honora Maury); John St. Polis (Serafin); Adrienne d'Ambricourt (Julie); Cissy Fitzgerald (Countess Longueval); Doris Lloyd (Paula Vrain); Augustino Borgato (Carlos); Ruth Weston (Viscountess); Alphonse De Cruz; Alphonse Ethier; Chris-Pin Martin; Rolfe Sedan.

Guilty Hands (MGM, 1931) 60 min. Released in New York on August 28, 1931, Capitol Theater.

Credits: Producer/supervisor, Hunt Stromberg; directors, W.S. Van Dyke, Lionel Barrymore (uncredited); story/screenplay, Bayard Veiller; camera, Merritt B. Gerstad; editor, Anne Bauchens; wardrobe, Rene Hubert; musical director, William Axt; recording director, Douglas Shearer; assistant director, Al Shenberg; art director, Cedric Gibbons; original music, L. Andrieu, Domenico Savino.

Cast: Lionel Barrymore (Richard Grant); Kay Francis (Marjorie West); Madge Evans (Barbara Grant); William Bakewell (Tommy Osgood); C. Aubrey Smith (Reverend Hastings); Polly Moran (Aunt Maggie); Alan Mowbray (Gordon Rich); Forrester Harvey (Spencer Wilson); Charles Crockett (H.G. Smith); Henry Barrows (Harvey Scott); Sam McDaniel (Jimmy); Robert McKenzie (Second Man on Train); Blue Washington (Johnny).

24 Hours (Paramount, 1931) 65 min. Released in New York on October 2, 1931, Paramount Theater.

Credits: Director, Marion Gering; associate director, Dudley Murphy; based on the novel by Louis Bromfield and the play by William C. Lengle, Lew Levenson; screenplay, Louis Weitzenkorn; camera, Ernest Haller.

Cast: Clive Brook (Jim Towner); Kay Francis (Fanny Towner); Miriam Hopkins (Rosie Dugan); Regis Toomey (Tony Bruzzi); George Barbier (Hector Champion); Adrienne Ames (Ruby Wintringham); Lucille La Verne (Mrs. Dacklehorst); Wade Boreler (Pat Healy); Minor Watson (David Melbourn); Charlotte Granville (Savina Jerrold); Bob Kortman (Dave the Slapper); Malcolm Waite (Murphy); Thomas E. Jackson (Police Commissioner); Charles D. Brown (Detective); Mary Gordon (Nurse); Robert Homans (Police Official); Nicholas Kobliansky (Extra); Imboden Parrish (Extra); Virginia Pickering (Baby); Ben Taggert (Detective).

Girls About Town (Paramount, 1931) 80 min. Released in New York on October 30, 1931, Paramount Theater.

Credits: Associate producer, Raymond Griffith; director, George Cukor; story, Zoe Akins; screenplay, Raymond Griffith, Brian Marlow; camera, Ernest Haller; costumes, Travis Banton.

Cast: Kay Francis (Wanda Howard); Joel McCrea (Jim Baker); Lilyan Tashman (Marie Bailey); Eugene Pallette (Benjamin Thomas); Allan Dinehart (Jerry Chase); Lucile Webster Gleason (Mrs. Benjamin Thomas); Anderson Lawler (Alex Howard); Lucille Browne (Edna);

George Barbier (Webster); Robert McWade (Simms); Judith Wood (Winnie); Adrienne Ames (Anne); Katherine DeMille (Girl); Patricia Caron (Billie); Claire Dodd (Dot); Hazel Howard (Joy); Louise Beavers (Hattie); Sheila Bromley (Girl); Veda Buckland (Girl).

The False Madonna (Paramount, 1932) 72 min. Released in New York on January 10, 1932, Loew's State Theater.

Credits: Director, Stuart Walker; associate director, Edward D. Venturini; based on the story "The Heart Is Young" by May Edginton; screenplay, Arthur Kober, Ray Harris; dialogue, Arthur Kober; camera, Henry Sharp; original music, Herman Hand, W. Franke Harling, Bernard Kaun, John Leipold.

Cast: Kay Francis (Tina); William "Stage" Boyd (Doctor Ed Marcy); Conway Tearle (Grant Arnold); John Breeden (Phillip Bellows); Marjorie Gateson (Rose); Chas. D. Brown (Peter Angel); Julia Swayne Gordon (Dowager); Almeda Fowler (Mrs. Swanson); Kent Taylor (Extra).

Strangers in Love (Paramount, 1932) 68 min. Released in New York on March 5, 1932, Paramount Theater.

Credits: Director, Lothar Mendes; based on the novel *The Shorn Lamb* by William J. Locke; screenplay, Grover Jones, William Slavens McNutt; camera, Henry Sharp; original music, Rudolph G. Kopp, John Leipold, Stephan Pasternacki.

Cast: Fredric March (Buddy/Robert and Arthur Drake); Kay Francis (Diane Merrow); Stuart Erwin (Stan Keeney); Juliette Compton (Muriel Preston); George Barbier (Mr. Merrow); Sidney Toler (Detective McPhail); Earle Foxe (Mr. Clarke); Lucien Littlefield (Professor Clark); Leslie Palmer (Bronson); Gertrude Howard (Snowball); Ben Taggart (Crenshaw); John M. Sullivan (Dr. Selous).

Man Wanted (Warner Bros., 1932) 60 min. Released in New York on April 15, 1932, Strand Theater.

Credits: Director, William Dieterle; story, Robert Lord; screenplay, Charles Kenyon; camera, Gregg Toland; editor, James Gibbon; musical director, Leo F. Forbstein; original music, Bernhard Kaun; gowns, Earl Luick; art director, Anton Grot.

Cast: Kay Francis (Lois Ames); David Manners (Tommy Sherman); Una Merkel (Ruthie Holman); Andy Devine (Andy Doule); Kenneth Thomson (Fred Ames); Claire Dodd

(Ann Le Maire); Elizabeth Patterson (Miss Harper); Edward Van Sloan (Manager); Junior Coghlan (Youngster in Store); Betty Farrington (New Secretary); Bess Flowers (Party Guest); Douglas Gerrard (Mr. Orca); Charlotte Merriam (Receptionist); Lee Phelps (Waiter); Eric Wilton (Extra); Robert Greig.

Street of Women (Warner Bros., 1932) 59 min. Released in New York on May 26, 1932, Strand Theater.

Credits: Supervisor, Hal B. Wallis; director, Archie Mayo; based on the novel by Polan Banks; screenplay, Mary McCall, Jr.; adaptation & dialogue, Charles Kenyon, Brown Holmes; art director, Anton Grot; settings supervised by W. & J. Sloane; music director, Leo F. Forbstein; original music, W. Franke Harling; camera, Ernest Haller; editor, James Gibbon.

Cast: Kay Francis (Natalie Upton); Alan Dinehart (Larry Baldwin); Marjorie Gateson (Lois Baldwin); Roland Young (Link Gibson); Gloria Stuart (Doris Baldwin); Allen Vincent (Clarke Upton); Louise Beavers (Mattie, the Maid); Adrienne Dore (Frances); William Burress (Doctor); Wilbur Mack (Mayor).

Jewel Robbery (Warner Bros., 1932) 63 min. Released in New York on July 21, 1932, Strand Theater.

Credits: Director, William Dieterle; associate director, William Keighley; based on the play *Ekszerrablas a Vaci-uccaban* by Ladislaus Fodor; screenplay, Erwin Gelsey, Bertram Bloch; camera, Robert Kurrle; editor, Ralph Dawson; music director, Leo F. Forbstein; original music, Bernhard Kaun; art director, Robert Haas.

Cast: William Powell (the Robber); Kay Francis (Baroness Teri von Hohenfels); Helen Vinson (Marianne Horne); Hardie Albright (Paul, Undersecretary of State); Andre Luguet (Count Andre); Henry Kolker (Baron Franz von Hohenfels); Spencer Charters (Johann Christian Lenz, the Night Watchman); Alan Mowbray (Fritz); Lee Kohlmar (Hollander, the Jeweler); Lawrence Grant (Professor Bauman); Harold Minjur/Minjir (Jewelry Clerk); Ivan Linow (Chauffeur); Charles Coleman (Charles, the Butler); Ruth Donnelly (Berta, the Maid); Clarence Wilson (President of Police); Leo White (Assistant Robber); Don Brodie, Eddie Kane (Robbers); Gordon "Wild Bill" Elliott (Girl-Chasing Gendarme); Herman Bing (Alpine Tourist); George Davis (Polachek); Robert Greig (Henri); Sheila Terry (the Blonde); Jacques Vanaire (Manager); Harold Waldridge (Leopold); Al Hill; John Davidson.

One Way Passage (Warner Bros., 1932) 67 min. Released in New York on October 13, 1932, Strand Theater.

Credits: Producers, Robert Lord, Hal B. Wallis; director, Tay Garnett; assistant director, Robert Fellows; story, Robert Lord; screenplay, Wilson Mizner, Joseph Jackson, Tay Garnett; camera, Robert Kurrle; editor, Ralph Dawson; lyrics, Al Dubin; conductor, Leo F. Forbstein; original music, Bernhard Kaun, W. Franke Harling; orchestrator, Bernhard Kaun, Ray Heindorf; costumes, Orry-Kelly; art director, Anton Grot.

Cast: William Powell (Dan Hardesty); Kay Francis (Joan Ames); Frank McHugh (Skippy); Aline MacMahon (Barrel House Betty/the Countess); Warren Hymer (Steve Burke); Frederick Burton (Doctor); Douglas Gerrard (Sir Harold); Herbert Mundlin (S.S. Maloa Steward); Wilson Mizner (Singing Drunk); Mike Donlin (Hong Kong Bartender); Roscoe Karns (Bartender on S.S. Maloa); Dewey Robinson (Honolulu Contact); William Halligan (Agua Caliente Bartender); Stanley Fields (Captain); Willie Fung (Hong Kong Curio Dealer); Heinie Conklin (Singer of "If I Had My Way"); Harry Seymour (Ship's Officer); Glen Cavender (French Bartender); William Gould (Singing Drunk); Ruth Hall (Joan's Friend); Jane Jones (Singer); Allan Lane (Joan's Friend); Charles Sherlock (Man Listening to Betty).

Trouble in Paradise (Paramount, 1932) 81 min. Released in New York on November 8, 1932, Rivoli Theater.

Credits: Producer/director, Ernst Lubitsch; based on the play *The Honest Finder* by Laszlo Aladar; screenplay, Samson Raphaelson; adaptation, Grover Jones; gowns, Travis Banton; song, W. Franke Harling, Leo Robin; camera, Victor Milner; still photographer, Earl Crowley; camera operator, William Miller; assistant camera, Guy Roe; sound, M.M. Paggi; art director, Hans Dreier.

Cast: Miriam Hopkins (Lily Vautier/Mlle. La Vautier); Kay Francis (Mariette Colet); Herbert Marshall (Gaston Monescu/La Valle]); Charlie Ruggles (the Major); Edward Everett Horton (Francois Filiba); C. Aubrey Smith (Adolph Giron); Robert Greig (Jacques, the Butler); George Humbert (Waiter); Rolfe Sedan (Purse Salesman); Luis Alberni (Annoyed Opera Fan); Leonid Kinskey (Radical); Hooper Atchley (Insurance Agent); Nella Walker (Mme. Boucher); Perry Ivins (Radio Commentator);

Larry Steers (Party Guest); Tyler Brooke (Commercial Singer); Fred Malatesta (Hotel Manager); Eva McKenzie (Duchess Chambreau); Hector Sarno (Prefect of Police); Gus Leonard (Elderly Servant).

Cynara (United Artists, 1932) 78 min. Released in New York on December 24, 1932, Rivoli Theater.

Credits: Producer, Samuel Goldwyn; director, King Vidor; screenplay, Lynn Starling, Frances Marion; from the play by H.M. Harwood and R. Gore Brown, and Brown's novel *An Imperfect Lover.* Film title taken from the Ernest Dowson poem, "Non sum qualis cram" (1896); photography, Ray June; art director, Richard Day; film editor, Hugh Bennett; musical score, Alfred Newman; assistant director, Sherry Shourds; sound, C. Noyer, Frank Maher; song, "Blue Skies" by Irving Berling (1926), sung by Phyllis Barry; Charlie Chaplin footage from *A Dog's Life* (1918).

Cast: Ronald Colman (Jim Warlock); Kay Francis (Clemency Warlock); Phyllis Barry (Doris Lea); Henry Stephenson (John Tring); Viva Tattersall (Milly Miles); Florine McKinney (Garla); Clarissa Selwyne (Onslow); Paul Porcasi (Joseph); George Kirby (Mr. Boots); Donald Stuart (Henry); Wilson Benge (Merton); C. Montague Shaw (Constable); Charlie Hall (Court Spectator); Halliwell Hobbes (Inquest Judge).

The Keyhole (Warner Bros., 1933) 70 min. Released in New York on March 30, 1933, Radio City Music Hall.

Credits: Director, Michael Curtiz; based on the story "Adventuress" by Alice D.G. Miller; screenplay, Robert Presnell; dialogue director, Arthur Greville Collins; art director, Anton Grot; gowns, Orry-Kelly; music director, Leo F. Forbstein; orchestrator, Ray Heindorf; original music, W. Franke Harling; camera, Barney McGill; editor, Ray Curtiss.

Cast: Kay Francis (Ann Brooks/Anne Vallee); George Brent (Neil Davis); Glenda Farrell (Dot); Allen Jenkins (Hank Wales); Monroe Owsley (Maurice Le Brun); Helen Ware (Portia DeWitt Brooks); Henry Kolker (Schuyler Brooks); Ferdinand Gottschalk (Brooks' Lawyer); Irving Bacon (Grover, the Chauffeur); Clarence Wilson (Weems, Head of the Acme Detective Agency); George Chandler (Joe, the Desk Clerk); Heinie Conklin (Mr. Smith, Room 210); Renee Whitney (Cheating Wife); Gordon "Wild Bill" Elliott (Dancing Extra); George Humbert (Hotel Metropole Waiter); Gino Corrado (Hotel Metropole

Waiter); Maurice Black (Cuban Jewelry Salesman); Leo White (Porter); John Sheehan (S.S. Santiago Bartender); Walter Brennan (Extra).

Storm at Daybreak (MGM, 1933) 78 min. Released in New York on July 21, 1933, Capitol Theater.

Credits: Associate Producer, Lucien Hubbard; director, Richard Boleslavsky; based on the play *Black-Stemmed Cherries* by Sandor Hunyady; adaptor, Bertram Millhauser; original music, Dr. William Axt; lyrics, Gus Kahn; camera, George Folsey; editor, Margaret Booth; art director, Alexander Toluboff; interior decorator, Edwin B. Willis; costumes, Adrian; sound, Douglas Shearer; sound mixer, William N. Sparks. Song: "Two Lips Like Cherries."

Cast: Kay Francis (Irina Radovic); Nils Asther (Captain Geza Petery); Walter Huston (Dushan Radovic); Phillips Holmes (Csaholyi); Louise Closser Hale (Militza Brooska); Jean Parker (Danitza); Charles Halton (Villager); Leonid Kinskey (Serbian Villager); Akim Tamiroff (Gypsy Fiddler); Mischa Auer (Assassin); Frank Conroy (Archduke Franz Ferdinand); Eugene Pallette (Janos); C. Henry Gordon (Panto Nikitch); James Bell (Peter); Clarence Wilson (Captain); Oscar Apfel (Counselor Velasch); Hal Boyer (Mitry, Deserter); Frankie Burke (Jankovitch); Richard Cramer (Stepan); Allan Fox (Greg, Deserter); Etienne Girardot (Hungarian Officer); Ferdinand Munier (Party Guest with White Beard); Russ Powell (Man); Lucien Prival (Hungarian Soldier); Harry Semels (Serbian Villager); Milton Wallace (Colonel Patou); Wilhelm von Brincken (Hungarian Officer).

Mary Stevens, M.D. (Warner Bros., 1933) 71 min. Released in New York on August 3, 1933, Strand Theater.

Credits: Supervisor, Hal B. Wallis; director, Lloyd Bacon; assistant director, Chuck Hansen; based on the story by Virginia Kellogg; adaptors, Rian James, Robert Lord; dialogue director, William Keighley; gowns, Orry-Kelly; music director, Leo F. Forbstein; original music, Bernhard Kaun; camera, Sid Hickox; assistant camera, Wesley Anderson; second camera operator, Thomas Brannigan; editor, Ray Curtiss; sound, Robert B. Lee; props, Pinky Weiss; art director, Esdras Hartley.

Cast: Kay Francis (Dr. Mary Stevens.); Lyle Talbot (Dr. Don Andrews); Glenda Farrell (Glenda); Thelma Todd (Lois Rising); Una O'Connor (Mrs. Arnell Simmons); Charles C. Wilson (Walter Rising); Hobart Cavanaugh (Alf

Simmons); Harold Huber (Tony); George Cooper (Pete); John Marston (Dr. Lane); Christian Rub (Gus); Reginald Mason (Hospital Superintendent); Walter Walker (Dr. Clark); Ann Hovey (Miss Gordon, the Receptionist); Constantine Romanoff (Dynamite Schultz); Harry Myers (Nervous Patient); Grace Hayle (Wealthy Lady); Edward Gargan (Cop); Sidney Miller (Sanford Nussbaum); Wilfred Lucas (Barry); Lloyd Ingraham (Ship's Captain); Harry Seymour (Ship's Officer Bringing Serum); Wallace MacDonald (Purser); Joseph E. Bernard (Steward Bringing Purse); Andre Chiron (French Official); Cora Sue Collins (Jane Simmons); Chuck Hamilton (Fireman); Theresa Harris (Alice, the Maid); Milton Kibee (Deck Steward); Henry Otho (Fireman); Inez Palange (Tony's Wife); Lee Phelps (Station Master).

I Loved a Woman (First National, 1933) 80 min. Released in New York on September 21, 1933, Strand Theater.

Credits: Director, Alfred E. Green; based on the book by David Karsner; screenplay, Charles Kenyon, Sidney Sutherland; camera, James Van Trees; editor, Hubert Levy; costume design, Earl Luick; art director, Robert M. Haas; original music, Leo F. Forbstein.

Cast: Edward G. Robinson (John Hayden); Kay Francis (Laura McDonald); Genevieve Tobin (Martha Lane Hayden); J. Farrell MacDonald (Shuster); Henry Kolker (Sanborn); Robert Barrat (Charles Lane); George Blackwood (Henry); Murray Kinnell (Davenport); Robert McWade (Larkin); Walter Walker (Oliver); Henry O'Neill (Farrell); Lorena Layson (Annette, the Maid); Sam Godfrey (Warren); E.J. Ratcliffe (Theodore Roosevelt); Paul Porcasi (Hotel Proprietor); William V. Mong (Bowen); Davison Clark (Doctor); Wallis Clark (Banker); Charles Coleman (Hayden's First Butler); James Donlan (Voting Returns Announcer); Douglass Dumbrille (U.S. Attorney Brandt); Claude Gillingwater (Banker); Howard C. Hickman (Businessman at Meeting); DeWitt Jennings (Banker); Edward Keane (Businessman at Meeting); Milton Kibbee (Lane's Secretary); Wallace MacDonald (Hayden's First Secretary); Edwin Maxwell (Gossiper); Amy Rayan (Gypsy); Edwin Stanley (Businessman at Meeting); Phil Tead (Reporter); Harry Walker (Hayden's Second Secretary); Morgan Wallace (Pollock); William Worthington (Jefferson).

The House on 56th Street (Warner Bros., 1933) 69 min. Released in New York on December 1, 1933, Hollywood Theater.

Credits: Supervisor, James Seymour; director, Robert Florey; story, Joseph Santley; screenplay, Austin Parker, Sheridan Gibney; art director, Esdras Hartley; dialogue director, William Keighley; gowns, Orry-Kelly, Earl Luick; assistant director, Russell Saunders; second assistant director, Arthur Lueker; camera, Ernest Haller; assistant camera, Ellsworth Fredericks; editor, Howard Bretherton; conductor, Leo F. Forbstein; original music, W. Franke Harling, Bernhard Kaun; grip, Dudley Slausson; hair stylist, Emily Moore; props, Keefe Maley; supervisor, James Seymour; still photographer, Charles Scott Welborn.

Cast: Kay Francis (Peggy Martin Van Tyle/Mrs. Stone); Ricardo Cortez (Bill Blaine); Gene Raymond (Monte Van Tyle); John Halliday (Lyndon Fiske); Margaret Lindsay (Eleanor Burgess); Frank McHugh (Chester Hunt); Sheila Terry (Dolly); William "Stage" Boyd (Bonelli); Hardie Albright (Henry Burgess); Phillip Reed (Freddy); Philip Faversham (Gordon); Henry O'Neill (Baxter); Walter Walker (Dr. Wyman); Nella Walker (Mrs. Eleanor Van Tyle); Symona Boniface (Blackjack Player); Frank Darien (Justice of the Peace); George Davis (French Waiter); Lester Dorr (Ship's Steward); Jim Farley (District Attorney); Mary Gordon (Justice of the Peace's Wife); Samuel S. Hinds (Curtis); Olaf Hytten (Peggy's Butler); Lorena Layton (Sextet Girl); Wilfred Lucas (Prosecuting Attorney); John Marston (Ship's Captain); John Mower (Blackjack Player/Bystander); Dennis O'Keefe (Extra); Henry O'Neill (Baxter); Russ Powell (Tom, the Bartender); George Reed (James, the Butler); Leo White (Beautician); Renee Whitney (Sextet Girl); Pat Wing (Sextet Girl).

Mandalay (Warner Bros., 1934) 65 min. Released in New York on February 15, 1934, Strand Theater.

Credits: Producer, Robert Presnell, Sr.; director, Michael Curtiz; based on the story by Paul Hervy Fox; screenplay, Austin Parker, Charles Kenyon; art director, Anton Grot; gowns, Orry-Kelly; camera, Tony Gaudio; editor, Thomas Pratt; technical director, Don Taylor; grip, William McNally; still photographer, Mac Julian; assistant camera, Stuart Higgs; conductor, Leo F. Forbstein; original music, Sammy Fain, Irving Kahal, Heinz Roemheld; sound, W.S. Brown; props, G.W. Bernstein; assistant director, Frank Shaw; hair stylist, Ruth Pursley.

Cast: Kay Francis (Tanya Borisoff/Spot White/Margaret Lang); Ricardo Cortez (Tony Evans); Lyle Talbot (Dr. Gregory Burton);

Warner Oland (Nick); Ruth Donnelly (Mrs. Peters); Reginald Owen (Police Commissioner); David Torrence (Captain of the Sirohi); Etienne Girardot (Mr. Abernathie); Rafaela Ottiano (Countess); Lucien Littlefield (Mr. Peters); Halliwell Hobbes (Colonel Dawson Ames); Bodil Rosing (Mrs. Kleinschmidt); Herman Bing (Professor Kleinschmidt); Lillian Harmer (Louisa Mae Harrington); Torben Meyer (Mr. Van Brinken); Harry C. Bradley (Henry P. Warren); James Leong (Ram Singh); Shirley Temple (Betty Shaw); Leonard Mudie (Police Lieutenant); Frank Baker (First Mate); Olaf Hytten (Cockney Purser); Eric Wilton (English Agent); Otto Frisco (Fakir); George Herrera (2nd Steward); Desmond Roberts (Police Sergeant); Hobart Cavanaugh (Purser); Henry Otho (2nd Sergeant); Lottie Williams (Peters' Friend).

Wonder Bar (First National, 1934) 85 min. Released in New York on February 28, 1934, Strand Theater.

Credits: Producer, Robert Lord; director, Lloyd Bacon; based on the play by Karl Farkas, Robert Katscher, and Geza Herczeg; screenplay, Earl Baldwin; songs, Harry Warren, Al Dubin; music director, Leo F. Forbstein; musical numbers created and directed by Busby Berkeley; camera, Sol Polito; editor, George Amy; art direction, Jack Okey, Willy Pogany; costumes, Orry-Kelly; assistant camera, L. De Angelis; electrician, Frank Flanagan; second camera operator, Mike Joyce; still photographer, Buddy Longworth.

Cast: Al Jolson (Al Wonder); Kay Francis (Liane Renaud); Dolores Del Rio (Inez); Ricardo Cortez (Harry); Dick Powell (Tommy); Guy Kibbee (Henry Simpson); Hugh Herbert (Corey Pratt); Robert Barrat (Captain Von Ferring); Ruth Donnelly (Mrs. Emma Simpson); Louise Fazenda (Mrs. Panzy Pratt); Fifi D'Orsay (Mitzi); Merna Kennedy (Claire); Henry Kolker (Mr. R.H. Renaud); Henry O'Neill (Richard); Kathryn Sergava (Ilke); Gordon De Main, Harry Woods (Detectives); Marie Moreau (Maid); Emile Chautard (Pierre, the Concierge); Pauline Garon (Operator); Alphonse Martel (Doorman); Jane Darwell (Baroness); Gordon "Wild Bill" Elliott (Norman); Michael Dalmatoff (Russian Count); Renee Whitney, Amo Ingraham, Rosalie Roy (Chorus Girls); Alfred James (Night Watchman); Clay Clement, William Stack (Businessmen); Grace Hayle (Fat Dowager); Hal LeRoy (Himself); Spencer Charters (Pete); Demetrius Alexis (Young Boy); William Anderson (Call Boy); Louis Ardizoni (Leon, the Cook);

Hobart Cavanaugh (Drunk); Gino Corrado (Second Waiter); Dick Good (Page Boy); William Granger (First Bartender); Robert Graves (Police Officer); Lottie Woods (Wardrobe Woman); Mia Ichioka (GeeGee); George Irving (Broker); Bud Jamison (Third Bartender); Eddie Kane (Frank); Edward Keane (Captain); John Marlowe (Young Man); Bert Moorhouse (Joe); Marie Moreau (Marie, Liane's Maid); Mahlon Norvell (Artist); Dave O'Brien (Chorus Boy); Dennis O'Keefe (Man at Bar); Henry Otho (2nd Bartender); Gene Perry (Gendarme); Paul Power (Chester); Rolfe Sedan (1st Waiter); Miriam Marlin (Chorine).

Dr. Monica (Warner Bros., 1934) 75 min. Released in New York on June 20, 1934, Strand Theater.

Credits: Executive producers, Jack L. Warner, Hal B. Wallis; producer, Henry Blanke; directors, William Keighley, William Dieterle; based on the play by Marja Morozowicz Sczcepkowska; screenplay, Charles Kenyon; English adaptation, Laura Walker Mayer; art director, Anton Grot; gowns, Orry-Kelly; music director, Leo F. Forbstein; original music, Heinz Roemheld; camera, Sol Polito; editor, William Clemens; assistant director, Lee Katz.

Cast: Kay Francis (Dr. Monica Braden); Warren William (John Braden); Jean Muir (Mary Hathaway); Verree Teasdale (Anna Littlefield); Phillip Reed (Bunny Burton); Emma Dunn (Mrs. Monahan); Herbert Bunston (Mr. Pettinghill); Ann Shoemaker (Mrs. Hazlitt); Virginia Hammond (Mrs. Chandor); Hale Hamilton (Dr. Brent); Virginia Pine (Louise); Pauline True (Betsey, Anna's Maid); Leila McIntyre (Elizabeth, Monica's Maid); Norma Drew (Anna's Second Maid); Edward McWade (Janitor); Harry Seymour (Taxi Driver); Eric Wilton (Spike, Chandor's Butler); Gordon "Wild Bill" Elliott (Rutherford, the Horseback Rider); Reginald Pasch (Mr. Swiegart); Marion Lessing (Mrs. Swiegart); Helen Jerome Eddy (Miss Gelsey); Louise Beavers (Sarah, Mary's Maid); Stanley Mack (Bob, Airplane Mechanic); Claire McDowall (Miss Bryerly); Paul Power (Clerk); Sam Rice (Extra at Dock).

British Agent (First National, 1934) 75 min. Released in New York on September 20, 1934, Strand Theater.

Credits: Director, Michael Curtiz; suggested by the novel by R.H. Bruce Lockhart; screenplay, Laird Doyle; British dialogue, Roland Pertwee; dialogue, Pierre Collings; art director, Anton Grot; music director, Leo F.

Forbstein; original music, Bernhard Kaun, Heinz Roemheld; camera, Ernest Haller; editor, Thomas Richards; dialogue director, Frank McDonald; technical director, Nicholas Kobliansky; gowns, Orry-Kelly.

Cast: Leslie Howard (Stephen Locke); Kay Francis (Elena); William Gargan (Bob Medill); Phillip Reed (Gaston LeFarge); Irving Pichel (Pavlov); Walter Byron (Undersecretary Stanley); Cesar Romero (Tito Del Val); J. Carroll Naish (Commissioner for War); Ivan Simpson (Evans); Gregory Gaye (Kolinoff); Halliwell Hobbes (Sir Walter Carrister); Arthur Aylesworth (Farmer); Mary Forbes (Lady Catherine Trehearne); Doris Lloyd (Lady Carrister); Alphonse Ethier (DeVigny); Paul Porcasi (Romano); Addison Richards (Zvododu); Marina Schubert (Maria Nikolaievna); George Pearce (Lloyd George, Cabinet Officer); Tenen Holtz (Lenin); Walter Armitage (Under Secretary Armitage); Frank Reicher (Mr. X); Thomas Braidon (Cabinet Member); Donald Crisp (Marshall O'Reilly); Winter Hall (Cabinet Member); Lew Harvey (Suspect); Olaf Hytten (Undersecretary); Frank Lackteen (Suspect); Basil Lynn (Cabinet Member); Leonid Snegoff (Russian Diplomat); Wyndham Standing (Englishman); Fred Walton (Cabinet Member); Robert Wilber (Suspect); Claire McDowell (Woman); Zozia Tanina (Dora Kaplan, Woman Who Shot Lenin); Vesey O'Daveren.

Living on Velvet First National, 1935) 77 min. Released in New York in March 1935, Strand Theater.

Credits: Producer, Edward Chodorov; director, Frank Borzage; story/screenplay, Jerry Wald, Julius Epstein; art director, Robert M. Haas; gowns, Orry-Kelly; music director, Leo F. Forbstein; original music, Al Dubin, Harry Warren, Bernhard Kaun, Heinz Roemheld; camera, Sid Hickox; editor, William Holmes.

Cast: Kay Francis (Amy Prentiss); Warren William (Walter "Gibraltar" Pritcham); George Brent (Terrence C. "Terry" Parker); Helen Lowell (Aunt Martha Prentiss); Henry O'Neill (Thornton); Samuel Hinds (Henry L. Parker); Russell Hicks (Major); Maude Turner Gordon (Mrs. Parker); Martha Merrill (Cynthia Parker); Edgar Kennedy (Counterman); Austa (Max, the Dachshund Dog); Lee Shumway (Officer); Walter Miller (Pilot, Formation Leader); Emmett Vogan (Officer); May Beatty, Mrs. Wilfrid North (Dowagers); Frank Dodd (Minister); David Newell (Jim Smalley); Bud Geary (Aunt Martha's Chauffeur); William Wayne (Butler); Gordon "Wild Bill" Elliott (Commuter); William Bailey (Ted Drew); Wade Boteler (Police Sergeant); Harry Bradley (Talkative Man at Party); Eddy Chandler (Policeman at Carnival); John Cooper (Messenger Boy); Jay Eaton (Man at Amy's Party); Frank Fanning (Doorman); Paul Fix (Intern); Sam Hayes (Air Show Announcer); Grace Hayle (Talkative Woman at Party); Harry Holman (Bartender); Selmer Jackson (Officer); Stanley King (Soldier); Jack Mower (Policeman in Park); Harold Nelson (Sexton); Eddie Phillips (Eddie at Party); Jack Richardson (Taxi Driver); Emmet Vogan (Officer); Niles Welch (Major's Aide); Lloyd Whitlock (Man at Amy's Party); Eric Wilton (Lawton, Walter's Butler); Neal Dodd (Minister).

Stranded (Warner Bros., 1935) 76 min. Released in New York on June 20, 1935, Strand Theater.

Credits: Supervisor, Sam Bischoff; director, Frank Borzage; based on the story "Lady with a Badge" by Frank Wead, Ferdinand Reyher; screenplay, Delmer Daves; additional dialogue, Carl Erickson; assistant director, Lew Borzage; art directors, Anton Grot, Hugh Reticker; gowns, Orry-Kelly; music director, Leo F. Forbstein; original music, Bernhard Kaun, Heinz Roemheld; camera, Sid Hickox; editor, William Holmes.

Cast: Kay Francis (Lynn Palmer); George Brent (Mack Hale); Patricia Ellis (Velma Tuthill); Donald Woods (John Wesley); Barton MacLane (Sharkey); Robert Barrat (Stanislaus Janauschek); June Travis (Jennie Holden); Henry O'Neill (Mr. Tuthill); Ann Shoemaker (Mrs. Tuthill); Frankie Darro (Jimmy Rivers); William Harrigan (Updyke); Joseph Crehan (Johnny Quinn); John Wray (Mike Gibbons); Edward McWade (Tim Powers); Gavin Gordon (Jack); Mary Forbes (Grace Dean); Emmett Vogan (Officer on Ferry); Sam McDaniel (Porter); Joan Gay (Diane Nichols); Edwin Mordant (Surgeon); Wilfred Lucas (Pat, a Worker); Mia Liu (Japanese Girl); Richard Loo (Groom); Rita Rozelle (Polish Girl); Louise Seidel (Danish Girl); Frank LaRue (Immigration Officer); Philo McCullough (Immigration Officer); Adrian Morris (River Boss); Milton Kibbee (Pat, the Timekeeper); Vesey O'Davoren (Tuthill's Butler); Spencer Charters (Boatman); Jessie Arnold (Scrubwoman); Harry Bradley (Train Conductor); Mae Busch (Lizzie); Burr Caruth (Old Man); Stan Cavanaugh (2nd Taxi Driver); Glen Cavender (Immigrant); Walter Clyde (Hospital Assistant); Frank Coghlan, Jr. (Page); Claudia Coleman (Madame); Georgie Cooper (Floor Nurse); Nick Copeland (Bridge Worker at Meeting); Don Downen (Clerk); Ralph Dunn (Bridge Worker); Florence Fair (Miss Walsh); Dick French (Clerk); Harrison Greene (Blustery Man); Shirley Grey (Marvel Young); Lillian Harmer (Desk Attendant); Edward Keane (Doctor); John Kelly (Sailor); Joe King (Dan Archer); Eily Malyon (Old Maid); Frank Marlowe (Agitator at Meeting); Pat Moriarty (Steve Brodie); Henry Otho (Bridge Worker); Sarah Padden (Workman's Wife); Paul Panzer (Updyke Agitator); Jack Richardson (1st Taxi Driver); Adrian Rosley (Headwaiter); Cy Schindell (Bridge Worker); Frank Sheridan (Boone); Edwin Stanley (Police Surgeon); Harry Tenbrook (Rollins, Updyke's Agitator); Zeffie Tilbury (Old Hag); Wally Wales (Peterson); Niles Welch (Safety Engineer); Eleanor Wesselhoeft (Mrs. Young); Leo White (Haines, the Drunken Worker); Tom Wilson (Immigrant); Lillian Worth (Blonde); Marbeth Wright (Switchboard Operator); Emma Young (Chinese Girl).

The Goose and the Gander (Warner Bros., 1935) 65 min. Released in New York on September 12, 1935, Strand Theater.

Credits: Supervisor, James Seymour; director, Alfred E. Green; story/screenplay, Charles Kenyon; art director, Robert M. Haas; gowns, Orry-Kelly; music director, Leo F. Forbstein; original music, Bernhard Kaun, Heinz Roemheld; assistant director, Chuck Hansen; camera, Sid Hickox; editor, Bert Lenard.

Cast: Kay Francis (Georgiana Summers); George Brent (Bob McNear); Genevieve Tobin (Betty Summers); John Eldredge (Lawrence Thurston); Claire Dodd (Connie Thurston); Helen Lowell (Aunt Julia Hamilton); Ralph Forbes (Ralph Summers); William Austin (Arthur Summers); Spencer Charters (Winklesteinbergher); Eddie Shubert (Sweeney); John Sheehan (Murphy); Charles Coleman (Jones, the Butler); Wade Boteler (Sprague, Hotel Detective); Davison Clark (Detective at Train Station); Nick Copeland (Mike, the Detective); Cliff Saum (Detective Snyder); Glen Cavender (George, the Detective); Al Woods (Bellboy); Milton Kibbee (Hotel Garageman); Edward McWade (Justice of the Peace); Jane Buckinham (Mrs. Burns); Gordon "Wild Bill" Elliott (Teddy); Olive Jones (Miss Brent); Carlyle Blackwell (Barkley); Eddy Chandler (Policeman); Eddie Graham (Beach Casino Guest); David Newell (Hotel Clerk); Guy Usher (Police Sergeant); Tom Wilson (Baggageman); Al Woods (Bellboy); Helen Woods (Violet).

I Found Stella Parish (First National, 1935) 84 min. Released in New York on November 4, 1935, Strand Theater.

Credits: Producer, Harry Joe Brown; director, Mervyn LeRoy; story, John Monk Saunders; screenplay, Casey Robinson; music director, Leo F. Forbstein; original music, Heinz Roemheld; art director, Robert M. Haas; gowns, Orry-Kelly; camera, Sid Hickox; editor, William Clemens; grip, Rudy Mashmeyer; still photographer, James Manatt; special effects, Fred Jackman, Willard Van Enger; sound, Robert B. Lee; props, Eddie Edwards; assistant director, William H. Cannon; hair stylist, Jane Romaine.

Cast: Kay Francis (Stella Parish/Elsa Jeffords/Aunt Lumilla Evans); Ian Hunter (Keith Lockridge); Paul Lukas (Stephan Norman); Sybil Jason (Gloria Parish); Jessie Ralph (Nana); Joseph Sawyer (Chuck); Eddie Acuff (Dimmy); Walter Kingsford (Reeves, the Editor); Robert Strange (Jed Duffy); Ferdinand Munier (Andrews); Rita Carlyle (First Waiting Woman); Shirley Simpson, Elspeth Dudgeon, Tempe Pigott (Waiting Women); Charles Evans (Old Actor); Lotus Liu (Lotus, Stella's Theater Maid); Olaf Hytten (Robert, Stephen's Butler); Elsa Buchanan (Stella's Maid); Vesey O'Davoren (Deck Steward); Lotus Thompson (Reeves' Secretary); Milton Kibbee (Costumer); John Dilson (Charles Einfeld, Producer's Assistant at the Joe Barnes Company); Harlan Briggs (Theater Manager); Alice Keating (New York Operator); Marie Wells (Hotel Operator); Phyllis Coghlan (London Operator); Emmett Vogan (Reporter); Lew Harvey (Reporter); Gordon "Wild Bill" Elliott (Reporter); Crauford Kent (Lord Chamberlain); Edward Cooper (Caligula); Hugh Huntley (Cemellus); Ralph Bushman (Eric); Vernon Downing (Slave); Vernon Steele (Slave); Mary Treen (Sob Sister); Barton MacLane (Clifton Jeffords); Harry Beresford (James); Harry Allen (Driver to Steamship); Nick Copeland (New York Taxi Driver); Bess Flowers (Party Guest); Sam Harris (The Major, Aboard Ship); Dell Henderson (Actor in Prison Scene); Charles Irwin (Purser); Wilfred Lucas (Custom's Official); Eily Malyon (Ship's Clothing Clerk); Alphonse Martell (Waiter); Wedgwood Nowell (Extra Leaving Ship); Lee Phelps (Photographer); John Graham Spacey (Reeves' Reporter); Will Stanton (Messenger); David Thursby (Tontan, Curtain Operator).

The White Angel (First National, 1936) 75 min. Released in New York on June 25, 1936, Strand Theater.

Credits: Producer, Henry Blanke; director, William Dieterle; based on a biographical sketch in *Eminent Victorians* by Lytton Strachey; screenplay, Michael Jacoby, Mordaunt Shairp; dialogue director, Stanley Logan; art director, Anton Grot; special photography, Fred Jackman; musical director, Leo F. Forbstein; original music, Heinz Roemheld; orchestrator, Hugo Friedhofer; camera, Tony Gaudio; editor, Warren Low; gowns, Orry-Kelly.

Cast: Kay Francis (Florence Nightingale); Ian Hunter (Fuller); Donald Woods (Charles Cooper); Nigel Bruce (Dr. West); Donald Crisp (Dr. Hunt); Henry O'Neill (Dr. Scott); George Curzon (Sir Sidney Herbert); Phoebe Foster (Mrs. Elizabeth Herbert); Charles Croker-King (Mr. Nightingale); Georgia Caine (Mrs. Nightingale); Billy Mauch (Tommy); Lillian Kemble-Cooper (Parthenope Nightingale); Ara Gerald (Mrs. Ella Stevens); Montagu Love (Mr. Bullock); Halliwell Hobbes (Lord Raglan); Frank Conroy (Mr. LeFroy); Eily Malyon (Sister Colombo); Egon Brecher (Pastor Fliedner); Barbara Leonard (Minna); Fay Holden (Queen Victoria); Ferdinand Munier (Alexis Soyer, the Cook); Tempe Pigott (Mrs. Waters, the Nurse); Daisy Belmore (Nurse); Alma Lloyd (Nurse); May Beatty (Nurse); Kathrin Clare Ward (Nurse); Dorothy Arville (Nurse); Lawrence Grant (Colonel); Nelson McDowell (Superintendent of Hospital); Eric Wilton (Servant); Robert Bolder (Doctor); James May (Doctor); Arthur Turner Foster (Doctor); Harry Allen (Soldier); Robert Bolder (Doctor); Clyde Cook (Soldier); Harry Cording (Storekeeper); Neil Fitzgerald (Officer in Barracks); Charles Irwin (Soldier); George Kirby (Soldier); Lowden Adams (Secretary); Jimmy Aubrey (Sentry); Frank Baker (Customs Official); Lionel Belmore (Captain); George Broughton (Corporal); George Bunny (Coachman); Rita Carlisle (Mrs. Mellon); Fay Chaldecott (Praying Child); Silvia Vaughan (Praying Child's Mother); E.E. Clive (Surgeon); Vesey O'Davoren (Thompson, the Butler); Edith Ellison.

Give Me Your Heart (Warner Bros., 1936) 87 min. Released in New York on September 17, 1936, New Criterion Theater.

Credits: Executive producer, Jack L. Warner; producer, Hal B. Wallis; supervising producer, Robert Lord; director, Archie L. Mayo; based on the play *Sweet Aloes* by Jay Mallory (Joyce Carey); screenplay, Casey Robinson; gowns, Orry-Kelly; music director, Leo F. Forbstein; songs, Harold Arlen, E.Y. Harburg; incidental music, W. Franke Harling, Heinz Roemheld; camera, Sid Hickox; editor, James Gibbon; sound recordist, Robert B. Lee; props, Pat Patterson; assistant director, Sherry Shourds; art directors, C.M Novi, Max Parker.

Cast: Kay Francis (Belinda "Bill," "Linda" Warren); George Brent (James "Jim" Baker); Roland Young (Edward "Tubbs" Barrow); Patric Knowles (Robert "Bob" Melford); Henry Stephenson (Edward, Lord Farrington); Frieda Inescort (Rosamond Melford); Helen Flint (Dr. Florence "Bones" Cudahy); Halliwell Hobbes (Oliver Warren); Zeffie Tilbury (Aunt Esther Warren); Elspeth Dudgeon (Alice Dodd); Russ Powell (Cab Driver); Dick French (Guest Who Is Leaving); Ethel Sykes (Guest Who Is Leaving); Bruce Warren (Harry, the Young Man); Elsa Peterson (Young Woman); Velma Wayne and Charles Teske (Dance Team); Tockie Trigg (Edward, the Baby); Helena Grant (Nurse); Louise Bates (Mrs. Ethel Hayle, the Hostess); Demetrius Emanuel (Waiter); Bess Flowers (Carleton Bar Extra); Phyllis Godfrey (Grace, the Maid); Mitchell Ingraham (Bartender); Alphonse Martell (Dining Room Captain); Carlyle Moore, Jr. (Elevator Operator); Edgar Norton (Jenkins, the Servant); Edmund Mortimer (Mr. Hayle, the Host); Eric Wilton (Johnson, the Butler).

Stolen Holiday (Warner Bros., 1937) 76 min. Released in New York on February 1, 1937, Strand Theater.

Credits: Executive producer, Hal B. Wallis; associate producer, Harry Joe Brown; director, Michael Curtiz; story, Warren Duff, Virginia Kellogg; screenplay, Casey Robinson; musical director, Leo F. Forbstein; original music, Al Dubin, Werner R. Heymann, Heinz Roemheld, Harry Warren; art director, Anton Grot; dialogue director, Stanley Logan; gowns, Orry-Kelly; special effects, Fred Jackman; camera, Sid Hickox; editor, Terry Morse.

Cast: Kay Francis (Nicole Picot); Claude Rains (Stefan Orloff); Ian Hunter (Anthony Wayne); Alison Skipworth (Suzanne, the Fortune Teller); Alexander D'Arcy (Leon Anatole, Orloff's Assistant); Betty Lawford (Helen Tuttle); Walter Kingsford (Francis Chalon, Publisher); Charles Halton (Marcel Le Grande, Mayor of Courney); Frank Reicher (Charles Ranier, Credit Municipal); Frank Conroy (Dupont, the Crooked Cop); Kathleen Howard (Mme. Delphine); Wedgewood Nowell (M. Borel, the Swiss Printer); Robert Strange (Prefect of Police); Egon Brecher (Deputy Bergery); Eddie Foster (Agitator); Leonard Mudie (Wedding

Guest); George Beranger (Swiss Waiter); Albert Conti (Photographer); Holmes Herbert (Nicole's Dance Partner); Brandon Hurst (Police Detective); Houseley Stevenson (Minister); Leo White (Taxi Driver).

Another Dawn (Warner Bros., 1937) 73 min. Released in New York on June 18, 1937, Radio City Music Hall.

Credits: Executive producer, Hal B. Wallis; associate producer, Harry Joe Brown; director, William Dieterle; screenplay, Laird Doyle; based on *The Ambassador's Wife* by W. Somerset Maugham; dialogue director, Stanley Logan; art director, Robert Haas; gowns, Orry-Kelly; music, Erich Wolfgang Korngold; orchestrators, Hugo Friedhofer, Milan Roder; assistant director, Frank Heath; sound, Robert B. Lee; camera, Tony Gaudio; editor, Ralph Dawson; choreographer, Michael Kidd; production manager, Tenny Wright.

Cast: Kay Francis (Julia Ashton); Errol Flynn (Captain Denny Roark); Ian Hunter (Colonel John Wister); Frieda Inescort (Grace Roark); Herbert Mundin (Wilkins); G.P. Huntley, Jr. (Lord Alden); Billy Bevan (Hawkins); Clyde Cook (Sergeant Murphy); Richard Powell (Henderson); Kenneth Hunter (Sir Charles Benton); Mary Forbes (Mrs. Benton); Eily Malyon (Mrs. Farnold); Charles Austin (Yeoman); Joseph Tozer (Butler); Ben Welden (Mr. Romkoff); Spencer Teakle (Fromby); David Clyde (Campbell); Charles Irwin (Kelly); Reginald Sheffield (Wireless Operator); Martin Garralaga (Ali, the Servant); George Regas (Achaben); Jack Richardson (Lang); Edward Dew (Glass); R.M. Simpson (Lloyd); Will Stanton (John's Caddy); Noel Kennedy (Julia's Caddy); Sam Harris (Guest); Stefan Moritz (Arab Horseman); Tyrone Brereton (Soldier); Leonard Mudie (Doctor); Yorke Sherwood (Station Master); Claire Verdera (Innkeeper).

Confession (Warner Bros., 1937) 91 min. Released in New York on August 19, 1937, Strand Theater.

Credits: Executive producer, Jack L. Warner; producer, Hal B. Wallis; supervisor, Henry Blanke; director, Joe May; based on the screenplay *Mazurka* by Hans Rameau; English adapters, Julius J. Epstein, Margaret LeVino; dialogue director, Stanley Logan; art director, Anton Grot; gowns, Orry-Kelly; music director, Leo F. Forbstein; piano, Max Rabinowitz; original music, Peter Kreuder, Heinz Roemheld, Jack Scholl; dialogue director, Stanley Logan; camera, Sid Hickox; editor, James Gibbon; publicist, Arthur J. Zellner; grip, Dudie Maschmeyer; women's wardrobe, Ida Greenfield; men's wardrobe, Rydo Loshak; assistant camera, Vernon Larson; still photographer, Madison S. Lacy; assistant editor, Rudi Fehr; best boy, Walter Burris; gaffer, Paul Burnett; script clerk, Fred Applegate; second camera operator, Wesley Anderson; sound, Oliver S. Garretson; props, Emmett Emerson; assistant directors, Sherry Shourds, Fred Tyler; production manager, Al Alleborn; makeup, Ruby Felker, Ward Hamilton.

Cast: Kay Francis (Vera Kowalska); Ian Hunter (Leonide Kirow/Koslov); Basil Rathbone (Michael Michailow); Jane Bryan (Lisa Koslov); Donald Crisp (Presiding Judge); Dorothy Petersen (Mrs. Koslov); Laura Hope Crews (Stella); Mary Maguire (Hildegard); Robert Barrat (Prosecuting Attorney); Ben Welden (Defense Attorney); Veda Ann Borg (Xenia); Helen Valkis (Wanda); Anderson Lawler (Reporter); Michael Mark (Russian Interpreter); Sam Rice, Albert Lloyd, Perc Teeple, Jack Richardson (Men at Station); Lyle Moraine (Usher at Theater); Ferdinand Munier (Bald Man at Theater); Peggy Keys, Jewel Jordan (Autograph Fans); Sam Ash (Waiter); Edward Keane (Cabaret Manager); Pierre Watkin (Lawyer); Dawn Bender (Lisa as a Baby); Janet Shaw, Jody Gilbert, Evelyn Mulhall, Symona Boniface, Elsa Peterson (Actress Friends); Edward Price, Jeffrey Sayre, John Mather, Lane Chandler, John Davidson, Maurice Brierre (Actor Friends); Lawrence Grant (Doctor); Maurice Cass (Music Professor); Glen Cavender (Bailiff); Gennaro Curci (Extra); Don Downen (Young Man in Court); Alan Gregg (Extra); John Harron (Extra); Herbert Heywood (Porter Carrying a Letter); Leyland Hodgson (Leading Man in Opera); Stuart Holmes (Policeman in Court); Matty King (Dancer); Rolf Lindau (Clerk at Candy Counter); Al Lloyd (Man at Station); Theodore Lorch (Man in Court); Alphonse Martell (Maitre D'Hotel); Paul Panzer (Man Bringing Suitcase); Henry Roquemore (Fat Man in Court); Cliff Saum (Reporter); Ferdinand Schumann-Heink (Man in Court); Harry Semels (Porter on Train); John Shelton (Actor); Bernard Siegel (Theater Doorman); Adele St. Mauer (Koslov's Maid); Myrtle Stedman (Nurse Maid); Don Turner (Man Leaving Theater); Dale Van Sickel (Diner in Cabaret); Emmett Vogan (American Frontiersman in Show); Patricia Walthall (Frontiersman's Assistant); Pierre Watkin (Lawyer Stagoff); Tom Wilson (Man in Court Sitting Next to Mrs. Koslov); Jack Wise (Reporter).

First Lady (Warner Bros., 1937) 82 min. Released in New York on December 23, 1937, Strand Theater.

Credits: Executive producers, Jack L. Warner, Hal B. Wallis; associate producer, Harry Joe Brown; director, Stanley Logan; based on the play by George S. Kaufman, Katharine Dayton; screenplay, Rowland Leigh; art director, Max Parker; music director, Leo F. Forbstein; original music, Max Steiner; gowns, Orry-Kelly; assistant director, Sherry Shourds; camera, Sid Hickox; editor, Ralph Dawson.

Cast: Kay Francis (Lucy Chase Wayne); Anita Louise (Emmy Page); Preston Foster (Stephen Wayne); Walter Connolly (Carter Hibbard); Victor Jory (Senator Gordon Keane); Verree Teasdale (Irene Hibbard); Louise Fazenda (Mrs. Lavinia Mae Creevey); Marjorie Gateson (Sophie Prescott); Marjorie Rambeau (Belle Hardwicke); Eric Stanley (Tom Hardwick); Henry O'Neill (George Mason); Lucille Gleason (Mrs. Ives); Sara Haden (Mrs. Mason); Harry Davenport (Charles); Gregory Gaye (Gregoravich); Olaf Hytton (Bleeker); Jackie Morrow (Boy); Jack Mower (Halloran); Elizabeth Dunne (Extra); Lillian Harmer (Extra); Joseph Romantini (Senor Ortega); Robert Cummings, Sr. (Extra); Wedgwood Nowell (Extra); Grant Mitchell (Ellsworth T. Banning); John Harron (Waiter).

Women Are Like That (Warner Bros., 1938) 78 min. Released in New York on April 11, 1938, Strand Theater.

Credits: Associate producer, Robert Lord; director, Stanley Logan; from the *Saturday Evening Post* story by Albert H.Z. Carr, "Return from Limbo"; screenplay, Horace Jackson; art director, Max Parker; gowns, Orry-Kelly; musical director, Leo F. Forbstein; original music, Heinz Roemheld; sound, Stanley Jones; camera, Sid Hickox; editor, Thomas Richards.

Cast: Kay Francis (Claire Landin); Pat O'Brien (Bill Landin); Ralph Forbes (Martin Brush); Melville Cooper (Leslie Mainwaring); Thurston Hall (Claudius King); Grant Mitchell (Mr. Franklin Snell); Gordon Oliver (Howard Johns); John Eldredge (Charles Braden); Herbert Rawlinson (Avery Flickner); Hugh O'Connell (George Dunlap); Georgia Caine (Mrs. Amelia Brush); Joyce Compton (Miss Hall); Sarah Edwards (Mrs. Hattie Snell); Josephine Whittell (Miss Douglas); Lola Cheaney (Miss Perkins); Edward Broadley (Holliwell, the Butler); Sam McDaniel (Porter); Symona Boniface

(Lady Behind Claudius on Boat); Harry Bradley (Mr. Frazier); Allan Cavan (Jimmy, the Bartender); William Hopper (Extra); George Humbert (Waiter); Anderson Lawler (Freddie); Lillian Harmer (Landlady); Bernice Pilot (Maude); Renie Riano (Hotel Maid); William Worthington (the Minister); Harvey Clark (Salesman).

My Bill (Warner Bros., 1938) 65 min. Released in New York on July 9, 1938, Strand Theater.

Credits: Producer, Bryan Foy; director, John Farrow; based on the play *Courage* by Tom Barry; screenplay, Vincent Sherman, Robertson White; art director, Max Parker; gowns, Orry-Kelly; musical director, Leo F. Forbstein; original music, Howard Jackson; sound, Charles Lang; camera, Sid Hickox; editor, Frank Magee; assistant director, Russell Saunders; dialogue director, Vincent Sherman.

Cast: Kay Francis (Mary Colbrook); Dickie Moore (Bill Colbrook); Bonita Granville (Gwen Colbrook); John Litel (Mr. John C. Rudlin); Anita Louise (Muriel Colbrook); Bobby Jordan (Reginald Colbrook); Maurice Murphy (Lynn Willard); Elisabeth Risdon (Aunt Caroline Colbrook); Helena Phillips Evans (Mrs. Adelaide Crosby); John Ridgely (Mr. Martin, the Florist); Jan Holm (Miss Kelly, Rudlin's Secretary); Sidney Bracy (Jenner, Aunt Caroline's Butler); Bernice Pilot (Beulah, the Colbrook Maid); Tommy Bupp (Football Player); Glen Cavender (Mr. Perry); William Gould (Dr. Judd); William Haade (Piano Mover); John Harron (Bank Clerk); Stuart Holmes (Passerby); Henry Otho (Piano Mover); Billy Wayne (Taxi Driver); Tom Wilson (Onlooker); Jack Wise (Man Who Buys Newspaper).

Secrets of an Actress (Warner Bros., 1938) 70 min. Released in New York on October 8, 1938, Strand Theater.

Credits: Producer, David Lewis; director, William Keighley; based on the screen story "Lovely Lady" by Milton Krims; screenplay, Milton Krims, Rowland Leigh, Julius J. Epstein; art director, Anton Grot; gowns, Orry-Kelly; musical director, Leo F. Forbstein; original music, Heinz Roemheld; sound, Charles Lang; camera, Sid Hickox; editor, Owen Marks; assistant director, Chuck Hansen.

Cast: Kay Francis (Fay Carter); George Brent (Dick Orr); Ian Hunter (Peter Snowden); Gloria Dickson (Mrs. Carla Orr); Isabel Jeans (Marian Plantagenet); Penny Singleton (Miss Reid); Dennie Moore (Miss Blackstone); Selmer

Jackson (Thompson); Herbert Rawlinson (Harrison); Emmett Vogan (Joe Spencer); James B. Carson (W.P. Carstairs, Theatrical Manager); Jerry Fletcher (Theater Usher); Theresa Harris (Blanche, the Maid); John Harron (Party Guest at Bar); Grace Hayle (Fat Visitor in Dressing Room); Leyland Hodgson (Man in Theater Lobby); Arthur Housman (Drunk Who Keeps Turning Off Lamp); Olaf Hytten (Reynolds, Peter's Butler); Anderson Lawler (Thompson's Assistant); Clayton Moore (Theater Usher); Jack Mower (Purser); Wedgwood Nowell (Man in Theater Lobby); Spec O'Donnell (Call Boy); George O'Hanlon (Delivery Boy); Jack Richardson (Man in Theater Lobby); Cliff Saum (Extra in Audience); Leo White (Florist); Peggy Moran (Actress Waiting to See Carstairs).

Comet Over Broadway (Warner Bros., 1938) 65 min. Released in New York on December 16, 1938, Palace Theater.

Credits: Executive producers, Jack L. Warner, Hal B. Wallis; associate producer, Bryan Foy; director, Busby Berkeley; based on a *Cosmopolitan* magazine story by Faith Baldwin; screenplay, Mark Hellinger, Robert Buckner; musical director, Leo F. Forbstein; original music, Ray Heindorf, M.K. Jerome, H. Roemheld; gowns, Orry-Kelly; art director, Charles Novi; sound, Charles Lang; camera, James Wong Howe; editor, James Gibbon; grip, Warren Yaple; still photographer, Madison S. Lacy; assistant director, Russell Saunders; makeup, Robert Cowan; hair stylist, Ruby Felker.

Cast: Kay Francis (Eve Appleton); Ian Hunter (Bert Ballin); John Litel (Bill Appleton); Donald Crisp (Joe Grant); Minna Gombel (Tim Adams); Sybil Jason (Jackie Appleton); Melville Cooper (Emerson); Ian Keith (John Banks); Leona Marical (Janet Eaton); Ray Mayer (Tommy Brogan); Vera Lewis (Mrs. Appleton); Nat Carr (Haines, Burlesque Manager); Chester Clute (Willis); Edward McWade (Harvey); Clem Bevans (Benson); Dorothy Comingore/Linda Winters (Mrs. McDermott); Jack Mower (Hotel Manager); Edgar Edwards (Walter); Alice Connors, Fern Barry, Susan Hayward (Amateur Actors); Owen King (Actor); Janet Shaw (Woman); Kay Gordon, Jessie Mae Jackson (Chorus Girls); Frank O'Connor (Officer); Henry Otho (Baggage Man); Frank Orth (Cab Driver); Sidney Bracy (English Porter); Jimmy Conlin (Comic); Charles Seel (Jury Foreman); Mitchell Ingraham (Court Clerk); Raymond Brown (Judge); Emmett Vogan (Prosecutor); Edwin Stanley (Doctor); Howard M. Mitchell (Court Officer); Loia

Cheaney (Extra); Dudley Dickerson (Porter); Lester Dorr (Performer); Edgar Edwards (Waiter); Jerry Fletcher (Bellhop); Jan Holm (Ticket Booth Girl); Henry Otho (Baggage Man); Victoria Elizabeth Scott (Jackie, Age 18 Months); Jack Wise (Stage Manager).

King of the Underworld (Warner Bros., 1939) 69 min. Released in New York on January 14, 1939, Rialto Theater.

Credits: Executive producer, Jack L. Warner; associate producer, Bryan Foy; director, Lewis Seiler; based on the serialized novel "Dr. Socrates" by W.R. Burnett; screenplay, George Bricker, Vincent Sherman; dialogue director, Vincent Sherman; musical director, Leo F. Forbstein; original music, Heinz Roemheld; assistant director, Frank Heath; art director, Charles Novi; gowns, Orry-Kelly; technical adviser, Dr. Leo Schulman; sound, Everett A. Brown; camera, Sidney Hickox; editor, Frank Dewar; technical advisor, Dr. Leo Shulman; sound, E.A. Brown; assistant director, Frank Heath.

Cast: Humphrey Bogart (Joe Gurney); Kay Francis (Carole Nelson); James Stephenson (Bill Stevens); John Eldredge (Dr. Niles Nelson); Jessie Busley (Aunt Josephine); Arthur Aylesworth (Dr. Sanders); Raymond Brown (Sheriff); Harland Tucker (Mr. Ames, the Head G-Man); Ralph Remley (Mr. Robert, the Grocer); Murray Alper (Eddie); Charley Foy (Slick); Joe Devlin (Porky); Elliott Sullivan (Mugsy); Alan Davis (Pete); John Harmon (Slats); John Ridgely (Jerry); Richard Bond (Intern); Paul MacWilliams (Anesthetist); Richard Quine (Medical Student); Stuart Holmes (Doorman); Vera Lewis (Woman); William Gould (Chief of Police); Clem Bevans, Carl Stockdale, Nat Carr (Villagers); Jack Mower, John Harron (G-Men); Sherwood Bailey (Boy); Jimmy O'Gatty, Frank Bruno, Paul Panzer, Cliff Saum, Doc Stone (Gangsters); Sidney Bracy (Farmer); Lottie Williams (Farmer's Wife); Tom Wilson, Glen Cavender (Deputies); Davison Clark (Foreman); Pierre Watkin (District Attorney); Charles Trowbridge (Dr. Ryan); Ed Stanley (Dr. Jacobs); Ralph Dunn (First Policeman); Jerry Fletcher (Young Man); Lew Harvey (Chic, a Gangster); Herbert Heywood (Clem); Max Hoffman, Jr. (Second Policeman); Al Lloyd (Drug Store Clerk); Peggy Moran (Young Man's Wife); Jack Richardson (Townsman Running); Ann Robinson (Second Nurse); Francis Sayles (Furniture Store Proprietor); Janet Shaw (Blonde Nurse); Charles Sullivan (Gangster).

Women in the Wind (Warner Bros., 1939) 63 min. Released in New York on April 13, 1939, Palace Theater.

Credits: Producer, Mark Hellinger; associate producer, Bryan Foy; director, John Farrow; based on the novel by Francis Walton; screenplay, Lee Katz, Albert DeMond; assistant director, Marshall Hageman; art director, Carl Jules Weyl; dialogue director, Jo Graham; technical adviser, Frank Clark; musical director, Leo F. Forbstein; gowns, Orry-Kelly; camera, Sid Hickox; editor, Thomas Pratt; sound, Charles Lang.

Cast: Kay Francis (Janet Steele); William Gargan (Ace Boreman); Victor Jory (Doc); Maxie Rosenbloom (Stuffy McInnes); Sheila Bromley (Frieda Boreman); Eve Arden (Kit Campbell); Eddie Foy, Jr. (Denny Carson); Charles Anthony Hughes (Bill Steele); Frankie Burke (Johnnie); John Dilson (Sloan); Spencer Charters (Henry, the Farmer); Vera Lewis (Farmer's Wife); Sally Sage, Alice Connors, Marian Alden, Iris Gabrielle, Diana Hughes (Aviatrixes); John Harron (Process Server); John Ridgely, Jack Mower, Frank Mayo (Salesmen); Lucille De Never, Marie Astaire (Women); Steven Darrell, David Kerman (Photographers); Emmett Vogan (Radio Announcer); George O'Hanlon (Bellboy); Eddie Graham (Microphone Man); Milton Kibbee (Burbank Official); William Gould (Palmer); Gordon Hart (Drew, Air Races Official); Ila Rhodes (Joan); Rosella Towne (Phyllis); Raymond Bailey (Attendant); Richard Bond (Salesman); Sidney Bracey (Burbank Official); Nat Carr (Salesman); Allan Cavan (Wichita Official); Joe Cunningham (Telegraph Office Attendant); Ralph Dunn (Policeman on Field); Edgar Edwards (Wichita Starter); Hudson Fausset (Attendant); Frank Faylen (Chuck, the Mechanic); Paul Panzer (Mechanic); Jack Gardner (Mechanic); George Guhl (Bartender); John Hiestand (Radio Announcer); Lew Kelly (Wichita Official); Reid Kilpatrick (Voice of Announcer); Alexander Leftwich (Cleveland Official); Al Lloyd (Wichita Official); Wilfred Lucas (Burbank Official); Carlyle Moore, Jr. (Cleveland Radio Operator); Will Morgan (Intern); Wedgwood Nowell (Cleveland Official); Lee Phelps (Wichita Official); Cliff Saum (Policeman); Tom Wilson (Attendant); Jack Wise (Welcoming Official); David Newell (Man in Crowd); Pat O'Malley (Cleveland Official).

In Name Only (RKO, 1939) 94 min. Released in New York, August 4, 1939, Radio City Music Hall.

Credits: Executive producer, Pandro S. Berman; producer, George Haight; director, John Cromwell; based on the novel *Memory of Love* by Bessie Breuer; screenplay, Richard Sherman; original music, Roy Webb; art directors, Van Nest Polglase, Perry Ferguson; set decorator, Darrell Silvera; Miss Lombard's gowns by Irene; other gowns, Edward Stevenson; assistant director, Dewey Starkey; sound, Hugh McDowell, Jr.; special effects, Vernon L. Walker; camera, J. Roy Hunt; editor, William Hamilton.

Cast: Carole Lombard (Julie Eden); Cary Grant (Alec Walker); Kay Francis (Maida Walker); Charles Coburn (Mr. Richard Walker); Helen Vinson (Suzanne Duross); Katharine Alexander (Laura Morton); Jonathan Hale (Dr. Edward "Ned" Gateson); Maurice Moscovich (Dr. Muller); Nella Walker (Mrs. Grace Walker); Peggy Ann Garner (Ellen Eden); Spencer Charters (Fred, the Gardener); Alan Baxter (Charley, the Drunk); Harriet Mathews, Sandra Morgan (Women on Boat); Harold Miller (Man on Boat); John Dilson (Head Train Steward); Douglas Gordon (Steward); James Adamson (Black Waiter on Train); Tony Merlo (Waiter); Frank Puglia (Tony, Café Manager); Alex Pollard (Butler); Charles Coleman (Archie Duross); Florence Wix, Clive Morgan, Major Sam Harris, Kathryn Wilson (Party Guests); Grady Sutton (Paul Graham, Suzanne's Escort); Bert Moorhouse (College Man Asking About Game); Mary MacLaren (Nurse at Desk); Robert Strange (Hotel Manager); Jack Chapin (First Bellhop); Allan Wood (Joe, a Bellhop); Harold Hoff (Bellhop Bringing Bottle); John Laing (John, the Chauffeur); Frank Mills (Bartender); Byron Foulger (Owen, an Office Clerk); Arthur Aylesworth (Farmer on Truck); Fern Emmett (Hotel Chambermaid); Edward Fliegle (Night Clerk); Gus Glassmire (Yawning Hospital Attendant); Lloyd Ingraham (Hospital Elevator Operator); George Rosener (Dr. Hastings, at the Hotel).

It's a Date (Universal, 1940) 103 min. Released in New York on March 22, 1940, Rivoli Theater.

Credits: Producer, Joseph Pasternak; director, William A. Seiter; story, Jane Hall, Frederick Kohner, Ralph Block; screenplay, Norman Krasna; orchestrator, Frank Skinner; musical director, Charles Previn; music, Lucien Denni ("Oceana Roll"), Prince Leleiohaku ("Hawaiian War Chant"), Queen Liliuokalani ("Aloha Oe"), Felix Mendelssohn-Bartholdy ("The Wedding March"), Pinky Tomlin and Harry Tobias ("Love Is All"), Ralph Freed and Frank Skinner

("It Happened in Kaloha"), Hans J. Salter (incidental music); Eddie Cherkose, Jacques Press, Leon Belasco ("Rhythm of the Islands"), Giacomo Puccini ("Musetta's Waltz Song"), Franz Schubert ("Ave Maria"); Lyrics, Ralph Freed; camera, Joseph Valentine; editor, Bernard W. Burton; sound supervisor, Bernard B. Brown; sound technician, Joseph Lapis; art director, Jack Otterson; associate art director, Martin Obzina; assistant director, Frank Shaw; gowns, Vera West; set decorator, R.A. Gausman.

Cast: Deanna Durbin (Pamela Drake); Kay Francis (Georgia Drake); Walter Pidgeon (John Arlen); Samuel S. Hinds (Sidney Simpson); S.Z. Sakall (Carl Ober); Lewis Howard (Freddie Miller); Cecilia Loftus (Sara Frankenstein); Henry Stephenson (Captain Andrew); Eugene Pallette (Governor Allen); Joe King (First Mate Kelly); Fritz Feld (Headwaiter); Charles Lane (Mr. Horner); John Arledge (Newcomer); Romaine Callender (Evans); Virginia Brissac (Miss Holden); Leon Belasco (Captain); Anna Demetrio (Cook); Mary Kelley (Governor's Wife); Eddie Acuff (Ship's Steward); Fay McKenzie, Linda Deane, Phyllis Ruth, Virginia Engels (Young Girls); Eddie Polo (Quartermaster); Mary Shannon (Wardrobe Mistress); Mark Anthony (Officer); Harry Owens and His Royal Hawaiians (Themselves); Randy Oness (Singer); John Daheim (Sleepy-Eyed Man); Landers Stephens (Business Executive); William Ruhl (Ship's Officer); David Oliver (Officer); Louis Natheaux (Party Guest); Eddie Lee (Captain Andrews' Servant); Jennifer Gray (Cable Office Girl).

When the Daltons Rode (Universal, 1940) 81 min. Released in New York on August 23, 1940, Loew's State Theater.

Credits: Director, George Marshall; based on the book by Emmett Dalton, Jack Jungmeyer; screenplay, Harold Shumate; musical director, Charles Previn; original music, Frank Skinner; art director, Jack Otterson; associate art director, Martin Obzina; assistant director, Vernon Keays; camera, Hal Mohr; editor, Ed Curtiss; sound supervisor, Bernard B. Brown; sound technician, Robert Pritchard; gowns, Vera West; set decorator, R.A. Gausman.

Cast: Randolph Scott (Tod Jackson); Kay Francis (Julie King); Brian Donlevy (Grat Dalton); George Bancroft (Caleb Winters); Broderick Crawford (Bob Dalton); Stuart Erwin (Ben Dalton); Andy Devine (Ozark Jones); Frank Albertson (Emmett Dalton); Mary Gordon (Ma Dalton); Harvey Stephens (Rigby); Edgar Dearing (Sheriff); Quen Ramsey (Clem Wilson);

Dorothy Grainger (Nancy); Bob McKenzie (Photographer); Fay McKenzie (Hannah); Walter Soderling (Judge Swain); Mary Ainslee (Minnie); Erville Alderson (District Attorney Wade); Sally Payne (Annabella); June Wilkins (Suzy); William Gould (Deputy on Train); Jack Clifford (Deputy); Pat West (Pete, the Restaurant Owner); Dorothy Moore (Girl); George Guhl (Deputy in Baggage Car); Robert Dudley (Juror Pete Norris); Edward Brady (Deputy); Walter Long (Deputy on Train); Bob Reeves (Henchman); Kernan Cripps (Freight Agent); Tom London (Lyncher); Mary Cassidy (Girl); Lafe McKee (Doctor); Russ Powell (Engineer); John Beck (Native); James C. Morton (Juror Ed Pickett); Edgar Buchanan (Narrator/Old-timer); Harry Cording (Jim Osburn); James Flavin (Annabella's Brother).

Little Men (RKO, 1940) 84 min. Released in New York on December 7, 1940, Rivoli Theater.

Credits: Producers, Gene Towne, Graham Baker; associate producer, Donald J. Ehlers; director, Norman Z. McLeod; based on the novel by Louisa May Alcott; screenplay, Mark Kelly, Arthur Caesar; art directors, Van Nest Polglase, Al Herman; musical director, Roy Webb; original music, Roy Webb; camera, Nicholas Musuraca; editor, George Hively; special effects, Vernon L. Walker; sound recordist, John E. Tribby; assistant director, Sam Ruman; costumes, Edward Stevenson; set decorator, Darrell Silvera.

Cast: Kay Francis (Jo); Jack Oakie (Willie, the Fox); George Bancroft (Major Burdle); Jimmy Lydon (Dan); Ann Gillis (Nan); Charles Esmond (Professor); Richard Nichols (Teddy); Elsie, the Moo Girl of the New York World's Fair (Buttercup); Casey Johnson (Robby); Francesca Santoro (Bess); Johnny Burke (Silas); Lillian Randolph (Asia); Sammy McKim (Tommy); Edward Rice (Demi); Anne Howard (Daisy); Jimmy Zaner (Jack); Bobbie Cooper (Adolphus); Schuyler Standish (Nat); Paul Matthews (Stuffy); Tony Neil (Ned); Fred Estes (Emmett); Douglas Rucker (Billy); Donald Rackerby (Frank); William Demarest (Constable); Sterling Holloway (Reporter); Isabel Jewell (Stella); Bud Jamison (Cop); Sarah Edwards (Landlady); Duke York (Poker Player); Howard Hickman (Doctor); Stanley Blystone (Bartender); Charles Arnt (Drunk); Nora Cecil (Matron); Hal K. Dawson (Telegraph Operator); George D. Green (Poker Player); Jack Henderson (Drunk); Bill Irving (Bartender); George Irving (Truant

Officer); Lew Kelly (Postman); Russ Powell (Railroad Conductor); Clarence Wilson (Reynolds); Nella Walker (Extra).

Play Girl (RKO, 1941) 76 min. Released in New York on January 29, 1941, Palace Theater.

Credits: Executive producer, Lee Marcus; producer, Cliff Reid; director, Frank Woodruff; story/screenplay, Jerry Cady; camera, Nicholas Musuraca; editor, Harry Marker; art director, Van Nest Polglase; set decorator, Darrell Silvera; assistant director, Sam Ruman; associate art director, Albert D'Agostino; sound recordist, Theron O. Kellum; special effects, Vernon L. Walker; musical director, Paul Sawtell; Miss Francis' gowns, I. Magnin & Co.; wardrobe, Edward Stevenson.

Cast: Kay Francis (Grace Herbert); James Ellison (Thomas Elwood "Tom" Dice); Mildred Coles (Ellen Daley); Nigel Bruce (William McDonald "Bill" Vincent); Margaret Hamilton (Josie, Grace's Maid); Katharine Alexander (Mrs. Dice); George P. Huntley (Van Payson); Charles Quigley (Lock, the Polo Player in Montage); Georgia Carroll (Alice Sawyer, Girl with Tom at Concert); Kane Richmond (Don Shawhan); Stanley Andrews (Joseph Shawhan); Selmer Jackson (Uncle Fred Dice); Dick Hogan (Bellhop); Ralph Byrd (Miami Doctor); Cecil Cunningham (Dowager, Next to Payson at Concert); Charles Arnt (Grady, the Private Detective); Marek Windheim (Dr. Alonso Corvini, the Orchestra Conductor); Oliver Cross (Cashier); Eddie Dew (Bartender); Douglas Evans (Concert Radio Announcer); Charles Flynn (Football Player); Boyd Irwin (Mike Kilroy, Man in Steam Bath); Frank Meredith (Brakeman); Joey Ray (Usher); Gwen Seager (Miss Seager, Vincent's Secretary); Larry Steers (Dance Extra); Gayne Whitman (Jeweller); Theodore von Eltz (Mr. Hunter, the Hotel Manager).

The Man Who Lost Himself (Universal, 1941) 72 min. Released on March 21, 1941.

Credits: Producer, Lawrence W. Fox, Jr.; associate producer, Ben Hersch; director, Edward Ludwig; based on the novel by H. De Vere Stacpoole; screenplay, Eddie Moran; camera, Victor Milner; special photographic effects, John Fulton; musical director, H.J. Salter; original music, Charles Previn, Hans J. Salter, Frank Skinner; editor, Milton Carruth; art director, Jack Otterson; associate art director, Richard H. Riedel; set decorator, R.A. Gausman; gowns, Vera West; sound supervisor, Bernard B. Brown;

assistant director, Seward Webb; technician, Hal Bumbaugh.

Cast: Brian Aherne (John Evans/Malcolm Scott); Kay Francis (Adrienne Scott); S.Z. Sakall (Paul); Henry Stephenson (Frederick Collins); Eden Gray (Venetia Scott); Wilson Benge (Butler); Nils Asther (Peter Ransome); Sig Ruman (Dr. Simms); Marc Lawrence (Frank De Soto); Henry Kolker (T.J. Mulhausen); Janet Beecher (Mrs. Milford); Dorothy Tree (Mrs. Van Avery); Russell Hicks (Mr. Van der Girt); Frederick Burton (Mr. Milford); Selmer Jackson (Mr. Green); Henry Roquemore (Bartender); Sarah Padden (Mrs. Cummings, the Maid); Ethel Clifton (Maid); Paul Bryar (Bar Waiter); Irene Coleman (Office Girl); Cyril Ring (Relative); Frank O'Connor (Cab Driver); Lloyd Whitlock (Attendant); William "Billy" Benedict (Messenger Boy); Billy Engle (Newsboy); William Gould (Mr. Ryan); Margaret Armstrong (Mrs. Van der Girt).

Charley's Aunt (Twentieth Century–Fox, 1941) 81 min. Released in New York on August 1, 1941, Roxy Theater.

Credits: Producer, William Perlberg; director, Archie Mayo; based on the play by Brandon Thomas; screenplay, George Seaton; original music, Alfred Newman; art directors, Richard Day, Nathan Juran; set decorator, Thomas Little; costumes, Travis Banton; camera, J. Peverell Marley; editor, Robert Bischoff; matte artist, Chesley Bonestell; sound, Joseph E. Aiken, Roger Heman.

Cast: Jack Benny (Babbs Babberly/Lord Fancourt); Kay Francis (Donna Lucia); James Ellison (Jack Chesney); Anne Baxter (Amy Spettigue); Edmund Gwenn (Stephen Spettigue); Reginald Owen (Mr. Redcliff); Laird Cregar (Sir Francis Chesney); Arleen Whelan (Kitty Verdun); Richard Haydn (Charley Wyckham); Ernest Cossart (Brassett); Morton Lowry (Harley Stafford); Lionel Pape (Babberly); Claud Allister, William Austin (Spectators); Russell Burroughs, Gilchrist Stuart, John Meredith (Teammates); Bob Conway, Bob Cornell, Basil Walker, Herbert Gunn (Students); Will Stanton (Messenger); C. Montague Shaw (Elderly Man); Maurice Cass (Octogenarian); Brandon Hurst (Coach); Stanley Mann (Umpire).

The Feminine Touch (MGM, 1941) 97 min. Released in New York on December 12, 1941, Capitol Theater.

Credits: Producer, Joseph L. Mankiewicz; director, Major W.S. Van Dyke II; screenplay,

George Oppenheimer, Edmund L. Hartmann, Ogden Nash; original music, Franz Waxman; song "Jealous" composed by Jack Little; lyrics, Dick Finch, Tommie Malie; art director, Cedric Gibbons; special effects, Warren Newcombe; camera, Ray June; editor, Albert Akst; set decorator, Edwin B. Willis; gowns, Adrian; hair stylist, Sydney Guilaroff; assistant director, Tom Andre; associate art director, Paul Groesse; recording director, Douglas Shearer.

Cast: Rosalind Russell (Julie Hathaway); Don Ameche (John Hathaway); Kay Francis (Nellie Woods); Van Heflin (Elliott Morgan); Donald Meek (Captain Makepeace Liveright); Gordon Jones (Rubber-Legs Ryan); Henry Daniell (Shelley Mason); Sidney Blackmer (Freddie Bond); Grant Mitchell (Dean Hutchinson); David Clyde (Brighton); Gino Corrado (Party Waiter); Robert Homans (Subway Cop); Harold Minjir (College Official); Bernard Nedell (Subway Snake); Jack Norton (Drunk at Party); Anne O'Neal (Lady on Subway); Robert Ryan (Extra); Dennie Travis (Piano Player).

Always in My Heart (Warner Bros., 1942) 92 min. Released in New York on March 13, 1942, Strand Theater.

Credits: Producers, Walter MacEwen, William Jacobs; director, Joe Graham; suggested by a play (*Fly Away Home*) by Dorothy Bennett, Irving White; screenplay, Adele Comandini; dialogue director, Frank Fox; music, H. Roemheld; "Una voce poca fa" from *Barber of Seville* by Rossini; "Always in My Heart" by Ernesto Lecuona; musical director; Leo F. Forbstein; vocal arrangements, Dudley Chambers; orchestrator, Frank Perkins; camera, Sid Hickox; editor, Thomas Pratt; art director, Hugh Reticker; gowns, Orry-Kelly; makeup, Perc Westmore; sound, Francis J. Scheid; special effects, Edwin A. DuPar, Byron Haskin.

Cast: Kay Francis (Marjorie Scott); Walter Huston (MacKenzie Scott); Gloria Warren (Victoria Scott); Patty Hale (Booley); Frankie Thomas (Martin Scott); Una O'Connor (Angie); Sidney Blackmer (Philip Ames); Armida (Lolita); Frank Puglia (Joe Borelli); Anthony Caruso (Frank); Elvira Curci (Rosita); Herbert Gunn (Dick); Harry Lewis (Steve); John Hamilton (Warden); Borrah Minevitch and His Rascals (Blackie and His Musicians); Leon Belasco (Violinist); Cliff Saum (Trusty); Lester Sharpe (Tuba Player); Frank Mayo (Tom, the Guard); Hank Mann (Truck Driver); Lon McCallister (Boy); Jean Ames, Juanita Stark, Mary Brodel (Girls); Frank Lackteen (Pedro); Bob Stevenson (Fisherman);

Pat O'Malley (Cop); Russell Arms (Red); Glen Cavender (Second Truck Driver); George Guhl (Café Proprieter); Herbert Heywood (Sailor); Jack Mower (Ames' Chauffeur); Spec O'Donnell (Ice Cream Vendor); Leo White (Studio Manager); Lottie Williams (Lady Buying Bread).

Between Us Girls (Universal, 1942) 89 min. Released in New York on September 4, 1942, Capitol Theater.

Credits: Producer, Henry Koster; associate producer, Philip P. Karlstein (Phil Karlson); director, Koster; based on the play *Le Fruit Vert* by Regis Gignoux, Jacques Thery; adapters, Hans Jacoby, John Jacoby; screenplay, Myles Connolly, True Boardman; art directors, Jack Otterson, Richard H. Riedel; gowns, Vera West; musical director, Charles Previn; camera, Joseph A. Valentine; editor, Frank Gross; sound director, Bernard B. Brown.

Cast: Diana Barrymore (Caroline Bishop); Robert Cummings (Jimmy Blake); Kay Francis (Christine Bishop); John Boles (Steven Forbes); Andy Devine (Mike Kilinsky); Ethel Griffies (Gallagher); Walter Catlett (Desk Sergeant); Guinn "Big Boy" Williams (Father of the Boys); Scotty Beckett (Leopold); Andrew Tombes (Doctor); Peter Jamerson (Harold); Mary Treen (Mary Belle); Lillian Yarbo (Phoebe); Irving Bacon (Soda Dispenser); Aileen Pringle, Charles Coleman, Virginia Engels (Guests); Edgar Dearing (Cop); Jack Mulhall, Leon Belasco (Waiters); Billy Lenhart (Boy); Bennie Bartlett (Kid); Walter Woolf King (Duke); Ed Gargan (Cab Driver); Edgar Licho (Ambassador); Bobby Barber (Waiter).

Four Jills in a Jeep (Twentieth Century–Fox, 1944) 89 min. Released in New York on April 6, 1944, Roxy Theater.

Credits: Producer, Irving Starr; director, William A. Seiter; story, Froma Sand, Fred Niblo, Jr.; based on the actual experiences of Kay Francis, Carole Landis, Martha Raye, Mitzi Mayfair; screenplay, Robert Ellis, Helen Logan, Snag Werris; orchestrator, Maurice De Packh; music and lyrics, Jimmy McHugh, Harold Adamson, Leo Robin, Harry Warren; choreographer, Don Loper; musical directors, Emil Newman, Charles Henderson; art directors, James Basevi, Albert Hogsett; set decorators Thomas Little; associate set decorator, Al Orenbach; camera, Peverell Marley; editor, Ray Curtiss; costumes, Yvonne Wood; assistant director, William Eckhardt; sound, Jesse Bastian, Murray Spivack; special effects, Fred Sersen; makeup artist, Guy Pearce.

Cast: Kay Francis, Carole Landis, Martha

Raye, Mitzi Mayfair (Themselves); Jimmy Dorsey & His Band (Themselves); John Harvey (Ted Warren); Phil Silvers (Eddie); Dick Haymes (Lieutenant Dick Ryan); Alice Faye, Betty Grable, Carmen Miranda (Guest Stars); George Jessel (Master of Ceremonies); Glenn Langan (Captain Stewart); Lester Matthews (Captain Lloyd); Miles Mander (Colonel Hartley); Frank Wilcox (Officer); Paul Harvey (General); Mary Servoss (Nurse Captain); B.S. Pulley, Dave Willock (Soldiers); Ralph Byrd (Sergeant); Renee Carson (French Maid); Edith Evanson (Swedish Maid); Betty Roadman (Housekeeper); Mary Field (Maid); Mel Schubert (Pilot); Winifred Harris (Lady Carlton-Smith); Crauford Kent (British Officer); Frances Morris (Surgical Nurse); James Flavin (M.P.); Jimmy Martin (Aide); Eddie Acuff (Sentry); Kirk Alyn (Pilot); Martin Black (Soldier); Lester Dorr (Soldier); Alex Pollard (Butler); Alec Harford (Priest); Mike Killian (Soldier); George Tyne (Soldier); Gordon Wynn (Soldier).

Divorce (Monogram, 1945) 71 min. Released in New York, August 18, 1945, Paramount Theater.

Credits: Executive director, Trem Carr; producers, Jeffrey Bernerd, Kay Francis; director, William Nigh; story, Sidney Sutherland; screenplay, Harvey H. Gates, Sidney Sutherland; original music, Edward J. Kay; musical director, Edward J. Kay; technical director, Dave Milton; set decorator, Vin Taylor; assistant director, Richard Harlan; sound recorder, Tom Lambert; camera, Harry Neumann; supervising editor, Richard Currier; production manager, William Strohbach; stylist, Lorraine MacLean; gowns, Odette Myrtil; hats, Keneth Hopkins.

Cast: Kay Francis (Dianne Hunter Carter); Bruce Cabot (Bob Phillips); Helen Mack (Martha Phillips); Jerome Cowan (Judge Jim Driscoll); Craig Reynolds (Bill Endicott); Ruth Lee (Liz Smith); Jean Fenwick (June Endicott); Mary Gordon (Ellen, the Housekeeper); Larry Olsen (Michael Phillips); Johny Calkins (Robby Phillips); Jonathan Hale (Judge Conlon); Addison Richards (Plummer, the Lawyer); Leonard Mudie (Harvey Hicks); Reid Kilpatrick (Dr. Andy Cole); Virginia Ware (Secretary); Napoleon Simpson (Train Porter); Pierre Watkin (John B. Carter).

Allotment Wives (Monogram, 1945) 80 min. Released in New York on December 29, 1945, Fox Theater, Brooklyn.

Credits: Executive director, Trem Carr; producers, Jeffrey Bernerd, Kay Francis; director, William Nigh; story, Sidney Sutherland; screenplay, Harvey Gates, Sidney Sutherland; art director, Dave Milton; set decorators, Vin Taylor, Charles Thompson; assistant director, Richard Harlan; sound, Tom Lambert; camera, Harry Neumann; editor, William Austin; Miss Francis' gowns, Odette Myrtil; Miss Francis' hats, Keneth Hopkins; stylist, Lorraine MacLean; production manager, Glenn Cook; musical director, Edward J. Kay; technical director, David Milton.

Cast: Kay Francis (Sheila Seymour); Paul Kelly (Pete Martin); Otto Kruger (Whitey Colton); Gertrude Michael (Gladys Smith); Teala Loring (Connie Seymour); Bernard Nedell (Spike Malone); Matty Fain (Louie Moranto); Anthony Warde (Joe Agnew); Jonathan Hale (General Gilbert); Selmer Jackson (Deacon Sam); Evelyn Eaton (Ann Farley); Reid Kilpatrick (Philip Van Brook); John Elliott (Officer); Terry Frost (Soldier).

Wife Wanted (Monogram, 1946) 73 min. Released November 2, 1946.

Credits: Producers, Jeffrey Bernerd, Kay Francis; director, Phil Karlson; suggested by the novel by Robert Callahan; screenplay, Caryl Coleman, Sidney Sutherland; technical director, Dave Milton; assistant director, Doc Joos; production manager, William Calihan; musical director, Edward J. Kay; sound, Tom Lambert; "There Wasn't a Moon," by Edgar Hayes; camera, Harry Neumann; editor, Ace Herman; stylist, Lorraine MacLean; production manager, Glenn Cook; Miss Francis' gowns, Athena.

Cast: Kay Francis (Carole Raymond); Paul Cavanagh (Jeffrey Caldwell); Robert Shayne (Bill Tyler); Veda Ann Borg (Nola Reed); Teala Loring (Mildred Hayes); John Gallaudet (Lee Kirby); Barton Yarborough (Walter Desmond); Selmer Jackson (Lowell Cornell); Bert Roach (Arthur Mayfield); John Hamilton (Judge); Jonathan Hale (Philip Conway); Anthony Warde (Man); Sara Berner (Agnes); Charles Marsh (Tenant); Claire Meade (Tenant); Will Stanton (Squint); Paul Everton (Toland); Buddy Gorman (Newsboy); Shelby Payne (Secretary); Mabel Todd (Florist); Tim Ryan (Bartender); Barbara Woodell (Miss Shelton); Maurice Prince (Messenger); Bob Alden (Messenger); Valerie Ardis (Nurse); Wilbur Mack (Doctor); Budd Fine (Cop); Joe Greene/Joseph J. Greene (Hector); Elaine Lange (Mrs. Wiley); George Carleton/George M. Carlton (Arthur Mayfield); John Hamilton (Judge); Edgar Hayes (Extra); Margo Woode (Miss Sheldon).

Notes

Abbreviations: MCNY = Museum of the City of New York, NYPL = New York Public Library for the Performing Arts, RLC = Robinson Locke Collection WCA = Kay Francis, Diaries, 1922–1953. Kay Francis Collection. Wesleyan Cinema Archives, Wesleyan University, Middletown, Connecticut.

Chapter 1

1. Elizabeth Wilson, Projections, *Silver Screen,* March 1937, p. 27.

2. *Daily Oakie,* January 14, 1905, p. 1.

3. The Threadgill, located at the northeast corner of N. Broadway and W. Second (300 N. Broadway), opened on April 2, 1904. Named for Dr. John Threadgill, the showplace featured tiled floors, marble wainscoting, and private bathrooms.

4. There is no birth certificate to verify Kay's exact name, as certificates were not required in Oklahoma at that time — the Bureau of Vital Statistics didn't exist until 1906. In a March 3, 1938, interview with *The Daily Oklahoman,* Dr. G. A. Wall, the presiding physician, claimed he gave a birth certificate to Kay's mother, and was adamant that Kay was born January 13, 1905. When Kay filled out her Social Security application in 1937, she stated she was born on January 13, 1905. Other evidence exists in a letter Kay's mother wrote to a friend, claiming Kay was born "Jy. 13, 1905." Some misinterpreted this to mean July, but it now seems clear that Jy. was Katherine Clinton's abbreviation for January. Kay also explained in an interview that Paramount did not want to give out her birth year, but simply told interviewers she was born on Friday the 13th. This accounts for the variety of birth years for Kay. It's possible that Kay's first name was spelled "Katherine." It's also possible she was named "Kathleen"—this name was provided by an aunt in an old newspaper clipping. The Edwina was in honor of Katherine Clinton's late brother, Edwin.

5. Ed Sullivan, Hollywood, unidentified clipping, NYPL.

6. Tarkington's novel was adapted for the 1942 Orson Welles film of the same name.

7. "The House of Gibbs," *Homer Index,* Oct. 16, 1901, p. 1.

8. Joseph remarried after his wife's death. His second wife, Eliza, died in 1877.

9. "Obituary [Helen Woolley]," *Homer Index,* January 24, 1894, unidentified page.

10. "A Good Man Gone. Death of Volney Gibbs—Last of a Prominent Family," November 22, 1899, *Homer Index,* unidentified page number.

11. Marcus Gibbs died in 1837—before Joe Gibbs' birth. Mason Gibbs died in a Battle Creek sanitarium, but the remaining siblings lived in the house until their deaths.

12. There were three students in Joe Gibbs' graduating class.

13. "Married," *Homer Index,* September 10, 1884, unidentified page.

14. Katherine Clinton Gibbs was also reportedly in Richard Mansfield's company, which rings a little truer.

15. Kay met Maxine Elliott in September 1934 on one of her European trips.

16. Rae S. Corliss, "Kay Francis Visited Ill Father in Albion Hospital," *Journal of Albion,* June 14, 1986, p. 1.

17. Hattie Darrow Gibbs—Joe's ex-wife—married Owen Townsend in 1896.

18. "House of Gibbs," October 16, 1901, *Homer Index,* p. 1.

19. *Illustrated Atlas and Directory of Free Holders of Calhoun County Michigan Including Brief Biographical Sketches of Enterprising Citizens: Compiled and Published from Official Records and Personal Examinations,* 1894, unidentified page number.

20. Coincidentally, Kay played a telegraph operator in *When the Daltons Rode,* a 1940 film.

21. "House of Gibbs," *Homer Index,* p. 1.

22. "Colorful Homer Citizen Was Father of Miss Kay Francis," unidentified clipping.

23. "Colorful Homer Citizen Was Father of Miss Kay Francis," unidentified clipping.

24. "Colorful Homer Citizen Was Father of Miss Kay Francis," unidentified clipping.

25. *Homer Index,* August 25, 1896.

26. According to the *Annals of the New York Stage,* Joe also appeared in *The Westerner* at the Windsor Theater in New York on July 12, 1890, and at the Bedford Avenue Theater during the week of April 11–16, 1891. This was probably around the time he met his second wife, Mary Connelly.

27. "Colorful Homer Citizen Was Father of Miss Kay Francis," unidentified clipping.

28. *Homer Index,* April 4, 1894, unidentified page.

29. Helen was rarely mentioned again, and there is no record of what happened to her. Mary stated in her 1907 will that she had no children.

30. "Beat the Railroads: J.S. Gibbs Travels from Chicago in His New Automobile," *Homer Index,* October 17, 1900, unidentified page.

31. According to the inheritance law, the first $5,000 in value was exempt, and the remainder was taxed at one percent, making the estate worth a little less than $28,000.

32. *Homer Index,* April 17, 1901, unidentified page.

33. *Battle Creek Moon,* November 20, 1900, unidentified page number.

34. Pedro is a card game, similar to euchre.

35. "Brilliant Social Events: Mr. and Mrs. Jos. S. Gibbs Entertain at Their Suburban Home," *Homer Index,* January 22, 1902, p. 1.

36. "The Pick of the Country: Are Among the Fine Horses at the Gibbs Farm: Joe's Extensive Deals in Fancy Horseflesh: Handles Only High-Class Coach Horses and Sells to the Aesthetic Eastern Trade," *Homer Index,* April 30, 1902, p. 1.

37. The property was sold to Henry Goldup and reported in *The Homer Index* on December 24, 1902.

38. The presiding judge was a Judge Hopkins.

39. Ed Sullivan, Hollywood, unidentified clipping, NYPL.

40. Herbert Cruikshank, "Lucky Thirteen," *Modern Screen.*

41. Founded in 1857 by musician and composer Robert Goldbeck, the school's name was changed to the Chicago Conservatory College. The school closed in 1981.

42. Alumni of the Augustin Daly Company included John Drew, Otis Skinner, Catherine Lewis, May Fielding, Hart Conway, and other notable stage actors.

43. Ada Rehan was the star of the Daly Company at this time. She was also rumored to be Daly's mistress.

44. Unidentified clipping, RLC.

45. Unidentified clipping, RLC.

46. Unidentified clipping, RLC.

47. "I know I need a rest, and no doubt it is the Spanish blood of my grandmother stirring in me." Jewel Smith, *Hollywood and the Great Fan Magazines,* p. 182. There was also a 1932 *Silver Screen* article that referred to Katherine Clinton's "Spanish ancestry." Dana Rush, "The Aristocrat of the Screen," *Silver Screen,* February 1932, p. 41.

48. In fact, Kay's dark hair and complexion led to a rumor that she was part black. Rumormongers went so far as to insist that Kay's dark-skinned maid was her own mother (á la Merle Oberon). Some African Americans assumed Kay had black blood. In Maya Angelou's autobiographical *I Know Why the Caged Bird Sings,* she and brother Bailey were stunned by how much Kay Francis resembled their mother.

49. According to Clinton's research, Lawrence Clinton arrived in the Massachusetts Bay Colony in 1665, served as an apprentice, and eventually bought his freedom. Furthermore, Moses B. and Jacob Franks came from London to America before the Revolution, and worked as the King's government agents in New York and Pennsylvania.

50. Dana Rush, "The Aristocrat of the Screen," *Silver Screen,* February 1932, p. 77.

51. Hattie V. Finch and Marie A. Connelly witnessed the event, and the Rev. George C. Houghton officiated. Joe and Katherine both listed their address as 137 W. 48th Street, probably a rooming house. Katherine was listed as unmarried, and Joe claimed to be widowed, which may have been what he told Katherine.

52. The Church, designated a national landmark in 1973, is still a popular place of worship for stage actors.

53. On September 26, 1931, the Hotel Threadgill changed its name to the Hotel Bristol. The Bristol closed on January 15, 1957, and was demolished to make room for a parking lot in February 1957. A six-storey parking garage — the Broadway-Kerr Garage — replaced the lot in August 1971. Yes, Kay's birthplace is now a parking garage.

54. Letter to Editor, *Daily Oklahoman,* June 18, 1944, p. 50.

55. "The Guests of Manager Gibbs: New Landlord of Threadgill Entertains a Coterie of Friends at a Dinner Party," *Daily Oklahoman,* June 17, 1904, p. 7.

56. The ad listed 21 East 6th Street as her contact address. According to a city directory, this was the home of Charles and Alice Lowery.

57. Katherine also participated in a 1904 Christmas Bazaar given by the Episcopal Guild. If Kay attended any church services as a child it was probably Episcopalian — and her first wedding was at an Episcopal church, as was Katherine Clinton's.

58. The ad for *Two Hours of Oblivion* ran in the September 25, 1904, edition of *The Daily Oklahoman.* Admission ranged from twenty-five cents to one dollar, and the production ran for one night only at the Overholser.

59. "Social Calendar," *Daily Oklahoman,* October 9, 1904, p. 11.

60. "Two Hours of Oblivion," *Daily Oklahoman,* October 6, 1904, p. 5.

61. "Sense and Nonsense [advertisement]," *Daily Oklahoman,* April 9, 1905, p. 13.

62. Katherine was sometimes credited as Catherine Clinton Gibbs.

63. "Amusements," *Daily Oklahoman,* May 3, 1905.

64. "Amusements," *Daily Oklahoman,* May 16, 1905, p. 10.

65. Letter to the Editor, *Daily Oklahoman,* June 18, 1944, p. 50.

66. Helen Starr, "My Daughter, Kay," unidentified clipping, NYPL.

67. Joe's other employers in Oklahoma City included the Hotel Lee and the Marquette Club. In November 1904, Joe was demoted from Threadgill's principal manager to food manager. This arrangement apparently didn't work out, and Joe left and became manager at the Marquette Club in February 1905, shortly after Kay's birth.

68. Kay banned any future interviews. According to a November 14, 1936, article in the *Hollywood Citizen News,* "Kay Francis has issued strict orders to the Warner publicity department that no one, absolutely NO ONE, is to be given the telephone number and street address of her mother. It isn't that Mrs. Gibbs is offish. Kay is the one who is building a wall of 'protection' around her. Seems some time ago a fan magazine writer did an interview with Mrs. Gibbs, and it was rather a saccharine story when it appeared in print. Kay was furious and intends to keep her mother incommunicado as far as the press is concerned."

69. Helen Starr, "My Daughter, Kay," unidentified clipping, NYPL.

70. Montecito is a small town near Santa Barbara, California. Around the time the Gibbs would have lived there, rich Easterners were building European-style mansions, and the area eventually became a wealthy resort town.

71. "Kay Francis Describes Early Days in Theatre, Love for Drama," unidentified clipping, MCNY.

72. Ben Maddox, "Kay Francis Wants Life," *Movie Mirror,* September 1934, p. 77.

73. Helen Starr, "My Daughter, Kay," unidentified clipping, NYPL.

74. The Lake Hotel was built in 1890 near Yellowstone Lake in the National Park.

75. Mary Gibbs' will was probated in September 1907. Her final will had been drawn in February 1907.

76. Linton's first name was variously reported as Edward and Edwin.

77. Linton was born in 1874 and married Mary Reichow on February 4, 1918. He sold the farm on May 21, 1927, to the Mestdagh family, who still own it today. A January 1950 fire destroyed most of the outbuildings, but did not damage the house, which still stands, though it's been renovated. Linton died on November 14, 1946, at the age of 72.

78. "Gets a Fortune," September 6, 1907, unidentified clipping.

79. The Republican House, located at 3rd and Cedar, was built in 1865 and torn down in 1961. It was here, in 1900, that the American League was created when representatives voted to change the baseball league's name from the Western League to the American League. A parking lot now occupies the site where the hotel once stood.

80. Justin T. Cook, the son of Louisa Woolley Cook (Helen Woolley's sister), was born in 1854 and died in 1929 of tertiary syphilis. His first wife, Harriet, died in 1903. He married Fanny Reed in 1905. She died in 1950. Her obituary made no mention of Kay Francis.

81. Lottie Tillotson , "Homer Claims Kay Francis," unidentified clipping.

82. Rae S. Corliss, "Kay Francis Visited Ill Father in Albion Hospital," *Journal of Albion*, June 14, 1986, p. 5.

83. The certifying physician in St. Louis was August Dulzi. Joe's age was given as 64 years and four days. He was actually younger — only 56 years old.

84. Joe was buried in an unmarked grave in Homer's Fairview Cemetery on January 25, 1919. He's likely in the Gibbs section, along with his grandparents, aunts, uncles, parents — and ex-wife Mary!

85. No record of a divorce between Joe and Katherine has been found. It's possible that Joe's marriage to Minnie was common-law.

Chapter 2

1. Helen Starr, "My Daughter, Kay," unidentified clipping, NYPL.

2. Helen Starr, "My Daughter, Kay," unidentified clipping, NYPL.

3. "Kay Francis Describes Early Days in Theatre, Love for Drama," unidentified clipping, MCNY.

4. Herbert Cruikshank, "Lucky Thirteen," *Modern Screen*, October 1931, p. 58. In another version of Kay's childhood incident, the plot point was suicide — not murder: "Kay's earliest recollection of the theatre was when, at the age of four, she was allowed to sit 'out front' one matinee day and watch her mother act. It was one of those melodramas so much in vogue at that time, and for the third act curtain her mother had to shoot herself. The shot rang out and the audience was frightfully impressed — then through the tense atmosphere piped up Kay's baby voice. 'Mother's not really dead — she's only acting.' Kay received her best spanking to date and was sent away to school."

5. Helen Starr, "My Daughter, Kay," unidentified clipping, NYPL.

6. British-born Lindsay Morison was a featured actor and singer with the Castle Square Theater Company. It may have been a case of an old friend doing a favor for a needy friend. It's likely the Morison Company was based in Boston.

7. Unidentified clipping, RLC.

8. Unidentified clipping, RLC.

9. Unidentified clipping, RLC.

10. Unidentified clipping, RLC.

11. Unidentified clipping, RLC.

12. Unidentified clipping, RLC.

13. Unidentified clipping, RLC.

14. *Hartford Courant*, May 2, 1916.

15. George Eells, *Ginger, Loretta, and Irene Who*, p. 187.

16. Kay Francis, Diary, March 22, 1927, Kay Francis Collection, Wesleyan Cinema Archives, Wesleyan University, Middletown, Connecticut.

17. Unidentified clipping, NYPL.

18. Kay met Pola Negri on May 8, 1931, at a Hollywood dinner party at Bebe Daniels' home.

19. 104. Unidentified clipping, NYPL.

20. Helen Starr, "My Daughter, Kay," unidentified clipping, NYPL.

21. Unidentified clipping, MCNY

22. The Academy of Holy Angels was located at Main Street and Linwood Avenue in Fort Lee, New Jersey. Founded in 1879, it relocated to Demarest, New Jersey, in 1965.

23. Notre Dame Academy was located at Washington and Marcella Streets in Roxbury, Massachusetts. Founded in 1853, it merged with Notre Dame Academy in Boston in 1954, and relocated to Hingham, Massachusetts, in 1964.

24. Holy Child Jesus School, founded in 1910, is located at 111–11 86th Avenue in Richmond Hill, New York.

25. Helen Starr, "My Daughter, Kay," unidentified clipping, NYPL.

26. Ossining was also the home of Sing Sing prison. In fact, the town was originally named Sing Sing, but in an effort to avoid the prison's notoriety, the city's name was changed to Ossining in 1901.

27. "Kay Francis Describes Early Days in Theatre, Love for Drama," unidentified clipping, MCNY.

28. Unidentified advertisement.

29. Unidentified advertisement.

30. "Kay Francis Describes Early Days in Theatre, Love for Drama," unidentified clipping, MCNY.

31. More than a million people watched Pershing lead some 25,000 veterans down Fifth Avenue, from 110th Street to Greenwich Village's Washington Square. It was New York's last war pageant.

32. Lucille Elfenbein, "So Now Kay Francis Wears Dark Glasses Everywhere; Tall Actress Travels Light," unidentified clipping, NYPL.

33. Kay also told the story when she complained about her lack of privacy. She described how reporters broke down her door while she was on a cruise. "'I told them,' chuckled Kay, with relish, 'that I was a strong girl who made a twelve second mark for the one hundred dash in school, and that I would be likely to break their cameras over their heads if they dared take any pictures.'"

34. Helen Starr, "My Daughter, Kay," unidentified clipping, NYPL.

35. Unidentified clipping, MCNY.

36. Unidentified clipping, MCNY.

37. George Eells, p. 188.

38. The title is sometimes reported as "You Never Can Tell."

39. Unidentified clipping, MCNY.

40. "Kay Francis Describes Early Days in Theatre, Love for Drama," unidentified clipping, MCNY. St. Paul's and St. Mary's were operated by the Episcopal Diocese of Long Island. The schools were closed in the 1990s. St. Mary's burned in June 2000 and was subsequently sold to a development company in July 2001. The building was demolished in December 2001, and eight single-family, luxury homes were built on the site. St. Paul's has been converted into a retirement home.

41. Unidentified clipping, MCNY.

42. Kay Francis, "Don't Try Your Luck Out Here!," *Pictorial Review,* January 1937, p. 50.

43. Unidentified clipping, MCNY. Kay and Reg might have stayed in touch. Kay reported seeing a "Reg" several times in 1922 when she was dating Dwight Francis. There was also a "Reggie" who sent congratulatory telegrams when she opened in *Crime* and *Venus.* In fact, Kay stayed in touch with several friends from her boarding school days, and occasionally mentioned in her diary revisiting Ossining after leaving the school.

44. The school was located at Park Avenue and 40th Street.

45. The Katharine Gibbs School, owned by Career Education Corporation, is now located at 50 West 40th Street.

46. Juliana Cutting's address was 565 Park Avenue, New York.

47. By coincidence, Frank Reicher, who staged *The Wife with the Smile,* appeared with Kay Francis more than ten years later in two films—*British Agent* (1934) and *Stolen Holiday* (1936).

Chapter 3

1. Francis Diary, July 4, 1922, WCA.

2. Lundihn, Inc. (Ladies Tailors) was located at 24 East 55th Street, now the heart of the women's luxury shopping district.

3. McMillan Emerson & Co. was located at 120 Broadway.

4. Sinclair Rubber Co. was located at 1679 Broadway.

5. Kay Francis, "Don't Try Your Luck Out Here!," *Pictorial Review,* January 1937, p. 50.

6. Elizabeth Wilson, "Projections," *Silver Screen,* March 1937, p. 27.

7. Francis Diary, April 23, 1922, WCA. Intriguingly, this was the first time Kay used shorthand to record a diary entry—she obviously feared someone reading her diary.

8. Francis Diary, June 27, 1922, WCA.

9. It's conceivable that the first pregnancy ended in a miscarriage, but it was more likely an abortion. Until Kay moved to California, she used the same doctor for all of her abortions, Dr. Donald Levy.

10. Twice, in 1917 and 1919, Dwight was asked to leave Harvard despite desperate—and repeated—requests from his parents that he be given another chance.

11. Kay and Dwight were married in the Chantry Chapel by Reverend E.M. Stires. Kay's address was listed as 41 W. 54th Street. Her maid of honor was a young woman named Buddy [she did not identify her last name], a schoolmate from Ossining.

12. Jerry Lane, "Kay Francis' Amazing Secret," *Screen Play,* March 1935, p. 23.

13. Kay's previous addresses included 224 East 49th Street and 41 West 54th Street.

14. Francis Diary, December 31, 1922, WCA.

15. Elizabeth Wilson, "Projections," *Silver Screen,* March 1937, p. 80.

16. The Inn, built in 1918, was located at 153 South Street.

17. The South Street Inn was sold in 1952, and the apartments converted into smaller units.

18. Kay and girlfriend Gwyneth had lunch with Cornell on April 16, 1923.

19. According to Katherine Clinton, Mrs. Dwight Morrow and Mrs. W. K. Vanderbilt hired Kay as a personal secretary, but Kay later said she was simply a secretary to *their* financial secretaries.

20. Ben Maddox, "Kay Francis Wants Life," *Movie Mirror,* September 1934, p. 76.

21. Francis Diary, October 11, 1924, WCA.

22. Virginia Maxwell, "Just 'Life and Love,'" *Photoplay,* June 1933, p. 85.

23. Faith Service, "Did $26,000 Outweigh a Honeymoon Trip for Kay Francis?," *Motion Picture,* November 1932, p. 78.

24. Francis Diary, November 9, 1924, WCA.

25. Frances Kellum, "The Men in Kay Francis' Life!," *Screen Book,* December 1936, p. 86.

26. Francis Diary, July 7, 1925, WCA.

27. Francis Diary, December 30, 1924, WCA.

28. Warner Fabian's real name was Samuel Hopkins Adams. *Flaming Youth* was made into a silent film with Colleen Moore. As Fabian, he was also responsible for *The Wild Party, The Men in Her Life,* and other sensational Jazz Age works. Using the name Adams, his works were adapted into more respectable films such as *It Happened One Night* and *The Harvey Girls.*

29. "Restless, seductive, greedy," Warner Fabian, *Flaming Youth,* p. 5.

30. Warner Fabian, *Flaming Youth,* p. 18.

31. Francis Diary, January 1, 1925, WCA.

32. Her telephone number was Plaza 0758.

33. The site today is the freight entrance of a large midtown office building.

34. Gerald Kelly was born in England in 1879 and died in 1972. Knighted by the King in 1945, Kelly painted many royal and celebrity portraits. Kelly's sister Rose was once married to Aleister Crowley, whom Kelly detested.

35. Personal correspondence, Erika Ingham, National Portrait Gallery, London, October 3, 2003.

36. Personal correspondence, Erika Ingham, National Portrait Gallery, London, October 3, 2003.

37. Derek Hudson, *For Love of Painting,* pp. 44–45.

38. *The Sphere,* May 26, 1926.

39. "The New Forehead Craze," *New York Evening Journal,* August 9, 1926.

40. The portrait, measuring 39 _ by 31 inches, was also included in a 1957 retrospective exhibition in the Diploma Gallery of the Royal Academy.

41. Derek Hudson, *For Love of Painting,* p. 45.

42. The painting is now owned by the Seeing Eye Inc. of Morristown, New Jersey, and hangs in the women's lounge of student housing.

43. *Harper's Bazar* was changed to *Harper's Bazaar* in November 1929.

44. Franklin Simon & Co. was located at 5th Avenue and 37th Street. Kay's coat was the least expensive. Another was priced at $50, but the others were $68 and $75. Kay modeled on December 9, 1924.

45. Hart Crane, quoted in Carol Mann, *Paris: Artistic Life in the Twenties & Thirties,* p. 15.

46. Eells, p. 190.

47. Phyllis Duganne, *Harper's Bazar,* October 1923, pp. 90–91.

48. The French franc had lost most of its value in comparison to the American dollar, making it inexpensive for Americans to live in France.

49. Charles Baskerville, also known as Top Hat, died at the age of 98 in 1994.

50. Lois Long, who retired in 1970 from *The New Yorker,* died in 1974. According to William Shawn in her *New York Times* obituary, "Lois Long invented fashion criticism."

51. Kay often worked as a model to supplement her income. One of the artists was reportedly Leo Mielziner, who would become her father-in-law in 1931. However,

we found no evidence of a sitting with him in the diary. We suspect he was confused with Sir Gerald Kelly.

52. Eells, p. 191.

53. Kay attended the fall fashion presentation by Jean Patou on August 29, 1925. Patou, the first couturier to include sportswear in his collection, sold his designs to Josephine Baker, Constance Bennett, the Dolly Sisters, Pola Negri, and other celebrities. His press agent was Elsa Maxwell, and she helped make his designs popular with Americans. She also helped market his perfume, Joy, "The most expensive scent in the world." Meredith Etherington-Smith, *Patou*, p. 98.

54. Eells, p. 191.

55. Born Julien Shackno in Brooklyn, he changed his name to Julien St. Charles Chaqueneau after marrying Adelaide Kip Rhinelander in November 1922 and moving to Paris. The society marriage ended in 1928, and he subsequently married Katherine Leslie in 1938. In that same year, he produced an unsuccessful Broadway play, *Waltz in Goose Step*. He later became president of Chaqueneau, Inc., a New York perfume company. He died in 1958 at the age of 60 while vacationing in Acapulco, Mexico.

56. Kay did not indicate in her diary whether she met the Mdivani brothers, but she apparently did. Years later in Hollywood, when her name was linked to one of them, she explained that she was simply a friend of Roussie's. She did enjoy a flirtation with Alexis in 1927 when she lived in New York. Sadly, there is no information about what happened to the bust.

57. Karl Shaw, *Royal Babylon*, p. 305.

58. Francis Diary, September 13, 1925, WCA.

59. Brian Herne, *White Hunter*, p. 74.

60. Other sources claim Kiki died of a drug overdose at a London hotel in 1939. Jerome died May 29, 1934, in Paris. Kiki appears as a character in Clint Jefferie's play *African Nights*. She was also depicted in a BBC television program, *The Queen's Lost Uncle*.

61. Ben Maddox, "Kay Francis Wants Life," *Movie Mirror*, September 1934, p. 76.

62. Kay had met Margaret in New York in the fall of 1922, and was apparently somewhat intimidated by her — for some time, her diary entries referred to her as "Miss Case." Margaret Case committed suicide at the age of 79 on August 25, 1974, when she jumped out of her 535 Park Avenue bedroom window. Still employed at *Vogue* at the time of her death, she left no survivors.

63. Ed Sullivan, Hollywood, unidentified clipping, NYPL.

64. "Kay Francis Returns to Playhouse," unidentified source, June 26, 1952, NYPL.

65. Helen Starr, "My Daughter, Kay," unidentified clipping, NYPL.

Chapter 4

1. Kay remained close to Dwight's uncle, Bob Francis, a designer at the textile mill. Bob, who never married, was also an amateur artist of note. Francis died in 1950.

2. Francis Diary, September 26, 1925, WCA.

3. Elinor was born in 1929, and Lesley Lee in 1931.

4. Henry was born in 1938, Robert in 1941, and Bartlett in 1942.

5. Unidentified obituary, received from Lesley Lee Francis.

6. Kay Francis, "Don't Try Your Luck Out Here!," *Pictorial Review*, January 1937, p. 50.

7. Kay later claimed that she refused alimony. Intriguingly, although Kay sometimes referred to herself in her diary as a gold digger, she never accepted alimony from any husband. After her divorce, which was paid for by Dwight's family, the Francis family may have helped support her for a time. In fact, there was continued good will between Kay and her in-laws, and she visited them in the 1930s.

8. Maude Cheatham, "Not What She Seems to Be," *Motion Picture*, March 1937, p. 82.

9. Helen Starr, "My Daughter, Kay," unidentified clipping, NYPL.

10. Kay's speech impediment is referred to as a lateral lisp. It is one of the more common speech problems, and there are several therapies and treatments.

11. The dramatic version of Michael Arlen's 1924 sensational novel began pre–broadway tryouts at the Garrick Theatre in the spring of 1925 in Detroit, then moved to the Selwyn Theatre in Chicago for 14 weeks, and finally opened in New York at the Broadhurst Theatre on Sept. 15, 1925. *The Green Hat* was a *success de scandale*, and Cornell's 231 performances as gallantly promiscuous Lady Iris March propelled her into the ranks of superstars. The play was filmed twice by MGM, first in 1929 as *A Woman of Affairs* with Greta Garbo, and in 1934 as *Outcast Lady* with Constance Bennett.

12. The misconception about Kay and *The Green Hat* may have gotten started because of a magazine article written by Jerry Lane for *Screen Play*. According to Lane, Baskerville introduced Kay to Edgar Selwyn, who then took Kay to Al Woods. Kay happened to be wearing a green hat, and Al Woods remarked on Kay's resemblance to Kit Cornell.

13. Francis Diary, January 19, 1926, WCA.

14. According to Jerry Lane's article in *Screen Play*, Kay used theater names she'd heard her mother mention to embellish her own stage experience.

15. Mrs. Leslie Carter was a renowned stage actress, nicknamed "the American Sarah Bernhardt."

16. Ed Sullivan, Hollywood, unidentified clipping. The role of Mother God Damn was played by Florence Reed when the play opened on Broadway, although Mrs. Leslie Carter toured in the play in the late 1920s and early 1930s. The role of Poppy went to Mary Duncan. The play, which opened February 1, 1926, went on for 206 performances before closing. Ironically, years later Kay almost played Mrs. Carter in a 1940 movie version of her life, *The Lady with Red Hair*. Miriam Hopkins ended up with the part.

17. Unidentified clipping, MCNY.

18. Eells, p. 192.

19. Jerry Lane, "Kay Francis' Amazing Secret," *Screen Play*, March 1935, p. 80.

20. Ed Sullivan, Hollywood, unidentified clipping, MCNY.

21. "The Girl on the Cover," unidentified source, NYPL.

22. "Plus Fours 'Hamlet' Here," *New York Times*, August 18, 1925, 8:5.

23. Burns Mantle, *Best Plays of 1925–1926*, pp. 4–5.

24. Jerry Lane, "Kay Francis' Amazing Secret," *Screen Play*, March 1935, p. 80.

25. On November 21, 1925, Kay wrote in her diary that she rehearsed the part of the Duchess of Portsmouth (the play is unidentified) in Adrienne Morrison's apartment.

26. "Kay Francis Describes Early Days in Theatre, Love for Drama," unidentified clipping, MCNY.

27. Morrison, born in 1883, was the daughter of actors Lewis Morrison and Rose Wood. She married Richard Bennett in 1903, and they divorced in 1925. Morrison married literary agent Eric Pinker in 1927 and remained married to him until her death in 1940. During *Hamlet*'s

run, Morrison's daughters were on the West Coast or in Europe, and Kay became Adrienne's "surrogate daughter." After *Hamlet,* Morrison retired from the stage and became a successful play broker.

28. Eells, p. 190.

29. When Bill Gaston reported for training to the naval air station at Squantum, Massachusetts, in 1917, his instructor was Winfield Spencer — married at the time to the future Duchess of Windsor.

30. Frances Kellum, "The Men in Kay Francis' Life!" *Screen Book,* December 1936, p. 86.

31. It wasn't until Kay's divorce from Kenneth MacKenna that the marriage was publicly revealed in court records. Up to that point, husband number two had been a secret.

32. Marjorie Haynes, "The Untold Love Stories of Kay Francis," *Movie Mirror,* November 1936, p. 98.

33. Francis Diary, October 19, 1925, WCA.

34. "The Untold Story of Kay's Secret Marriage!," May 1934, unidentified source, p. 58, NYPL.

35. "The Untold Story of Kay's Secret Marriage!," May 1934, unidentified source, p. 58, NYPL.

36. Basil Sydney, born in England in 1894, made his film debut in 1920. His best known films included *Hamlet* (1948), *Salome* (1953), and *Around the World in 80 Days* (1956). His stage credits included other Shakespeare plays — and a stage version of *Jewel Robbery* in 1932. He divorced first wife Doris Keane in 1925, and was also married to Mary Ellis and Joyce Howard. He died in London in January 1968.

37. Marjorie Haynes, "The Untold Love Stories of Kay Francis," *Movie Mirror,* November 1936, pp. 98–99.

38. An interviewer once dared to ask Rosamond Pinchot if she'd been the cause of Kay's divorce. "We both loved Billy," Rosamond replied, "but at different times. I wouldn't presume to think I could take anyone away from a person as lovely as Miss Francis." Geraldine Smith, "Triple Failure to Break Love Jinx," *Philadelphia Inquirer,* November 2, 1941.

39. Kay visited Bill and Rosamond in March 1929 after the birth of their first child.

40. Amos Pinchot was a founder of the Progressive Party and the American Civil Liberties Union.

41. Gaston also had a daughter, Theodora Louise Gaston.

42. An amusing anecdote concerned Gaston and his purported forgetfulness. While entertaining two female friends at Fefe's Monte Carlo Beach Club, one woman spied Kay Francis. Bill argued that it most certainly wasn't Kay. "Bill wanted to bet. But he lost the wager. The strikingly handsome woman was Kay Francis, his first wife." Geraldine Smith, "Triple Failure to Break Love Jinx," *Philadelphia Inquirer,* November 2, 1941.

43. Francis Diary, January 1, 1926, WCA.

44. Her telephone number was Regent 7155. Kay moved from her previous 150 E. 54th Street address to 60th Street in October 1925. Another typical brownstone, the building is still there today, although quite altered by the invasion of commerce. Number 37 now has a restaurant on the ground floor and a nail salon on the floor above.

45. Raquel Meller made her U.S. debut at the Empire Theatre on April 14, 1926, and gave 38 performances.

46. "Kay Francis Describes Early Days in Theatre, Love for Drama," unidentified clipping, MCNY.

47. Ilka Chase, *Past Imperfect,* p. 52. During her stint with Stuart Walker, Ilka reported that she, too, fell madly in love with a gay actor. It may very well have been McKay Morris.

48. Six years later Stuart Walker directed Kay in the 1932 Paramount film *False Madonna.*

49. The interurban cars Kay so vividly recalled were operated by the Dayton and Western Traction Company, and the Cincinnati, Dayton and Toledo Traction Company. In the 1920s and '30s, the cities and towns of the Midwest were still connected by hundreds of miles of streetcar tracks and overhead wires. The large inter-city trolleys ran hourly, and the fares were much cheaper than the competing steam railroads, an obvious concern to a struggling stage company.

50. "Kay Francis Describes Early Days in Theatre, Love for Drama," unidentified clipping, MCNY.

51. The number of choices for the George with whom Kay had an affair in 1926 is almost laughable — like something from a French farce by Jacques Feydeau. Her diary simply indicated the man was named George. As there were several members of the troupe named George, it's not entirely certain he's the right George. Other Georges include Gaul, Somnes, Kinsey, and Alison.

52. Francis Diary, June 19, 1926, WCA.

53. George Meeker was born in Brooklyn in 1904. His first film was *Four Sons* (1928), and he made other appearances in *Gone with the Wind* (1939) and *Casablanca* (1942).

54. Unidentified clipping, NYPL.

55. Covington, Kentucky, is just across the river from Cincinnati.

56. Unidentified clipping, MCNY.

57. Unidentified clipping, MCNY.

58. Unidentified clipping, MCNY.

59. Unidentified clipping, MCNY.

60. Elizabeth Wilson, "Projections," *Silver Screen,* March 1937, p. 80.

61. Kay sometimes blamed the broken bone on a fall down stairs.

62. Unidentified clipping, MCNY.

63. Dana Rush, "The Aristocrat of the Screen," *Silver Screen,* February 1932, p. 77.

64. The gift was not noted in the diary. According to George Eells, it was some time before Kay discovered the source of the funds. A few years later, Lois Long wired Kay for a loan, reminding her of the long ago favor. Kay didn't answer, but did transfer $1,000 into Long's bank account. Lois replied with a grateful telegram on August 11, 1936.

65. Wilda Bennett was a popular operetta star whose credits included *The Only Girl, The Riviera Girl, Apple Blossoms, The Lady in Ermine,* and *Mme. Pompadour.*

66. The Hotel Marlton is still there, just around the corner from Fifth Avenue.

67. Eells, p. 193.

68. Kay sometimes used the shorthand symbol for queer when she wrote about McKay Morris.

69. Eells, p. 192. Frank Costello (1891–1973) was a notorious mobster whose colleagues included Lucky Luciano, Albert Anastasia, and other well known Mafia figures.

70. Dana Rush, "The Aristocrat of the Screen," *Silver Screen,* February 1932, p. 77.

71. Elizabeth Wilson, "Projections," *Silver Screen,* March 1937, pp. 27, 80. Actually, Kay lived in the Park Avenue–area apartment for less than a month. A combination of indoor polo matches and high rent may have contributed to the short stay.

72. Greene & Laurie, *Showbiz,* p. 223.

73. Greene & Laurie, *Showbiz,* p. 223.

74. Jon Bradshaw, *Dreams That Money Can Buy,* p. 76.

75. "The Girl on the Cover," unidentified source, NYPL.

76. Julia Hoyt, also known as Mrs. Lydig Hoyt, was born Julia Robbins in New York in 1897. She was a society

beauty whose marriage to Lydig Hoyt in 1914 — when she was only 17 — was one of that year's important social events. She received a Paris divorce in 1924. A beautiful brunette, she bore a slight resemblance to her friend, Kay. Her portrait was painted by renowned artists, including Sargent. She worked with the Stuart Walker stock company, had a co-starring role in a Norma Talmadge silent film, and even started her own clothing line. Married to actor Louis Calhern from 1927 to 1932, and then to Aquila C. Giles in 1935, she died of a heart attack in her New York home — 214 East 62nd Street — in 1955. According to Kay's diary entries, she was quite a character. This is from June 16, 1931: "Lunch at studio with Julia — back with her for cocktails. [Julia] fainted twice, tried to jump out of the window." Ilka Chase was also briefly married to Louis Calhern. After Hoyt married Calhern, Chase found lovely engraved calling cards stored in her trunk. Since the name on the cards was Mrs. Louis Calhern, Chase no longer had any use for them. "They were the best cards — thin, flexible parchment, highly embossed — and it seemed a pity to waste them, and so I mailed the box to my successor. But aware of Lou's mercurial marital habits, I wrote on the top one, 'Dear Julia, I hope these reach you in time.' I received no acknowledgment." Ilka Chase, *Past Imperfect*, p. 59.

77. This was another instance of Katharine Francis using Kay Francis as a stage name before her film career started. On January 18, Kay noted in her diary that her mother had arrived to help fit one of the costumes.

78. Another source listed 11 performances for *Damn the Tears.*

79. Alexander Woollcott, "The Stage," *New York World,* January 23, 1927.

80. Burton Davis, "Damn the Tears and the Sneers," *New York Telegraph,* January 23, 1927.

81. Gaston, who apparently desired a creative profession, also acted in a musical revue, *Harry Delmar's Revels,* which opened November 28, 1927, at the Shubert Theatre. The revue, produced by Samuel Baerwitz and Harry Delmar, included music by Jimmy Monaco, Jesse Greer, and Lester Lee. The book was written by William K. Wells, with lyrics by Billy Rose and Ballard MacDonald. It ran for 112 performances. The cast also included Frank Fay, Dorothea James, Patsy Kelly, Bert Lahr, the Trado Twins, and others.

82. Neysa McMein (1888–1949), born in Quincy, Illinois, was part of the Algonquin Roundtable. She produced magazine covers for *Photoplay, McCall's,* and *Saturday Evening Post.* She also drew advertising illustrations for Palmolive and Lucky Strike, and created the image of Betty Crocker. McMein worked out of her West 57th studio near Central Park. Posing for the portrait probably took place in January 1927. Kay noted in her diary that she had dinner at Neysa's on January 26, 1927.

83. Francis Diary, February 10, 1927, WCA.

84. *Crime* opened in New York on February 22, 1927, at the Eltinge Theater.

85. Burns Mantle, *Best Plays of 1926–1927,* p. 13.

86. Eells, p. 194.

87. "Kay Francis Describes Early Days in Theatre, Love for Drama," unidentified clipping, MCNY.

88. Kay Francis was reported to have been a stand-in for Kay Johnson in a Manhattan stage play, though the date and title are unknown. It may have been during *Crime* that Kay understudied Johnson.

89. The entries about Swanee were written in shorthand, which usually meant the content was of a sexual nature. Swan, born in 1904, lived in New York in the 1920s, where she acted and wrote theatrical reviews. She

apparently followed Kay to Hollywood because a 1932 magazine article described her as working in Paramount's scenario department. She later married artist Donald Works and lived with him in California, where she became a painter. Swan died in 1998.

90. Somnes, who grew up in Boston, Massachusetts, enjoyed a long career as actor, producer, and director. He traveled to Europe in 1916, and made a notable appearance with England's Old Vic Repertory Theater as King Claudius in *Hamlet.* He also directed four movies. Somnes married Helen Bonfils, secretary-treasurer of the *Denver Post,* in 1936, and became director of the Elitch's Garden Theatre stock company. He and his wife established the Bonfils Memorial Theatre in Denver. Somnes died in 1956.

91. Francis Diary, August 1, 1927, WCA.

92. *The Command to Love* was written by Rudolph Lothar and Fritz Gottwald, adapted by Herman Berstein and Brian Marlow, produced by William A. Brady, Jr. and Dwight Deere Wiman, in association with John Tuerk, and staged by Lester Lonergan. Kay was either replaced by Violet Kemble Cooper or Mary Nash. Other cast members included Thomas Louden, Henry Stephenson, Walter Colligan, Basil Rathbone, Anthony Kemble Cooper, Percy Hemus, Ferdinand Gottschalk, and David Glassford.

93. Francis Diary, August 14, 1927, WCA.

94. Francis Diary, September 25, 1927, WCA.

95. Tommy Hitchcock's address was 54 East 52nd Street.

96. Hitchcock's roommates included John Gaston (apparently no relation to William), George Gordon Moore, and Percy Pyrne, Jr. In addition, Averill Harriman was a frequent guest.

97. Nelson Aldrich, Jr., *Tommy Hitchcock: An American Hero,* p. 165.

98. On September 10, 1928, it was announced that Bebe Daniels and Hitchcock were engaged. They weren't — it was a publicity stunt for the silent film actress. Hitchcock married Margaret Mellon Laughlin on December 15, 1928, at the Plaza Hotel. Tommy Hitchcock, who'd enlisted during World War II, died on April 12, 1944, when the airplane he was testing crashed in Salisbury, England. The airplane, a P-51 Mustang, was one he'd helped design.

99. Kay also read for the role of Sharon Falconer in Patrick Kearney's *Elmer Gantry.* She indicated in a diary entry on October 21, 1927, that the role had been offered to her. However, she wrote nothing additional after this date. The play opened on Broadway on August 7, 1928, with Vera Allen in the Falconer role. Jean Simmons played the role in the 1960 film.

100. Probably wisely, Gertrude Bryan used the pen name G.M. Fair for her writing credit.

101. Eells, p. 194.

102. *Billboard,* January 7, 1928.

103. *New York Times,* unknown date.

104. Francis Diary, December 30, 1927, WCA.

105. Rumors of an affair with Mdivani continued into the 1930s, though Kay insisted they were just good friends.

106. According to the Social Register, Kay's 1927 New York address was 140 East 39th Street. Her roommate was Lois Long. The small, three-story building now bears a plaque indicating it is the Permanent Mission of the Republic of Guinea to the United Nations.

Chapter 5

1. Francis Diary, January 1, 1928, WCA.

2. Adela Rogers St. Johns, "Working Girl," *New Movie Magazine,* March 1931, p. 86.

3. Francis Diary, November 12, 1927, WCA.

4. Goulding, born in England in 1891, was also a song-writer who collaborated with Elsie Janis and Mack Gordon. He married dancer Marjorie Moss on November 28, 1931 (Kay attended their reception at Goulding's North Linden Drive mansion), but was bisexual. After Marjorie's death in 1935, he did not remarry. In the early days of Hollywood, Eddie was known for hosting orgies. "There were stories of outrageous bisexual galas, one of which allegedly landed two women in the hospital and prompted Irving Thalberg to send Goulding to Europe until the furor died down." William J. Mann, *Behind the Screen,* p. 89. There were also stories hinting that Goulding was a tad kinky. Screenwriter Frederica Sagor Maas described him as "depraved" and suggested that he, along with director Marshall Neilan, "initiated more young women—and men—into more kinky sexual practices than one can possibly imagine. The carrot stick that they dangled was the promise of a screen test, a good part in some picture in which they were involved, or that they would use their clout with some other director shooting a picture on the lot." Frederica Sagor Maas, *The Shocking Miss Pilgrim,* p. 74. Goulding directed *Love* (1927), *Grand Hotel* (1932), *Dark Victory* (1939), and many others. Goulding died in Los Angeles on December 24, 1959.

5. Matthew Kennedy, *Edmund Goulding's Dark Victory: Hollywood's Genius Bad Boy,* p. 100.

6. Frances Kellum, "The Men in Kay Francis' Life!" *Screen Book,* December 1936, p. 87.

7. Evelyn's husband, Harry Thaw, had murdered architect Stanford White in 1906, supposedly in defense of Evelyn's virtue. She appeared in several silent films. She has also been portrayed in at least two films. Joan Collins played her in *The Girl in the Red Velvet Swing* (1955), and Elizabeth McGovern was Evelyn in *Ragtime* (1981).

8. Theodore Newton, born in 1904, began his Broadway career in 1928. He died in 1963.

9. Francis Diary, June 16, 1928, WCA.

10. Harold Healy appeared in the 1922 and 1924 productions of *Rain* with Jeanne Eagels. He also appeared in *Enemies of the Law* (1931) and *Sign of the Cross* (1932). His other film appearances were bit parts.

11. Francis Diary, July 13, 1928, WCA.

12. Jerry Lane, "Kay Francis' Amazing Secret," *Screen Play,* March 1935, p. 23.

13. Francis Diary, September 4, 1928, WCA.

14. Francis Diary, September 15, 1928, WCA. Grant is actor Grant Mills. She did eventually succeed in getting him to sleep with her on September 21, 1928.

15. Ernie—last name unknown—remained a friend for many years, and Kay visited him and wife Kitty whenever she was in Chicago.

16. While in Chicago, Kay also met Jeanette MacDonald for the first time. According to her diary, they attended the same parties on June 30 and July 1, 1928.

17. Kay mentioned in her November 23, 1928, diary entry that Dwight stopped in for cocktails. On that same night, Humphrey Bogart also stopped by.

18. Francis Diary, October 27, 1928, WCA.

19. Unidentified clipping, MCNY.

20. Unidentified clipping, MCNY.

21. Unidentified clipping, MCNY.

22. Otis Chatfield-Taylor was born in Lake Forest, Illinois, in 1900. He died in 1948.

23. Francis Diary, December 5, 1928, WCA.

24. Bayard Livingston Kilgour, Jr., was born in 1904, and died in 1984. Heir to the Cincinnati Bell fortune, he graduated from Harvard in 1927. His rare book collection included many Russian items, which he'd collected on several visits.

25. Adela Rogers St. Johns, "Working Girl," *New Movie Magazine,* March 1931, p. 86.

26. Other 1929 films produced at Astoria included *The Letter,* with Broadway legend Jeanne Eagels; *The Hole in the Wall,* with Claudette Colbert and Edward G. Robinson; *Nothing but the Truth,* with Richard Dix and Helen Kane; *The Cocoanuts,* with the Marx Brothers, Mary Eaton, and Kay; *Jealousy,* Jeanne Eagels' second and last talkie; *The Lady Lies,* with Walter Huston and Claudette Colbert; *Glorifying the American Girl,* with Ziegfeld star Mary Eaton, Eddie Cantor, Rudy Vallee, and Technicolor production numbers; *Applause,* with nightclub legend Helen Morgan; *The Battle of Paris,* with musical comedy queen Gertrude Lawrence; *The Return of Sherlock Holmes;* and *The Laughing Lady,* with Ruth Chatterton replacing Jeanne Eagels, who died during production.

27. "The Girl on the Cover," unidentified clipping, NYPL.

28. Frances Kellum, "The Men in Kay Francis' Life!" *Screen Book,* December 1936, p. 87.

29. It's unlikely that Kay got the part through Millard Webb, because his name didn't appear in the diary until *after* her screen test.

30. Morehouse, *Forty-Five Minutes Past Eight,* pp. 85–86.

31. Unidentified clipping, MCNY. Written and directed by John McGowan, *Nigger Rich* was eventually produced in September 1929 by Lee Shubert. Cast members included Helen Flint, Don Beddoe, and Spencer Tracy.

32. "Kay Francis Describes Early Days in Theatre, Love for Drama," unidentified source, MCNY.

33. "Kay Francis Returns to Playhouse," June 26, 1952, unidentified source, MCNY.

34. In the early days of talkies, dialogue directors were assigned to help actors learn their lines.

35. "Kay Francis Describes Early Days in Theatre, Love for Drama," unidentified source, MCNY.

36. Ed Sullivan, Hollywood, unidentified clipping, NYPL. Kay signed the Paramount contract on December 28, 1928. In addition to paying her $300 a week for her on-camera work, Paramount also agreed to pay her $150 a week for rehearsals.

37. She was identified as Katharine Francis. The photographer was fashion legend Baron De Meyer.

38. Kay's first Hollywood advertisement was probably for Lux Soap in 1930. She appeared, along with Pauline Stark, Kathryn Carver, and Anne Cornwall, in an ad that ran in several magazines and newspapers. Lux enlisted the help of Kay's friend, photographer John Engstead, when they later needed Kay's signature on a release. Engstead, who'd known Kay at Paramount, reluctantly went to the Warner Brothers lot where he was warmly welcomed by Kay. "'Johnny, what in the world are you doing here?' I hesitated. 'Ike [St. Johns—a *Photoplay* magazine editor and husband of Adela] wants you to sign this Lux release.' With great exasperation, Kay said, 'Give me that damned paper. Who's got a pen?' She scribbled her name. 'There!' she said. 'Now sit down and talk to me.' For his help, Engstead received a case of Lux soap every month for the next twenty-five years. John Engstead, *Star Shots,* p. 116.

39. "Kay Francis Describes Early Days in Theatre, Love for Drama," unidentified source, MCNY.

40. The Paramount Studio, designated a National Landmark, is now the Astoria-Kaufman Studio. The studio fills an entire city block in the middle of a heavily built-up, working-class residential neighborhood in Long Island City—technically, not Astoria. Single-family homes, small apartment buildings, and tree-lined streets look almost the same today as they did in 1929. The entire

block east of the Paramount studio was originally used as the back lot for outdoor sets and scenes. Today, most of this block is the studio parking lot, although a few small storage buildings and shops are still standing. The Museum of the Moving Image is also located there, just across the street from the main entrance to the studio.

41. S.R. Mook, "I Can't Wait to Be Forgotten," *Photoplay,* March 1939, p. 72.

42. Walter Winchell, *Your Broadway and Mine,* April 2, 1928, unidentified source.

43. Attorney Joel E. Mann wrote in court papers filed in December 1968 that Kay provided little information about her marriages. "In the years that I knew Miss Francis, she never discussed her marital affairs other than to say that she had been married and divorced several times.... It is apparent that Miss Francis was extremely reticent about discussing her marital affairs, and we have been unable to discover further information." State of New York, Surrogate's Court, County of New York, Probate Proceeding, Will of Katharine G. Francis, also known as Kay Francis, December 2, 1968.

44. Born in Canada in 1890, Meehan enjoyed a lengthy career in New York theater and then in Hollywood. He'd even been a leading man in one of Katharine Clinton's stage companies. He also worked with George M. Cohan in the early 1920s and began writing plays in the late '20s, including *The Lady Lies,* which was adapted into a movie with Walter Huston. After working on *Gentlemen of the Press,* he headed west to Hollywood where he worked on scripts for MGM's *The Painted Veil, Sadie McKee,* and *The Prizefighter and the Lady,* and collaborated with his playwright son John Meehan, Jr. In 1939 Meehan left MGM to work for producer Walter Wanger. Nominated for Oscars for writing *The Divorcee* (1930) and *Boys Town* (1938), he died on November 12, 1954, at the Motion Picture Country Home, leaving behind a wife, son, and two daughters.

45. According to the New York City Department of Records and Information Services Municipal Archives, there is no record of a marriage between John Meehan and Katharine Francis in 1928 or 1929.

46. Jeanine Basinger, *A Woman's View,* p. 153.

47. *Photoplay,* October 1929.

48. Adamson, *Groucho, Harpo, Chico, and Sometimes Zeppo,* p. 78.

49. Adamson, p. 78.

50. Kay indicated in her diary that she saw *Animal Crackers* twice — on November 30 and December 18, 1928.

51. Ed Sullivan, Hollywood, unidentified clipping, NYPL.

52. "Kay Francis Describes Early Days in Theatre, Love for Drama," unidentified source, MCNY.

53. Francis Diary, April 10, 1929, WCA.

54. At the time Kay made her trip, the trains would not have had air conditioning. The Santa Fe Chief was air conditioned in 1934 and renamed the Super Chief in 1936. If Kay had been in a hurry, she could have flown to the West Coast in 48 hours — Transcontinental Air Transport inaugurated a limited service coast-to-coast by air in 1929. However, since the Ford tri-motor airplanes could only fly during daylight hours, the trip involved an overnight trip by train from New York to Columbus, Ohio, then by airplane to Waynoka, Oklahoma, another overnight train to Clovis, New Mexico, and then the final lap of the trip by airplane.

55. Francis Diary, April 12, 1929, WCA.

56. Elizabeth Wilson, "Projections," *Silver Screen,* March 1937, p. 81.

57. Unidentified clipping, NYPL.

Chapter 6

1. Francis Diary, April 17, 1929, WCA.

2. The legendary hotel, named for Theodore Roosevelt, opened in May 1927. Investors included Mary Pickford, Douglas Fairbanks, and Louis B. Mayer. The first Academy Awards were presented in the hotel's Blossom Room in May 1929. The hotel is still used for movie and TV sets, and is supposedly haunted by previous guests, including Montgomery Clift and Marilyn Monroe.

3. Adela Rogers St. Johns, "Working Girl," *New Movie Magazine,* March 1931, p. 124.

4. Adela Rogers St. Johns, "Working Girl," *New Movie Magazine,* March 1931, p. 124.

5. Chicago-born Alan Brock began his Broadway career at the age of fifteen in *The Moon's a Gong,* with Helen Chandler and Allyn Joslyn. He appeared in films — including *24 Hours* with Kay — and on stage, eventually becoming a producer, writer, and finally an agent. Other clients included Lillian Gish, Madge Evans, Irene Castle, Mrs. Patrick Campbell, Lois Wilson, Nita Naldi, Blanche Sweet, Nancy Carroll, and many others. He died at the age of 85 in 1995 at his longtime home in Hastings-on-Hudson.

6. Leonard Hall, "Vamping with Sound," *Photoplay,* October 1929, p. 126.

7. Leonard Hall, "Vamping with Sound," *Photoplay,* October 1929, p. 126.

8. Kay had actually met Ruth Chatterton at a party on January 27, 1927, in New York, and they occasionally socialized on the East Coast. However, it wasn't until both were in Hollywood that they became close friends.

9. The Cromwells divorced in the late 1940s.

10. According to William Mann, most gays in Hollywood identified Kay Francis as a lesbian. "Costume designer Miles White recalled an 'all-gay' pool party at Francis' house in the 1930s; that Francis was a lesbian was something he and the others simply presumed." William J. Mann, *Behind the Screen,* p. 83.

11. Francis Diary, June 1, 1929, WCA.

12. Ben Maddox, "Kay Francis Wants Life," *Movie Mirror,* September 1934, pp. 76–77.

13. At the time of the breakup, Millard Webb was working on *Glorifying the American Girl,* where he met future wife Mary Eaton. Eaton had co-starred with Kay in *The Cocoanuts.* Webb died in a private Hollywood hospital at the age of 40 on April 21, 1935. His cause of death was an intestinal ailment.

14. Francis Diary, June 21, 1929, WCA.

15. Telephone interview with Jimmy Bangley, January 23, 2004; Buddy Rogers interviewed in person by Jimmy Bangley at Pickfair, July 1993.

16. Paul Lukas, born in Budapest in 1887, came to Hollywood in 1927. He married Daisy Benes in 1927, and they remained married until her death in 1962. Paul Lukas not only saw Kay again, he co-starred with her in *The Vice Squad* (1931).

17. *Variety,* January 15, 1930.

18. Telephone interview with Jimmy Bangley, February 23, 2004; Fay Wray interviewed via telephone by Jimmy Bangley, October 1998.

19. Francis Diary, July 25, 1929, WCA.

20. Kay moved from Fountain Avenue to 8487 Franklin Avenue in February 1931, another rental home. Both modest bungalows, her first two homes are long gone. In 1932, Kay was living at 1117 North Alta Loma Road before she moved into William S. Hart's 8218 De Longepre house.

21. Kay first met Kenneth MacKenna on February 18, 1926, at a New York party. She indicated in her diary entry for July 13, 1929, that Kenneth was her 24th man.

22. MacKenna's great-aunt was actress Charlotte Cushman.

23. Levald, the Mielziner's first child, died shortly after birth.

24. Before transferring to an English school, Kenneth attended the Ecole L'Alsacienne with classmate Eva Le Gallienne.

25. William Brady, Sr. was the father of Bill Brady, Jr., Kay's paramour in New York in the late 1920s.

26. MacKenna also performed with the Jesse Bonstelle company in Detroit. Coincidentally, Katherine Clinton had worked with Jesse Bonstelle in Rochester, New York, in 1903.

27. Mary C. Henderson, *Mielziner*, p. 47.

28. Helen Hayes was quite fond of Kenneth, and numerous diary entries indicate that Kay and Kenneth socialized with Hayes and husband Charles MacArthur.

29. Mary C. Henderson, *Mielziner*, p. 67.

30. Francis Diary, November 2, 1929, WCA.

31. Unidentified clipping, MCNY.

32. Kay's diary entry for May 14, 1929, noted an interview with Ruth Hall from *Photoplay.*

33. Leonard Hall, "Vamping with Sound," *Photoplay,* October 1929, p. 126.

34. John Engstead, *Star Shots,* p. 116.

35. Elsie Janis, "Class with a Capital K," *The New Movie Magazine,* March 1934, pp. 50, 51–84.

36. Dana Rush, "The Aristocrat of the Screen," *Silver Screen,* February 1932, p. 77.

37. Dana Rush, "The Aristocrat of the Screen," *Silver Screen,* February 1932, p. 77.

38. Jane Clark followed Kay to Hollywood, too. Clark, Kay's stand-in at Warners, had previously worked with Kay on stage. She moved to Hollywood around the same time Kay did, and became her principal stand-in for many films. Clark was also a stand-in for Verree Teasdale. Gloria Raymond was Kay's stand-in at Paramount.

39. Unidentified clipping, MCNY.

40. Helen Starr, "My Daughter, Kay," unidentified source, NYPL.

41. Helen Starr, "My Daughter, Kay," unidentified source, NYPL.

42. Francis Diary, December 31, 1929, WCA.

43. Francis Diary, January 2, 1930, WCA.

44. The collision was blamed on sun blindness and flying too close together. Hawks' last film, *Such Men Are Dangerous,* was released in March 1930.

45. To no one's great surprise, the couple divorced in 1931. Gilbert married Virginia Bruce, with whom Kay also socialized. Gilbert died of a heart attack in January 1936. Legend suggests he was stricken while sharing a bed with Marlene Dietrich.

46. Kay did *not* like Florence Eldridge and referred to her disparagingly in her diary.

47. *Film Daily,* July 27, 1930.

48. Harry Evans, "The Personal Touch," *Family Circle,* August 3, 1934, p. 10.

49. John Engstead, *Star Shots,* pp. 115–116. This incident has also been reported as occurring on the *Mandalay* set.

50. Francis Diary, March 22, 1930, WCA.

51. Francis Diary, April 7, 1930, WCA.

52. David O. Selznick, *Memo from David O. Selznick,* p. 32.

53. David O. Selznick, *Memo from David O. Selznick,* p. 32.

54. Louella O. Parsons, *Los Angeles Examiner,* February 21, 1930.

55. Lucille Elfenbein, "So Now Kay Francis Wears Dark Glasses Everywhere; Tall Actress Travels Light," unidentified clipping, MCNY.

56. W.E. Oliver, *Los Angeles Evening Herald,* June 28, 1930.

57. Telephone interview with Jimmy Bangley, January 23, 2004; Billie Dove interviewed via telephone by Jimmy Bangley, August 1994.

58. Elizabeth Yeaman, *Hollywood Daily Citizen,* September 12, 1930.

59. Marjorie Ross, *Hollywood Daily Citizen,* October 10, 1930.

60. Paramount also picked up the options of Carole Lombard and Rosita Moreno around the same time.

61. The other co-director was the infamous Louis Gasnier, chiefly known for the 1936 cult film *Reefer Madness.*

62. *Variety,* October 29, 1930.

63. Bickford, *Bulls Balls Bicycles & Actors* , p. 253.

64. *New York Times,* December 22, 1930.

65. *Variety,* December 24, 1930.

66. Unidentified source, MCNY.

67. "Kay Francis of the Films," *Vanity Fair,* May 1931, p. 65.

68. Katharine Roberts, "Acting in a Business Way," *Colliers,* March 16, 1935, p. 32.

69. Adela Rogers St. Johns, "Working Girl," *New Movie Magazine,* March 1931, p. 124.

70. Lyle Rooks, "Superstitious Lady: Kay Francis Was Born on a Friday the Thirteenth, Perhaps That Explains This Whole Story," unidentified source, MCNY.

71. Maude Cheatham, "Not What She Seems to Be," *Motion Picture,* March 1937, p. 83.

72. Maude Cheatham, "Not What She Seems to Be," *Motion Picture,* March 1937, p. 83.

73. *New York World Telegram,* July 6, 1935, unknown page number.

74. "Secret of Good Grooming by Kay Francis," unidentified clipping, MCNY.

75. Reine Davies, "Hollywood Parade," *Los Angeles Examiner,* September 28, 1935. Allan Ryan gave Kay an emerald in Europe in 1934, which she lost at a London party in 1935. Kay also told an interviewer that green was her favorite color, and she admitted to knitting at least ten green sweaters.

76. Dorothy Emerson, *Silver Screen,* March 1931.

77. Malcolm Oettinger, "Is Stardom Worth It?," unidentified clipping, MCNY.

78. Unidentified clipping, MCNY.

79. Gladys McVeigh, "Who's Afraid of the Big Screen Wolf?," unidentified clipping, MCNY.

80. "Dark Lady," *Vanity Fair,* October 1932, p. 28.

81. "Movie Boudoirs," *New Movie Magazine,* April 1931.

82. Hedda Hopper, *From Under My Hat,* p. 206.

83. Unidentified clipping, NYPL.

84. According to Vincent Sherman, Orry-Kelly once shared a Midtown Manhattan apartment with boyfriend Cary Grant, which they'd turned into a speakeasy. Before Grant and Orry-Kelly left for Hollywood they sold many of their possessions, and Sherman and his wife bought drapes and a daybed.

85. Tom Tierney, *Thirty from the 30s,* unnumbered pages.

86. Eells, p. 203.

87. Kay once suggested to Orry-Kelly that he invent slippers that used varying heel sizes.

88. Eells, p. 204.

89. Telephone interview with Jimmy Bangley, February 23, 2004; Dorothy Jeakins interviewed via telephone by Jimmy Bangley, January 1995.

90. Malcolm Oettinger, "Is Stardom Worth It?," unidentified source, MCNY.

91. The house is now part of the William S. Hart Park. Originally purchased for $25,000 by Hart in 1920, he and sister Mary Ellen moved in after extensive renovations. Hart married Winifred Westover in 1921, and they moved to a ranch in 1927, which was when the house became a rental. The property was donated to the city of Los Angeles in 1944. When Kay was his tenant, Hart often signed correspondence to her, "Your Tyrant Landlord."

92. Maude Cheatham, "Not What She Seems to Be," *Motion Picture*, March 1937, p. 59.

93. Adela Rogers St. Johns, "Working Girl," *New Movie Magazine*, March 1931, p. 124.

94. Ruth Rankin, "O-Kay Francis!," unidentified clipping, NYPL.

95. Guests at the parties Kay attended ran the gamut from Jean Harlow to Sergei Eisenstein, and Marilyn Miller to Mrs. Patrick Campbell.

96. Kay had known Jessica since the early 1920s in New York. Society woman Jessica Haynes was first married to Harry Brooks Sargeant. Jessica and Richard Barthelmess married in 1928. Kay was godmother to their son, Stewart Barthelmess.

97. Bea Stewart finally announced she could take no more parties. The Stewarts then held a "Nervous Breakdown" party, which started at noon, and featured Louella Parson's arrival in an ambulance and Elsa Maxwell pretending to be a psychiatrist.

98. Maude Cheatham, "Not What She Seems to Be," *Motion Picture*, March 1937, p. 82.

99. Fred Lawrence Guiles, *Hanging on in Paradise*, p. 17. Kay recorded at least three dinner parties at the Goldwyns in 1930.

100. Kenneth L. Geist, *Pictures Will Talk: The Life & Films of Joseph L. Mankiewicz*, p. 23.

101. Telephone interview with Jimmy Bangley, February, 2004; Douglas Fairbanks, Jr. interviewed in person by Jimmy Bangley at the Bel Air Hotel, August 1999. Fairbanks also remarked that his favorite Kay Francis film was *British Agent* with Leslie Howard.

102. Charles Higham, *Charles Laughton: An Intimate Biography*, p. 54.

103. Maude Cheatham, "Not What She Seems to Be," *Motion Picture*, March 1937, p. 59.

104. Sara Hamilton, "Okay Francis!" *Photoplay*, March 1936, p. 31.

105. Lloyd Pantages, *I Cover Hollywood*, March 5, 1935.

106. Francis Diary, December 24, 1930, WCA.

Chapter 7

1. Francis Diary, January 12, 1931, WCA.

2. Hopkins' name was often noted in Kay's diary as a frequent host/guest at social functions. Kay immediately regretted sleeping with him: "Slept with Arthur — My god, what a little prick!" Francis Diary, February 12, 1930, WCA. Hopkins, born in Cleveland in 1878, was a playwright-producer-director. His 1933 marriage to Doris Kenyon was annulled. Hopkins died in 1950.

3. Francis Diary, July 26, 1930, WCA.

4. Adela Rogers St. Johns, "Working Girl," *New Movie Magazine*, March 1931, p. 124.

5. Francis Diary, January 11, 1931, WCA.

6. Elizabeth Wilson, "Projections," *Silver Screen*, March 1937, p. 80.

7. *Hollywood Daily Citizen*, January 13, 1931.

8. One witness at Kay's wedding was supposedly a hotel cook.

9. Francis Diary, January 18, 1931, WCA.

10. Elizabeth Wilson, "Projections," *Silver Screen*, March 1937, p. 80.

11. Kenneth's co-director was William Cameron Menzies, who'd worked as art director on *Raffles*. Kenneth also directed *The Spider* (1931), *Good Sport* (1931), *Careless Lady* (1932), *Walls of Gold* (1933), and *Sleepers East* (1934) before Fox fired him.

12. The Earl of Warwick was the owner of the castle that Kay visited during her Paris divorce. He was born Charles Guy Fulke Greville in London in 1904. Known as the seventh Greville Earl, he changed his name to Michael Brooke, and made his film debut in 1938 in Errol Flynn's *Dawn Patrol*, after more than a year of screen tests. Considered quite handsome, Brooke was handicapped by what was euphemistically referred to as a "plump" torso. According to Edmund Goulding's biographer, Matthew Kennedy, Brooke was Goulding's live-in lover in the late 1930s.

13. Joan Fontaine, *No Bed of Roses*, p. 152.

14. According to Graham Lord, David Niven's biographer, a similar event happened in 1937 when Kay and Niven were neighbors on De Longpre Avenue. A frantic Kay telephoned David, begging him to come to her house, as a man was at her home and wouldn't leave. When David arrived, he discovered Kay using a sofa to separate herself from the Duke of Sutherland, who indeed thought Kay was Lee Francis.

15. Virginia Maxwell, "Just 'Life and Love,'" *Photoplay*, June 1933, p. 76.

16. Louella O. Parsons, *Los Angeles Examiner*, January 21, 1931.

17. Harry Mines, *Los Angeles Illustrated Daily News*, August 4, 1932. Although he probably *was* disappointed in the material he was given to direct, Kenneth MacKenna was, in fact, fired by Fox.

18. Francis Diary, January 21, 1930, WCA.

19. "What It Has Taken from Me," unidentified clipping, MCNY.

20. Kay Roberts, "They Hope to Stay Married," *Photoplay Magazine*, December 1932, p. 120.

21. *Screen Book Magazine*, December 1932.

22. "What It Has Taken from Me," unidentified clipping, MCNY.

23. Kay's fondness for the East Coast was known by friend Elsa Maxwell. "Kay cares only about money. Were she to stop making it tomorrow she would be aboard an eastbound train the day after."

24. Faith Service, "Did $26,000 Outweigh a Honeymoon Trip for Kay Francis?," *Motion Picture*, November 1932, p. 78. Kenneth paid several thousand dollars for the cottage, which was located on the north side of Truro's Pamet River. After his divorce from Kay, Kenneth added a heating system and allowed his parents to live there until Leo's death on August 11, 1935. Kenneth never returned to Little Hollow Downs. He rented it out for a time, and then, in 1949, sold the house and its contents (including family letters and photographs), along with 52 adjoining acres, to Dr. and Mrs. Donald Schlesinger.

25. Faith Service, "Did $26,000 Outweigh a Honeymoon Trip for Kay Francis?," *Motion Picture*, November 1932, p. 78.

26. Elizabeth Yeaman, *Hollywood Citizen News*, November 18, 1931. Kay met Greta Garbo at a Basil and Ouida Rathbone party on April 19, 1942.

27. Yeaman, *Hollywood Citizen News*, November 18, 1931.

28. Francis Diary, January 1, 1932, WCA.

29. Undated (1931) letter from Kay to Mrs. Leo Mielziner, Mielziner family papers, 1890–1935, Special Collections, Billy Rose Theatre Collection, The New York Public Library for the Performing Arts. The Mielziner family archives contains only a few letters from Kay Francis. At the time of Kay's marriage to Kenneth, Leo and Ella lived at 47 Washington Square in New York City. In another letter, dated in 1932, Kay apologized for not writing, and blamed "sheer bad manners and my horrible laziness." Undated (1932) letter from Kay Francis to Mrs. Leo Mielziner, Mielziner family papers, 1890–1935, Special Collections, Billy Rose Theatre Collection, The New York Public Library for the Performing Arts. The letters are charming, and show that Kay was well aware of the social graces.

30. This incident was reported by the press, but no mention was made in Kay's diary.

31. Leonard Hall, "Just Three Years," *Photoplay*, October 1932, p. 48.

32. Elizabeth Yeaman, *Hollywood Daily Citizen*, January 23, 1931.

33. Louella O. Parsons, *Los Angeles Examiner*, January 29, 1931.

34. Llewellyn Miller, *Los Angeles Record*, January 16, 1931.

35. *Variety*, February 11, 1931.

36. Undated (1931) letter from Kay Francis to Mrs. Leo Mielziner, Mielziner family papers, 1890–1935, Special Collections, Billy Rose Theatre Collection, The New York Public Library for the Performing Arts.

37. *Los Angeles Evening Herald*, June 5, 1931.

38. Nance O'Neil, born in Oakland, California, in 1874, made her film debut in 1915, and appeared in 33 films. Although married to Alfred Hickman, she had close friendships with women, including Lizzie Borden. The alleged affair with Borden took place between 1904 and 1906 when O'Neil was a renowned Boston stage actress. O'Neil died in 1965.

39. *New York Times*, June 15, 1931.

40. Gladys McVeigh, "Who's Afraid of the Big Screen Wolf? Not Kay Francis— She Leaves Worry Over Jinx to Others," unidentified clipping, MCNY.

41. Marquis Busby, *Los Angeles Examiner*, September 3, 1931.

42. Harriet Parsons, *Los Angeles Examiner*, October 2, 1931.

43. *Variety*, November 3, 1931.

44. Elizabeth Yeaman, *Hollywood Citizen News*, November 18, 1931.

45. Elsa Maxwell, "It's Romance Again for Kay Francis," p.25.

46. Jimmy Starr, *Los Angeles Evening Herald Express*, January 22, 1932. *Week-End Marriage* was finally made in 1932 — and starred Loretta Young.

47. Eleanor Barnes, *Los Angeles Illustrated Daily News*, January 8, 1932.

48. *Variety*, March 8, 1932.

49. Harry Mines, *Los Angeles Illustrated Daily News*, April 1, 1932.

50. Interview with Jimmy Bangley, January 23, 2004; Gloria Stuart interviewed via telephone by Jimmy Bangley, January 23, 2004.

51. Interview with Jimmy Bangley; Gloria Stuart interviewed via telephone by Jimmy Bangley, January 23, 2004.

52. Harry Mines, *Los Angeles Illustrated Daily News*, June 17, 1932.

53. Harrison Carroll, *Los Angeles Evening Herald Express*, July 29, 1932.

54. Elizabeth Yeaman, *Hollywood Daily Citizen*, July 29, 1932.

55. Elizabeth Yeaman, *Hollywood Daily Citizen*, May 25, 1932.

56. Eells, p. 203.

57. Eells, p. 203.

58. Although *One Way Passage* ended up being a drama, it also included lighter moments amidst the melodrama, mainly due to the antics of the supporting cast members.

59. Brother of David, Myron Selznick was also Kay's agent.

60. Tay Garnett, *Light Your Torches and Pull Up Your Tights*, p. 120.

61. Tay Garnett, *Light Your Torches and Pull Up Your Tights*, p. 120.

62. Tay Garnett, *Light Your Torches and Pull Up Your Tights*, p. 122.

63. Irene Thirer, *Daily News*, October 14, 1932.

64. "Farewell to Francis," unidentified clipping, NYPL.

65. "Farewell to Francis," unidentified clipping, NYPL.

66. *Man Wanted* and *Trouble in Paradise* also offer brief exercise scenes in which she wears shorts.

67. Francis Diary, June 13, 1932, WCA.

68. Faith Service, "Did $26,000 Outweigh a Honeymoon Trip for Kay Francis?," *Motion Picture*, November 1932, p. 51.

69. Faith Service, "Did $26,000 Outweigh a Honeymoon Trip for Kay Francis?," *Motion Picture*, November 1932, p. 51.

70. Scott Eyman, *Ernst Lubitsch*, p. 191.

71. Undated (1932) letter from Kay Francis to Mrs. Leo Mielziner, Mielziner family papers, 1890–1935, Special Collections, Billy Rose Theatre Collection, The New York Public Library for the Performing Arts.

72. Telephone interview with Jimmy Bangley, February 23, 2004; Curt Siodmak interviewed via telephone by Jimmy Bangley, September 1999.

73. Fred Lawrence Guiles, *Hanging on in Paradise*, p. 19.

74. Fred Lawrence Guiles, *Hanging on in Paradise*, p. 21.

75. *New York American*, November 9, 1932.

76. Louella O. Parsons, *Los Angeles Examiner*, December 30, 1932.

77. Francis Diary, July 30, 1932, WCA.

78. S.R. Mook, "I Can't Wait to Be Forgotten," *Photoplay*, March 1939, p. 72.

79. Unidentified clipping, NYPL.

80. Harry Mines, *Los Angeles Illustrated Daily News*, August 4, 1932.

81. Sheilah Graham, *Garden of Allah*, p. 213.

82. Francis Diary, January 23, 1932, WCA.

83. Francis Diary, November 9, 1932, WCA.

84. Louella O. Parsons, *Los Angeles Examiner*, November 9, 1932.

85. Jimmy M. Fidler, "Spiking the Rumors," *Silver Screen*, August 1934, p. 62.

86. Leonard Hall, "Just Three Years," *Photoplay Magazine*, October 1932, p. 113.

Chapter 8

1. Gladys McVeigh, "Who's Afraid of the Big Screen Wolf? Not Kay Francis— She Leaves Worry Over Jinx to Others," unidentified clipping, MCNY.

2. *Film Daily*, March 31, 1933.

3. *New York Times*, July 22, 1933.

4. Eleanor Barnes, *Los Angeles Illustrated Daily News*, July 28, 1933.

5. Wallis & Highham, *Starmaker: The Autobiography of Hal Wallis*, p. 47.

6. *Variety*, September 26, 1933.

7. Katharine Roberts, "Acting in a Business Way," *Colliers*, March 16, 1935, p. 32.

8. Lawrence J. Quirk, *The Great Romantic Films*, pp. 23, 25.

9. Jerry Hoffman, *Los Angeles Examiner*, January 5, 1934.

10. "A really well dressed woman," Mollie Merrick, *Hollywood Citizen News*, October 31, 1932.

11. Kay must have enjoyed *Design for Living*, because she saw it again on January 26. Perhaps she wondered if she'd be up for the female lead. She didn't get it. Lynn Fontanne originated the role on stage, and Miriam Hopkins won the screen lead.

12. The ex-lovers hovering around Kay had to drive Kenneth batty. Bill and Allan continued to be in the picture even after Kay's divorce from Kenneth.

13. The picture was unidentified in her diary, but was probably either *Storm at Daybreak* or *Mary Stevens, M.D.*

14. Born Dorothy Taylor in 1888 in Watertown, New York, she inherited $12 million from her father, a wealthy leather manufacturer. Briefly married to aviator Claude Graham White, she then married Italian Count Carlo Dentice di Frasso in 1923 — and eagerly accepted his title. Their mansion, Villa Madama, was a showplace. "The villa, which is the Frasso home, is just outside the gates of Rome. The entire villa is a masterpiece of 16th century architecture. It was built during the period from 1516–1525 by Cardinal Giulio de Medici (later Pope Clement VII) from designs by the illustrious Raphael. In the buildings are three ceilings decorated by Raphael which are rated among the art treasures of the world." Harry Evans, "The Personal Touch," *Family Circle*, August 3, 1934, p. 10. The Countess left for America when Mussolini took over her residence. The Countess character in Clare Booth Luce's *The Women* was said to be based on di Frasso — down to her cowboy actor boyfriend. Count di Frasso, born in 1876, died in Italy in 1945. The Countess died on January 5, 1954.

15. The Colony was a favorite hangout for Kay, Kenneth, di Frasso, Cooper, and others. On that same day — June 15, 1933 — Kay recorded in her diary an argument with Hal Wallis over *I Loved a Woman*.

16. Kay had previously kissed Asther at a party about two weeks before. Quite handsome, Nils was gay, and though he was no doubt flattered, there was little chance of a full-blown romance. They had worked together on *Storm at Daybreak*, which was filmed in the spring of 1933.

17. On this visit to New York, before the divorce announcement, Kay saw her usual friends, including Arthur Hornblow, Louis Bromfield, Donald and Bea Stewart, Lois Long, Julia Hoyt, Allan Ryan, and Bill Gaston. She also enjoyed cocktails with Dorothy Parker and husband Alan Campbell.

18. "Kay Francis Parts from Her Husband," *New York Times*, December 20, 1933.

19. Marjorie Haynes, "The Untold Love Stories of Kay Francis," *Movie Mirror*, November 1936, p. 99.

20. Francis Diary, March 11, 1934, WCA.

21. Francis Diary, May 31, 1934, WCA.

22. "Kay Francis Asks Divorce," unidentified clipping, NYPL.

23. "Divorce to Kay Francis," unidentified clipping, NYPL.

24. During her divorce proceedings, Mary Astor's explicit diary entries were introduced into evidence. They graphically detailed her adulterous affair with George S. Kaufman while Astor was married to Dr. Franklin Thorpe. The resulting publicity was one of Hollywood's most infamous scandals.

25. *Bill Collins Book of Movies*, p. 158.

26. W.E. Oliver, *Los Angeles Evening Herald Express*, March 2, 1934.

27. Rudy Behlmer, *Inside Warner Bros. 1935–1951*, p. 14.

28. Rudy Behlmer, *Inside Warner Bros. 1935–1951*, p. 15.

29. S.R. Mook, "Unguarded Moment," *Picture Play*, November 1934, p. 27.

30. James M. Fidler, "Spiking the Rumors," *Silver Screen*, August 1934, p. 62.

31. *Variety*, March 6, 1934.

32. S.R. Mook, "Unguarded Moment," *Picture Play*, November 1934, p. 27.

33. S.R. Mook, "Unguarded Moment," *Picture Play*, November 1934, p. 27.

34. Peter Fry, "Behold Them Minus Hokum," *Hollywood Citizen News*, March 31, 1934.

35. Dorothy Cartwright, "On the Set with Kay Francis," unidentified clipping, NYPL.

36. "Kay Francis Off to the Continent," unidentified clipping, NYPL.

37. S.R. Mook, "Unguarded Moment," *Picture Play*, November 1934, p. 54.

38. *Variety*, June 26, 1934.

39. Harry Evans, "The Personal Touch," *Family Circle*, August 3, 1934, p. 10.

40. Harry Evans, "The Personal Touch," *Family Circle*, August 3, 1934, p. 10.

41. Opened in 1926, La Quinta was a desert resort, located near Palm Springs. It was around this time, on March 21, 1934, that Kay's friend Lilyan Tashman died of cancer in New York. Oddly, there was no mention in Kay's diary of her death or funeral.

42. On October 27, 1937, while staying at Tookie De Zappola's New York home, Cole Porter broke both legs in a horse riding accident. Although he didn't die until October 1964, he never fully recovered from the accident.

43. W.E. Oliver, *Los Angeles Evening Herald Express*, September 15, 1934.

44. "Kay Francis Has Narrow Escape," *Los Angeles Times*, May 21, 1934, unidentified page, NYPL.

45. Elizabeth Yeaman, *Hollywood Citizen News*, May 23, 1934.

46. William M. Drew, *At the Center of the Frame*, p. 304.

47. Paolo died in Monte Carlo in August 1989 at the age of 86.

48. Francis Diary, July 29, 1934, WCA. "B" is unidentified. It could be Bert or Aileen B ... or someone else.

49. Francis Diary, July 30, 1934, WCA.

50. "P" refers to Paolo.

51. Francis Diary, August 5, 1934, WCA.

52. Francis Diary, August 8, 1934, WCA.

53. Francis Diary, August 13, 1934, WCA. "HRH" was either Prince Christopher of Greece or Prince Frederick.

54. Francis Diary, August 15, 1934, WCA. "Michael" might be Michael Robinson.

55. Francis Diary, September 2, 1934, WCA.

56. While in France, Kay and Elsa Maxwell had dinner and cocktails with 66-year-old stage legend Maxine Elliott, who had retired to France. Elliott died in 1940.

57. Harold J. Kennedy, *No Pickle, No Performance*, p. 71.

58. Unidentified clipping, NYPL.

59. Unidentified clipping, MCNY.

60. Helen Morgan, "No Romance — Chevalier," unidentified clipping, NYPL.

61. The doctor also socialized with Kay, and his name was recorded as a frequent party guest. Kay presented Branch, a polo player, with a trophy cup on August 2, 1936.

62. Lloyd Pantages, "I Cover Hollywood," *Los Angeles Examiner*, December 3, 1934.

63. *New York Times,* March 8, 1935.

64. "I like pictures," Harrison Carroll, Los Angles Evening Herald, December 7, 1934.

65. Francis Diary, January 4, 1935, WCA. A couple of days after the radio show with Brent, Kay, who apparently resolved to learn French, took a lesson from Georges "Frenchy" Jaumier. It may have been her first and last lesson, as there were no additional entries about the lessons. Jaumier's other students included Mabel Normand, who was tutored at the time of the 1922 William Desmond Taylor murder; Mary Pickford; and others.

66. Frances Kellum, "The Men in Kay Francis' Life!," *Screen Book,* December 1936, p. 34.

67. After his divorce from Kay, Kenneth MacKenna appeared on Broadway in *Accent on Youth, Othello,* and *Macbeth.* He and set designer brother Jo Mielziner co-produced *Co-Respondent Unknown.* According to Jo, it was Ken's idea that James Michenor's novel *Tales of the South Pacific* be made into a musical play; he casually mentioned it one night at the opening of *Mister Roberts* to stage director Joshua Logan. Eventually Kenneth became director of MGM's story department, taking time out to serve during World War II, and earning the Legion of Merit. He resigned from MGM in 1959 to return to Broadway acting in *The Highest Tree.* He also acted on TV and appeared in the film *Judgment at Nuremburg.* MacKenna died of cancer in a Santa Monica hospital at the age of 62 in 1962.

68. Eells, p. 184.

69. "Film Actress Says Good-Bye in Big Way," *Los Angeles Examiner,* February 18, 1935.

70. *Los Angeles Illustrated Daily News,* February 21, 1935.

71. Harrison Carroll, *Los Angeles Evening Herald Express,* September 7, 1935.

72. After Gilbert Roland began dating — and eventually married — Kay's good friend Constance Bennett, Kay often socialized with the couple. "I first met the lovely Miss Francis at Pickfair," Roland told an interviewer. "She was bubbly, interesting, and full of fun. Kay loved parties, and parties loved Kay. Nowadays, people forget what a big star Kay was. She indeed shined very bright." Telephone interview with Jimmy Bangley, March 22, 2004; Gilbert Roland interviewed in person by Jimmy Bangley, February 24, 1994.

73. Eells, pp. 209–210.

74. Elizabeth Wilson, "Projections," *Silver Screen,* March 1937, p. 81.

75. Louella O. Parsons, *Los Angeles Examiner,* February 16, 1935.

76. Westmore and Davidson, *The Westmores of Hollywood,* p. 108. The House of Westmore was located at 6638 Sunset Boulevard. A tourist attraction for many years, it closed in 1965. The building still stands.

77. Louella O. Parsons, *Los Angeles Examiner,* April 5, 1935.

78. Anderson's legal name was Sidney Anderson Lawler. He was a favorite escort of many Hollywood actresses, including Lilyan Tashman, Tallulah Bankhead, Ina Claire, Hedda Hopper, Ruth Chatterton, Constance Bennett, and others.

79. Andy Lawler also appeared in *Confession, Women Are Like That,* and *Secrets of an Actress.*

80. Eells, p. 185.

81. *Lynchburg Virginia Daily Advance,* July 10, 1935. According to the newspaper, the reporters arrived at Lawler's mother's house at 5 P.M., only to find Andy still in his pajamas and dressing gown — "which is probably more of a compliment to Lynchburg's night life than it deserves. He sat down, crossed his ankles over a footstool and asked if it has been this hot all summer." *Lynchburg Virginia Daily Advance,* July 10, 1935. Later in the article, he was quoted as saying he'd "had a gay time abroad." The implication that Lawler was a homosexual was transparent. Myrna Loy was on the *Normandie* with Kay and Andy, and Andy was thought by some to be engaged to Myrna, too!

82. Andy Lawler lived on East 52nd Street.

83. Kay often socialized with Kitty Miller, wife of producer Gilbert Miller.

84. Located in the Banff National Park in Canada, the area is considered one of the most beautiful in the world. At the time Kay and Del stayed there, it was quite rustic and sparsely populated.

85. "What It Has Taken From Me," unidentified clipping, MCNY.

86. *Time,* July 1, 1935.

87. *Variety,* June 26, 1935.

88. *Newsweek,* September 21, 1935.

89. *New York Times,* September 12, 1935.

90. Elsie Janis, "Class with a Capital Kay," *The New Movie Magazine,* March 1934, p. 50.

91. Eileen Creelman, *The New York Sun.*

92. Harrison Carroll, *Los Angeles Evening Herald Express,* September 20, 1935.

93. Eells, p. 211. In the 1930s, a movie magazine asked various stars to pose as the character they'd most like to play. Kay chose Cleopatra.

94. Louella O. Parsons, *Los Angeles Examiner,* November 6, 1935.

Chapter 9

1. Francis Diary, January 1, 1936, WCA.

2. Francis Diary, January 2, 1936, WCA.

3. Gay character actor Clifton Webb lived for years with mother Maybelle, who often accompanied her son to Hollywood's social functions. The two supposedly haunted their Rexford Drive house after their deaths (Maybelle died in 1959, and Clifton in 1966) until the house was demolished. Coincidentally, Grace Moore, Kay's opera singer friend, had lived in the same house, and she, too, was rumored to haunt it. Clifton, a friend of both Grace and Kay, told friends he'd seen Grace's ghost after her plane crash in Denmark on January 26, 1947.

4. *Los Angeles Examiner,* March 25, 1936.

5. *Los Angeles Evening Herald Express,* March 25, 1936.

6. Harrison Carroll, *Los Angeles Evening Herald Express,* April 3, p. 936.

7. Lyle Rooks, "Superstitious Lady: Kay Francis Was Born on a Friday the Thirteenth, Perhaps That Explains This Whole Story," unidentified source, MCNY.

8. Graham Greene, *Pleasure-Dome,* p. 121.

9. Harold Heffernan, "Quickie Plans Fail to Upset," *Daily Oklahoman,* May 11, p. 9.

10. "French, Give Yourself a Break," *Woman's World,* p. 12.

11. Wallis & Higham, p. 57.

12. Lydia Calvert, "Kay Francis 'Mad' About Footwear," unidentified clipping, MCNY.

13. *New York Evening Journal,* September 17, 1936.

14. Sidney Skolsky, "Film-Flam," *Hollywood Citizen News,* May 20, 1936.

15. Harry Mines, *Los Angeles Illustrated Daily News,* May 5, 1938.

16. A detailed account of the incident can be found in *Wisecracker,* William J. Mann's biography on William Haines.

17. Francis Diary, June 12, 1936, WCA.

18. Francis Diary, June 16, 1936, WCA. Kay had seen the opera *Tristan and Isolde* in New York City on January 6, 1923, while married to Dwight Francis.

19. Francis Diary, October 12, 1936, WCA.

20. Francis Diary, August 30, 1936, WCA.

21. Victor Fleming eventually replaced George Cukor during filming of *Gone with the Wind*.

22. "Kay Greets Writer with a Tap Dance," unidentified source, MCNY.

23. Harrison Carroll, *Los Angeles Evening Herald Express,* November 16, 1936.

24. "Kay Greets Writer with a Tap Dance," unidentified source, MCNY.

25. Maude Cheatham, "Not What She Seems to Be," *Motion Picture,* March 1937, p. 59.

26. Maude Cheatham, "Not What She Seems to Be," *Motion Picture,* March 1937, p. 82. Every Kay Francis film required numerous costumes. In truth, she could successfully wear even the most bizarre outfit — and often did. In November 1936, the Fashion Academy of New York honored Kay by naming her the best-dressed woman in America, making her the first actress to win the award. Kay was presented with a gold medal from Academy director Emil Alvin Hartman.

27. Lydia Calvert, "Kay Francis 'Mad' About Footwear," unidentified clipping, MCNY.

28. Malcolm Oettinger, "Is Stardom Worth It?," unidentified source, MCNY.

29. S.R. Mook, "Unguarded Moment," *Picture Play,* November 1934, p. 27.

30. S.R. Mook, "Unguarded Moment," *Picture Play,* November 1934, p. 27.

31. Malcolm Oettinger, "Is Stardom Worth It?," unidentified source, MCNY.

32. James Francis Crow, *Hollywood Citizen News,* April 1, 1937.

33. "It's K.O. Francis Now," *Picturegoer,* October 2, 1937.

34. Ginger Rogers, *Ginger: My Story,* p. 178.

35. Francis Diary, March 7, 1937, WCA.

36. S.R. Mook, "I Can't Wait to Be Forgotten," *Photoplay,* March 1939, p. 72.

37. Lyle Rooks, "Kay Francis Can't Believe Her Fans Care If She Eats Spinach — or Not," unidentified clipping, NYPL.

38. Telephone interview with Jimmy Bangley, February 23, 2004; Allan Ellenberger interviewed via phone by Jimmy Bangley, February 23, 2004.

39. Kay's salary as reported to the IRS: $115,167 (1935); $227,100 (1936); $209,100 (1937). Generally, her weekly salary was in the range of $3,000 to $4,500 a week during her early years at Warner Brothers. In comparison, comedian Joe E. Brown earned $201,562; Leslie Howard, $185,000; and Irene Dunne, $102,777. Kay was the highest paid actor at Warner Brothers. In comparison, the President of the United States made $75,000, and the highest paid business executive was Harvey S. Firestone, who earned $85,000.

40. Kay met Jean Harlow for the first time on January 16, 1930. She occasionally socialized with Harlow's husband Paul Bern, who committed suicide on September 5, 1932.

41. Wilkerson & Borle, *The Hollywood Reporter,* p. 102. Kay recorded no diary entries between June 1 and June 17, 1937.

42. On Del's previous birthday, Kay had given him a gold watch.

43. Kay wrote very little about her mother in her diary, though she was included in some holiday events, especially in the earlier years. Sylvia was a house servant. Kay hired Harry and Sylvia (last names unknown) in August 1935. On January 2, 1938, Kay wrote that Harry and Sylvia were fired. She began interviews for new servants the next day.

44. Lyle Rooks, "Kay Francis Can't Believe Her Fans Care If She Eats Spinach — or Not," unidentified clipping, MCNY.

45. "Farewell to Francis," unidentified clipping, NYPL.

46. *Variety,* September 1, 1937.

47. "Free! By Kay Francis," unidentified clipping, MCNY.

48. Katharine Roberts, "Acting in a Business Way," *Colliers,* March 16, 1935, p. 32.

49. Gladys McVeigh, "Who's Afraid of the Big Screen Wolf? Not Kay Francis— She Leaves Worry Over Jinx to Others," unidentified clipping, MCNY.

50. Adela Rogers St. Johns, "Working Girl," *New Movie Magazine,* March 1931, p. 124.

51. "Democratic," *Los Angeles Times,* June 11, 1934.

52. Elizabeth Wilson, "Projections," *Silver Screen,* March 1937, p. 82. In 1941, it was conjectured that Kay had managed to save close to a million dollars over a ten-year period, obviously planning for the time when she wouldn't be receiving such lucrative contracts.

53. Reine Davies, "The Hollywood Parade," *Los Angeles Examiner,* January 9, 1935.

54. Helen Starr, "My Daughter, Kay," unidentified source, NYPL.

55. Elsa Maxwell, "It's Romance Again for Kay Francis," p. 25.

56. Kay recorded several entries in September 1936 when she and Del argued over pinochle games played at the cabin. In fact, they argued so frequently over these games that Kay made a special note when they *didn't*: "Irving Thalberg died! Del here for dinner — pinochle — no fight!" Francis Diary, September 14, 1936. Kay attended Thalberg's funeral on September 16.

57. Known as the "Witch of Wall Street," Hetty Green was a legendary millionaire who lived like a pauper.

58. Eells, p. 186.

59. "More Good News," *Modern Screen,* April 1936, p. 126.

60. Eells, p. 198.

61. Eells, p. 209.

62. Dick Mook, "She Wanted to Be Forgotten," *Silver Screen,* April 1941, p. 46.

63. Elsie Janis, "Class with a Capital Kay," *The New Movie Magazine,* March 1934, p. 84.

64. Stuart Jerome, *Those Crazy Wonderful Years,* p. 41.

65. Marjorie Haynes, "The Untold Love Stories of Kay Francis," *Movie Mirror,* November 1936, p. 26.

66. Lydia Calvert, "Kay Francis 'Mad' About Footwear," unidentified clipping, MCNY.

67. Kay's usual breakfast order at Warner Brothers was a ham sandwich, pickle, and ice cream!

68. Katharine Roberts, "Acting in a Business Way," *Colliers,* March 16, 1935, p. 32.

69. Katharine Roberts, "Acting in a Business Way," *Colliers,* March 16, 1935, p. 32.

70. Katharine Roberts, "Acting in a Business Way," *Colliers,* March 16, 1935, p. 32.

71. Elizabeth Wilson, "Projections," *Silver Screen,* March 1937, p. 81.

72. Sara Hamilton, "Okay Kay!" *Photoplay,* March 1936, p. 105.

73. Malcolm Oettinger, "Is Stardom Worth It?," unidentified source, MCNY.

74. Kay apparently didn't blame Claudette, describing her as "one of the nicest persons out there." After re-

signing, Kay's new contract was scheduled to expire in July 1942. She'd earn $5,250 a week, and, if Warner exercised their options, $6,000 per week in 1939–1940, and $7,000 in the last year of her contract. Furthermore, Warner Brothers had the right not to use her services for eight weeks per year. After the settlement, this contract became moot.

75. Eells, p. 215. Kay reported in her diary that she'd attended a meeting with agent Myron Selznick and attorneys on August 23, 1937. On August 28, she reported problems with the studio, specifically concerning their refusal of her request to have two days off during her menstrual period.

76. *Variety*, March 30, 1938.

77. *Film Daily*, April 13, 1938.

78. Francis Diary, September 20, 1937, WCA.

Chapter 10

1. Dick Mook, "Why Kay Francis Fascinates Men," unidentified clipping, NYPL.

2. Eells, p. 215. Born in San Francisco in 1904, Daves graduated from Stanford University. After his breakup with Kay, he became a successful writer/director, working on such films *Destination Tokyo, Dark Passage,* and *Broken Arrow.* Daves married writer Mary Lou Lawrence on July 11, 1938, and they had three children, Michael, Deborah and Donna. Daves died in August 1977.

3. Ted Magee, unidentified clipping, MCNY.

4. Francis Diary, December 25, 1937, WCA.

5. While Kay was busy interviewing servants and unpacking in her house, she noted Rosamond Pinchot Gaston's suicide on January 24, 1938. Kay phoned Bill that same day to offer her condolences.

6. S.R. Mook, "I Can't Wait to Be Forgotten," *Photoplay,* March 1939, p. 72.

7. "Kay Francis Lives Here," *House and Garden,* October 1939, p. 52. Kay's house was also featured in an *Architectural Digest* profile.

8. Tom Douglas, born in Kentucky in 1896, had acted on stage in Europe and in silent movies. His last film, *West of Singapore,* was made in 1933. His close friends included George Cukor, Billy Haines, and Edmund Goulding. Douglas died in Mexico in 1978.

9. "Kay Francis Lives Here," *House and Garden,* October 1939, p. 52.

10. Annette Tapert, *Power of Glamour,* p. 121.

11. Ted Magee, unidentified clipping, MCNY.

12. Harold Heffernan, "Quickie Plans Fail to Upset," *Daily Oklahoman,* May 11, 1938, p. 9.

13. Bette Davis played the tragic role of Empress Carlotta in *Juarez and Maximilian* in 1939.

14. Harold Heffernan, "Quickie Plans Fail to Upset," *Daily Oklahoman,* May 11, 1938, p. 9.

15. Rudy Behlmer, *Inside Warner Brothers,* p. 75.

16. At one time David O. Selznick even considered Greta Garbo and Fredric March for *Dark Victory.*

17. Francis Diary, March 5, 1938, WCA.

18. An equivalent salary today would be approximately $2,718,300. Kay made more than her boss Hal Wallis, who earned $208,083, and her fellow actor Dick Powell who made $176,249.

19. *New York Times,* July 7, 1938.

20. Vincent Sherman, *Studio Affairs,* pp. 75–76.

21. *Motion Picture Herald,* March 4, 1939.

22. Personal communication with Sybil Jason.

23. Tony Thomas, *The Busby Berkeley Book,* p. 119.

24. Irene Thirer, unidentified clipping, NYPL.

25. Harold Heffernan, "Quickie Plans Fail to Upset," *Daily Oklahoman,* May 11, 1938, p. 9.

26. Coincidentally, during the making of *King of the Underworld,* Kenneth MacKenna, Kay's ex-husband, was on the verge of marrying Humphrey Bogart's ex-wife, Mary Philips. MacKenna and Phillips married in August 1938. Bogart, meanwhile, married Mayo Methot, his wife prior to Lauren Bacall, in 1938.

27. Vincent Sherman, *Studio Affairs,* p. 75.

28. *New York Times,* January 7, 1939, p. 6.

29. James Francis Crow, *Hollywood Citizen News,* January 13, 1939.

30. "Farewell to Francis," unidentified clipping, NYPL.

31. "Farewell to Francis," unidentified clipping, NYPL.

32. Stuart Jerome, *Those Crazy Wonderful Years,* p. 37. Jerome rightly pointed out that Kay was luckier than others who'd incurred the studio's wrath in years past. The Screen Actors Guild's new contract specified that an actor could only be employed "for acting services." Otherwise, the studio could ask their employee to clean toilets, bus tables, or mop a floor in order to force his/her hand. Someone who'd worked with Kay commented that, if forced to waitress, "Knowing Francis, she would not only report, but she would also keep the tips, right down to the last goddam dime!" Stuart Jerome, *Those Crazy Wonderful Years,* p. 40.

33. Stuart Jerome, *Those Crazy Wonderful Years,* p. 38.

34. Stuart Jerome, *Those Crazy Wonderful Years,* p. 38.

35. Stuart Jerome, *Those Crazy Wonderful Years,* p. 41. An April 1935 article about the Warner Brothers commissary noted that many big stars often had their meals brought to their bungalows or dressing rooms, but some stars, including Kay, weren't so picky. "Warner Brothers have the Green Room for stellar players and distinguished studio visitors, but it is surprising how many stars prefer to sit with the extras and bit players, or even at the counter with the stage crews." According to Katherine Higgins, who was in charge of the commissary for many years at Warner, "'Kay Francis has only one peculiarity regarding food. When she has breakfast at the studio, she usually orders eggs, the whites soft and the yolks well done. She always sits at the counter for breakfast." Reine Davis, "Hollywood Parade," *Los Angeles Examiner,* April 14, 1935.

36. Harold Heffernan, "Hollywood Is Flooded by Cowboys," *Daily Oklahoman,* June 4, 1938, p. 7. Unfortunately, no evidence has been found that Kay ever started work on a manuscript.

37. Stuart Jerome, *Those Crazy Wonderful Years,* p. 40.

38. Miriam Hopkins ended up with the role in the adaptation of Mrs. Carter's memoirs.

39. "Farewell to Francis," unidentified clipping, NYPL.

40. Francis Diary, April 5, 1938, WCA. During this time, Erik made numerous business trips to San Francisco.

41. Francis Diary, June 28, 1938, WCA.

42. Francis Diary, July 21, 1938, WCA.

43. According to Gary Carey in his Anita Loos biography, Kay occasionally checked into the Las Encinas Sanitarium in Pasadena, California, to lose weight.

44. "Farewell to Francis," unidentified source, NYPL.

45. S.R. Mook, "I Can't Wait to Be Forgotten," *Photoplay,* March, 1939, p. 72.

46. S.R. Mook, "I Can't Wait to Be Forgotten," *Photoplay,* March, 1939, p. 32.

47. S.R. Mook, "I Can't Wait to Be Forgotten," *Photoplay,* March, 1939, p. 72.

48. Archer Winsten, unidentified clipping, NYPL.

49. On September 26, 1938 — two days before Kay's last

day at Warner Brothers— studio lawyer Roy Obringer wrote a memo to Hal Wallis, requesting Kay Francis' dressing room for Bette Davis: "If Francis's dressing room is available, then I am of the opinion that Bette Davis, being our top ranked female artist, would undoubtedly be entitled to it." Rudy Behlmer, *Inside Warner Brothers*, p. 79. Obringer was prompted to write Wallis by Davis' attorney, Oscar Cummins.

50. S.R. Mook, "I Can't Wait to Be Forgotten," *Photoplay*, March 1939, p. 72.

51. Stuart Jerome, *Those Crazy Wonderful Years*, p. 41.

52. S.R. Mook, "I Can't Wait to be Forgotten," *Photoplay*, March 1939, p. 32.

53. Kay hired Dorothy Wagner on January 8, 1938.

54. Louella O. Parsons, *Los Angeles Examiner*, October 13, 1938.

55. Kay sailed from Galveston, Texas, on the freighter *S.S. Velma Lykes*. On June 4, 1942, the ship was sunk near Mexico by a torpedo from German submarine U-158. Fifteen crew members died.

56. Louella O. Parsons, *Los Angeles Examiner*, December 1, 1938.

57. Louella O. Parsons, *Los Angeles Examiner*, December 8, 1938.

58. "Baron Barnekow," Erskine Johnson, *Los Angeles Examiner*, January 21, 1939.

59. Francis Diary, January 16, 1939, WCA.

60. S.R. Mook, "I Can't Wait to Be Forgotten," *Photoplay*, March 1939, p. 72.

61. Lucille Elfenbein, "So Now Kay Francis Wears Dark Glasses Everywhere; Tall Actress Travels Light," unidentified clipping, NYPL.

62. Francis Diary, February 21, 1939, WCA.

63. On December 11, 1939, Kay, Cary, and Carole performed in the radio adaptation of *In Name Only* on the *Lux Radio Theatre*.

64. Carl Combs, *Hollywood Citizen News*, August 26, 1939.

65. Dick Mook, "She Wanted to Be Forgotten," p. 91.

66. "Free! By Kay Francis," unidentified source, MCNY.

67. "Free! By Kay Francis," unidentified source, MCNY.

68. "Free! By Kay Francis," unidentified source, MCNY.

69. Morella & Epstein, *Loretta Young*, p. 99.

70. Faith Service, unidentified clipping, MCNY.

71. Eells, p. 220.

72. Eells, p. 220.

73. For a while, Erik Barnekow was known only as Kay Francis' fiancé. The FBI went to considerable trouble trying to track down first his name, and finally his whereabouts. According to the FBI file, "Informant advises Dr. A.M. Zenzes, an acquaintance, had in a conversation which casually brought up the name of Kay Francis' fiancé, nonchalantly mentioned that he was or had been interested in the development of poisonous gases." It should be noted, too, that one of the Baron's FBI files was destroyed.

74. Hans Herlin, *Udet: A Man's Life*, p. 213. Erik Barnekow's conversation with Udet reportedly took place shortly before Udet's suicide.

75. Francis Diary, September 3, 1939, WCA.

76. Directed by Charles Vidor, the 1940 film starred Brian Aherne and Madeleine Carroll.

77. Ella Wickersham, "Hollywood Parade," *Los Angeles Examiner*, December 20, 1939.

78. Dorothy Kilgallen, unidentified clipping, NYPL.

79. Hornblow and Loy would divorce in June 1942. Although Loy didn't mention his womanizing in her candid autobiography, she did describe him as cruel and controlling. Born in New York in 1893, Hornblow was the son of a novelist and theater critic. He worked as a lawyer before going into show business, starting first as a stage producer. One of his first productions was the controversial *The Captive*, which was shut down because of its lesbian theme. Before his marriage to Loy, he'd married and divorced actress Juliette Crosby. His last marriage was to Leonora Schinasi, with whom he collaborated on several children's books. Hornblow received Oscar nominations for *Hold Back the Dawn* (1941), *Gaslight* (1944), and *Witness for the Prosecution* (1958). He died at the age of 83 in 1976 — while working on a film adaptation of *The Captive*— leaving behind wife Leonora and two sons, John and Michael.

80. Hans Herlin, *Udet: A Man's Life*, p. 211.

81. Dick Mook, "She Wanted to Be Forgotten," p. 91.

82. Herb Caen, *San Francisco Chronicle*, January 29, 1940, cited in FBI file. Kay's diary didn't mention Barnekow's heart attack.

83. On July 23, 1940, Mary Pickford, Chairman of the Women's Committee of the Motion Picture Division of the Red Cross, wrote Kay, congratulating her on her work for the organization. Mamoulian, born in Russia in 1897, directed *Love Me Tonight* (1932), *Queen Christina* (1933), *Golden Boy* (1939) and other notable films. Kay's affair with Mamoulian took place between his work on *Golden Boy* (1939) and *The Mark of Zorro* (1940). He married portrait artist Azadia Newman in 1945 — she painted the portrait of Gene Tierney for the film *Laura*. Mamoulian died in 1987.

84. Sheilah Graham, *Garden of Allah*, p. 152. Born in New York in 1896, Eddie Mayer wrote his autobiography, *A Preface to Life*, while still in his twenties. Soon after, he had a hit play with *The Firebrand*. Although he continued to occasionally write plays, Mayer moved to Hollywood to work in film. Mayer married Frances O'Neill McIntyre in 1927, but they divorced in 1937. He died at the age of 63 in 1960 in New York. Mayer's son, Paul Avila Mayer, co-created the TV soap opera *Ryan's Hope* and later quit show business to become a psychotherapist. Eddie's granddaughter is writer-director Daisy von Scherler Mayer.

85. Francis Diary, May 1, 1940, WCA.

86. Mayer was prepared to divorce wife Margaret, and offered Jean a sizeable premarital agreement. Jean, however, broke Mayer's heart when she finally confessed that she was in love with Feldman. "I knew he [Mayer] liked me but I had no idea that he was so serious. I was wildly in love with Charlie Feldman. He loved me too; it was a chemical reaction, we were always dashing for the bedroom whenever we were together. We made love all the time." Samuel Marx, *Mayer and Thalberg: The Make-Believe Saints*, p. 229.

87. Kay attended a party at Jean's on May 14, 1941. Although Charlie and Jean divorced in 1948, they remained friends, and Jean dedicated her lavish photo book, *Jean Howard's Hollywood*, to Charles K. Feldman. The book included photos of many of Kay's friends— though there were none of Kay.

88. Harry Crocker eventually became the co-host of Romanoff's. He died in 1958.

89. Ernst Udet, born April 26, 1896, was the highest scoring German ace to survive World War I. After the war, he was a test pilot and movie stunt pilot, and even appeared as himself in the 1933 movie *S.O.S. Eisberg*. This film also featured Leni Riefenstahl and Rod La Rocque. Udet was a Luftwaffe Quartermaster General in Berlin at the time of his suicide. He committed suicide while talking on the phone to girlfriend Inge Bleier. The gun he used— a Mexican 12mm Colt — had been given to him

in Hollywood when he worked as a stuntman. Carl Zuckmayer's play *The Devil's General* was based on Udet's life and death. The government provided Udet with a state funeral. Goering, head of the Luftwaffe, himself committed suicide on October 15, 1946 — two hours before he was to be executed for war crimes.

90. *New York Times,* December 9, 1940.

91. On July 7, 1940, Kay reported in her diary that she'd seen *I Married a Nazi.* The film, also known as *The Man I Married,* starred Joan Bennett. Kay made no other comment about the film, but it's intriguing to consider what she might have been thinking while viewing the picture.

92. Reinhardt, born in Berlin in 1913, was the son of Max Reinhardt. A producer/director/writer, his credits included *Two Faced Woman* (1941), *The Great Sinner* (1949), and *Town Without Pity* (1961). He died in 1994.

93. Patrick McGilligan, *Fritz Lang: The Nature of the Beast,* p. 236. Fritz Lang, a brilliant director, was a ladies' man. Born in Vienna in 1890, he died in Beverly Hills in 1976. Lang, who directed such classics as *Metropolis* (1927), *Woman in the Window* (1945), and *Big Heat* (1953), had affairs with Miriam Hopkins, Joan Bennett, Virginia Gilmore, Marlene Dietrich, and many others. He also had a dark side, and there were suspicions about his involvement with the mysterious 1921 death of his first wife, Lisa Rosenthal.

94. Goff, born in Perth in 1910, began writing screenplays in the late 1940s with writing partner Ben Roberts. Their credits included *Portrait in Black, Man of a Thousand Faces, Goodbye, My Fancy;* and *Midnight Lace.* Goff and Roberts later became successful television writers/producers, creating such shows as *The Rogues, Burke's Law, Mannix,* and *Charley's Angels.* Goff, who married and divorced Natalie Draper, died in 1999.

95. Francis Diary, December 31, 1940, WCA.

Chapter 11

1. Lyle Rooks, "Kay Francis Can't Believe Her Fans Care If She Eats Spinach — or Not," unidentified clipping, MCNY.

2. According to the FBI, no file was kept on Kay Francis. This seems odd, considering her relationship with Erik Barnekow, but that's the official word from the Bureau.

3. Federal Bureau of Investigation Freedom of Information/Privacy Acts Section: Marlene Dietrich.

4. Federal Bureau of Investigation Freedom of Information/Privacy Acts Section: Marlene Dietrich. The FBI file also claimed that Dietrich had an affair with a married woman — her name was blacked out for privacy reasons. This woman, also a "known Lesbian," was supposedly given a large sapphire ring in a Los Angeles nightclub by Dietrich. The woman in question was probably Jack Warner's wife, Ann. Federal Bureau of Investigation Freedom of Information/Privacy Acts Section: Marlene Dietrich.

5. This statement was echoed years later by Phil Silvers when he worked with Kay on *Four Jills in a Jeep.*

6. Boze Hadleigh, *Bette Davis Speaks,* p. 114.

7. Kay made a cryptic entry in her diary on January 4, 1941, that simply referred to Margaret Lindsay and trouble. This may have been a reference to the scandal.

8. Stage actress, interior designer, *and* onetime Kay Francis neighbor, Elsie de Wolfe married British diplomat Lord Charles Mendl in 1926 when she was 61. Born in New York in 1865, she was stage producer/agent Elizabeth Marbury's longtime partner. Lady Mendl, who

among other things, was credited with inventing the Pink Lady cocktail and the blue rinse hair dye, died in France in 1950. Elsie's address when she lived next door to Kay was 1018 Benedict Canyon Drive.

9. Born Elsie Bierbower in Columbus, Ohio, in 1889, Elsie Janis was a composer, writer, and actor. A child star in vaudeville and then on Broadway, she became world-famous during World War I while entertaining troops. She was a playwright, novelist, magazine writer, songwriter — and one of the movie industry's first female writers, directors, and producers. She was also radio's first female announcer. Janis died in 1956.

10. Elsa Maxwell, born in Iowa in 1883, was best known for hosting parties. She purportedly invented the scavenger hunt. A former vaudeville performer, she wrote several books and many songs and occasionally appeared in movies — as herself. She later made regular appearances on Jack Paar's *Tonight* TV show. She once admitted on a radio show "that she not only did not like men but could never have contemplated going to bed with one." Meredith Etherington-Smith, *Patou,* p. 89. Elsa's longtime lover was Dorothy (Dickie) Fellows-Gordon. Purported conquests — both unsuccessful — included Maria Callas and Rita Hayworth. Maxwell died in 1963.

11. Frances Kellum, "The Men in Kay Francis' Life!" *Screen Book,* p. 34.

12. Faith Service, "Did $26,000 Outweigh a Honeymoon Trip for Kay Francis?," *Motion Picture,* November 1932, p. 78.

13. Faith Service, "Did $26,000 Outweigh a Honeymoon Trip for Kay Francis?," *Motion Picture,* November 1932, p. 78.

14. Faith Service, "Did $26,000 Outweigh a Honeymoon Trip for Kay Francis?," *Motion Picture,* November 1932, p. 78.

15. No relation to Otto, Jetti, who now goes by Jetti Ames, used Preminger as a stage name.

16. Lois Long, quoted in Eells, pp., 204–205.

17. Elizabeth Wilson, "Projections," *Silver Screen,* March 1937, p. 82.

18. Lydia Calvert, "Kay Francis 'Mad' About Footwear," unidentified clipping, MCNY.

19. Elsa Maxwell, "It's Romance Again for Kay Francis," p. 26.

20. *Variety,* December 18, 1940.

21. Gilbert Kanour, unidentified clipping, NYPL.

22. Wanda Hale, unidentified clipping, NYPL

23. Telephone interview with Jimmy Bangley, February 23, 2004; Sydney Guilaroff interviewed in person by Jimmy Bangley, October 1996.

24. Francis Diary, January 12, 1941, WCA.

25. Francis Diary, March 8, 1941, WCA.

26. Kay often socialized with director Lewis Milestone and wife Kendall Lee, a onetime actress.

27. Amy Schapiro, *Millicent Fenwick,* pp. 65–66.

28. Legendary New Jersey Republican Congresswoman Millicent Fenwick was thought to be the model for *Doonesbury's* Lacey Davenport. Hugh Fenwick married Millicent on June 11, 1932. Supposedly Millicent's stepmother, Daisy, was so against the marriage that she followed the photographer, unplugging his lights. Only a few wedding photographs remain — those that were taken outdoors. Hugh and Millicent had two children. Mary Stevens Fenwick was born February 25, 1934; Hugh (Hugo) Hammond Fenwick was born January 28, 1937. By the way, Daisy was right. When Hugh abandoned Millicent and the children in 1938, he also left behind debts, which forced Millicent to go to work to support herself and the children. Hugh asked for a reconciliation in 1940,

but Millicent refused — she'd had enough of his womanizing and lies (mainly the lies, according to Millicent's biographer, Amy Schapiro). The couple divorced in 1945.

29. Amy Schapiro, *Millicent Fenwick*, p. 65.

30. Dolly O'Brien, born Willow Laura Hylan, was once married to Julius Fleischmann, owner of the yeast company. O'Brien was courted by Clark Gable in the 1940s before he married Sylvia Ashley Fairbanks.

31. Grace Moore, *You're Only Human Once*, p. 210.

32. Francis Diary, December 13, 1941, WCA.

33. Johnny McMullen was one of Kay's gay friends in Hollywood. Although she was not as close to him as she was to Andy Lawler, they occasionally played cards, and he was a frequent guest at her dinners and parties. Johnny was a social gadfly who lived in Paris and London in the 1920s and '30s, and wrote a column for *Vogue*, "As Seen By Him," commenting on the world of society and fashion from a man's point of view. He was very close to Elsie Mendl, who considered him her "adopted son." He moved with her to Los Angeles during World War II and lived with her as a companion–social secretary. McMullen died suddenly of a heart attack in 1945 at age 56.

34. Francis Diary, January 1, 1942, WCA.

35. Press release, Lou Smith, Universal Studio, NYPL.

36. Wanda Hale, unidentified clipping, MCNY.

37. Charles Higham, *Charles Laughton: An Intimate Biography*, pp. 112–113.

38. Personal e-mail correspondence with Gloria Jean, July 5, 2004.

39. Oddly, Kay made no mention in her diary of the Carole Lombard tragedy.

40. Hugh Fenwick's speech later became an article in the *New York Times*. In 1954, Hugh married a third time, this time to Barbara West. They lived in Aiken, South Carolina, with daughter Maureen, who was born May 19, 1955. Barbara, a widow with a significant inheritance, already had four children of her own. Supposedly Maureen was named after Lady Maureen Stanley, the British woman with whom Hugh had the affair during World War II. Hugh died at the age of 86 on July 24, 1991, in Aiken. He was opening a second-floor window when he was stricken with a heart attack and fell to his death.

41. Kotsilibas-Davis & Loy, *Being and Becoming*, p. 169.

42. Kotsilibas-Davis & Loy, *Being and Becoming*, p. 169. The raid alarm started at approximately 2:25 A.M. and was lifted at 7:21 A.M. The alarm was triggered by the reported sighting of enemy aircraft approaching Los Angeles. Although the 37th Coast Artillery Brigade used anti-aircraft weaponry, no aircraft were shot down. However, numerous houses and businesses were destroyed by friendly fire, and three people died of heart attacks.

43. "Connie and Kay Give Cause, Gob's Fist Creates Effect," *Daily Oklahoman*, April 9, 1942, p. 9.

44. Francis Diary, June 6, 1942, WCA.

45. Francis Diary, July 30, 1942, WCA. Kay knew Larry Fox from her early days in Hollywood. He also produced *The Man Who Lost Himself.*

46. In his autobiography, Preminger described being seduced by a star after attending a dinner party at her house. "I left early, explaining that I was starting a picture the next morning and had to get up very early. Around four in the morning my telephone rang. The hostess was on the line: 'Everybody has left. Would you like to come over?' The distance between our houses was forty minutes by car. She summoned me that way several times while I was shooting. It gratified her that she could make me sacrifice my precious sleep for her. I didn't mind because she was very attractive." Preminger, *Preminger: An Autobiography*, p. 92.

47. The USO (United Service Organizations) was started on February 4, 1941, in New York. Thomas Dewey was its first fundraiser. When he resigned in 1942 to run for governor of New York, Prescott Bush — grandfather of George W. Bush — took over.

48. Born Dorothea Stephens, her nickname has been variously reported as Stephie, Stevie, and Steve. She and Kay remained friends until Kay's death in 1968.

49. In the November 1946 issue of *Photoplay*, Carole's sister identified Kay and Mary Astor as Carole's two favorite stars. Dorothy added that their photographs covered Carole's bedroom wall.

50. Jean Maddern Pitrone, *Take It from Big Mouth*, pp. 52–53.

51. Jean Maddern Pitrone, *Take It from Big Mouth*, p. 53.

52. Jean Maddern Pitrone, *Take It from Big Mouth*, p. 53.

53. Jean Maddern Pitrone, *Take It from Big Mouth*, p. 53.

54. Jean Maddern Pitrone, *Take It from Big Mouth*, p. 54.

55. "Actresses 'Casualties' Touring Camps in Britain," November 27, 1942, unidentified clipping, NYPL.

56. Jean Maddern Pitrone, *Take It from Big Mouth*, p. 54.

57. "Actresses Bombed, but Show Went On," unidentified clipping, NYPL.

58. "Actresses Bombed, but Show Went On," unidentified clipping, NYPL.

59. "Actresses Bombed, but Show Went On," unidentified clipping, NYPL.

60. Kirk Crivello, *Fallen Angels*, p. 95.

61. Sgt. Francis K. Gleason, quoted in Sidney Skolsky's *New York Post* column, February 22, 1943.

62. Francis Diary, January 26, 1943, WCA. For the most part, Kay wrote few diary entries on her USO tour.

63. Grace Moore, *You're Only Human Once*, p. 210.

64. Herbert (Bart) Marshall divorced Edna Best in 1940. He married Lee Russell that same year. Kay was godmother to their daughter Ann, born in late February 1943.

65. Friedlob, born in Illinois in 1906, produced six films, including *Untamed*, before his death in 1956. He was married to Eleanor Parker from 1946 to 1953.

66. Willi Frischauer, *Behind the Scenes of Otto Preminger*, p. 91.

67. Francis Diary, May 1, 1943, WCA.

68. Founded by John Garfield and Bette Davis, the Canteen was located at 1451 Cahuenga Boulevard in what had once been a stable and then a small theater. Opened in October 1942, virtually every Hollywood star volunteered at least once, including Eddie Cantor, Rudy Vallee, Kay Kyser, Duke Ellington, Harry James, Betty Grable, Marlene Dietrich, Fred MacMurray, Jean Gabin, Louis Calhern, George Murphy, Basil Rathbone, Edgar Bergen, Gene Tierney, Hedy Lamarr, and many more. Stars were recruited to wait on tables, wash dishes, dance with the enlisted men, etc. On November 22, 1945, the Canteen was closed. The site is now a parking garage.

69. Telephone interview with Jimmy Bangley, February 23, 2004; Roddy McDowall interviewed in person by Jimmy Bangley, June 1996.

70. Letter from Kay Francis to Corporal Ambrose M. DuBek, July 16, 1943.

71. Francis Diary, October 14, 1943, WCA.

72. Eells, p. 222.

73. Phil Silvers, *This Laugh Is on Me*, p. 122.

74. *New York Times*, April 6, 1944.

75. Francis Diary, December 14, 1943, WCA.

76. Phil Silvers, *This Laugh Is on Me*, p. 122.

Chapter 12

1. Francis Diary, January 1, 1944, WCA.
2. Francis Diary, January 11, 1944, WCA.
3. Teddi was the daughter of producer Harry Sherman.
4. Marsha Hunt, *The Way We Wore*, p. 315.
5. Marsha Hunt, *The Way We Wore*, p. 312.
6. Marsha Hunt, *The Way We Wore*, p. 312.
7. Marsha Hunt, *The Way We Wore*, p. 314.
8. Marsha Hunt, *The Way We Wore*, p. 315.
9. Married at the time to Hollywood star Tyrone Power, Jr., Annabella was a French actress who came to Hollywood in 1938. The play, which ran for almost a year, also featured Louis Calhern and E.G. Marshall in a small role.
10. Gypsy Rose Lee, married at the time to Alexander Kirkland, kept the identity of Erik's real father a secret until Erik was an adult. Erik was born on December 11, 1944. Otto, who eventually divorced Marion Mill, married model Mary Gardner in 1951. That marriage ended in divorce in 1958. He also had a celebrated romance with actress Dorothy Dandridge, whom he directed in *Carmen Jones* (1954) and *Porgy and Bess* (1959). Otto married again in 1971 — this time to his longtime companion, costume designer Hope Bryce. They remained married until his death from cancer and Alzheimer's disease in 1986. Preminger, considered one of America's finest directors, received three Oscar nominations — and played Mr. Freeze on TV's *Batman*.
11. Francis Diary, March 22, 1944, WCA.
12. Francis Diary, March 28, 1944, WCA.
13. Personal correspondence, MCNY, July 25, 1944.
14. Kay Francis letter, MCNY, July 25, 1944.
15. Wilkerson & Borie, *The Hollywood Reporter*, p. 154.
16. Kay Francis letter, MCNY, July 25, 1944.
17. Kay Francis letter, MCNY, July 25, 1944.
18. George and Valentina Schlee were close friends of Greta Garbo when she lived in New York. The friendship cooled when George and Greta had an affair.
19. Hedda Hopper, "Stanwyck Slated for Good Part in Bond Rally Film," *Daily Oklahoman*, December 26, 1944, p. 6. Kay often mentioned gossip columnists Hedda Hopper and Louella Parsons in her diary. She did not like Hedda — at all. However, she occasionally socialized with Louella and husband, Dockie.
20. "Farewell to Francis," unidentified clipping, NYPL.
21. Telephone interview with Jimmy Bangley, January 23, 2004; Bob Hope interviewed in person by Jimmy Bangley at the Roundtable West, Beverly Wilshire Hotel, October 21, 1997.
22. Located at 1725–35 Fleming (Hoover) Street in East Hollywood, the site had a lengthy and convoluted history. By the time Monogram bought the property in 1942, the lot had changed hands several times. Monogram added a third sound stage and bought nearby property. The studio eventually merged with Allied Artists. The lot was later used as a rental for a number of years before being sold to the PBS station KCET. Part of the lot is now used as an administration building.
23. Mick LaSalle, "B Movie Bad Girls," *San Francisco Chronicle*, May 9, 1999, p. 51.
24. As bad as *Wife Wanted* is, an argument could be made that it's so bad it's good. The same cannot be said of the Warner pictures.
25. *Harrison's Reports*, October 26, 1946.
26. Kay made no mention in her diary of VJ Day on August 14, 1945, or the atomic bombs that brought the war to an end.
27. Despite our best efforts, we have not been able to identify "Miss P," though she was a frequent companion of Kay's.
28. Elsie Janis, "Class with a Capital K," *The New Movie Magazine*, March 1934, p. 84.
29. James M. Fidler, "Spiking the Rumors," *Silver Screen*, August 1934, p. 62. According to the 1934 interview, Kay revealed a lack of confidence about her stage ability: "I want to be featured with a successful actor who is more accustomed to the stage than I who have been away from the footlights for years. I prefer a smaller role with a good cast, rather than to be the whole show, alone, and perhaps prove a failure." James M. Fidler, "Spiking the Rumors," *Silver Screen*, August 1934, p. 62.
30. Patsy Ruth Miller, *My Hollywood*, p. 230.
31. Two reviews specifically mentioned Judy Holliday's performance. *Variety* (August 22, 1945) wrote, "Judy Holliday, the amiable tramp from last season's legiter, 'Kiss Them for Me,' uses a similar voice and style for the role of actress-friend — and steals the show each time she's on." *The Newark Sunday Call* (August 19, 1945) echoed the sentiment. "Judy Holliday, whom many of us applauded last season in 'Kiss Them for Me,' has a similar dumb-bunny role in 'Windy Hill' and manages to steal the scenes uncaptured by smooth Lawrence Fletcher."
32. Patsy Ruth Miller, *My Hollywood*, p. 116.
33. Francis Diary, August 4, 1945, WCA.
34. Francis Diary, August 20, 1945, WCA.
35. *Variety*, August 22, 1945.
36. William Leonard, *Theatre World 1945–1946*, p. 136.
37. *Cleveland Press*, February 19, 1946.
38. Patsy Ruth Miller, *My Hollywood*, pp. 116–117.
39. Eells, p. 224.
40. "I nearly lost my mind," Patsy Ruth Miller, *My Hollywood*, p. 116.
41. Patsy Ruth Miller, *My Hollywood*, p. 117.
42. Roger Pryor married Ann Sothern in September 1936. They divorced in May 1943. Pryor quit show business in 1947 and became a New York advertising executive. He retired in 1962 to Florida and died in 1974.
43. According to Kay's diary, Ruth Chatterton phoned on November 10, 1945, to tell her about the "new girl." Three days later, Jetti arrived, and Kay began rehearsing with her. Born in Evansville, Indiana, Jetti (her given name was Jetaline) graduated from the University of Iowa and appeared in *Angel Street* in 1942 with Vincent Price and Judith Evelyn. Preminger eventually became known as Jetti Ames — she had married television executive Lou Ames in 1942 while he was in the military — and continued to do stage work and occasional television shows. She and her husband, who also became a close friend of Kay's after finishing his military stint, had two sons. Kay became a "surrogate godmother" to their children. Now in her mid–80s, Ames is still a working actress in local theater, dividing her time between Nantucket and Tucson. In a telephone interview she said this about Kay: "She was a fine actor and a fine person." Telephone interview with Jetti Ames, May 18, 2004.
44. Francis Diary, November 23, 1945, WCA.
45. Francis Diary, March 16, 1946, WCA. Ironically, on March 14, 1946, Kay saw *The Lost Weekend*. A couple of weeks earlier, she'd seen *The Bells of St. Mary's*. One of the maddening things about the diary is that Kay often provided only the title of a film she'd seen, usually with no editorial comments.
46. Gladys McVeigh, "Who's Afraid of the Big Screen Wolf? Not Kay Francis — She Leaves Worry Over Jinx to Others," unidentified clipping, MCNY.
47. This was Connie Bennett's fifth — and last — marriage.

She had just divorced Gilbert Roland on June 20, and then married John Theron Coulter on June 22, 1946.

48. Francis Diary, June 26, 1946, WCA.

49. Francis Diary, July 3, 1946, WCA.

50. Founded in 1917 by Gilmor Brown, the Pasadena Playhouse produced hundreds of plays, and was best known for its College of Theatre Arts, whose graduates included Gloria Grahame, Gloria Stuart, Gene Hackman, Dustin Hoffman, and many others. It was named the State Theatre of California in 1937.

51. Kay had had a brief affair with Bayard, or Bydie as she called him, in 1928.

52. *New York Post,* September 29, 1946.

53. Kay's role was taken over by Edith Atwater until Kay's return in January 1947.

Chapter 13

1. Francis Diary, January 26, 1947, WCA.

2. Grace Moore, *You're Only Human Once,* p. 210. Kay hosted a dinner party in honor of Grace Moore on April 27, 1934. Grace and Kay often saw each other throughout the years in New York, California, and Europe.

3. Despite their differences, Grace Moore sang at Thalberg's funeral in 1936.

4. Legend has it that Elvis Presley's Graceland mansion was named for Grace Moore. Others, however, insist the property was named for previous owners.

5. Kay was one of thirteen women presented with gold medals from the New York-based Fashion Academy. Other notable names included Mrs. George Marshall, Louise Albritton, Maggie McNellis, Rise Stevens, Patricia Travers, Doris Duke, and Mrs. Walter Thornton.

6. The Chevalier show opened on March 10 and closed on April 19, 1947.

7. *Finian's Rainbow* opened on January 10, 1947, at the 46th Street Theatre and closed on October 2, 1948. Sets were designed by Kay's former brother-in-law, Jo Mielziner.

8. Francis Diary, April 13, 1947, WCA.

9. *Morning Call,* Allentown, Pennsylvania, September 25, 1947. Kay was presented with the key to the city by the Harrisburg, Pennsylvania, mayor's wife on September 27, 1947.

10. Faith Service, unidentified clipping, MCNY.

11. Playbill, the Playhouse, Wilmington, DE.

12. Francis Diary, October 25, 1947, WCA.

13. Unidentified clipping, MCNY.

14. "Colorful Homer Citizen Was Father of Miss Kay Francis," unidentified clipping.

15. "Kay Francis, Here with Play, Is Passing Up Visit to Homer," *Battle Creek Enquirer & News,* October 29, 1947, unidentified page.

16. "Kay Francis, Here with Play, Is Passing Up Visit to Homer," *Battle Creek Enquirer & News,* October 29, 1947, unidentified page.

17. "Kay Francis, Here with Play, Is Passing Up Visit to Homer," *Battle Creek Enquirer & News,* October 29, 1947, unidentified page.

18. "Kay Francis, Here with Play, Is Passing Up Visit to Homer," *Battle Creek Enquirer & News,* October 29, 1947, unidentified page.

19. "Kay Francis, Ill with Cold, Stars in State of the Union," unidentified clipping, MCNY.

20. "Kay Francis, Here with Play, Is Passing Up Visit to Homer," *Battle Creek Enquirer & News,* October 29, 1947, unidentified page.

21. Lottie Tillotson, "Homer Claims Kay Francis," unidentified clipping, MCNY.

22. "Kay Francis, Ill with Cold, Stars in State of the Union," unidentified clipping, MCNY.

23. Kay reported a pleasant visit with Dr. Wall, the physician who had delivered her more than 42 years before.

24. Lucille Elfenbein, "So Now Kay Francis Wears Dark Glasses Everywhere; Tall Actress Travels Light," unidentified clipping, NYPL.

25. Francis Diary, January 22, 1948, WCA.

26. Francis Diary, January 23, 1948, WCA.

27. *Los Angeles Evening Herald,* January 23, 1948.

28. "Kay Francis Mysteriously Ill," *Columbus Citizen,* January 23, 1948. Kay had no understudy. Erin O'Brien-Moore, part of another touring company of *State of the Union,* replaced Kay in Columbus, and continued for the rest of the tour. O'Brien-Moore asked that she be paid only $60 weekly plus expenses because of her loyalty to Lindsay and Crouse. The authors insisted, however, that she be paid her normal rate.

29. Graham had a small role as a bellboy in *State of the Union.*

30. *Los Angeles Evening Herald,* January 23, 1948.

31. "'Union' Closing Tour; Kay Francis Improved," *Variety,* January 28, 1948.

32. Malabar Farm is now a working farm and state park. Bromfield entertained many Hollywood friends here, and hosted the Lauren Bacall–Humphrey Bogart wedding in 1945.

33. Francis Diary, February 24, 1948, WCA.

34. Francis Diary, March 29, 1948, WCA.

35. Dwight Francis was one of Kay's visitors in May at her new apartment.

36. In later years, Adnia Rice became best known for playing Alma Hix in the stage and film version of *The Music Man.* She also made television appearances and had an act at New York's Blue Angel, where she appeared with the Mademoiselles.

37. 31 West 61st Street is now a large office building.

38. S.R. Mook, "Unguarded Moment," *Picture Play,* November 1934, p. 54.

39. S.R. Mook, "Unguarded Moment," *Picture Play,* November 1934, p. 54.

40. S.R. Mook, "Unguarded Moment," *Picture Play,* November 1934, p. 54.

41. Gladys McVeigh, "Who's Afraid of the Big Screen Wolf? Not Kay Francis— She Leaves Worry Over Jinx to Others," unidentified clipping, MCNY.

42. Torben Prestholdt, *Theatre World, 1946–1947,* pp. 141–142.

43. A third film version, with Greer Garson, titled *The Law and the Lady,* would be filmed in 1950.

44. Francis Diary, June 7, 1948, WCA.

45. Kay was in Boston during the week of July 5, 1948, when 29-year-old Carole Landis committed suicide in California, supposedly over a failed love affair with Rex Harrison. According to researcher Eric Gans, there is no record of Kay sending a card or flowers for Carole's funeral service. Kay also didn't comment on the suicide in her diary.

46. *Fitchburg Sentinel,* July 22, 1948. Kay's frequent colds and respiratory illnesses were likely due to heavy cigarette smoking.

47. Barbara Rodgers (sometimes credited as Rogers) appeared in about ten movies between 1933 and 1936, including *42nd Street* and *Footlight Parade.*

48. Earle Foxe founded the military school. He was a former stage and silent screen actor who appeared in *Strangers in Love* with Kay Francis in 1932.

49. In later years, Joel Ashley appeared on television, on such 1950s TV shows as *Studio One, Lux TV Play-*

house, Boots and Saddles, and *Hallmark Hall of Fame.* He re-entered movies in 1956 via *The Ten Commandments* and *The Vagabond King,* and then appeared in at least ten low-budget westerns in the late 1950s. Ashley ended his career in dozens of TV westerns, such as *Gunsmoke, Annie Oakley,* and *Have Gun Will Travel.*

50. Margalo's father, Francis Wilson, was the founding president of Actors Equity. Her godmother — and namesake — was actor Margalo Gillmore, daughter of Frank Gillmore, founding executive secretary of Actors Equity.

51. E-mail correspondence from Margalo Ashley-Farrand, May 19, 2004. Also, telephone interview, June 7, 2004.

52. *Star Gazette,* December 26, 1948.

53. *Cleveland Press,* December 28, 1948.

54. Unidentified Fort Worth newspaper, March 8, 1949, MCNY.

55. Francis Diary, April 2, 1949, WCA.

56. Francis Diary, April 1, 1949, WCA.

57. Kay also considered touring in *Portrait in Black* in 1951, but again turned it down.

58. *The Saratogian,* June 22, 1949.

Chapter 14

1. Unidentified clipping, NYPL.

2. Marjorie Gateson, unlike Kay, embraced television work and enjoyed a long run on *The Secret Storm.*

3. Unidentified clipping, MCNY.

4. Unidentified clipping, MCNY.

5. Unidentified clipping, MCNY.

6. George S. Kaufman was banned from the show after a December 21, 1952, episode in which he commented, "Let's make this one program on which no one sings 'Silent Night!'" Alex McNeil, *Total Television,* p. 650. The program went off the air in March 1954, but was revived by Irving Mansfield in 1956. Panelists included his wife Jacqueline Susann, along with Abe Burrows and Walter Slezak.

7. "When All the Stars Came Out/Part II," *The Marblehead Messenger,* unknown date, page number.

8. Producer Richard Barr had a long career, which included producing Ruth Draper's Broadway show, as well as *Who's Afraid of Virginia Woolf, A Delicate Balance,* and *Sweeney Todd.* He died of AIDS in 1989.

9. It was probably in late February to early March 1951 when Kay vacationed in Mexico(no year was indicated in her diary, so this remains an educates guess). Kay spent two weeks traveling to cities famous for their colonial architecture, native handicrafts, and scenic beauty. While in Mexico City, Kay climbed the pyramids at Teotihuacan, and then rode a trolley to Xochimilco to spend an afternoon on the flower boats at the famous floating gardens. She also flew to Acapulco, which had just become a popular getaway for members of the movie colony, noting that she spent her days at the resort eating, drinking, and reading mystery novels. The diary entries differ from her usual ones in that they're much more descriptive — and contain nothing about her sex life. Here's a sample: "very nice room over 2 balconies — went to cathedral which is dusty pink and gold — down into steep streets in the markets." Francis Diary, March 7, unknown year, WCA.

10. "Members of the Sardi set," *Boston Globe,* unidentified clipping, MCNY.

11. According to James A. Pegolotti's biography, Taylor's wives included writer Jane Anderson and Broadway actress Mary Kennedy. Deems and Mary had one daughter, Joan. Taylor and Lucille Watson-Little received an annulment in 1953. In 1955, Lucille married Borrah Minevitch, who'd appeared with Kay in *Always in My Heart.* Unfortunately, Minevitch, who'd shelved the harmonica to produce French films, died of a stroke three weeks after the wedding. Taylor told Lucille he'd marry her again, but she refused. She later married French movie producer Alain Terouanne. Deems Taylor died in New York in July 1966.

12. Francis Diary, April 2, 1951, WCA.

13. On May 10, Kay and Basil Rathbone received plaques for their contributions to the advancement of summer theater at a luncheon at the Astor Hotel. Gertrude Lawrence, who was appearing in *The King and I,* was guest of honor.

14. Unidentified clipping, MCNY.

15. Jerry Lane, "Kay Francis' Amazing Secret," *Screen Play,* March 1935, p. 23.

16. Unidentified clipping, MCNY.

17. Eells, pp. 226–227.

18. Lucille Elfenbein, "So Now Kay Francis Wears Dark Glasses Everywhere; Tall Actress Travels Light," unidentified clipping, NYPL.

19. Lucille Elfenbein, "So Now Kay Francis Wears Dark Glasses Everywhere; Tall Actress Travels Light," unidentified clipping, NYPL. The article described Joel as 6'3" and Kay's height as 5'7".

20. Lucille Elfenbein, "So Now Kay Francis Wears Dark Glasses Everywhere; Tall Actress Travels Light," unidentified clipping, NYPL.

21. Lucille Elfenbein, "So Now Kay Francis Wears Dark Glasses Everywhere; Tall Actress Travels Light," unidentified clipping, NYPL.

22. Lucille Elfenbein, "So Now Kay Francis Wears Dark Glasses Everywhere; Tall Actress Travels Light," unidentified clipping, NYPL.

23. Eells, p. 227.

24. *Albany Times Union,* July 19, 1951.

25. Unfortunately, suit Miss Francis," unidentified clipping, MCNY.

26. Francis Diary, September 8, 1951, WCA.

27. Lucille Elfenbein, "So Now Kay Francis Wears Dark Glasses Everywhere; Tall Actress Travels Light," unidentified clipping, NYPL.

28. Francis Diary, September 13, 1951, WCA.

29. *New York World-Telegram and Sun,* unidentified date. One Fifth Avenue is still there, but the ground floor now houses a restaurant. The building is only a short distance from the Marlton Hotel, where Kay briefly lived in 1926.

30. Telephone interview, Margalo Ashley-Farrand, June 7, 2004.

31. Margalo Ashley-Farrand, June 7, 2004.

32. Francis Diary, November 10, 1951, WCA.

33. Coincidentally, ex-husband Dwight Francis lived only blocks from her on East 66th Street.

34. Unidentified clipping, MCNY.

35. Lyle Rooks, "Kay Francis Can't Believe Her Fans Care if She Eats Spinach — or Not," unidentified source.

36. "Kay Francis in photo highlight," *TV Guide.*

37. Kay frequently socialized with Tony's father, Osgood Perkins, particularly in the summer of 1931.

38. Charles Winecoff, *Split Image,* p. 60.

39. Charles Winecoff, p. 60.

40. *The Saratogian,* August 26, 1952.

41. Eells, p. 227

42. Eells, pp. 228–229.

43. Francis Diary, April 3, 1952, WCA.

44. Lillian Gish was in South America, and sister Dorothy accepted for her.

45. Mart Martin, *Did She or Didn't She?*, p. 60.
46. Unidentified clipping, MCNY.
47. Eells, p. 229.
48. Unidentified clipping, MCNY.
49. Francis Diary, July 19, 1953, WCA.
50. Francis Diary, September 27, 1953, WCA.
51. Francis Diary, August 26, 1953, WCA.
52. Unidentified clipping, MCNY.
53. Francis Diary, December 31, 1953, WCA.
54. *Miami Daily News,* June 23, 1954.
55. Unidentified clipping, MCNY.
56. Unidentified clipping, MCNY.
57. Eells, p. 205.
58. Dennis had changed the final scene in *Theatre* so the character, supposedly avoiding her fans outside the stage door, exited the stage through the actual audience. Kay loved it — and so did her audiences.

Chapter 15

1. Malcolm Oettinger, "Is Stardom Worth It?," unidentified source, MCNY.
2. *Cape Cod Standard Times,* July 14, 1955.
3. Goldie's real name was Louis Goldson Hawkins, and he was from Fort Deposit, Alabama.
4. *An Evening at Goldie's New York.*
5. *New York Journal American,* November 1, 1955.
6. Unidentified letter, MCNY.
7. Letter from Katherine Clinton, MCNY.
8. Weissberger, who specialized in entertainment law, was attorney — and confidante — to many stars, including Marilyn Monroe and Orson Welles. He was also an amateur photographer of note. His book, *Famous Faces: A Photograph Album of Personal Reminiscences,* was published in 1973. The book includes a photo of Kay and Anna taken in 1960. Weissberger died in 1986.
9. Joel Lobenthal, *Tallulah! The Life and Times of a Leading Lady,* p. 253. Goldman's clients included Tallulah Bankhead.
10. *New York Journal,* September 18, 1957, unknown page number.
11. Dennis Allen married the woman he met at Fire Island that summer.
12. "The Love Creed of Kay Francis," unidentified clipping, MCNY.
13. Dwight Deere Wiman was one of Broadway's most successful producers. Born in Moline, Illinois, in 1895, he graduated from Yale. His family hoped he'd work in the family business, Deere & Co. However, Dwight preferred show business. He was a partner for six years with Bill Brady, Jr. His productions included *The Little Show* (1929), *The Vinegar Tree* (1930), *The Gay Divorcee* (1932), and many others. Wife Dorothea Stephens, nicknamed Steve, was also from Moline. They divorced in 1942. Wiman died in January 1951.
14. Clay Shaw was arrested in March 1967 and charged with conspiring to kill President Kennedy. In March 1969, Shaw was acquitted.
15. Lipson was born in Brooklyn but raised in Pittsfield, Massachusetts. Kay was likely amused by this link to her early married life. Lipson was best known for playing Tevye in *Fiddler on the Roof.* Described in 1965 as "a gentle-mannered, warm-hearted, 51-year-old bachelor," he died in 1996. Norman Nadel, "Lipson a Replacement Expert," *New York World Telegram,* October 30, 1965.
16. Billy Matthews, born in Austin, Texas, began his show business career as a child actor at Zachary Scott's Austin Little Theatre. He later became a model, most notably on military recruitment posters — "You, too, can be an Aviation cadet" — and a Camel cigarette billboard that was displayed in New York's Times Square for many years. Active in the Society of Stage Directors & Choreographers, he directed Broadway plays, including *Thirteen Daughters* and *Beg, Borrow or Steal.* He died in London in 1997 at the age of 76.
17. Fedora Dorato, now in her eighties and still Fedora's manager/hostess, was interviewed at the restaurant (239 W. 4th Street) by John Rossman on October 20, 2004.
18. Kay often stayed at the Boxwood Inn, 100 Dillingham, in Falmouth. The Inn is now the Nimrod Restaurant.
19. Personal correspondence with James Robert Parish.
20. Personal correspondence with James Robert Parish.
21. Harold J. Kennedy, *No Pickle, No Performance,* p. 71.
22. Harold J. Kennedy, *No Pickle, No Performance,* p. 71.
23. Malcolm Oettinger, "Is Stardom Worth It?," unidentified source, MCNY.
24. Ben Maddox, "Kay Francis Wants Life," *Movie Mirror,* September 1934, p. 76.
25. Dick Mook, "She Wanted to Be Forgotten," p. 92.
26. Leonard Lyons, "The Lyons Den," *New York Post,* August 29, 1968. Here is the actual wording from Kay's will: "I direct that my body be cremated but that no other and further funeral expenses of any character be had, and that the undertaker shall dispose of my ashes in a manner to be determined by him, but under no circumstances shall my ashes be retained in any urn or receptacle of any kind, nor shall my ashes be interred, nor shall my ashes be scattered over the seas, nor shall my remains be displayed or viewed by anyone, nor shall services of any type be held."
27. Specifically, Kay bequeathed a bracelet, earrings, and gold bagel pin; topaz and ruby earrings and ring; topaz and ruby necklace, bracelet and clips to Hilda Coppage, with the hope that Hilda would eventually pass the jewelry on to her daughter, Judy Reynolds, and then to Reynolds' daughter, Barbara. As for the bequest to Mrs. Wiman, Kay specified that Wiman would receive every piece of Kay's jewelry that contained an emerald or emeralds, along with the single round diamond used to connect the emerald necklace; the connecting snap on the emerald necklace made up of eighteen round diamonds; and two baguette diamonds. Furthermore, she hoped that Mrs. Wiman would divide the jewelry between herself, Virginia Chambers, and Kendall Milestone. There's no record of how *that* particular transaction was finally settled.
28. Katherine Clinton's doctors included John MacDonald and John P. Lordan. Kay's doctors included William H. Kammerer and Herbert Conway. Kay left $1,000 each to MacDonald and Lordan, and $2,000 each to Kammerer and Conway.
29. Alfred Albelli, "Kay Francis Leaves $1M to Seeing-Eye Dog Fund," *New York Daily News,* December 7, 1968.
30. Throughout her life, Kay Francis usually had a beloved pet, and often attended events with other dog lovers. For example, on February 5, 1934, she participated in a dog christening for Warren Williams' four wirehaired terriers. Other guests included the Richard Barthelmesses, George Barnes and Joan Blondell, the Leslie Howards, the Edward G. Robinsons, Mary Astor, Dick Powell, William Powell, and many others. Like the other attendees, Kay arrived at the party with her dog.
31. Kay's star is located at 6764 Hollywood Boulevard.
32. Telephone interview with Jimmy Bangley, February

23, 2004; Cari Beauchamp interviewed via phone by Jimmy Bangley, February 23, 2004.

33. Telephone interview with Jimmy Bangley, March 22, 2004; Margaret Burk letter to Jimmy Bangley, March 5, 2004.

34. Telephone interview with Jimmy Bangley, July 21, 2004; Christopher Nickens telephone interview with Jimmy Bangley, July 21, 2004.

Bibliography

Adamson, Joe (1973). *Groucho, Harpo, Chico, and Sometimes Zeppo: A Celebration of the Marx Brothers.* New York: Simon and Schuster.

"Allotment Wives, Inc." (November 1945). *Screen Romances,* pp. 52–53, 113–120.

"The Amateur Cracksman Again" (1930, July 25) [Review of *Raffles*]. *The New York Times,* 20:2.

Arce, Hector (1979). *Gary Cooper: An Intimate Biography.* New York: William Morrow.

Arden, Eve (1985). *Eve Arden: Three Phases of Eve.* New York: St. Martin's Press.

Atkinson, J. Brooks (1927, February 23). "Crook Drama, Modern Style" [Review of *Crime*]. *The New York Times,* 27:3.

"An Attorney Confesses" (1930, July 19) [Review of *For the Defense*]. *The New York Times,* 27:7.

Barbour, Alan G. (1973). *Humphrey Bogart: The Pictorial Treasury of Film Stars.* New York: Gallahad Books.

Barrymore, Diana (1957). *Too Much Too Soon.* New York: Henry Holt.

Basinger, Jeanine (1993). *A Woman's View: How Hollywood Spoke to Women 1930–1960.* New York: Alfred A. Knopf.

Behlmer, Rudy (1985). *Inside Warner Bros. 1935–1951: The Battles, Brainstorms, and the Bickering — from the Files of Hollywood's Greatest Studio.* New York: Simon & Schuster.

Bergman, Ingrid, and Alan Burgess (1980). *Ingrid Bergman: My Story.* New York: Delacorte Press.

Bernard, April (January 1990). "Screen Gem" [Interview with Sylvia Sidney]. *Interview,* pp. 54–56, 104.

Berry, Sarah (2000). *Screen Style: Fashion and Femininity in 1930s Hollywood.* Minneapolis: University of Minnesota Press.

Bickford, Charles (1965). *Bulls Balls Bicycles & Actors.* New York: Paul S. Eriksson.

Billups, Connie, and Arthur Pierce (1995). *Lux Presents Hollywood: A Show-by-Show History of the Lux Radio Theatre and the Lux Video Theatre, 1934–1957.* Jefferson, N.C.: McFarland.

Black, Shirley Temple (1988). *Child Star.* New York: McGraw-Hill.

Bradshaw, Jon (1985). *Dreams That Money Can Buy: The Tragic Life of Libby Holman.* New York: William Morrow.

"Brief Reviews of Current Pictures" (October 1934). *Photoplay,* p. 6, 110, 115.

_____ (March 1936). *Photoplay,* p. 5.

Brooks, Tim, and Earle Marsh (1979). *The Complete Directory to Prime Time Network TV Shows 1946–Present.* New York: Ballantine Books. .

Brown, Gene (1995). *Movie Time: A Chronology of Hollywood and the Movie Industry from Its Beginnings to the Present.* New York: Macmillan.

Bryce, Robert (October 1999). "Without a Net." *Polo Magazine.*

Bubbeo, Daniel (2002). "Kay Francis: 'Trouble in Paradise.'" In *The Women of Warner Brothers: The Lives and Careers of 15 Leading Ladies.* Jefferson, N.C.: McFarland, pp. 86–101.

Calanquin, Leon V. (April 1980). "The Tragedy of Kay Francis." *The World of Yesterday,* pp. 15–19.

Carey, Gary (1988). *Anita Loos: A Biography.* London: Bloomsbury.

Chase, Ilka (1942). *Past Imperfect.* Garden City, N.Y.: Doubleday & Doran.

Cheatham, Maude (March 1934). "Not What She Seems to Be — That's Kay." *Motion Picture,* pp. 59, 82–83.

Chevalier, Maurice (1960). *With Love.* Boston: Little & Brown.

Chierichetti, David (2003). *Edith Head: The Life and Times of Hollywood's Celebrated Costume Designer.* New York: HarperCollins.

Cocchi, John (1991). *Second Feature: The Best of the "B" Films.* New York: A Citadel Press Book.

Coffee, Frank (1991). *Always Home: 50 Years of the USO: The Official Photographic History.* Washington, D.C.: Brassey's.

Collins, Bill (1974, June 8). "Kay Francis, Hollywood's Fallen Angel." *TV Times,* pp. 16–18.

_____ (1977). *Bill Collins' Book of Movies.* Australia: Cassell.

Corliss, Rae S. (1986, June 14). "Kay Francis Visited Ill Father in Albion Hospital." *Journal of Albion,* pp. 1, 5.

Cosio, Robyn (2000). *The Eyebrow.* New York: ReganBooks.

Crivello, Kirk (1988). *Fallen Angels: The Lives and Untimely Deaths of 14 Hollywood Beauties.* New Jersey: Citadel Press.

Cruikshank, Herbert (October 1931). "Lucky Thirteen." *Modern Screen,* unknown page numbers.

"Dangerous Curves" [review] (1929, July 15). *The New York Times,* 25:1.

Daniel, Clifton, ed. (1989). *Chronicle of America.* Mount Kisco, N.Y.: Chronicle.

Davis, Bette, with Whitney Stine (1975). *Bette Davis "Mother Goddam."* New York: Berkley Medallion.

Denver City Directories, 1906–1909.

Dooley, Roger (1981). *From Scarface to Scarlett: American Film in the 1930s.* New York: Harcourt Brace Jovanovich.

Drew, William M. (1999). *At the Center of the Frame: Leading Ladies of the Twenties and Thirties.* Lanham, M.D.: Vestal Press.

Druxman, Michael B. (1975). *Basil Rathbone: His Life and His Films.* New York: A.S. Barnes.

Edelson, Edward (1976). *Funny Men of the Movies.* Garden City, N.Y.: Doubleday.

Eells, George (1976). *Ginger, Loretta and Irene Who?* New York: G.P. Putnam's Sons.

Emerson, Dorothy (March 1931). "Reading Their Writing." *Silver Screen,* pp. 28–29, 60–61.

Engstead, John (1978). *Star Shots: Fifty Years of Pictures and Stories by One of Hollywood's Greatest Photographers.* New York: E.P. Dutton.

Etherington-Smith, Meredith (1983). *Patou.* New York: St. Martin's.

Evans, Harry (1934, August 3). "The Personal Touch: Chats with Kay Francis, Jessie and Dick Barthelmess, Louella Parsons, and Countess Frasso at Bert Taylor's Party." *Family Circle,* pp. 10–11, 22.

An Evening at Goldie's New York (no date). Mercury Records MG 20544.

Eyman, Scott (1993). *Ernst Lubitsch: Laughter in Paradise.* New York: Simon & Schuster.

Eyman, Scott (1997). *The Speed of Sound.* New York: Simon & Schuster.

Fabian, Warner (1923). *Flaming Youth.* New York: Boni and Liveright.

Farrar, Rowena Rutherford (1982). *Grace Moore and Her Many Worlds.* New York: Cornwall Books.

"A Fashionable Rogue" (1931, May 1) [Review of Ladies' Man]. *The New York Times,* 30:3.

Felheim, Marvin (1956). *The Theater of Augustin Daly: An Account of the Late Nineteenth Century American Stage.* Cambridge: Harvard University Press.

Fidler, James M. (August 1934). "Spiking the Rumors: Kay Francis Answers the Gossips." *Silver Screen,* pp. 61–62.

"Film Stars Flee on Yacht: Kay Francis and Kenneth MacKenna Silent on Marriage Plans" (1931, January 17). *The New York Times,* p. 23.

"First Lady" [review] (November 1937). *Silver Screen,* p. 58.

Ford, Hugh (1975). *Published in Paris: American and British Writers, Printers, and Publishers in Paris, 1920–1939.* New York: Macmillan.

Francis, Kay. Diaries, 1922–1953. Kay Francis Collection. Wesleyan Cinema Archives, Wesleyan University, Middletown, CT.

Francis, Kay (January 1937). "Don't Try Your Luck Out Here! *Pictorial Review,* 16–17, 50.

Frank, Sam. (1997). *Ronald Colman: A Bio-Bibliography.* Westport, C.T.: Greenwood Press.

Franks, Norman, Frank Bailey, and Rick Duiven (1996). *The Jasta Pilots.* London: Grub Street.

Freedland, Michael (1972). *Jolson.* New York: Stein and Day.

_____ (1979). *The Two Lives of Errol Flynn.* New York: William Morrow.

French, William Fleming (August 1936). "Kay Francis Says: Give Yourself a Break." *Woman's World,* pp. 12–13, 16.

Frick, John W., and Carlton Ward (1987). *Directory of Historic American Theatres.* Westport, C.T.: Greenwood Press.

Frischauer, Willi (1974). *Behind the Scenes of Otto Preminger: An Unauthorized Biography.* New York: William Morrow.

Galbraith, John Kenneth (1962). *The Great Crash 1929.* New York: Time Reading Program Special Program.

Gallagher, Brian (1987). *Anything Goes: The Jazz Age Adventures of Neysa McMein and Her Extravagant Circle of Friends.* New York: Times Books.

Gargan, William (1969). *Why Me?* Garden City, N.Y.: Doubleday.

Garnett, Tay (1973). *Light Your Torches and Pull Up Your Tights.* New Rochelle, N.Y.: Arlington House.

Geist, Kenneth L. (1978). *Pictures Will Talk: The Life & Films of Joseph L. Mankiewicz.* New York: Da Capo Press.

"A General Falls in Love" (1930, November 2) [Review of The Virtuous Sin]. *The New York Times,* 5:2.

"Gentlemen of the Press" [Review] (1929, May 13). *The New York Times,* 27:2.

Graham, Sheilah (1970). *The Garden of Allah.* New York: Crown.

Grams, Jr., Martin (1998). *The History of the Cavalcade of America.* Kearney, N.B.: Morris.

Gray, Sonya F. (July 9, 2002). "Making a Difference: Katharine Ryan Gibbs." *http://www.projo.com/specials/women/94root13.htm.*

Green, Abel, and Joe Laurie, Jr. *Show Biz: From Vaude to Video.* New York: Henry Holt.

Greene, Graham (1980). *The Pleasure-Dome: The Collected Film Criticism 1935–40.* Edited by John Russell Taylor. Oxford: Oxford University Press.

Griffith, Richard (1971). *The Talkies: Articles and Illustrations from a Great Fan Magazine 1928–1940.* New York: Dover.

Grobel, Lawrence (1989). *The Hustons.* New York: Charles Scribner's Sons.

Guest, Val (1933, December 30). "Oh Kay–That's Francis." *Film Pictorial,* p. 10.

Guiles, Fred Lawrence (1975). *Hanging on in Paradise.* New York: McGraw-Hill.

Hadleigh, Boze (1996). *Bette Davis Speaks.* New York: Barricade Books.

Hall, Ben M. (1988). *The Best Remaining Seats: The Golden Age of the Movie Palace.* New York: Da Capo Press.

Hall, Leonard (October 1929). "Vamping with Sound." *Photoplay,* pp. 51, 126.

_____ (October 1932). "Just Three Years." *Photoplay,* pp. 48, 112–113.

Hall, Mordaunt (1929, May 25). "Groucho and His Brethren" [Review of The Cocoanuts]. *The New York Times,* p. 17:3.

_____ (1929, September 28). "Queer Happenings" [Review of Illusion]. *The New York Times,* 17:3.

_____ (1929, December 14). "The Children" [Review

of *The Marriage Playground*]. *The New York Times*, 22:4.

_____ (1929, December 22). "Children of Divorce: Edith Wharton's Novel Makes an Interesting Talker — 'This Thing Called Love'" [Review of *Marriage Playground*]. *The New York Times*, VIII, 1.

_____ (1930, January 18). "The Lout" [Review of *Behind the Make-Up*]. *The New York Times*, 21:1.

_____ (1930, February 3). "A Rothstein Shadow" [Review of *Street of Chance*]. *The New York Times*, 17:1.

_____ (1930, April 21). "A Hollywood Studio Frolic" [Review of *Paramount on Parade*]. *The New York Times*, 20:4.

_____ (1930, April 26). "A Notorious Affair Given" [Review of *A Notorious Affair*]. *The New York Times*, 11:2.

_____ (1930, August 30). "Merry Tomfoolery" [Review of *Let's Go Native*]. *The New York Times*, 7:4.

_____ (1930, December 22). "Love and Infatuation" [Review of *Passion Flower*]. *The New York Times*, 16:2.

_____ (1931, February 9). "Hoist with His Own Petard" [Review of *Scandal Sheet*]. *The New York Times*, 25:4.

Hall, Mordaunt (1931, June 6). "The Stool Pigeon" [Review of *The Vice Squad*]. *The New York Times*, 15:5.

_____ (1931, June 15). "The Missing Letter" [Review of *Transgression*]. *The New York Times*, 23:3.

_____ (1931, August 29). "Murder as an Art" [Review of *Guilty Hands*]. *The New York Times*, 16:3.

_____ (1931, October 3). "A Sinister Record" [Review of *Twenty-Four Hours.*] *The New York Times*, 20:2.

_____ (1931, November 2). "Gold-Diggers on Parade" [Review of *Girls About Town*]. *The New York Times*, 27:1.

Hamann, G.D. (2003). *Kay Francis in the '30s*. Hollywood: Filming Today Press.

Hamilton, Sara (March 1936). "Okay Francis!" *Photoplay*, pp. 30–31, 104–105.

"Hamlet Modishly" (1925, November 10). *The New York Times*, p. 23.

Haver, Ronald (1980). *David O. Selznick's Hollywood*. New York: Bonanza Books.

Haynes, Marjorie (November 1936). "The Untold Love Stories of Kay Francis." *Movie Mirror*, pp. 26–27, 98–99.

Heffernan, Harold (1938, May 11). "Quickie Plans Fail to Upset." *The Daily Oklahoman*, p. 9.

Henderson, Mary C. (2001). *Mielziner: Master of Modern Stage Design*. New York: Watson-Guptill.

Herlin, Hans (1960). *Udet: A Man's Life*. Translated by Mervyn Savill. London: MacDonald.

Herne, Brian (2001). *White Hunters: The Golden Age of African Safaris*. New York: Owl.

Higham, Charles (1976). *Charles Laughton: An Intimate Biography*. Garden City, N.Y.: Doubleday.

_____, and Roy Moseley. *Cary Grant: The Lonely Heart*. New York: Harcourt Brace Jovanovich.

Hill, Beverly (December 1932). "Keep This Under Your Hat." *Screen Book Magazine*, p. 32.

Hollywood Newsreel (June 1937). "Okay, Kay!" *Hollywood*, p. 11.

Hopper, Hedda (1952). *From Under My Hat: The Fun and Fury of a Stage, Screen and Column Career*. Garden City: N.Y.: Doubleday.

"The House of Gibbs: History of One of Homer's Oldest Families" (1901, October 16). *The Homer Index*, p. 1.

House, Marie (March 1931). "Tips on Tempting from Kay Francis." *Screenland*, pp. 23, 107.

"How the Stars Rate in Popularity" (December 1932). *Screen Book Magazine*, p. 38.

Howard, Jean, with James Watters (1989). *Jean Howard's Hollywood: A Photo Memoir*. New York: Harry N. Abrams.

Hudson, Derek (1975). *For Love of Painting: The Life of Sir Gerald Kelly, K.C.V.O., P.R.A.* London: Peter Davies.

Hulse, Ed (1996). *The Films of Betty Grable*. Burbank: Riverwood Press.

Hunt, Marsha (1996). *The Way We Wore: Styles of the 1930s and '40s and Our World Since Then*. Fallbrook, C.A.: Fallbrook.

Illustrated Atlas and Directory of Free Holders of Calhoun County Michigan Including Brief Biographical Sketches of Enterprising Citizens: Compiled and Published from Official Records and Personal Examinations (1894). Fort Wayne, I.N.: Atlas.

"It's K.O. Francis Now" (1937, October 2). *Picturegoer*.

Janis, Elsie (March 1934). "Class with a Capital Kay." *The New Movie Magazine*, pp. 50–51, 84.

Jerome, Stuart (1983). *Those Crazy Wonderful Years When We Ran Warner Bros.* Secaucus, N.J.: Lyle Stuart.

Johnston, Alva (1962). "Hollywood's Ten Per Centers." In *Hello Hollywood!* (pp. 193–205). Originally published in *Saturday Evening Post*, 8/8/42 and 8/22/42.

Jones, Jennifer (1998). "Rebels of Their Sex: Nance O'Neil and Lizzie Borden." In R.A. Schanke and K. Marra, eds., *Passing Performances: Queer Readings of Leading Players in American Theater History* (pp. 83–103). Ann Arbor: The University of Michigan Press.

Karney, Robyn (1997). *Chronicle of the Cinema*. New York: DK Publishing.

"Kay Francis, Actress, Dies at 63; Epitome of Glamour in the 30s" (1968, August 27). *The New York Times*, p. 41.

"Kay Francis Back from S. American Army Tour" (1945, May 1). *Hollywood Reporter*.

"Kay Francis Lives Here" (October 1939). *House and Garden*, pp. 52–53.

"Kay Francis Parts from Her Husband" (1933, December 20). *The New York Times*, 27.

Keats, Patricia (January 1934). "Kay Francis 'as 'eard the East a'Callin.'" *Silver Screen*, p. 49, 63–64.

Kellow, Brian (2004). *The Bennetts: An Acting Family*. Lexington: University Press of Kentucky.

Kellum, Frances (December 1936). "The Men in Kay Francis' Life!" *Screen Book*, pp. 34, 86–87.

Kennedy, Harold J. (1978). *No Pickle, No Performance: An Irreverent Theatrical Excursion from*

Tallulah to Travolta. Garden City, N.Y.: Double-day.

Kennedy, Matthew (2004). *Edmund Goulding's Dark Victory: Hollywood's Genius Bad Boy*. Madison: University Press of Wisconsin.

Lambert, Gavin (1997). *Nazimova*. New York: Alfred A. Knopf.

Lane, Jerry (March 1935). "Kay Francis' Amazing Secret." *Screen Play*, pp. 23, 80.

LaSalle, Mick (1999, May 9). "B Movie Bad Girls," *San Francisco Chronicle*, p. 51.

_____ (2000). *Complicated Women: Sex and Power in Pre-Code Hollywood*. New York: St. Martin's Press.

_____ (2000, April 30). "Dark Side of the 20th Century." *San Francisco Chronicle*, p. 58.

Lasky, Bessie Mona (1957). *Candle in the Sun*. Los Angeles: DeVorss.

Lasky, Jesse L. (1975). *Whatever Happened to Hollywood?* New York: Funk & Wagnalls.

Lawrence, Greg (May 2001). "Ballets Over Broadway." *Vanity Fair*, pp. 122–148.

Leff, Leonard J., and Jerold L. Simmons (2001). *Dame in the Kimono: Hollywood, Censorship, and the Production Code*. Lexington: University Press of Kentucky.

Leonard, William (1946). "Chicago Season." In *Theatre World Season, 1945–1946*. Daniel Blum, ed. New York: Guide.

"Let's Talk About Hollywood: More News and Chit-Chat about the Film City and Its Folks" (June 1933). *Modern Screen*, p. 80.

Levin, Martin (1970). *Hollywood and the Great Fan Magazines*. New York: Castle Books.

Little Church http://www.littlechurch.org/history. html

Lobenthal, Joel (2004). *Tallulah! The Life and Times of a Leading Lady*. New York: ReganBooks.

Lord, Graham (2004). *NIV: The Authorized Biography of David Niven*. New York: Thomas Dunne Books.

Los Angeles City Directories, 1906 — 1909.

Loy, Myrna, and James Kotsilibas-Davis (1987). *Being and Becoming*. New York: Alfred A. Knopf.

Maas, Frederica Sagor (1999). *The Shocking Miss Pilgrim: A Writer in Early Hollywood*. Lexington: University Press of Kentucky.

Maddox, Ben (September 1934). "Kay Francis Wants Life." *Movie Mirror*, pp. 31, 76–77.

_____ (November 1937). "Pets for Pals." *Silver Screen*, pp. 30–31, 66–68.

Maltin, Leonard (1985). *Movie Comedy Teams*. New York: New American Library.

_____ (1995). *1996 Movie & Video Guide*. New York: Plume.

Mandelbaum, Howard, and Eric Myers (1985). *Screen Deco: A Celebration of High Style in Hollywood*. New York: St. Martin's Press.

Mann, Carol (1996). *Paris: Artistic Life in the Twenties & Thirties*. London: Laurence King.

Mann, William J. (1998). *Wisecracker: The Life and Times of William Haines: Hollywood's First Openly Gay Star*. New York: Penguin Books.

_____ (2001). *Behind the Screen: How Gays and Lesbians Shaped Hollywood 1910–1969*. New York: Viking.

Mantle, Burns, ed. (1945). *Best Plays of 1925–1926*. New York: Dodd & Mead.

_____ (1945). *Best Plays of 1926–1927*. New York: Dodd & Mead.

"Marsha Hunt Home with Report on Troops in Arctic" (20 March, 1944). *Hollywood Reporter*.

Martin, Mart (1996). *Did She or Didn't She? Behind the Bedroom Doors of 201 Famous Women*. New York: Citadel Press.

Marx, Samuel (1975). *Mayer and Thalberg: The Make-Believe Saints*. New York: Random House.

Mattfield, Julius (1968). *Variety Music Cavalcade 1620–1961: A Chronology of Vocal and Instrumental Music Popular in the United States*. New Jersey: Prentice-Hall.

Maxwell, Elsa (May 1938). "It's Romance Again for Kay Francis." *Photoplay*, pp. 24–25, 71.

Maxwell, Virginia (June 1933). "Just 'Life and Love.'" *Photoplay*, pp. 76, 85.

McGilligan, Patrick (1997). *Fritz Lang: The Nature of the Beast*. New York: St. Martin's Press.

McLellan, Diana (2000). *The Girls: Sappho Goes to Hollywood*. New York: LA Weekly.

McNeil, Alex (1984). *Total Television: A Comprehensive Guide to Programming from 1948 to the Present*. New York: Penguin.

Meryman, Richard (1978). *Mank: The Wit, World, and Life of Herman Mankiewicz*. New York: William Morrow.

Meyer, William R. (1978). *Warner Brothers Directors: The Hard-Boiled, the Comic, and the Weepers*. New Rochelle, N.Y.: Arlington House.

Miles, Mary (Spring 2001). "Life Before Nantucket: Never Bored, Always Busy." http://www.yesterdaysisland.com/spring_01/lifebefore/bored.html

Miller, Patsy Ruth (1988). *My Hollywood: When Both of Us Were Young: The Memories of Patsy Ruth Miller*. O'Raghailligh Ltd. Publishers.

Mills, Brian (1991). *Movie Star Memorabilia: A Collector's Guide*. London: B. T. Batsford.

"The Modern Screen Directory of Pictures ... These brief reviews are to serve as a guide when you do your movie shopping. From them you can get an idea whether the picture is good or bad and whether it is the sort of story you go for" (June 1933). *Modern Screen*, p. 90.

Mook, Dick (April 1941). "Pictures on the Fire." *Silver Screen*, pp. 66–72, 98.

_____ (April 1941). "She Wanted to Be Forgotten." *Silver Screen*, pp. 46–47, 91–92.

Mook, S.R. (November 1934). "Unguarded Moment." *Picture Play*, pp. 26–28, 54.

_____ (March 1939). "'I Can't Wait to Be Forgotten' Kay Francis Looks Ahead." *Photoplay*, pp. 32, 72.

Moore, Grace (1944). *You're Only Human Once*. Garden City, N.Y.: Country Life Press.

Mordden, Ethan (1983). *Movie Star: A Look at the Women Who Made Hollywood*. New York: St. Martin's Press.

Morehouse, Ward (1939). *Forty-Five Minutes Past Eight*. New York: Dial Press.

Morella, Joe, and Edward Z. Epstein (1986). *Loretta*

Young: An Extraordinary Life. New York: Delacorte Press.

Morrow, Lee Alan (1998). "Elsie Janis: 'A Comfortable Goofiness.'" In R.A. Schanke and K. Marra, eds., *Passing Performances: Queer Readings of Leading Players in American Theater History* (pp. 151–172). Ann Arbor: The University of Michigan Press.

Moses, Robert (1999). *American Movie Classics Classic Movie Companion.* New York: Hyperion.

Munn, Michael (1999). *X-Rated: The Paranormal Experiences of the Movie Star Greats.* London: Robson Books.

New York City Directories, 1921–1922.

New York Social Register, 1922–1929.

Norman, Barry (1987). *The Story of Hollywood.* New York: New American Library.

Nowlan, Robert A., and Gwendolyn Wright Nowlan (1989). *Cinema Sequels and Remakes, 1903–1987.* Jefferson, N.C.: McFarland.

Oakie, Jack (1980). *Jack Oakie's Double Takes.* San Francisco: Strawberry Hill Press.

Oakie, Victoria Horne (2001). *Life with Jack Oakie.* Waterville, M.E.: Five Star.

O'Brien, Pat (1964). *The Wind at My Back: The Life and Times of Pat O'Brien.* New York: Doubleday.

O'Brien, Scott (Winter 1995/1996). "Kay Francis: Portrait on Silk." *Films of the Golden Age,* pp. 56–62.

"Oklahoma Wrapped in Zero Weather" (1905, January 14). *Daily Oklahoman,* p. 1.

Okuda, Ted (1987). *The Monogram Checklist: The Films of Monogram Pictures Corporation, 1931–1952.* Jefferson, N.C.: McFarland.

Oller, John (1999). *Jean Arthur: The Actress Nobody Knew.* New York: Limelight Editions.

O'Toole, Lawrence (October 1989). "New York Story: The Blockbuster Saga of a Filmmaker's Dream—One Hundred Years in the Making." *American Film* (62–74).

Palmer, Gretta (1970). "This Year's Love Market." In *Hollywood and the Great Fan Magazines,* p. 115.

Parish, James Robert (1976). *The Jeanette MacDonald Story.* New York: Mason/Charter.

_____ (1977). *Hollywood's Great Love Teams.* New York: Arlington House.

_____ (1978). *The Hollywood Beauties.* New Rochelle, N.Y.: Arlington House.

_____ (1980). *The Hollywood Reliables.* Westport, C.T.: Arlington House.

_____ (2002). *Hollywood Divas: The Good, the Bad, and the Fabulous.* Chicago: Contemporary Books.

Parish, James R., and Gene Ringgold (February 1964). "Kay Francis." *Films in Review.*

Pegolotti, James A. (2003). *Deems Taylor: A Biography.* Boston: Northeastern University Press.

Petaja, Emil (1975). *Photoplay Edition.* San Francisco: SISU.

Peters, Margot (1990). *The House of Barrymore.* New York: Touchstone.

Phillips, Gene D. (1982). *George Cukor.* Boston: Twayne Publishers.

Pitrone, Jean Maddern (1999). *Take It from Big Mouth: The Life of Martha Raye.* Lexington: University of Kentucky Press.

"Plus Fours 'Hamlet' Here: Erlanger Production to Observe Dry Law in Modernist Effort" (1925, August 28). *The New York Times,* 8:5.

Pratley, Gerald, (1971). *The Cinema of Otto Preminger.* New York: A.S. Barnes.

Preminger, Otto (1977). *Preminger: An Autobiography.* New York: Doubleday.

Prestholdt, Torben (1947). "Summer Theatre Circuit." In *Theatre World, 1946–1947.* Daniel Blum, ed. New York: Stuyvesant Press.

Pyle, E. (1943, March 29). "Four Good Soldiers." *Senior Scholastic,* p. 2.

Quirk, Lawrence J. (1974). *The Great Romantic Films.* Secaucus, NJ: Citadel Press.

_____ (1990). *Fasten Your Seat Belts: The Passionate Life of Bette Davis.* New York: William Morrow.

"Reviews—A Tour of Today's Talkies" (June 1933). *Modern Screen,* p. 82.

Rich, Sharon (1994). *Sweethearts: The Timeless Love Affair—on Screen and Off—Between Jeanette MacDonald and Nelson Eddy.* New York: Donald I. Fine.

Roberts, Katharine (1935, March 16). "Acting in a Business Way." *Colliers,* pp. 14, 32.

Roberts, Kay (December 1932). "They Hope to Stay Married." *Photoplay,* pp. 34, 119–120.

Robinson, Edward G. (1973). *All My Yesterdays.* New York: Signet.

Rogers, Ginger (1991). *Ginger: My Story.* New York: HarperCollins.

Rosen, Marjorie (1974). *Popcorn Venus: Women, Movies and the American Dream.* New York: Avon Books.

Roth, Andrew (1996). *Infamous Manhattan.* New York: Citadel Press Book.

Rubin, Hanna, and Cynthia Grisolia (October 1989). "Star Quality." *American Film* (58–61, 76–89).

Rush, Dana (February 1932). "The Aristocrat of the Screen: Kay Francis Lives in a Thoroughbred World." *Silver Screen,* pp. 41, 77.

St. Johns, Adela Rogers (March 1931). "Working Girl." *New Movie Magazine,* pp. 84–86, 124.

"Savages and Ink" [Review of *Gentlemen of the Press*] (1929, May 19). *The New York Times,* IX, 7:2.

Schapiro, Amy (2003). *Millicent Fenwick: Her Way.* Piscataway, N.J.: Rutgers University Press.

Schatz, Thomas (1988). *The Genius of the System: Hollywood in the Studio Era.* New York: Pantheon Books.

Schickel, Richard (1983). *Cary Grant: A Celebration.* Boston: Little, Brown.

Screen Parliament [Letters to the editor] (1933, December 30). "Presentable—Kay Francis has a dignity and a 'presence' lacking entirely in any other film star on the screen to-day." John Hiddy, Bournemouth.

Selznick, David O. (2000). *Memo from David O. Selznick.* Edited by Rudy Behlmer. New York: Modern Library.

Sennett, Ted (1971). *Warner Brothers Presents.* New York: Arlington House.

Service, Faith (November 1932). "Did $26,000 Outweigh a Honeymoon Trip for Kay Francis?" *Motion Picture,* pp. 51, 78.

"Shadow Stage: A Review of the New Pictures" (October 1934). *Photoplay,* p. 53.

Shaw, Karl (2001). *Royal Babylon: The Alarming History of European Royalty.* New York: Broadway Books.

Sherman, Vincent (1996). *Studio Affairs: My Life as a Film Director.* Lexington: University Press of Kentucky.

Shipman, David (1979). *The Great Movie Stars: The Golden Years.* New York: Da Capo Press.

Silver, Gordon R. "Their Favourite Rooms: Did You Know Stars Have Favourite Rooms— Pet Nooks and Corners in their Luxurious Mansions? They do!" *The Film-Lovers' Annual.* London: Dean &Son Ltd., pp. 27–30.

Silvers, Phil (1973). *This Laugh Is on Me: The Phil Silvers Story.* Englewood Cliffs, N.J.: Prentice-Hall.

Skinner, Cornelia Otis (1976). *Life with Lindsay & Crouse.* Boston: Houghton Mifflin.

Smith, Geraldine (1941, November 2). "Triple Failure to Break Love Jinx." *Philadelphia Inquirer.*

Smith, Jewel (1970). "Kay's Dream of Romance: Kay Francis Outlines Her Conception of an Ideal Honeymoon." In *Hollywood and the Great Fan Magazines,* pp. 58, 182. Edited by Martin Levin. New York: Castle Books.

Spergel, Mark (1993). *Reinventing Reality — The Art and Life of Rouben Mamoulian.* Metuchen, NJ: The Scarecrow Press.

Stenn, David (2000). *Clara Bow Runnin' Wild.* New York: Cooper Square Press.

Stewart, Donald Ogden (1975). *By a Stroke of Luck!* New York: Paddington Press.

Stewart, Roy P. (1974). *Born Grown: An Oklahoma City History.* Oklahoma City: Fidelity Bank.

Stine, Whitney (1985). *Stars & Star Handlers: The Business of Show.* Santa Monica: Roundtable.

Stuart, Gloria (1999). *I Just Kept Hoping.* Boston: Little, Brown and Company.

Tague, William H., Robert B. Kimball, and Richard V. Happel (1961). *Berkshire: Two Hundred Years in Pictures: 1761–1961.* Pittsfield, M.A.: Eagle.

Tapert, Anne (1998). *The Power of Glamour.* New York: Crown.

Teichmann, Howard (1972). *George S. Kaufman: An Intimate Portrait.* New York: Atheneum.

Thomas, Tony (1973). *The Busby Berkeley Book.* New York: A & W Visual Library.

"Thoughts, Some Sad, on New Films" [Review of *Dangerous Curves*] (1929, July 21). *The New York Times,* VIII, p. 3.

Tierney, Tom (1974). *Thirty from the 30s.* Englewood Cliffs, N.J.: Prentice-Hall.

Turk, Edward Baron (2000). *Hollywood Diva.* Berkeley: University of California Press.

Udet, Ernst (1970). *Ace of the Iron Cross: The Autobiography of the Red Baron's Leading Ace.* New York: Ace Books.

Underwood, Peter (1992). *Death in Hollywood.* London: Clio Press.

Van Ishoven, Armand (1977). *The Fall of an Eagle: The Life of Fighter Ace Ernst Udet.* London: Translated by Chaz Bowyer, William Kimber.

Vermilye, Jerry (1982). *The Films of the Thirties.* Secaucus, N.J.: Citadel Press.

Vieira, Mark A. (1999). *Sin in Soft Focus: Pre-Code Hollywood.* New York: Harry N. Abrams.

Walker, Alexander (1979). *Shattered Silents.* New York: William Morrow.

Walker, Helen Louise (September 1930). "How Men Annoy Us: Kay Francis Gives the Woman's Side." *Motion Picture,* pp. 71, 98.

Wallace, David (2001). *Lost Hollywood.* New York: St. Martin's Press.

Wallis, Hal, and Charles Higham (1980). *Starmaker: The Autobiography of Hal Wallis.* New York: Macmillan.

Weibel, Kathryn (1977). *Mirror Mirror: Images of Women Reflected in Popular Culture.* New York: Anchor Books.

Westmore, Frank, and Muriel Davidson (1976). *The Westmores of Hollywood.* New York: J. B. Lippincott.

Wilkerson, Tichi, and Marcia Borle (1984). *The Hollywood Reporter: The Golden Years.* New York: Arlington House.

Williams, Whitney (November 1937). "Which Will Win the Golden Apple of Success?" *Silver Screen,* pp. 24–25, 80–81.

Wilson, Elizabeth (March 1937). "Projections." *Silver Screen,* pp. 26–27, 80–82.

Winecoff, Charles (1996). *Split Image: The Life of Anthony Perkins.* New York: Dutton.

Wise, James E. Jr., and Paul W. Wilderson, III (2000). *Stars in Khaki: Movie Actors in the Army and the Air Services.* Annapolis, Maryland: Naval Institute Press.

Wray, Fay (1989). *On the Other Hand: A Life Story.* New York: St. Martin's Press.

Wright's Directory of Milwaukee, 1908.

Yurka, Blanche (1970). *Bohemian Girl: Blanche Yurka's Theatrical Life.* Athens: Ohio University Press.

Zinman, David (1973). *Saturday Afternoon at the Bijou.* New Rochelle, N.Y.: Arlington House.

Index